WRITING FICTION

WRITING FICTION

A Guide to Narrative Craft

FOURTH EDITION

Janet Burroway
Florida State University

HarperCollins*College*Publishers

Acquisitions Editor: Lisa Moore
Developmental Editor: Randee Falk
Project Coordination: Interactive Composition Corporation
Text and Cover Designer: Interactive Composition Corporation
Cover Photograph: © 1994 by Mark Bumgarner
Electronic Production Manager: Eric Jorgensen
Manufacturing Manager: Willie Lane
Electronic Page Makeup: Interactive Composition Corporation
Printer and Binder: RR Donnelley & Sons Company
Cover Printer: The Lehigh Press, Inc.

HarperCollins has made available an impressive array of high quality video and audiotape productions of literary works to enhance students' experience of literature. For more information contact your local HarperCollins representative or Marketing Manager for Literature: College Division, HarperCollins Publishers, 10 East 53rd Street, NY, NY 10022.

For permission to use copyrighted material, grateful acknowledgment is made to the copyright holders on page 372, which are hereby made part of this copyright page.

Writing Fiction: A Guide to Narrative Craft, Fourth Edition

Library of Congress Cataloging-in-Publication Data

Burroway, Janet.
    Writing fiction : a guide to narrative craft / Janet Burroway. —
4th. ed.
    Includes bibliographical references and index.
    ISBN 0–673–52345–4
    1. Fiction—Technique.   I. Title
PN3355.B79   1995
808.3—dc20   95-3562
                                                                                      CIP

        98 9 8 7 6

For David Daiches, mentor and friend

CONTENTS

PREFACE

When the first edition of this book appeared in 1982, the workshop was already a thriving phenomenon, but to be a student or a teacher of writing was still slightly eccentric. Writers on both sides of the classroom were likely to have more hair than our peers in literature, more attitude; we were more likely to wear sandals than a tie. We tended to greet each other conspiratorially in the halls, as if we weren't sure we belonged there. Now full-scale writing programs are so accepted a part of university life that those entering the program are probably not aware of its relatively short history. Intended lawyers and executives often opt for the writing major, and workshop students fairly consider themselves part of the mainstream.

Like most of my colleagues in the past two decades I have sometimes felt a nagging ambivalence about the popularity of creative writing. Were we diluting the power of fiction, giving false hopes to young writers, and spawning dozens of amateurish little journals? Or were we the monks of the new Dark Ages, keeping the language alive in our workshop cloisters? Was the truth somewhere in the middle, or at both extremes?

Then at some point I began to realize that the workshops and the literary quarterlies filled an immediate need. As telecommunications swallowed the custom of writing letters, the "little magazines" became a kind of correspondence, a place for people to share their interest; and as the corporate giants swallowed the trade publishers, the best of these journals provided an alternative and prestigious place for good writers to get published.

In the classroom, I saw that writing fiction could lead students toward reading, and would need to. Literacy has been diminishing even as we realize that our ideas of literature are provincial. Literature and creative writing, both, will now have to be taught in universities for the same reason that philosophy is taught—because they are not part of the everyday experience of most people.

Moreover, I observed a curious anomaly: that students who had grown up with few books beyond their school assignments could nevertheless, out of their massive television experience, turn a joke, tag a character, shape a plot, produce a recognition scene, foreshadow, reveal, and write lively dialogue.

It now seems to me no longer an anomaly, but a *mystery*, that students who have not read for pleasure nevertheless arrive at university wanting, often passionately, to write. They have some kind of connection with the language that is not satisfied by the passive relationship they have had with it through television. Yes, they want to express themselves—there's a therapeutic aspect in all writing—but they also perceive, perhaps dimly, that language has to do with being human, and that they need it at the deepest level, for identity.

In a survey done in the mid-eighties for the National Endowment for the Arts, it was shown that *a quarter of the adults in America believe they write fiction or poetry*. This cannot be true. But it argues for something else than widespread self-deception. In spite of the grim trashy things that are being done with and to the language by all the wielders of pomp, power, and finance, people still want to connect through the written word. It is ironic that in the same period that has seen the acceptance of creative writing as an academic discipline, computer technology has begun to restore the popularity of "letter" writing. Technology taketh away and technology giveth.

A friend of mine recently wrote scathingly of this new and unnecessary verb "to workshop," as if, he said, "to discuss" were not a perfectly adequate word. I agreed the term is cumbersome—not as graphic as *menu* or *virus*, not elegant like *détente*—but I defended it as describing an activity that is particular, complex, and relatively recent.

The workshop process entails much more than discussion. It implies a commitment on the part of everyone concerned to give close attention to work that is embryonic. As much as workshops vary, they inevitably entail a close reading, a personal response, an interpretation, and an assessment of the work's strengths and weaknesses. A workshop is intense by nature, and I have experienced no workshop that was not. The writer is vulnerable, the critic powerful. Fiction reveals the inner world, and the act of writing is tied to ego. You are setting your baby out for love or slaughter—how could it be otherwise than intense?

This intensity carries certain dangers: that the writer will be discouraged; that the writer will be flattered; that the writer will be tempted to write for the teacher or the group. Most writers instinctively want to explain or defend, and it is hard to learn that these are counterproductive responses to criticism. Often the most gifted writers are full of self-doubt, the least gifted self-assured; and there is no guarantee that a workshop can reverse these tendencies, convince the sufferers to celebrate and the cocky to revise.

But the intensity of the workshop is also the source of its positive power. People want to be here. They are almost never in it for the grade. The quality of attention and the level of energy are high, and in such an atmosphere a workshop can help a writer to find his or her own story and to tell it.

There are a number of practical ways that a workshop can help. It imposes a deadline, forcing the writer to produce. It guarantees an audience, something that even the most successful professional can never be quite certain of finding. Usually it offers course credit, which is the same thing as getting paid for writing. And it offers a quantity of response: if one person says, "This passage is unclear," it's always possible to feel that the critic is stupid or inattentive; but if fifteen or twenty critic peers agree that "This passage is unclear," it is convincing that the fault lies in the text, and the responsibility with the writer.

Beyond these practical matters, at its best the workshop offers an approximation at an early stage of the literary circle, with all the implied stimulus of collaboration, a shared desire for excellence, and judicious help. A workshop requires many acts of judgment; it's crucial that judgment is not an end but a means toward help. Striking a productive balance between tact and incisiveness is the responsibility of everyone in the room. The attitude that seems to work best is that literary standards are absolute, and—except for bad spelling, grammar, punctuation, and sloth—forgiveness is also absolute. The quality of the communication is under judgment; the author's character is not.

Usually this balance is struck. The most common pattern of a semester's writing course is that students and teacher alike begin discouraged with the quality of the writing and end with a certain sense of astonishment at how far so many have come.

Who will have come how far is not always predictable. At the end of two or three years in a writing program, some who arrived with talent will not have moved on, while some who showed nothing but dedication and cliché will have become writers. Some will have acquired dedication. Some will make an evolutionary leap.

It is a truism of the workshop that not everyone will "become a writer", but it is also true that everyone *is* a writer, and it is undoubtedly the case that our "star system" mentality, our focus on grades, contests, awards and celebrity, falsifies the distance between the gifted and the mere citizens.

Writing ought, in my view, to hold a position in our society more or less like playing tennis. A passable amateur tennis player may exercise her skill often, even obsessively, can involve some few others as partners and spectators, can struggle to improve and feel exhilarated by the struggle. It's impressive if she turns pro, but no one despises her for devoting a portion of most days to the game, even if no one will ever pay money to watch her play. Nobody says that because tennis requires innate talent, the buff is an embarrassment.

By the same token, the amateur—that is, lover of the game—does not suppose that because he can catch felt on catgut three returns out of five, he is just a lucky break away from Wimbledon. He does it for the doing. Because although it's hard to get revved up for it, once you start the momentum carries you; because you get better when you work at it; because the effort makes you sweat; and it feels good to have done it.

I think we ought to think of writing more like that.

I have many people to thank for help on the fourth edition of *Writing Fiction*: as usual my colleagues in the Writing Program at Florida State University, and especially Claudia Johnson in the Film School. Jacqueline Hendricks asked the right questions. My husband Peter Ruppert fed me more ways than one while I was at work. I am grateful to my reviewers Lisa J. Church; Judith Beth Cohen, Lesley College; Anthony Grooms, University of Georgia; William Hunt, Northwestern Connecticut Community College; Fred Leebron, Fine Arts Work Center, Provincetown; Robert Phillips, University of Houston; David Sharp, Maple Woods Community College; Chester Sullivan, University of Kansas; and especially Susan Weinberg, Appalachian State University, whose suggestions were always on the mark; and to my editors Randee Falk and Lisa Moore.

Janet Burroway

1

WHATEVER WORKS
The Writing Process

- *Get Started*

- *Keep Going*

- *A Word About Theme*

You want to write. Why is it so hard?

There are a few lucky souls for whom the whole process of writing is easy, for whom the smell of fresh paper is better than air, whose minds chuckle over their own agility, who forget to eat, and who consider the world at large an intrusion on their good time at the typewriter. But you and I are not among them. We are in love with words except when we have to face them. We are caught in a guilty paradox in which we grumble over our lack of time, and when we have the time, we sharpen pencils, make phone calls, or clip the hedges.

Of course, there's also joy. We write for the satisfaction of having wrestled a sentence to the page, the rush of discovering an image, the excitement of seeing a character come alive. Even the most successful writers will sincerely say that these pleasures—not money, fame, or glamour—are the real rewards of writing. Nevertheless, we forget what such joy and satisfaction feel like when we confront a blank page.

The narrator of Anita Brookner's novel *Look at Me* records a familiar pattern.

Sometimes it feels like a physical effort simply to sit down at the desk and pull out the notebook. Sometimes I find myself heaving a sigh when I read through what I have already written. Sometimes the effort of putting pen to paper is so great that I literally feel a pain in my head, as if all the furniture of my mind were being rearranged, as if it were being lined up, being got ready for delivery from the storehouse. And yet when I start to write, all this heaviness vanishes, and I feel charged with a kind of electricity. . .

It helps to know that most writers share the paradox of least wanting to do what we most want to do. It also helps to know some of the reasons for our reluctance. Jacques Barzun, in "A Writer's Discipline," suggests that it stems first of all from fear. The writer's intention, he says:

> . . . is to transfer a part of our intellectual and emotional insides into an independent and self-sustaining outside. It follows that if we have any doubts about the strength, truth or beauty of our insides, the doubt acts as an automatic censor which quietly forbids the act of exhibition.

Novelist Richard Koster offers a blanket absolution for what writers tend to think of as "wasting time"—that hour or two of muddled glaring at the page before a word will allow itself to be placed there. In the process of creating a fiction we must divorce ourselves from the real world, he points out. And that is hard. The real world is insistent not only in its distractions but also in its brute physical presence. To remove ourselves from that sphere and achieve a state in which our mental world is more real requires a disciplined effort of displacement.

We may even sense that it is unnatural or dangerous to live in a world of our own creation. People love to read stories about the dreamer nobody thinks will amount to much, and who turns out to be a genius inventor, scientist, artist, or savior. Part of the reason such stories work is that we like to escape from the way the world really works, including the way it works in us. We all feel the pressure of the practical. The writer may sympathize with the dreamer but forget to sympathize with the dreamer-in-himself-or-herself.

There's another impediment to beginning, expressed by a writer character in Lawrence Durrell's *Alexandria Quartet*. Durrell's Pursewarden broods over the illusory significance of what he is about to write, unwilling to begin in case he spoils it. Many of us do this: The idea, whatever it is, seems so luminous, whole, and fragile, that to begin to write about that idea is to commit it to rubble. Knowing in advance that words will never exactly capture what we mean or intend, we must gingerly and gradually work ourselves into a state of accepting what words can do instead. No matter how many times we find out that what words can do is quite all right, we still shy again from the next beginning. Against this wasteful impulse I have a motto over my desk that reads: "Don't Dread; Do." It's a fine motto, and I contemplated it for several weeks before I began writing this chapter.

The mundane daily habits of writers are apparently fascinating. No author offers to answer questions at the end of a public reading without being asked: *Do you write in the morning or at night? Do you write every day? Do you compose on a word processor?* Sometimes such questions show a hagiographic interest in the workings of genius. More often, I think, they are a plea for practical help: *Is there something I can do to make this job less horrific? Is there a trick that will unlock my words?*

Get Started

The variety of authors' habits suggests that there is no magic to be found in any particular one. Donald Hall will tell you that he spends a dozen hours a day at his desk, moving back and forth between as many projects. Philip Larkin said that he wrote a poem only every eighteen months or so, and never tried to write one that was not a gift. Gail Godwin goes to her workroom every day "because what if the angel came and I wasn't there?" Diane Wakowski thinks that to sit at work against your will is evidence of bourgeois neurosis. Maria Irene Fornes begins her day with a half hour of loosening up exercises, finding a comfortable center of gravity before she sits down to work. Mary Lee Settle advises that writers who teach must work in the morning, before the analytical habits of the classroom take over the brain; George Cuomo replies that he solves this problem by taking an afternoon nap. Dickens could not deal with people when he was working: "The mere consciousness of an engagement will worry a whole day." Hemingway and Thomas Wolfe wrote standing up. Some writers can plop at the kitchen table without clearing the breakfast dishes; some need total seclusion, a beach, a cat, a string quartet.

There is something to be learned from all this, though. It is not an open sesame but a piece of advice older than fairy tales: Know thyself. The bottom line is that if you do not at some point write your story down, it will not get written. Having decided that you will write it, the question is not how do you get it done? but how do *you* get it done? Any discipline or indulgence that actually helps nudge you into position facing the page is acceptable and productive. If jogging after breakfast energizes your mind, then jog before you sit. If you have to pull an all-nighter on a coffee binge, do that. Some schedule, regularity, pattern in your writing day (or night) will always help, but only you can figure out what pattern is for you.

JOURNAL KEEPING

There are, though, a number of tricks you can teach yourself in order to free the writing self, and the essence of these is to give yourself permission to fail. The best place for such permission is a private place, and for that reason a writer's journal is an essential, likely to be the source of originality, ideas, experimentation, and growth.

Keep a journal. A journal is an intimate, a friend that will accept you as you are. Pick a notebook you like the look of, one you feel comfortable with, as you would pick a friend. I find a bound blank book too elegant to live up to, preferring instead a loose-leaf because I write my journal mainly at the computer and can stick anything in at the flip of a three-hole punch. But you can glue scribbled napkins into a spiral, too.

Keep the journal regularly, at least at first. It doesn't matter what you write and it doesn't matter very much how much, but it does matter that you make a steady habit of the writing. A major advantage of keeping a journal regularly is that it will put you in the habit of observing in words. If you know at dawn that you are committed to writing so-and-so many words before dusk, you will half-consciously tell the story of your day to yourself as you live it, finding a phrase to catch whatever catches your eye. When that habit is established, you'll begin to find that whatever invites your attention or sympathy, your anger or curiosity, may be the beginning of invention. Whoever catches your attention may be the beginning of a character.

But before the habit is developed, you may find that even a blank journal page has the awesome aspect of a void, and you may need some tricks of permission to let yourself start writing there. The playwright Maria Irene Fornes says that there are two of you: one who wants to write and one who doesn't. The one who wants to write had better keep tricking the one who doesn't. Or another way to think of this conflict is between right brain and left brain—the spatial, playful, detail-loving creator, and the linear, cataloging, categorizing critic. The critic is an absolutely essential part of the writing process. The trick is to shut him or her up until there is something to criticize.

FREEWRITING

Freewriting is a technique that allows you to take very literally the notion of getting something down on paper. It can be done whenever you want to write, or just to free up the writing self. The idea is to put

> anything on paper and I mena anything, it doesn't matter as long as it's coming out of your head nad hte ends of your fingers, down ont the page I wonder if;m improving, if this process gets me going better now than it did all those—hoewever many years ago? I know my typing is geting worse, deteriorating even as we speak (are we speaking? to whom? IN what forM? I love it when i hit the caps button by mistake, it makes me wonder whether there isn;t something in the back or bottom of the brain that sez PAY ATTENTION now, which makes me think of a number of things, freud and his slip o tonuge, self-deception, the myriad way it operates in everybody's life, no not everybody's but in my own exp. llike Aunt Ch. mourniong for the dead cats whenevershe hasn't got her way and can't disconnect one kind of sadness from another, I wonder if we ever disconnect kinds of sadness, if the first homesickness doesn;t operatfor everybody the same way it does for me, grandma's house the site of it, the grass out the window and the dog rolling a tin pie plate under the willow tree, great heavy hunger in the belly, the empty weight of loss, loss, loss

That's freewriting. Its point is to keep going, and that is the only point. When the critic intrudes and tells you that what you're doing is awful, tell the critic to take a dive, or acknowledge her/him (*typing is getting worse*) and keep writing. If you work on a computer, try dimming the screen so you can't see what you're doing. If you freewrite often, pretty soon you'll be bored with writing about how you don't feel like writing (though that is as good a subject as any; the subject is of no importance and neither is the quality of the writing) and you will find your mind and your phrases running on things that interest you. Fine. It doesn't matter.

Freewriting is the literary equivalent of scales at the piano or a short gym workout. All that matters is that you do it. The verbal muscles will develop of their own accord.

Though freewriting is mere technique, it can affect the freedom of the content. Many writers feel themselves to be *an instrument through which*, rather than a *creator of*, and whether you think of this possibility as humble or holy, it is worth finding out what you say when you aren't monitoring yourself. Fiction is written not so much to inform as to find out, and if you force yourself into a mode of informing when you haven't yet found out, you're likely to end up pontificating, or lying some other way.

In *Becoming a Writer*, a book that only half facetiously claims to do what teachers of writing claim cannot be done—to teach genius—Dorothea Brande suggests that the way to begin is not with an idea or a form at all, but with an unlocking of your thoughts at the typewriter. She advises that you rise each day and go directly to your desk (if you have to have coffee, put it in a thermos the night before) and begin writing whatever comes to mind, before you are quite awake, before you have read anything or talked to anyone, before reason has begun to take over from the dream-functioning of your brain. Write for twenty or thirty minutes and then put away what you have written without reading it over. After a week or two of this, pick an additional time during the day when you can salvage a half hour or so to write, and when that time arrives, write, even if you "must climb out over the heads of your friends" to do it. It doesn't matter what you write. What does matter is that you develop the habit of beginning to write the moment you sit down to do so.

CLUSTERING

Clustering is a technique, described in full by Gabriele Rico in her book *Writing the Natural Way*, that helps you organize on the model of the right brain rather than the left, organically rather than sequentially. Usually when we plan a piece of writing in advance, it is in a linear fashion—topic sentences and subheadings in the case of an essay, usually an outline of the action in the case of fiction. Clustering is a way of quite literally making spatial and visual the organization of your thoughts.

To practice the technique, choose a word that represents your central subject, write it in the center of the page, and circle it. Then for two or three minutes free-associate by jotting down around it any word—image, action, abstraction, or part of speech—that comes to mind. Every now and again, circle the words you have written and draw lines or arrows between words that seem to connect. As with freewriting, it is crucial to keep going, without self-censoring and without worrying about whether you're making sense. What you're doing is *making*; sense will emerge. When you've clustered for two or three minutes, you will have a page that looks like a cobweb with very large dewdrops, and you will probably sense when it is enough. Take a few seconds, no more, to look at what you have done. (*Look at* seems more relevant here than *read over*, because the device does make you see the words as part of a visual composition.) Then start writing. Don't let the critic in yet. This will not be a genuine freewrite because you've chosen the subject, but think of it as a freedraft or focused freewrite, and keep writing.

Here is a sample cluster of the preceding passage.

When I first encountered this device, I was aware that it was widely used for English composition classes and that it had also led to poetry and prose poems, but

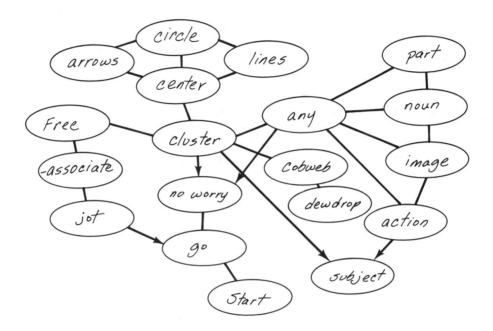

I was doubtful how much use it would be to a fiction writer. I decided to try it, though, so I sat down to the first exercise offered in Rico's book, which was to cluster on the word "fear." I was not very thrilled with the project, but I wrote the word in the center of my page. As soon as I circled it, I realized that in the novel I was then writing, there was a lot of fear in the mind of the heroine, a Baltimore Catholic headed for the desert Southwest in 1914. I started free-associating her fear rather than my own, and images erupted out of nowhere, out of her childhood—a cellar, the smell of rotting apples and mice droppings, old newspapers, my heroine as a little girl squatting in the dank dark, the priest upstairs droning on about the catechism. Where had it all come from? Within fifteen minutes I had a two-paragraph memory for my character that revealed her to me, and to my reader, more clearly than anything I had yet written.

Now I cluster any scene, character, narrative passage, or reflection that presents me with the least hint of resistance. When I have a complicated scene with several characters in it, I cluster each character so I have a clear idea at the beginning how each is feeling in that situation. Even if, as is usually the case, the passage is written from the point of view of only one of them, I will know how to make the other characters react, speak, and move if I've been gathering cobwebs in their minds.

To take a simple example, suppose you are writing a scene in which Karl is furiously berating Jess for being late when an important guest was expected for dinner. The dialogue comes easily. But you're unclear about Jess's reaction. So you cluster what's going on in her mind:

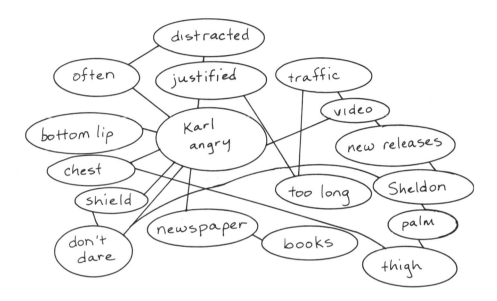

Naturally your cluster would be entirely different from this one, and suited to your story. But though I started without any concept of these characters, the clustering tossed up these ideas in a few minutes: Karl's justified, Jess thinks; she got distracted at the video store when she ran into her old boyfriend Sheldon sifting through the new releases, and she stopped to talk to him for too long and got caught in rush hour traffic—none of which she dares say to Karl. She's often distracted these days. Right now she can't concentrate on what Karl is saying because she's so interested in the way his bottom lip shakes when he's angry, and the way his newspaper is held like a shield over his chest—Sheldon always cupped his books in his palm and swung them against his thigh, she remembers. She wouldn't dare mention that either.

If the story were told from inside Jess's mind, then you might use much of this directly. But even if it were told from Karl's angry point of view, it would help you (and him) see her—the way she tries to poke the video out of sight in her handbag, the way she seems to be concentrating on his newspaper as if she were trying to read it off his chest. It might also help you hear her, how she mumbles complaining about rush hour, how she starts a sentence and then gives up on it.

Clustering is an excellent technique for journal keeping. It focuses your thoughts, cuts out extraneous material, and reduces writing time. In composing fiction, I recommend frequent clustering, followed by freedrafting and light editing. Then put the passage away for twenty-four hours. Like most recommendations, all this one means is that it seems to work for me.

A similar process was my forced habit for many years before I discovered that I could make it work for me instead of against. I would sit at my desk from mid morning to noon paralyzed by the cosmic weight of needing to write something absolutely wonderful. I would lunch at my desk regularly in despair. By mid afternoon I would hate myself so thoroughly that I'd decide to splash anything down, any trash at all, just to be free of the blank page and feel justified in fleeing my paper prison. The whole evening would be tainted by the knowledge of having written such garbage. Next morning I would find that although it was mostly orange peels and eggshells, there was a little bit of something salvageable here and there. For a couple of intent hours I would work on that to make it right, feeling better, feeling good. Then I'd be faced with a new passage to begin, which, unlike that mess I'd cleaned up from yesterday, was going to emerge in rough draft as Great Literature. Lunch loomed in gloom.

Now, most days (allow for a few failures, a few relapses into old habits), I write the junk quite happily straight away. Then I begin to tinker, usually with something I did yesterday or last week—which is where I concentrate, lose myself, and am transported into the word world. Often it's two o'clock before I remember to stop for my apple and chunk of cheese.

Cluster, freedraft, lightly edit, put away. I do urge you at least to try this, several times. What you are at this moment reading is no doubt a many-times turned-around, picked at, honed, and buffed version of my paragraphs on clustering. But as I finish the first version, the document on my computer screen runs to three and a half pages, and only seventeen minutes have passed on my desk clock since I sat down to cluster the word "clustering." Moreover, I'm alert and having fun, and I feel like going on to say something about the computer.

THE COMPUTER

A very real and considerable disadvantage of a computer is that unless you have a notebook model you can't take it to the park or the beach. I think it's important for a writer to try a pencil from time to time so as not to lose the knack of it, or the reminder of the cave walls where it all started.

But apart from its cumbersomeness and its need for some energy source other than the writer's mind, a computer is a great boon, and it's a rare idiosyncratic author who will not benefit from one. Freewriting frees more freely on a computer. The knowledge that you can so easily delete makes it easier to quiet the internal critic and put down whatever comes. The "wraparound" feature of the computer means that you need never be aware, visually, through sound, or in the muscles of your carriage-throwing arm, that what you write is chopped into lines of type on the page. Turn down the screen or ignore it, look at your fingers (they make a hypnotic sight), or stare out the window into middle space. You can follow the thread of your thought through the labyrinth to the center without a pause.

Enter the critic. The cautionary note that needs to be sounded regarding all the techniques and technology that free you to write is that the critic is absolutely essential afterwards. Because revision, the heart of the writing process, will continue until you finally finish or abandon a piece of work, a chapter on revision is the last in this book. But the revising process is continuous, and begins as soon as you choose to let your critic in. Clustering and freedrafting allow you to create before you criticize, do the essential play before the essential work. Don't forget the essential work. The computer lets you write a lot because you can so easily cut. Don't forget to do so.

CHOOSING A SUBJECT

Some writers, again, are lucky enough never to be faced with the problem of choosing a subject. The world presents itself to them in terms of conflict, crisis, and resolution. Ideas for stories pop into their heads day after day; their only difficulty is choosing among them. In fact, the habit of mind that produces stories *is* a habit and can be cultivated, so that the more and the longer you write, the less likely you are to run out of ideas.

But sooner or later you may find yourself faced with the desire (or the deadline necessity) to write a story when your mind is a blank. The sour and untrue impulse crosses your thoughts: Nothing has ever happened to me. The task you face then is to recognize among all the paraphernalia of your mind a situation, idea, perception, or character that you can turn into a story.

Some teachers and critics advise beginning writers to write only from their personal experience, but I feel that this is a misleading and demeaning rule. If your imagination never gets beyond your age group or off campus, never tackles issues larger than dormitory life, then you are severely underestimating the range of your imagination. It is certainly true that you must draw on your own experience (including your experience of the shape of sentences). But the trick is to identify what is interesting, unique, original in your experience (including your experience of the shape of sentences), which will therefore surprise and attract the reader. John Gardner, in *The Art of Fiction*, agrees that "nothing can be more limiting to the imagination" than the advice that you write about what you know. He suggests instead that you "write the kind of story you know and like best."

This is a better idea, because the kind of story you know and like best has also taught you something about the way such stories are told, how they are shaped, what kind of surprise, conflict, and change they involve. Many beginning writers who are not yet avid readers have learned from television more than they realize about structure, the way characters behave and talk, how a joke is arranged, how a lie is revealed, and so forth. The trouble is that if you learn fiction from television, or if the kind of story you know and like best is genre fiction—science fiction, fantasy, romance, mystery—you may have learned about technique without having learned anything about the unique contribution you can make to such a story. The result is that you end up writing imitation soap opera or space odyssey, second-rate somebody else instead of first-rate you.

The essential thing is that you write about something you really care about, and the first step is to find out what that is. Playwright Claudia Johnson advises her students to identify their real concerns by making a "menu" of them. Pick the big emotions and make lists in your journal: *What makes you angry? What are you afraid of? What do you want? What hurts?* Or consider the crucial turning points of your life: *What really changed you? Who really changed you?* Those will be the areas to look to for stories, whether or not those stories are autobiographical. Novelist Ron Carlson says, "I always write from my own experiences, whether I've had them or not."

Another journal idea is to jot down the facts of the first seven years of your life under several categories: *Events, People, Your Self, Inner Life, Characteristic Things.* What from those first seven years still occupies your mind? Underline or highlight the items on your page(s) that you aren't done with yet. Those items are clues to your concerns, and a possible source of storytelling.

A related device for your journal might be borrowed from the *Pillow Book* of Sei Shonagun. A courtesan in tenth-century Japan, she kept a diary of the goings-on at court and concealed it in her wooden pillow—hence *pillow book*. Sei Shonagun made lists under various categories of specific, often quirky *Things*. This device is capable of endless variety and can reveal yourself to you as you find out what sort of thing you want to list: *Things I wish had never been said. Red things. Things more embarrassing than nudity. Things to put off as long as possible. Things to die for. Acid things. Things that last only a day.*

Such devices may be necessary because identifying what we care about is not always easy. We are surrounded by a constant barrage of information, drama, ideas, and judgments offered to us live, printed, and electronically. It is so much easier to know what we ought to think and feel than what we actually do. Worthy authorities constantly exhort us to care about worthy causes, only a few of which really touch us, whereas what we care about at any given moment may seem trivial, self-conscious, or self-serving.

This, I think, is in large part the value of Brande's first exercise, which forces you to write in the intuitively honest period of first light, when the half sleeping brain is still dealing with its real concerns. Often what seems unworthy is precisely the thing that contains a universal, and by catching it honestly, then stepping back from it, you may achieve the authorial distance that is an essential part of significance. (All you really care about this morning is how you'll look at the dance tonight? This is a trivial obsession that can hit anyone, at any age, anywhere. Write about it as honestly as you can. Now who else might have felt this way? Someone you hate? Someone remote in time from you? Look out: You're on your way to a story.) Sometimes pursuing what you know and feel to its uttermost limits will take you into the realms of fantasy. Sometimes your fantasies will transform themselves into reality.

Brande advises that once you have developed the habit of regular freewriting, you should read your pages over and pick a passage that seems to suggest a simple story. Muse on the idea for a few days, find its shape, and then fill that shape with people, settings, details from your own experience, observation, and imagination. Turn the story over in your mind. Sleep on it—more than once. Finally, pick a time when you are going to write the story, and when that time comes, go to the desk and write a complete first draft as rapidly as possible. Then put it away, at least overnight. When you take it out again, you will have something to work with, and the business of the reason may begin.

Eventually you will learn what sort of experience sparks ideas for your sort of story—and you may be astonished at how such experiences accumulate, as if your life were arranging itself to produce material for you. In the meantime, here are a half dozen suggestions for the kind of idea that may be fruitful.

The Dilemma, or Catch-22.   You find yourself facing, or know someone who is facing, or read about someone who is facing, a situation that offers no solution whatsoever. Any action taken would be painful and costly. You have no chance of solving this dilemma in real life, but you're a writer, and it costs nothing to solve it with imaginary people in an imaginary setting, even if the solution is a tragic one. Some writers use newspaper stories to generate this sort of idea. The situation is there in the bland black and white of this morning's news. But who are these people, and how did they come to be in such a mess? Make it up, think it through.

The Incongruity.   Something comes to your attention that is interesting precisely because you can't figure it out. It doesn't seem to make sense. Someone is breeding pigs in the backyard of a mansion in the most affluent section of town. Who is it? Why is she doing it? Your inventing mind can find the motives and the meanings. An example from my own experience: Once when my phone was out of order, I went out very late at night to make a call from a public phone at a supermarket plaza. At something like two in the morning all the stores were closed but the plaza was not empty. There were three women there, one of them with a baby in a stroller. *What were they doing there?* It was several years before I figured out a possible answer, and that answer was a short story.

The Connection.   You notice a striking similarity in two events, people, places, or periods that are fundamentally unlike. The more you explore the similarity, the more striking it becomes. My novel *The Buzzards* came from such a connection: The daughter of a famous politician was murdered, and I found myself in the position of comforting the dead girl's fiancé, at the same time as I was writing lectures on the *Agamemnon* of Aeschylus. Two politicians, two murdered daughters—one in ancient Greece and one in contemporary America. The connection would not let go of me until I had thought it through and set it down.

The Memory.   Certain people, places, and events stand out in your memory with an intensity beyond logic. There's no earthly reason you should remember the smell of Aunt K's rouge. It makes no sense that you still flush with shame at the thought of that ball you "borrowed" when you were in fourth grade. But for some reason these things are still vivid in your mind. That vividness can be explored, embellished, given form. Stephen Minot in *Three Genres* wisely advises, though, that if you are going to write from a memory, it should be a memory more than a year old. Otherwise you are likely to be unable to distinguish between what happened and what must happen in the story, or between what is in your mind and what you have conveyed on the page.

The Transplant.   You find yourself having to deal with a feeling that is either startlingly new to you or else obsessively old. You feel incapable of dealing with it. As a way of distancing yourself from that feeling and gaining some mastery over it, you write about the feeling as precisely as you can, but giving it to an imaginary someone in an imaginary situation. What situation other than your own would produce such a feeling? Who would be caught in that situation? Think it through.

The Revenge.   An injustice has been done, and you are powerless to do anything about it. But you're not really, because you're a writer. Reproduce the situation with another set of characters, in other circumstances or another setting. Cast the outcome to suit yourself. Punish whomever you choose. Even if the story ends in a similar injustice, you have righted the wrong by enlisting your reader's sympathy on the side of right. (Dante was particularly good at this: He put his enemies in the inferno and his friends in paradise.) Remember too that as human beings we are intensely, sometimes obsessively, interested in our boredom, and you can take revenge against the things that bore you by making them absurd or funny on paper.

Keep Going

A story idea may come from any source at any time. You may not know you have an idea until you spot it in the random jottings of your journal. Once you've identified the idea, the process of thinking it through begins, and doesn't end until you finish (or abandon) the story. Most writing is done between the mind and the hand, not between the hand and the page. It may take a fairly competent typist about three hours to type a twelve-page story. It may take days or months to write it. It follows that, even when you are writing well, most of the time spent writing is not spent putting words on the page. If the story idea grabs hard hold of you, the process of thinking through may be involuntary, a gift. If not, you need to find the inner stillness that will allow you to develop your characters, get to know them, follow their actions in your mind; and it may take an effort of the will to find such stillness.

The metamorphosis of an idea into a story has many aspects, some deliberate and some mysterious. "Inspiration" is a real thing, a gift from the subconscious to the conscious mind. But over and over again, successful writers attest that unless they prepare the conscious mind with the habit of work, the gift does not come. Writing is mind-farming. You have to plow, plant, weed, and hope for growing weather. Why a seed turns into a plant is something you are never going to understand, and the only relevant response to it is gratitude. You may be proud, however, of having plowed.

Many writers besides Dorothea Brande have observed that it is ideal, having turned your story over in your mind, to write the first draft at one sitting, pushing on through the action to the conclusion, no matter how dissatisfied you are with this paragraph, that character, this phrasing, or that incident. There are two advantages to doing this. The first is that you are more likely to produce a coherent draft when you come to the desk in a single frame of mind with a single vision of the whole, than when you write piecemeal, having altered ideas and moods. The second is that fast writing tends to make for fast pace in the story. It is always easier, later, to add and develop than it is to sharpen the pace. If you are the sort of writer who stays on page one for days, shoving commas around and combing the thesaurus for a word with slightly better connotations, then you should probably force yourself to try this method (more than once). A note of caution, though: If you write a draft at one sitting, it will not be the draft you want to show anyone, so schedule the sitting well in advance of whatever deadline you may have.

However, this method does not always work, for a variety of reasons. Obviously it won't work for a novel (though the British author Gabriel Josipovici once startled me by observing that the first draft of a novel could be written in a month: "Ten pages a day for thirty days gives you three hundred—and then you rewrite it seventeen times"). Novelist Sheila Taylor recounts how she accomplished her first book: She decided that she would give herself permission to write one bad page a day for a year. At the end of the year she had three hundred and sixty-five pages. She will not show them to anyone, but she had proved that she could write a novel, and her second, third, and fourth novels are in print in several languages.

It may happen—always keeping in mind that a single-sitting draft is the ideal—that as you write, the story will take off of its own accord in some direction totally other than you intended. You thought you knew where you were going and now you don't, and you know that unless you stop for a while and think it through again, you'll go wrong. You may find that although you are doing precisely what you had in mind, it doesn't work, and it needs more imaginative mulching before it will bear fruit. Or you may find, simply, that your stamina gives out, and that though you have done your exercises, been steadfast, loyal, and practiced every writerly virtue known, you're stuck. You have writer's block.

Writer's block is not so popular as it was a few years ago. I suspect people got tired of hearing or even talking about it—sometimes writers can be sensitive even to their own clichés. But it may also be that writers began to understand and accept their difficulties. Sometimes the process seems to require working yourself into a muddle and past the muddle to despair; until you have done this, it may be impossible suddenly to see what the shape of a thing ought to be. When you're writing, this feels terrible. You sit spinning your wheels, digging deeper and deeper into the mental muck. You decide you are going to trash the whole thing and walk away from it—only you can't, and you keep coming back to it like a tongue to an aching tooth. Or you decide you are going to sit there until you bludgeon it into shape—and as long as you sit there it remains recalcitrant. W. H. Auden observed that the hardest part of writing is not knowing whether you are procrastinating or must wait for the words to come.

I know a newspaper editor who says that writer's block always represents a lack of information. I thought this inapplicable to fiction until I noticed that I was mainly frustrated when I didn't know enough about my characters, the scene, or the action—when I had not gone to the imaginative depth where information lies.

So I learned something, but it led to the familiar guilt: *procrastinating again!* Victoria Nelson, in *On Writer's Block: A New Approach to Creativity* says that if you accuse yourself of procrastinating, you aren't a procrastinator, you're an accuser.

Whenever I ask a group of writers what they find most difficult about writing, a significant number answer that they feel they aren't good enough, that the empty page intimidates them, that they are in some way afraid. Many complain of their own laziness, but I have a wise friend who says she doesn't believe in laziness, which, like money, doesn't really exist except to represent something else—in this case fear, severe self-judgment, or possibly, the natural needs of the imaginal process.

Guilt, inadequacy, self-accusation, fear—all these stopper the imagination, and probably the best way out of a block is any way at all that helps you avoid what Natalie Goldberg calls "the cycle of guilt, avoidance, and pressure."

The stubborn fact remains that at some point we have to go to the desk or the story will not get written. This chapter has suggested some techniques to help us get there, and encouragement also comes from the poet William Stafford, who advised his students always to write to their lowest standard. Somebody always corrected him: "You mean your highest standard." No, he meant your lowest standard. Victoria Nelson means the same thing when she points out that "there is an almost mathematical ratio between soaring, grandiose ambition. . . and severe creative block." More writers prostitute themselves "up" than "down"; more are false in the determination to write great literature than to throw off a romance. A rough draft is rough; that's its nature. Let it be rough. Think of it as making clay. The molding and the gloss come later.

Remember: Writing is easy. Not writing is hard.

A Word About Theme

The process of discovering, choosing, and revealing the theme of your story begins as early as a first freewrite and continues, probably, beyond publication. The theme is what your story is about and what you think about it, its core and the spin you put on it. John Gardner points out that theme "is not imposed on the story but evoked from within it—initially an intuitive but finally an intellectual act on the part of the writer."

What your story has to say will gradually reveal itself to you and to your reader through every choice you as a writer make—the actions, characters, setting, dialogue, objects, pace, metaphors and symbols, viewpoint, atmosphere, style, even syntax and punctuation, and even in some cases typography.

Because of this comprehensive nature of theme, I have placed the discussion of it in chapter 10, after the individual story elements have been addressed. But this is not entirely satisfactory, since each of those elements contribute to the theme as it unfolds. You may want to skip ahead to take a look at that chapter, or you may want to anticipate the issue by asking at every stage of your manuscript: What really interests me about this? How does this (image, character, dialogue, place. . .) reveal what I care about? What connections do I see between one image and another? How can I strengthen those connections? Am I saying what I really mean, telling my truth about it?

All the later chapters in this book are followed by short stories that operate as examples of the elements of fiction under consideration. What follows here, however, are three excerpts by writers on the writing process from books of exceptional quality, very different from each other in content, tone, and form.

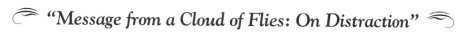 *"Message from a Cloud of Flies: On Distraction"*

BONNIE FRIEDMAN

I spent this morning smashing flies. I meant to be writing my novel. In fact, I'd already read over a few pages of it to hear the narrator's voice again, and copied onto a fresh piece of unlined yellow paper the last sentences from yesterday, and I was just about to come up with something new—when my ears buzzed. On the glass before me hung the black thick body of a fly. I decided to get rid of it so I could concentrate.

I rolled up a section of The Globe and returned to the desk. The fly remained in the exact same spot, as if glued. I swung, struck, thought, There, that's done— but when I lifted the baton: nothing. The fly hovered so close my bare arm tickled. Then it swooped to another window. I slammed—a direct hit!—but at that very instant two more flies sprang off the glass as if popped into the universe. I was surprised: all our windows have screens. This was a humid, hot day, though, the last sigh of summer after two crisp weeks, and perhaps that had drawn them.

I killed one fly against the doorjamb. Another I stalked into the kitchen and got against the fridge. A third fly wavered by the kitchen window. When I swatted, a wild ferocious swing, a whole trembling crowd shot from the window like pebbles from a blunderbuss, then settled back.

My heart pounded. I felt flushed with disgust and irritation. Why must I always have such obstacles to my writing? I craved to be submerged, to be "into" my novel, to be in that state when words come fast, and the characters walk and talk the way characters in your dreams do—without your conscious desire. It is like snorkeling: you go under, and there is a whole secret life. You go under, and scarlet fish shimmer past, fluttering like silk, watched perhaps by a gaping blue-striped grunt with a yellow eye, or there's a barracuda, all set to lunge. Outside, you saw just the water's surface mirroring back your own choppy face and the familiar, corrugated world. Submerged, breathing through a tube, you have a strange freedom from gravity, and an awareness of beauty like a bodily hum.

I craved that world, not this. I longed to go under. So frequently, though, there were obstacles: a bag of Growth Iambs my cat needed, an oil leak in the Civic (the landlady left a surly message about it on my answering machine), an insurance form I had to fill out and send to Minneapolis regarding last month's strep throat.

So many flies! I killed one against the window frame. Another buzzed against the glass as if it hoped to drown in it, and, when I swung, the breeze split the one in two and then I killed them both. I killed five, six, seven flies—I was furious! The more I wanted to end them, though, the more I had to study them, and they repulsed me more and more—the plump iridescent bluish bodies, the shifting plates, the gigantic reddish heads above the fragile legs. Once I struck the glass so hard it cracked. I sat down once, composed my mind, picked up my pen, and just as I was about to start writing saw a fly's wings and blood clinging to my hand. Another time I sat down, wrote two sentences, and heard—could it be?—a faint buzz, then the thud as a small body hit glass.

I would not learn. I was a human being controlled by a fly. Education, discipline, artistic vision—gone. My eyes were mesmerized and my arms followed scrupulously the movements of an insect. It ruled me. I let it. I wanted to get everything in that room just right before my writing began. I was afraid that just as a good idea was about to come to me, about to leap the synapse and appear fullblown, a fly would appear, and jar me, and the idea would fall in the gap and be lost forever, something impossible to recall because it was never really *known*.

It was my very commitment to writing that kept me from it. I wanted so much for it to be that ideal, submerged experience that I put it off. I saved it up. I longed for it, missed it, got bitchy about it, petulant, then again thought of it with a pang—an adored but long-gone love. What if the cherished one really isn't so beautiful after all? What if he turns out to be, upon reunion, slow, dumb, greedy, with lips that are thin and colorless—not at all as you'd remembered!

You love your work, so you don't touch it. You love your writing, so it's the very thing you must not do at all. You could not tolerate it if it didn't come out well. You could not tolerate yourself. You are thinking about the work, thinking about yourself, looking at the surface of the water, looking at the choppy face looking back.

"To distract" originally meant to rend into parts. It's from the Latin for "to draw in different directions, to pull asunder," and calls to mind the ancient torture of roping a man to horses and having them charge off in opposite directions. Distraction wrenches apart; it scatters and divides. The word also meant, as it does now, to draw someone from his or her actual destination, to perplex, and to derange in mind.

Those flies divided me up in a dozen tangled ways. Part of me craved my writing, part of me craved killing flies, part of me saw myself killing flies and said this makes no sense, and part said this *makes* sense, and part of me was aware of myself looking at myself like looking down a hall of mirrors. Eyes complex as an insect's stared back. An insect has compound eyes, each eye an array of facets, a crowded honeycomb of lenses. Images splinter in, the world a prism place, full of distraction.

Distraction said to me, I am the true path. I am the way to your beloved destination. Follow me and soon you'll be able to undistractedly write. I am the way to Concentration, Distraction said. It spoke in the voice of logic. It always took as its subject just this one last fly. It consumed tremendous energy. I whirled like a dervish, in place. I flapped like a human with an ant mask on. My cheeks were flushed with it, my head buzzed with it—the more distracted I was, the more distracted I became. The more I wanted cleanliness, the more my hands were smeared with filth. The more I yearned to be into my writing, the more I was decisively out.

On the Jewish New Year there is a prayer: "On New Year's Day the decree is inscribed and on the Day of Atonement it is sealed . . . who shall have rest and who go wandering; who shall be tranquil and who shall be disturbed; who shall be at ease and who shall be afflicted."

When I was a girl, I wondered at this prayer. I thought it was no curse to go wandering. All the best people were off wandering in those days, in painted vans, or hitching rides by the roadside. Almost all eventually settled somewhere or other. It is the curse of the pariah, of Cain himself, to be "a ceaseless wanderer." Unknown and unknowing, it is a living death. One can follow any road. Any road's just as good. Up every lane pipes a voice: "Follow me!"

I am drawn into distraction because I want to be distracted. It is a common choice. Compare the number of people who are "blocked" with the number who actually write, and you'd probably find a vast, shadow people, a ghostly populace caught within the lack of words. "Just do it," is the frequent advice, like a Nike ad. When I heard the tiny thud of yet another fly landing on the window, though, I rose from the desk. I knew about the sticky, seductive nature of distraction, yet I chose it.

I thought, if I can't control this room, how can I control my writing? Yet the essence of writing is not control, but release. Plan your story's path too narrowly, blinder it like a hack horse lugging a bunch of characters up the street—no, you may not go down that alley; no, to you that road must be a painted backdrop—and the damn thing balks. The story won't budge. Or else it shatters in tiny pieces, like a pencil ground too sharp, pressed too hard. Graphite clutters the page, and the point just lies there, an amputated thing.

When writing is going well it is not like pushing. It's like falling. You fall the way you do in dreams. You fall and fall. There is that same disorientation and breathlessness and speed and tension. You fall past the ground floor, past the sub-basement, past the creatures that live in the center of the earth, big black lobster-like figures working machines you glimpse as you fall toward blue sky. What joy! And yet, it's scary. For all its vast pleasure, it's scary because falling stops, words end, and it is always just you again at your desk in your room, judgment already beginning.

We have an aversion to loss of control, as much as we love it. We have an almost instinctive revulsion to people and things that are out of control or whom reason doesn't rule: drunk people, rioting people, the snake suddenly underfoot, the cockroach in the kitchen, unbridled nature, big as death. American history is an onslaught against wildness. All that chopping and burning and shooting at Indians reveal men appalled by what seemed untamed. We are terrified as much as we are enthralled by what seems wild, and by our own wildness. We don't know what will come out of it. We don't know what will come out of us. Perhaps something good. Perhaps ugly things, awful sentiments, perhaps hideous crawling bugs. We may awake in our writing to find ourselves Gregor Samsa.

I killed the bugs outside me because I longed to kill the bugs inside. I was afraid, I've said, that just as a good idea was about to come to me, a fly would appear. I was afraid the good idea would *be* a fly, an ugly appalling thing, something I wished would disappear.

Yet the things that disgust also fascinate. We don't want to look, but our eyes dart over. We sleep and they loom in our dreams. En masse we gaze at what we dare not see alone: bodies decomposing, you can see the worms; a mummy-faced creature with fingers that are knives; a machine that murders and murders—there's no stopping it, it's crushed but repairs itself, always ending up gleaming like new. Horror films, bloody movies—we laugh, but go. It's a thrill. Or we don't go but the images reach us anyway. In dreams, we are locked together. The night is dark, the body paralyzed with sleep. One is helpless before one's own thoughts. They arise and arise, although you prohibit them. They are impervious as the Martians in *War of the Worlds*. We don't know how to make them stop. One last defense works for a while. Dawn comes, and we wake to forget.

"It often happens," Freud notes, "that the account first given of a dream is incomplete and that the memory of the omitted portions only emerges in the course of analysis ... a part of a dream that has been rescued from oblivion in this way is invariably the most important part."

Freud likens the nonjudgmental mood necessary for remembering dreams to the attitude needed to write creatively: "The adoption of the required attitude of mind towards ideas that seem to emerge 'of their own free will' and the abandonment of the critical function that is normally in operation against them seem to be hard of achievement for some people. The 'involuntary thoughts' are liable to release a most violent resistance, which seeks to prevent their emergence. If we may trust that great poet and philosopher Friedrich von Schiller, however, poetic creation must demand an exactly similar attitude."

My resistance this morning was certainly "violent." I waged a furious attack. I acted out the role of censor, annihilating the unbidden with my paper bat. Freud calls the peculiarities of dreams "repugnant" to waking thought. He describes their "transitory character, the manner in which waking thought pushes them on one side, as something alien to it, and mutilates or extinguishes them in memory." All that disgust this morning— from what instinct did it spring?

We want to abandon ourselves in our writing, to experience images that come to us "of their own free will," and yet we are opposed to it. We are, in fact, ambivalent. Ambivalence, Harold Bloom reminds us, was used by Freud to mean "a simultaneous love and hatred directed toward the same object."

Writer's "block" embodies this ambivalence. One calls oneself a writer, but one who is "blocked." The block obstructs the passageway. It is a thing lodged in the throat, prohibiting speech. It is a boulder jammed in the mouth of the cave. The repressed cannot exit. The buried is kept below. Of course we know the repressed *will* out—but if you have a good solid block, at least it won't disgorge itself all over the unequivocal page. The block is like a man's Adam's apple, a sign of sin, of one's own suspected sin, stuck almost painfully in one's throat.

Not-writing has the same source as writing. It is the secret sharer. It is the yin of writing's yang. It is the tapeworm in the belly, the parasite that feeds at the host's expense, debilitating, hard to see, potent and obscure. It consumes the words one would have said. It hides them in itself, able to absorb as intensely as a black hole, collapsing entire worlds inside it and remaining dark as before. "Tap into what you don't want to say," urges movie director Arthur Penn. "Tap into that secret place, despite the agony, despite the personal pain, over and above the fatigue. This one little piece of me I want to get down on film."

This is the piece that craves words *and* silence.

We are afraid of writing, even those of us who love it. And there are parts of it we hate. The necessary mess, the loss of control, its ability to betray us, as well as the possibility that what we write might be lousy, it might just stink (it might just stink and we'll know it's ours, or worse, we might think it's lovely and show it to others only to realize by their constrained, uncomfortable response, that in fact we let loose a bad one)—how to feel at ease with all this? How just to let one's work be?

Our horror of the spontaneous emission and our obsession with perfection make us mute. We want beauty so badly we're speechless. We want the face of Dorian Gray: perfect no matter what. Never mind the poor soul was driven to ever greater corruption, provoked by his beautiful, impervious face. We want it. And what terrifies is the possibility that instead we'll end up with his cracked, decaying portrait, the pustules, the leer. Keep it in the closet! Lock it up and throw away the key!

But no, we keep the key in a deep vest pocket. We hide it on ourselves. We finger it from time to time. There it is: the key. It is a small, solid thing, like a stump of pencil. It takes up a definite space. Hard to believe so small a thing could hold such power. You toss it in the air while strolling. You slip it in your pants, jangle it against your change. It is a secret you keep with yourself—a little private joke. But oh, if it should fall into the wrong hands! So you keep it, and when you change your pants or your vest, your shirt or your shoes, you don't for a minute forget where it is. Afraid of losing it, you want it lost. It weighs a ton, it weighs nothing at all. What is it? Give up? If only you could! Give up, and the answer appears. Give up, and you are released. Give up, give up—let the bells toll it throughout your land. Struggle, and clarity of mind disperses. Surrender, and somehow it's yours.

The quality of concentration is not strained. "It droppeth as the gentle rain of heaven / Upon the place below." A writer's concentration is not only like mercy, it is mercy, mercy toward oneself. It is allowing imperfection. It is allowing mess. Even what stinks must be allowed into one's heaven. Even what has been considered paltry, contemptible, must have its place. Bar the lowly, and no one worthwhile will enter. Accept, and a teeming crowd appears, a whole mixed multitude of beggars and billionaires, quiet louts and loudmouth saints. The mutter, the cracked voice, the false start, the false start again, all precede the song. Those who write do have a trick. They lean on the process of writing the way an unsteady person leans on a cane. Not by sheer genius alone does the work advance. Not by an inchoate blaze from the head.

If you have few expectations for a piece, if you don't load it up with the baggage of the ego like an immigrant cart strapped with every single pot and pillow to be carried into the new life, surprisingly, the story or poem often gets good. That's the tricky part, not letting its goodness get in your way. Not being afraid to touch the half-finished piece for fear of messing it up. Letting yourself surrender your hopes for it again and again.

In New York I saw a Buddhist monk making a sand mandala. He had six or seven bowls of colored sand—egg-yolk orange, midnight blue, dusty gray among them—and a metal cone the size of a bull's horn, which had a tiny hole at the end. The monk scooped a bit of sand into the cone, and when he tapped, a trickle of sand beaded out of the hole a few grains at a time. With this he painted elaborate, complicated scenes: a procession of elephants looped tail to trunk, many-tiered palaces, flying birds, regal tigers, each intricate quarter of the design mirroring the opposite quarter in byzantine symmetry, the entire disk perhaps four feet across. In the hour I watched—this was in the Museum of Natural History, at the raging height of an apocalyptically hot summer—the monk shaped the tail of a lion. First he used yellow. Then he shaded with an echoing curve of red, then white. The tail shimmered like a flame.

It was a meditation to construct this mandala. It was being drawn for the spiritual benefit of the artist and of those people who would see it. The monk leaned intently over his trickle of sand. It would take three months to finish the work. It would take hundreds of hours of steady focus. Then, when it was done—kaput! He'd throw it to the wind. Or he would take it and toss it into the sea "for," a sign explained, "the spiritual benefit of the fish."

That is how it is with sand mandalas. With them, it's all in the doing. When they're done, they're gone. How can he bear it? I thought. In every tap of the funnel there is farewell. In every movement of the wrist, good-bye. The reward for the effort is giving it to the wind, giving it to the fish in the sea, doing it to be doing it, not to have it done.

Oh, to write openhandedly! To do it letting go! I've wanted that and wanted that, and sometimes it's just come to me like the gentle rain of heaven, but more often I've received it after practice, after much practice managing to outdistance even my acquisitive self.

I knew a man who believed a bee had been sent to earth to give him a message. He was sitting on a hilltop in Mexico, after smoking peyote. A bee hovered near him. It hovered and did not depart. It stayed so long he began to think it had a reason to be with him. It had chosen him, he thought. It was a spirit, a soul, a familiar. It brought a message of blessing and peace. It reassured him, sitting there.

A few days later this man found out his mother was dying in New York. He returned to that city and stayed in a room in a rent-by-the-week hotel in Chelsea while she slowly died. His room was cold and shabby and gave onto an airshaft. He was either at the hospital or he was there. He remembered that bee at that time. Years later he still remembered it.

If a bee in Mexico can bring a message, then a fly in Massachusetts can, too. My fly says, "Let me hover near you. Kill me and kill me, and I will come back. You will exhaust yourself in useless struggle. Let me be, and soon you will forget I'm here." Accept the fly before you, accept the fly that appears on the page. Who knows? You may even come to find beauty in its strange company.

From *The Writing Life*

ANNIE DILLARD

When you write, you lay out a line of words. The line of words is a miner's pick, a wood-carver's gouge, a surgeon's probe. You wield it, and it digs a path you follow. Soon you find yourself deep in new territory. Is it a dead end, or have you located the real subject? You will know tomorrow, or this time next year.

You make the path boldly and follow it fearfully. You go where the path leads. At the end of the path, you find a box canyon. You hammer out reports, dispatch bulletins.

The writing has changed, in your hands, and in a twinkling, from an expression of your notions to an epistemological tool. The new place interests you because it is not clear. You attend. In your humility, you lay down the words carefully, watching all the angles. Now the earlier writing looks soft and careless. Process is nothing; erase your tracks. The path is not the work. I hope your tracks have grown over; I hope birds ate the crumbs; I hope you will toss it all and not look back.

The line of words is a hammer. You hammer against the walls of your house. You tap the walls, lightly, everywhere. After giving many years' attention to these things, you know what to listen for. Some of the walls are bearing walls; they have to stay, or everything will fall down. Other walls can go with impunity; you can hear the difference. Unfortunately, it is often a bearing wall that has to go. It cannot be helped. There is only one solution, which appalls you, but there it is. Knock it out. Duck.

Courage utterly opposes the bold hope that this is such fine stuff the work needs it, or the world. Courage, exhausted, stands on bare reality: this writing weakens the work. You must demolish the work and start over. You can save some of the sentences, like bricks. It will be a miracle if you can save some of the paragraphs, no matter how excellent in themselves or hard-won. You can waste a year worrying about it, or you can get it over with now. (Are you a woman, or a mouse?)

The part you must jettison is not only the best-written part; it is also, oddly, that part which was to have been the very point. It is the original key passage, the, passage on which the rest was to hang, and from which you yourself drew the courage to begin. Henry James knew it well, and said it best. In his preface to *The*

Spoils of Poynton, he pities the writer, in a comical pair of sentences that rises to a howl: "Which is the work in which he hasn't surrendered, under dire difficulty, the best thing he meant to have kept? In which indeed, before the dreadful done, doesn't he ask himself what has become of the thing all for the sweet sake of which it was to proceed to that extremity?"

So it is that a writer writes many books. In each book, he intended several urgent and vivid points, many of which he sacrificed as the book's form hardened. "The youth gets together his materials to build a bridge to the moon," Thoreau noted mournfully, "or perchance a palace or temple on the earth, and at length the middle-aged man concludes to build a wood-shed with them." The writer returns to these materials, these passionate subjects, as to unfinished business, for they are his life's work.

It is the beginning of a work that the writer throws away.

A painting covers its tracks. Painters work from the ground up. The latest version of a painting overlays earlier versions, and obliterates them. Writers, on the other hand, work from left to right. The discardable chapters are on the left. The latest version of a literary work begins somewhere in the work's middle, and hardens toward the end. The earlier version remains lumpishly on the left; the work's beginning greets the reader with the wrong hand. In those early pages and chapters anyone may find bold leaps to nowhere, read the brave beginnings of dropped themes, hear a tone since abandoned, discover blind alleys, track red herrings, and laboriously learn a setting now false.

Several delusions weaken the writer's resolve to throw away work. If he has read his pages too often, those pages will have a necessary quality, the ring of the inevitable, like poetry known by heart; they will perfectly answer their own familiar rhythms. He will retain them. He may retain those pages if they possess some virtues, such as power in themselves, though they lack the cardinal virtue, which is pertinence to, and unity with, the book's thrust. Sometimes the writer leaves his early chapters in place from gratitude; he cannot contemplate them or read them without feeling again the blessed relief that exalted him when the words first appeared—relief that he was writing anything at all. That beginning served to get him where he was going, after all; surely the reader needs it, too, as groundwork. But no.

Every year the aspiring photographer brought a stack of his best prints to an old, honored photographer, seeking his judgment. Every year the old man studied the prints and painstakingly ordered them into two piles, bad and good. Every year the old man moved a certain landscape print into the bad stack. At length he turned to the young man: "You submit this same landscape every year, and every year I put it on the bad stack. Why do you like it so much?" The young photographer said, "Because I had to climb a mountain to get it."

A cabdriver sang his songs to me, in New York. Some we sang together. He had turned the meter off; he drove around midtown, singing. One long song he sang twice; it was the only dull one. I said, You already sang that one; let's sing something else. And he said, "You don't know how long it took me to get that one together."

How many books do we read from which the writer lacked courage to tie off the umbilical cord? How many gifts do we open from which the writer neglected to remove the price tag? Is it pertinent, is it courteous, for us to learn what it cost the writer personally?

You write it all, discovering it at the end of the line of words. The line of words is a fiber optic, flexible as wire; it illumines the path just before its fragile tip. You probe with it, delicate as a worm . . . .

When you are stuck in a book; when you are well into writing it, and know what comes next, and yet cannot go on; when every morning for a week or a month you enter its room and turn your back on it; then the trouble is either of two things. Either the structure has forked, so the narrative, or the logic, has developed a hair-line fracture that will shortly split it up the middle—or you are approaching a fatal mistake. What you had planned will not do. If you pursue your present course, the book will explode or collapse, and you do not know about it yet, quite.

In Bridgeport, Connecticut, one morning in April 1987, a six-story concrete-slab building under construction collapsed, and killed twenty-eight men. Just before it collapsed, a woman across the street leaned from her window and said to a passerby, "That building is starting to shake." "Lady," he said, according to the Hartford *Courant*, "you got rocks in your head."

You notice only this: your worker—your one and only, your prized, coddled, and driven worker—is not going out on that job. Will not budge, not even for you, boss. Has been at it long enough to know when the air smells wrong; can sense a tremor through boot soles. Nonsense, you say; it is perfectly safe. But the worker will not go. Will not even look at the site. Just developed heart trouble. Would rather starve. Sorry.

What do you do? Acknowledge, first, that you cannot do nothing. Lay out the structure you already have, x-ray it for a hairline fracture, find it, and think about it for a week or a year; solve the insoluble problem. Or subject the next part, the part at which the worker balks, to harsh tests. It harbors an unexamined and wrong premise. Something completely necessary is false or fatal. Once you find it, and if you can accept the finding, of course it will mean starting again. This is why many experienced writers urge young men and women to learn a useful trade.

Every morning you climb several flights of stairs, enter your study, open the French doors, and slide your desk and chair out into the middle of the air. The desk and chair float thirty feet from the ground, between the crowns of maple trees. The furniture is in place; you go back for your thermos of coffee. Then, wincing, you step out again through the French doors and sit down on the chair and look over the desktop. You can see clear to the river from here in winter. You pour yourself a cup of coffee.

Birds fly under your chair. In spring, when the leaves open in the maples' crowns, your view stops in the treetops just beyond the desk; yellow warblers hiss and whisper on the high twigs, and catch flies. Get to work. Your work is to keep cranking the flywheel that turns the gears that spin the belt in the engine of belief that keeps you and your desk in midair. . . .

The reason to perfect a piece of prose as it progresses—to secure each sentence before building on it—is that original writing fashions a form. It unrolls out into nothingness. It grows cell to cell, bole to bough to twig to leaf; any careful word may suggest a route, may begin a strand of metaphor or event out of which much, or all, will develop. Perfecting the work inch by inch, writing from the first word toward the last, displays the courage and fear this method induces. The strain, like Giacometti's penciled search for precision and honesty, enlivens the work and impels it toward its truest end. A pile of decent work behind him, no matter how small, fuels the writer's hope, too; his pride emboldens and impels him. One Washington writer—Charlie Butts—so prizes momentum, and so fears self-consciousness, that he writes fiction in a rush of his own devising. He leaves his house on distracting errands, hurries in the door, and without taking off his coat, sits at a typewriter and retypes in a blur of speed all of the story he has written to date. Impetus propels him to add another sentence or two before he notices he is writing and seizes up. Then he leaves the house and repeats the process; he runs in the door and retypes the entire story, hoping to squeeze out another sentence the way some car engines turn over after the ignition is off, or the way Warner Bros.' Wile E. Coyote continues running for several yards beyond the edge of a cliff, until he notices.

The reason not to perfect a work as it progresses is that, concomitantly, original work fashions a form the true shape of which it discovers only as it proceeds, so the early strokes are useless, however fine their sheen. Only when a paragraph's role in the context of the whole work is clear can the envisioning writer direct its complexity of detail to strengthen the work's ends.

Fiction writers who toss up their arms helplessly because their characters "take over"—powerful rascals, what is a god to do?—refer, I think, to these structural mysteries that seize any serious work, whether or not it possesses fifth-column characters who wreak havoc from within. Sometimes part of a book simply gets up and walks away. The writer cannot force it back in place. It wanders off to die. . . .

You climb a long ladder until you can see over the roof, or over the clouds. You are writing a book. You watch your shod feet step on each round rung, one at a time; you do not hurry and do not rest. Your feet feel the steep ladder's balance; the long muscles in your thighs check its sway. You climb steadily, doing your job in the dark. When you reach the end, there is nothing more to climb. The sun hits you. The bright wideness surprises you; you had forgotten there was an end. You look back at the ladder's two feet on the distant grass, astonished.

The line of words fingers your own heart. It invades arteries, and enters the heart on a flood of breath; it presses the moving rims of thick valves; it palpates the dark muscle strong as horses, feeling for something, it knows not what. A queer picture beds in the muscle like a worm encysted—some film of feeling, some song forgotten, a scene in a dark bedroom, a corner of the woodlot, a terrible dining room, that exalting sidewalk; these fragments are heavy with meaning. The line of words peels them back, dissects them out. Will the bared tissue burn? Do you want to expose these scenes to the light? You may locate them and leave them, or poke the spot hard till the sore bleeds on your finger, and write with that blood. If the sore spot is not fatal, if it does not grow and block something, you can use its power for many years, until the heart resorbs it.

The line of words feels for cracks in the firmament.

The line of words is heading out past Jupiter this morning. Traveling 150 kilometers a second, it makes no sound. The big yellow planet and its white moons spin. The line of words speeds past Jupiter and its cumbrous, dizzying orbit; it looks neither to the right nor to the left. It will be leaving the solar system soon, single-minded, rapt, rushing heaven like a soul. You are in Houston, Texas, watching the monitor. You saw a simulation: the line of words waited still, hushed, pointed with longing. The big yellow planet spun toward it like a pitched ball and passed beside it, low and outside. Jupiter was so large, the arc of its edge at the screen's bottom looked flat. The probe twined on; its wild path passed between white suns small as dots; these stars fell away on either side, like the lights on a tunnel's walls.

Now you watch symbols move on your monitor; you stare at the signals the probe sends back, transmits in your own tongue, numbers. Maybe later you can guess at what they mean—what they might mean about space at the edge of the solar system, or about your instruments. Right now, you are flying. Right now, your job is to hold your breath. . . .

What is this writing life? I was living alone in a house once, and had set up a study on the first floor. A portable green Smith-Corona typewriter sat on the table against the wall. I made the mistake of leaving the room.

I was upstairs when I felt the first tremor. The floor wagged under my feet — what was that?—and the picture frames on the wall stirred. The house shook and made noise. There was a pause; I found my face in the dresser mirror, deadpan. When the floor began again to sway, I walked downstairs, thinking I had better get down while the stairway held.

I saw at once that the typewriter was erupting. The old green Smith-Corona typewriter on the table was exploding with fire and ash. Showers of sparks shot out of its caldera—the dark hollow in which the keys lie. Smoke and cinders poured out, noises exploded and spattered, black dense smoke rose up, and a wild, deep fire lighted the whole thing. It shot sparks.

I pulled down the curtains. When I leaned over the typewriter, sparks burnt round holes in my shirt, and fire singed a sleeve. I dragged the rug away from the sparks. In the kitchen I filled a bucket with water and returned to the erupting typewriter. The typewriter did not seem to be flying apart, only erupting. On my face and hands I felt the heat from the caldera. The yellow fire made a fast, roaring noise. The typewriter itself made a rumbling, grinding noise; the table pitched.

Nothing seemed to require my bucket of water. The table surface was ruined, of course, but not aflame. After twenty minutes or so, the eruption subsided.

That night I heard more rumblings—weak ones, ever farther apart. The next day I cleaned the typewriter, table, floor, wall, and ceiling. I threw away the burnt shirt. The following day I cleaned the typewriter again—a film of lampblack still coated the caldera—and then it was over. I have had no trouble with it since. Of course, now I know it can happen. . . .

The sensation of writing a book is the sensation of spinning, blinded by love and daring. It is the sensation of rearing and peering from the bent tip of a grassblade, looking for a route. At its absurd worst, it feels like what mad Jacob Boehme, the German mystic, described in his first book. He was writing, incoherently as usual, about the source of evil. The passage will serve as well for the source of books.

"The whole Deity has in its innermost or beginning Birth, in the Pith or Kernel, a very tart, terrible *Sharpness*, in which the astringent Quality is very horrible, tart, hard, dark and cold Attraction or Drawing together, like *Winter*, when there is a fierce, bitter cold Frost, when Water is frozen into Ice, and besides is very intolerable."

If you can dissect out the very intolerable, tart, hard, terribly sharp Pith or Kernel, and begin writing the book compressed therein, the sensation changes. Now it feels like alligator wrestling, at the level of the sentence.

This is your life. You are a Seminole alligator wrestler. Half naked, with your two bare hands, you hold and fight a sentence's head while its tail tries to knock you over. Several years ago in Florida, an alligator wrestler lost. He was grappling with an alligator in a lagoon in front of a paying crowd. The crowd watched the young Indian and the alligator twist belly to belly in and out of the water; after one plunge, they failed to rise. A young writer named Lorne Ladner described it. Bubbles came up on the water. Then blood came up, and the water stilled. As the minutes elapsed, the people in the crowd exchanged glances; silent, helpless, they quit the stands. It took the Indians a week to find the man's remains.

At its best, the sensation of writing is that of any unmerited grace. It is handed to you, but only if you look for it. You search, you break your heart, your back, your brain, and then—and only then—it is handed to you. From the corner of your eye you see motion. Something is moving through the air and headed your way. It is a parcel bound in ribbons and bows; it has two white wings. It flies directly at you; you can read your name on it. If it were a baseball, you would hit it out of the park. It is that one pitch in a thousand you see in slow motion; its wings beat slowly as a hawk's.

One line of a poem, the poet said—only one line, but thank God for that one line—drops from the ceiling. Thornton Wilder cited this unnamed writer of sonnets: one line of a sonnet falls from the ceiling, and you tap in the others around it with a jeweler's hammer. Nobody whispers it in your ear. It is like something you memorized once and forgot. Now it comes back and rips away your breath. You find and finger a phrase at a time; you lay it down cautiously, as if with tongs, and wait suspended until the next one finds you: Ah yes, then this; and yes, praise be, then this.

Einstein likened the generation of a new idea to a chicken's laying an egg: *"Kieks—auf einmal ist es da."* Cheep—and all at once there it is. Of course, Einstein was not above playing to the crowd. . . .

Push it. Examine all things intensely and relentlessly. Probe and search each object in a piece of art. Do not leave it, do not course over it, as if it were understood, but instead follow it down until you see it in the mystery of its own specificity and strength. Giacometti's drawings and paintings show his bewilderment and persistence. If he had not acknowledged his bewilderment, he would not have persisted. A twentieth-century master of drawing, Rico Lebrun, taught that "the draftsman must aggress; only by persistent assault will the live image capitulate and give up its secret to an unrelenting line." Who but an artist fierce to know—not fierce to seem to know—would suppose that a live image possessed a secret? The artist is willing to give all his or her strength and life to probing with blunt instruments those same secrets no one can describe in any way but with those instruments' faint tracks.

Admire the world for never ending on you—as you would admire an opponent, without taking your eyes from him, or walking away.

One of the few things I know about writing is this: spend it all, shoot it, play it, lose it, all, right away, every time. Do not hoard what seems good for a later place in the book, or for another book; give it, give it all, give it now. The impulse to save something good for a better place later is the signal to spend it now. Something more will arise for later, something better. These things fill from behind, from beneath, like well water. Similarly, the impulse to keep to yourself what you have learned is not only shameful, it is destructive. Anything you do not give freely and abundantly becomes lost to you. You open your safe and find ashes.

After Michelangelo died, someone found in his studio a piece of paper on which he had written a note to his apprentice, in the handwriting of his old age: "Draw, Antonio, draw, Antonio, draw and do not waste time. . . . "

∽∽∽∽∽∽∽∽∽∽

Suggestions for Discussion

1. Bonnie Friedman takes a "just do it" approach to writing, while Annie Dillard stresses the difficulty and intensity of the work. Which most nearly describes your own process? Could you improve your work by leaning toward the other mode?

2. What insights into the writing process surprise you, discourage you, make you want to get to work?

3. What incidents, insights, moments of realization remind you of moments you have already experienced as a writer?

4. What elements of fiction does each of the essays employ?

Writing Assignments

Keep a journal for two weeks. Decide on a comfortable amount to write daily, and then determine not to let a day slide. In addition to the journal suggestions already in this chapter—freewriting, page 4; the Dorothea Brande exercise, page 5; clustering, pages 5–8; a menu of concerns, page 10; a review of your first seven years, page 10; a set of *Pillow Book* lists, page 10—you might try these:

1. Prove to yourself the abundance of your invention by opening this book and pointing at random. Take the noun nearest where your finger falls, cluster it for two or three minutes, and freedraft a paragraph on the subject.

2. Sketch a floor plan of the first house you remember. Place an X on the spots in the plan where significant events happened to you. Write a tour of the house as if you were a guide, pointing out its features and its history.

3. Identify the kernel of a short story from your experience of one of the following:
   - first memory
   - a dream
   - parents
   - loss
   - unfounded fear
   - your body
   - yesterday

   Cluster the word and freedraft a passage about it. Outline a story based on it. Write the first page of the story.

4. Identify a passage in one of the three excerpts above that seems to parallel or echo your own experience. Cluster, then freedraft, a response to it.

5. Write a short memoir of some moment that has to do with reading or writing—the moment you discovered that you could read, for example, or could write your name; or an early influence that has led you toward writing.

6. A classroom exercise: After you have written every day for a week, bring in what you consider your *worst* piece of writing. Tell the class what's wrong with it. The others' assignment is to point out its strengths and all the possibilities in it.

At the end of the two weeks, assess yourself and decide what habit of journal keeping you can develop and stick to. A page a day? A paragraph a day? Three pages a week? Then do it. Probably at least once a day you have a thought worth wording, and sometimes it's better to write one sentence a day than to let the habit slide. Like exercise and piano practice, a journal is most useful when it's kept up regularly and frequently. If you pick an hour during which you write each day, no matter how much or how little, you may find yourself looking forward to, and saving things up for, that time.

2

THE TOWER AND THE NET

Story Form and Structure

- *Conflict, Crisis, and Resolution*

- *Story and Plot*

- *The Short Story and the Novel*

What makes you want to write?

It seems likely that the earliest storytellers—in the tent or the harem, around the campfire or on the Viking ship—told stories out of an impulse to tell stories. They made themselves popular by distracting their listeners from a dull or danger-ous evening with heroic exploits and a skill at creating suspense: What happened next? And after that? And then what happened?

Natural storytellers are still around, and a few of them are very rich. Some are on the best-seller list; more are in television and film. But it's probable that your impulse to write has little to do with the desire or the skill to work out a plot. On the contrary, you want to write because you are sensitive. You have something to say that does not answer the question, What happened next? You share with most—and the best—twentieth-century fiction writers a sense of the injustice, the absurdity, and the beauty of the world; and you want to register your protest, your laughter, and your affirmation.

Yet readers still want to wonder what happened next, and unless you make them wonder, they will not turn the page. You must master plot, because no matter how profound or illuminating your vision of the world may be, you cannot convey it to those who do not read you.

E. M. Forster, in *Aspects of the Novel*, mourns the necessity of storytelling.

Let us listen to three voices. If you ask one type of man, "What does a novel do?" he will reply placidly: "Well—I don't know—it seems a funny sort of question to ask—a novel's a novel—well, I don't know—I suppose it kind of tells a story, so to speak." He is quite good-tempered and vague, and probably driving a motor bus at the same time and paying no more attention to literature than it merits. Another man, whom I visualize as on a golf-course, will be aggressive and brisk. He will reply: "What does a novel do? Why, tell a story of course, and I've no use for it if it didn't. I like a story. Very bad taste on my part, no doubt, but I like a story. You can take your art, you can take your literature, you can take your music, but give me a good story. And I like a story to be a story, mind, and my wife's the same." And a third man, he says in a sort of drooping regretful voice, "Yes—oh dear yes—the novel tells a story." I respect and admire the first speaker. I detest and fear the second. And the third is myself. Yes—oh dear yes—the novel tells a story. That is the fundamental aspect without which it could not exist. That is the highest factor common to all novels, and I wish that it was not so, that it could be something different— melody, or perception of the truth, not this low atavistic form.

When editors take the trouble to write a rejection letter to a young author (and they do so only when they think the author talented), the gist of the letter most frequently is: "This piece is sensitive (perceptive, vivid, original, brilliant, funny, moving), but it is not a *story*."

How do you know when you have written a story? And if you're not a natural-born wandering minstrel, can you go about learning to write one?

It's interesting that we react with such different attitudes to the words "formula" and "form" as they apply to a story. A *formula* story is hackwork, the very lowest "atavistic" form of supplying a demand. To write one, you read three dozen copies of *Cosmopolitan* or *Amazing Stories*, make a list of what kinds of characters and situations the editors buy, shuffle nearly identical characters around in slightly altered situations, and sit back to wait for the check. Whereas *form* is a term of the highest artistic approbation, even reverence, with overtones of *order, harmony, model, archetype*.

And "story" is a "form" of literature. Like a face, it has necessary features in a necessary harmony. We're aware of the infinite variety of human faces, aware of their unique individuality, which is so powerful that you can recognize a face you know even after twenty years of age and fashion have done their work on it. We're aware that minute alterations in the features can express grief, anger, or joy. If you place side by side two photographs of, say, Debra Winger and Geronimo, you are instantly aware of the fundamental differences of age, race, sex, class, and century; yet these two faces are more like each other than either is like a foot or a fern, both of which have their own distinctive forms. Every face has two eyes, a nose between them, a mouth below, a forehead, two cheeks, two ears, and a jaw. If a face is missing one of these features, you may say, "I love this face in spite of its lacking a nose," but you must acknowledge the *in spite of*. You can't simply say, "This is a wonderful face."

The same is true of a story. You might say, "I love this piece even though there's no crisis action in it." You can't simply say, "This is a wonderful story."

Conflict, Crisis, and Resolution

Fortunately, the necessary features of the story form are fewer than those of a face. They are *conflict, crisis, and resolution*.

Conflict is the first encountered and the fundamental element of fiction, fundamental because in literature, only trouble is interesting.

Only trouble is interesting. This is not so in life. Life offers periods of comfortable communication, peaceful pleasure, and productive work, all of which are extremely interesting to those involved. But such passages about such times by themselves make for dull reading; they can be used as lulls in an otherwise tense situation, as a resolution, even as a hint that something awful is about to happen; they cannot be used as a whole plot.

Suppose, for example, you go on a picnic. You find a beautiful deserted meadow with a lake nearby. The weather is splendid and so is the company. The food's delicious, the water's fine, and the insects have taken the day off. Afterward, someone asks you how your picnic was. "Terrific," you reply, "really perfect." No story.

But suppose the next week you go back for a rerun. You set your picnic blanket on an anthill. You all race for the lake to get cold water on the bites, and one of your friends goes too far out on the plastic raft, which deflates. He can't swim and you have to save him. On the way in you gash your foot on a broken bottle. When you get back to the picnic, the ants have taken over the cake and a possum has demolished the chicken. Just then the sky opens up. When you gather your things to race for the car, you notice an irritated bull has broken through the fence. The others run for it, but because of your bleeding heel the best you can do is hobble. You have two choices: try to outrun him or stand perfectly still and hope he's interested only in a moving target. At this point, you don't know if your friends can be counted on for help, even the nerd whose life you saved. You don't know if it's true that a bull is attracted by the smell of blood.

A year later, assuming you're around to tell about it, you are still saying, "Let me *tell* you what happened last year." And your listeners are saying, "What a story!"

If this contrast is true of so trivial a subject as a picnic, it is even more so of the great themes of life: birth, love, sex, work, and death. Here is a very interesting love story to live: Jan and Jon meet in college. Both are beautiful, intelligent, talented, popular, and well adjusted. They're of the same race, class, religion, and political persuasion. They are sexually compatible. Their parents become fast friends. They marry on graduating, and both get rewarding work in the same city. They have three children, all of whom are healthy, happy, beautiful, intelligent, and popular; the children love and respect their parents to a degree that is the envy of everyone. All the children succeed in work and marriage. Jan and Jon die peacefully, of natural causes, at the same moment, at the age of eighty-two, and are buried in the same grave.

No doubt this love story is very interesting to Jan and Jon, but you can't make a novel of it. Great love stories involve intense passion and a monumental impediment to that passion's fulfillment. So: They love each other passionately, but their parents are sworn enemies (*Romeo and Juliet*). Or: They love each other passionately, but he's black and she's white, and he has an enemy who wants to punish him (*Othello*). Or: They love each other passionately, but she's married (*Anna Karenina*). Or: He loves her passionately, but she falls in love with him only when she has worn out his passion ("Frankly, my dear, I don't give a damn").

In each of these plots, there is both intense desire and great danger to the achievement of that desire; generally speaking, this shape holds good for all plots. It can be called 3-D: *Drama* equals *desire* plus *danger.* One common fault of talented young writers is to create a main character who is essentially passive. This is an understandable fault; as a writer you are an observer of human nature and activity, and so you identify easily with a character who observes, reflects, and suffers. But such a character's passivity transmits itself to the page, and the story also becomes passive. Aristotle rather startlingly claimed that a man *is* his desire. It is true that in fiction, in order to engage our attention and sympathy, the central character must *want*, and want intensely.

The thing that the character wants need not be violent or spectacular; it is the intensity of the wanting that introduces an element of danger. She may want, like *The Suicide's Wife* in David Madden's novel, no more than to get her driver's license, but if so she must feel that her identity and her future depend on her getting a driver's license, while a corrupt highway patrolman tries to manipulate her. He may want, like Samuel Beckett's Murphy, only to tie himself to his rocking chair and rock, but if so he will also want a woman who nags him to get up and get a job. She may want, like the heroine of Margaret Atwood's *Bodily Harm*, only to get away from it all for a rest, but if so she must need rest for her survival, while tourists and terrorists involve her in machinations that begin in discomfort and end in mortal danger.

It's important to realize that the great dangers in life and in literature are not necessarily the most spectacular. Another mistake frequently made by young writers is to think that they can best introduce drama into their stories by way of muggers, murderers, crashes, and monsters, the external stock dangers of pulp and TV. In fact, all of us know that the most profound impediments to our desire usually lie close to home, in our own bodies, personalities, friends, lovers, and families. Fewer people have cause to panic at the approach of a stranger with a gun than at the approach of mama with the curling iron. More passion is destroyed at the breakfast table than in a time warp.

A frequently used critical tool divides possible conflicts into several basic categories: man against man, man against nature, man against society, man against machine, man against God, man against himself. Most stories fall into these categories, and they can provide a useful way of discussing and comparing works. But the employment of categories can be misleading to someone behind the typewriter, insofar as it suggests that literary conflicts take place in these abstract, cosmic dimensions. A writer needs a specific story to tell, and if you sit down to pit "man" against "nature," you will have less of a story than if you pit seventeen-year-old James Tucker of Weehawken, New Jersey, against a two-and-a-half-foot bigmouth bass in the backwoods of Toomsuba, Mississippi. (The value of specificity is a point to which we will return again and again.)

Once conflict is sharply established and developed in a story, the conflict must end. There must be a crisis and a resolution. This is not like life either, and although it is so obvious a point, it needs to be insisted on. Order is a major value that literature offers us, and order implies that the subject has been brought to closure. In life this never quite happens. Even the natural "happy endings," marriage and birth, leave domesticity and childrearing to be dealt with; the natural "tragic endings," separation and death, leave trauma and bereavement in their wake. Literature absolves us of these nuisances. Whether or not the lives of the characters end, the story does, and we are left with a satisfying sense of completion. This is one reason we enjoy crying or feeling terrified or even nauseated by fiction; we know in advance that it's going to be over, and by contrast with the continual struggle of living, all that ends, ends well.

What I want to do now is to present several ways—they are all essentially metaphors—of seeing this pattern of *conflict-crisis-resolution* in order to make the shape and its many variations clearer, and particularly to indicate what a crisis action is.

The editor and teacher Mel McKee states flatly that "a story is a war. It is sustained and immediate combat." He offers four imperatives for the writing of this "war" story.

(1) get your fighters fighting, (2) have something—the stake—worth their fighting over, (3) have the fight dive into a series of battles with the last battle in the series the biggest and most dangerous of all, (4) have a walking away from the fight.

The stake over which wars are fought is usually a territory, and it's important that this "territory" in a story be as tangible and specific as the Gaza Strip. For example, in William Carlos Williams's story "The Use of Force," found at the end of this chapter, the war is fought over the territory of the little girl's mouth, and the fight begins narrowing to that territory from the first paragraph. As with warring nations, the story territory itself can come to represent all sorts of serious abstractions—self-determination, domination, freedom, dignity, identity—but the soldiers fight yard by yard over a particular piece of grass or sand.

Just as a minor "police action" may gradually escalate into a holocaust, story form follows its most natural order of "complications" when each battle is bigger than the last. It begins with a ground skirmish, which does not decide the war. Then one side brings in spies, and the other, guerrillas; these actions do not decide the war. So one side brings in the air force, and the other answers with antiaircraft. One side takes to missiles, and the other answers with rockets. One side has poison gas, and the other has a hand on the nuclear button. Metaphorically, this is what happens in a story. As long as one antagonist can recoup enough power to counter-attack, the conflict goes on. But, at some point in the story, one of the antagonists will produce a weapon from which the other cannot recover. *The crisis action is the last battle and makes the outcome inevitable;* there can no longer be any doubt who wins the particular territory—though there can be much doubt about moral victory. When this has happened the conflict ends with a significant and permanent change—which is the definition, in fiction, of a resolution.

Notice that although a plot involves a desire and a danger to that desire, it does not necessarily end happily if the desire is achieved, nor unhappily if it is not. In *Hamlet*, Hamlet's desire is to kill King Claudius, and he is prevented from doing so for most of the play by other characters, intrigues, and his own mental state. When he finally succeeds, it is at the cost of every significant life in the play, including his own. Although the hero "wins" his particular "territory," the play is a tragedy. In Margaret Atwood's *Bodily Harm,* on the other hand, the heroine ends up in a political prison. Yet the discovery of her own strength and commitment is such that we know she has achieved salvation.

Novelist Michael Shaara described a story as a power struggle between equal forces. It is imperative, he argued, that each antagonist have sufficient power that the reader is left in doubt about the outcome. We may be wholly in sympathy with one character and even reasonably confident that she or he will triumph. But the antagonist must represent a real and potent danger, and the pattern of the story's complications will be achieved by *shifting the power back and forth from one antagonist to the other.* Finally, an action will occur that will shift the power irretrievably in one direction.

It is also important to understand that "power" takes many forms, some of which have the external appearance of weakness. Anyone who has ever been tied to the demands of an invalid can understand this: Sickness can be great strength. Weakness, need, passivity, an ostensible desire not to be any trouble to anybody—all these can be used as manipulative tools to prevent the protagonist from achieving his or her desire. Martyrdom is immensely powerful, whether we sympathize with it or not; a dying man absorbs all our energies.

The power of weakness has generated the central conflict in many stories and plays. Here is a passage in which it is swiftly and deftly sketched:

> This sepulchral atmosphere owed a lot to the presence of Mrs. Taylor herself. She was a tall, stooped woman with deep-set eyes. She sat in her living room all day long and chain-smoked cigarettes and stared out the picture window with an air of unutterable sadness, as if she knew things beyond mortal bearing. Sometimes she would call Taylor over and wrap her arms around him, then close her eyes and hoarsely whisper, "Terence, Terence!" Eyes still closed, she would turn her head and resolutely push him away.

> Tobias Wolff, *This Boy's Life*

Some critics of recent years have pointed out the patriarchal nature of narrative seen as a war or power struggle. Seeing the world in terms of conflict and crisis, of enemies and warring factions, not only limits the possibilities of literature, they argue, but also promulgates an aggressive and antagonistic view of our own lives. Further, the notion of resolution is untrue to life, and holds up perfection, unity, and singularity as goals at the expense of acceptance, nuance, and variety.

Speaking of the "gladiatorial view of fiction," Ursula Le Guin writes:

> People are cross-grained, aggressive, and full of trouble, the storytellers tell us; people fight themselves and one another, and their stories are full of their struggles. But to say that that *is* the story is to use one aspect of existence, conflict, to subsume all other aspects, many of which it does not include and does not comprehend.
>
> *Romeo and Juliet* is a story of the conflict between two families, and its plot involves the conflict of two individuals with those families. Is that all it involves? Isn't *Romeo and Juliet* about something else, and isn't it the something else that makes the otherwise trivial tale of a feud into a tragedy?

I'm indebted to dramatist Claudia Johnson for this further—and, it seems to me, crucial—insight about that "something else": Whereas the hierarchical or "vertical" nature of narrative, the power struggle, has long been acknowledged, there also appears in all narrative a "horizontal" pattern of connection and disconnection between characters which is the main source of its emotional effect. In discussing human behavior, psychologists speak in terms of "tower" and "network" patterns, the need to climb (which implies conflict) and the need for community, the need to win out over others and the need to belong to others; and these two forces also drive fiction.

In *Romeo and Juliet,* for example, the Montague and Capulet families are fiercely disconnected, but the young lovers manage to connect in spite of that. Throughout the play they meet and part, disconnect from their families in order to connect with each other, finally part from life in order to be with each other eternally. Their ultimate departure in death reconnects the feuding families.

The nineteenth-century German critic Gustav Freitag analyzed plot in terms of a pyramid of five actions: an exposition, followed by a complication (or *nouement* "knotting up" of the situation), leading to a crisis, which is followed by a "falling action" or anticlimax, resulting in a resolution (or *dénouement,* "unknotting").

In the compact short story form, the falling action is likely to be very brief or nonexistent, and often the crisis action itself implies the resolution, which is not necessarily stated but exists as an idea established in the reader's mind.

So for our purposes, it is probably more useful to think of story shape not as a pyramid with sides of equal length but as an inverted check mark. If we take the familiar tale of Cinderella and diagram it on such a shape in terms of the power struggle, we can see how the various elements reveal themselves even in this simple children's story.

At the opening of the tale we're given the basic conflict: Cinderella's mother has died, and her father has married a brutal woman with two waspish daughters. Cinderella is made to do all the dirtiest and most menial work, and she weeps among the cinders. The Stepmother has on her side the strength of ugliness and evil (two very powerful qualities in literature as in life). With her daughters she also has the strength of numbers, and she has parental authority. Cinderella has only beauty and goodness, but (in literature and life) these are also very powerful.

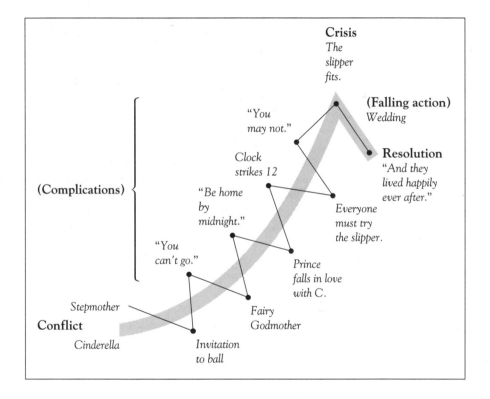

At the beginning of the struggle in "Cinderella," the power is very clearly on the Stepmother's side. But the first event (action, battle) of the story is that an invitation arrives from the Prince, which explicitly states that *all* the ladies of the land are invited to a ball. Notice that Cinderella's desire is not to triumph over her Stepmother (though she eventually will, much to our satisfaction); such a desire would diminish her goodness. She simply wants to be relieved of her mistreatment. She wants equality, so that the Prince's invitation, which specifically gives her a right equal to the Stepmother's and Stepdaughters' rights, shifts the power to her.

The Stepmother takes the power back by blunt force: You may not go; you must get us ready to go. Cinderella does so, and the three leave for the ball.

Then what happens? The Fairy Godmother appears. It is *very* powerful to have magic on your side. The Fairy Godmother offers Cinderella a gown, glass slippers, and a coach with horses and footmen, giving her more force than she has yet had.

But the magic is not all-potent. It has a qualification that portends bad luck. It will last only until midnight (unlike the Stepmother's authority), and Cinderella must leave the ball before the clock strikes twelve or risk exposure and defeat.

What happens next? She goes to the ball and the Prince falls in love with her— and love is an even more powerful weapon than magic in a literary war. In some versions of the tale, the Stepmother and Stepsisters are made to marvel at the beauty of the princess they don't recognize, pointing to the irony of Cinderella's new power.

And then? The magic quits. The clock strikes twelve, and Cinderella runs down the steps in her rags to her rats and pumpkin, losing a slipper, bereft of her power in every way.

But after that, the Prince sends out a messenger with the glass slipper and a dictum (a dramatic repetition of the original invitation in which all ladies were invited to the ball) that every female in the land is to try on the slipper. Cinderella is given her rights again by royal decree.

What happens then? In most good retellings of the tale, the Stepmother also repeats her assumption of brute authority by hiding Cinderella away, while our expectation of triumph is tantalizingly delayed with grotesque comedy: one sister cuts off a toe, the other a heel, trying to fit into the heroine's rightful slipper.

After that, Cinderella tries on the slipper and it fits. *This is the crisis action.* Magic, love, and royalty join to recognize the heroine's true self; evil, numbers, and authority are powerless against them. At this point, the power struggle has been decided; the outcome is inevitable. When the slipper fits, no further action can occur that will deprive Cinderella of her desire. The change in the lives of all concerned is significant and permanent.

The tale has a brief "falling action" or "walking away from the fight": the Prince sweeps Cinderella up on his white horse and gallops away to their wedding. The story comes to closure with the classic resolution of all comedy: They lived happily ever after.

If we look at "Cinderella" in terms of connection/disconnection we see a pattern as clear as that represented by the power struggle. The first painful disconnection is that Cinderella's mother has died; her father has married (connected with) a woman who spurns (disconnects from) her; the Prince's invitation offers connection, the Stepmother's cruelty alienates again. The Fairy Godmother connects as a magical friend, but the disappearance of the coach and gown disconnect Cinderella temporarily from that grand and glorious fairytale union, marriage to the Prince. If we consult the emotions that this tale engenders—pity, anger, hope, fear, romance, anticipation, disappointment, triumph—we see that both the struggle between antagonist/protagonist and the pattern of alienation/connectedness is necessary to ensure, not only that there is an action, but also that we care about its outcome. The traditional happy ending is the grand connection, marriage; the traditional tragic outcome is the final disconnection, death.

In the *Poetics*, the first extensive work of extant Western literary criticism, Aristotle referred to the crisis action of a tragedy as a *peripeteia*, or reversal of the protagonist's fortunes. Critics and editors agree that a reversal of some sort is necessary to all story structure, comic as well as tragic. Although the protagonist need not lose power, land, or life, he or she must in some significant way be changed or moved by the action. Aristotle specified that this reversal came about because of *hamartia*, which has for centuries been translated as a "tragic flaw" in the protagonist's character, usually assumed to be, or defined as, pride. But more recent critics have defined and translated hamartia much more narrowly as a "mistake in identity" with the reversal coming about in a "recognition."

It is true that recognition scenes have played a disproportionately large role in the crisis actions of plots both comic and tragic, and that these scenes frequently stretch credibility; in real life, you are unlikely to mistake the face of your mother, son, uncle, or even friend, and yet such mistakes have provided the turning point of many a plot. If, however, the notion of "recognition" is extended to more abstract and subtle realms, it becomes a powerful metaphor for moments of "realization." In other words, the "recognition scene" in literature may stand for that moment in life when we "recognize" that the man we have considered good is evil, the event we have considered insignificant is crucial, the woman we have thought out of touch with reality is a genius, the object we have thought desirable is poison. There is in this symbolic way a recognition in "Cinderella." We knew that she was essentially a princess, but until the Prince recognizes her as one, our knowledge must be frustrated.

James Joyce developed a similar idea when he spoke of, and recorded both in his notebooks and in his stories, moments of what he called *epiphany*. Epiphany as Joyce saw it is a crisis action in the mind, a moment when a person, an event, or a thing is seen in a light so new that it is as if it has never been seen before; at this recognition, the mental landscape of the viewer is permanently changed.

In many of the finest modern short stories and novels, the true territory of struggle is the main character's mind, and so the real crisis action must occur there. Yet it is important to grasp that Joyce chose the word *epiphany* to represent this moment of reversal, and that the word means "a manifestation of a supernatural being"; specifically, in Christian doctrine, "the manifestation of Christ to the gentiles." By extension, then, in a short story any mental reversal that takes place in the crisis of a story must be *manifested*; it must be triggered or shown by an action. The slipper must fit. It would not do if the Stepmother just happened to change her mind and give up the struggle; it would not do if the Prince just happened to notice that Cinderella looked like his love. The moment of recognition must be manifested in an action.

This point, that the crisis must be manifested or externalized in an action, is absolutely central, although sometimes difficult to grasp when the struggle of the story takes place in a character's mind.

It is easy to see, for example, how the conflict in a revenge story must come to crisis. The common revenge plot, from *Hamlet* to *Death Wish 4* takes this form:

Someone important to the hero (father, sister, lover, friend) is killed, and for some reason the authorities who ought to be in charge of justice can't or won't avenge the death. The hero must do so, then, and the crisis action is manifested in the swing of the dagger, the blast of the gun, the swallowing of the poison, whatever.

But suppose the story is about a struggle between two brothers on a fishing trip, and the change that takes place is that the protagonist, believing for most of the action that he holds his older brother in contempt, discovers at the end of the story that they are deeply bound by love and family history. Clearly this change is an epiphany, a mental reversal. A writer insufficiently aware of the nature of crisis action might signal the change in a paragraph that begins "suddenly Larry remembered their father and realized that Jeff was very much like him." Well, unless that memory and that realization are manifested in an action, the reader is unable to share them, and therefore cannot be moved with the character.

> Jeff reached for the old net and neatly bagged the trout, swinging round to offer it with a triumphant, "Got it! We got it, didn't we?" The trout flipped and struggled, giving off a smell of weed and water and fecund mud. Jeff's knuckles were lined with grime. The knuckles and the rich river smell filled him with a memory of their first fishing trip together, the sight of their father's hands on the same scarred net. . . .

Here the epiphany, a memory leading to a realization, is triggered by an action and sensory details that the reader can share; the reader now has a good chance of also being able to share the epiphany.

Much great fiction, and the preponderance of serious modern fiction, echoes life in its suggestion that there are no clear or permanent solutions, that the conflicts of character, relationship, and the cosmos cannot be permanently resolved. Most of the stories in this volume have the feel of the twentieth century, with its ambiguities and unfinished struggles; none could end "they lived happily ever after" or even "they lived unhappily ever after."

Yet the story form demands a resolution. Is there such a thing as a no-resolution resolution? Yes, and it has a very specific form. Go back to the metaphor that "a story is a war." After the skirmish, after the guerrillas, after the air strike, after the poison gas and the nuclear holocaust, imagine that the two surviving combatants, one on each side, emerge from their fallout shelters. They crawl, then stumble to the fence that marks the border. Each possessively grasps the barbed wire with a bloodied fist. The "resolution" of this battle is that neither side will ever give up and that no one will ever win; *there will never be a resolution.* This is a distinct reversal (the recognition takes place in the reader's mind) of the opening scene, in which it seemed eminently worthwhile to open a ground skirmish. In the statement of the conflict was an inherent possibility that one side or another could win. Inherent in the resolution is a statement that no one can ever win. That is a distinct reversal and a powerful change.

Story and Plot

So far, I have used the words "story" and "plot" interchangeably. The equation of the two terms is so common that they are often comfortably understood as synonyms. When an editor says, "This is not a story," the implication is not that it lacks character, theme, setting, or even incident, but that it has no plot.

Yet there is a distinction frequently drawn between the two terms, a distinction that although simple in itself, gives rise to manifold subtleties in the craft of narrative and that also represents a vital decision that you as a writer must make: Where should your narrative begin?

The distinction is easily made. A *story* is a series of events recorded in their chronological order. A *plot* is a series of events deliberately arranged so as to reveal their dramatic, thematic, and emotional significance.

Here, for example, is a fairly standard story: A sober, industrious, and rather dull young man meets the woman of his dreams. She is beautiful, brilliant, passionate, and compassionate; more wonderful still, she loves him. They plan to marry, and on the eve of their wedding his friends give him a stag party in the course of which they tease him, ply him with liquor, and drag him off to a whorehouse for a last fling. There he stumbles into a cubicle . . . to find himself facing his bride-to-be.

Where does this story become interesting? Where does the *plot* begin?

You may start, if you like, with the young man's *Mayflower* ancestry. But if you do, it's going to be a very long story, and we're likely to close the book about the middle of the nineteenth century. You may begin with the first time he meets the extraordinary woman, but even then you must cover at least weeks, probably months, in a few pages; and that means you must summarize, skip, and generalize, and you'll have a hard time both maintaining your credibility and holding our attention. Begin at the stag party? Better. If you do so, you will somehow have to let us know all that has gone before, either through dialogue or through the young man's memory, but you have only one evening of action to cover, and we'll get to the conflict quickly. Suppose you begin instead the next morning, when the man wakes with a hangover in bed in a brothel with his bride on his wedding day. Is that, perhaps, the best of all? An immediate conflict that must lead to a quick and striking crisis?

Humphry House, in his commentaries on Aristotle, defines *story* as everything the reader needs to know to make coherent sense of the plot, and *plot* as the particular portion of the story the author chooses to present—the "present tense" of the narrative. The story of *Oedipus Rex*, for example, begins before Oedipus's birth with the oracle predicting that he will murder his father and marry his mother. It includes his birth, his abandonment with hobbled ankles, his childhood with his foster parents, his flight from them, his murder of the stranger at the crossroads, his triumph over the Sphinx, his marriage to Jocasta and his reign in Thebes, his fatherhood, the Theban plague, his discovery of the truth, and his self-blinding and self-banishment. When Sophocles set out to plot a play on this story, he began at dawn on the very last day of it. All the information about Oedipus's life is necessary to understand the plot, but the plot begins with the conflict: How can Oedipus get rid of the plague in Thebes? Because the plot is so arranged, it is the revelation of the past that makes up the action of the play, a process of discovery that gives rise to the significant theme: Who am I? Had Sophocles begun with the oracle before Oedipus's birth, no such theme and no such significance could have been explored.

Forster makes substantially the same distinction between plot and story. A story, he says, is:

> the chopped off length of the tape worm of time . . . a narrative of events arranged in their time sequence. A plot is also a narrative of events, the emphasis falling on causality. "The king died, and then the queen died," is a story. "The king died, and then the queen died of grief," is a plot. The time sequence is preserved, but the sense of causality overshadows it. Or again: "The queen died, no one knew why, until it was discovered that it was through grief at the death of the king." This is a plot with a mystery in it, a form capable of high development. It suspends the time sequence, it moves as far away from the story as its limitations will allow. Consider the death of the queen. If it is in a story we say, "and then?" If it is in a plot we ask, "why?"

The human desire to know why is as powerful as the desire to know what happened next, and it is a desire of a higher order. Once we have the facts, we inevitably look for the links between them, and only when we find such links are we satisfied that we "understand." Rote memorization in a science bores almost everyone. Grasp and a sense of discovery begin only when we perceive *why* "a body in motion tends to remain in motion" and what an immense effect this actuality has on the phenomena of our lives.

The same is true of the events of a story. Random incidents neither move nor illuminate; we want to know why one thing leads to another and to feel the inevitability of cause and effect.

Here is a series of uninteresting events chronologically arranged.

Ariadne had a bad dream.
She woke up tired and cross.
She ate breakfast.
She headed for class.
She saw Leroy.
She fell on the steps and broke her ankle.
Leroy offered to take notes for her.
She went to a hospital.

This series of events does not constitute a plot, and if you wish to fashion it into a plot, you can do so only by letting us know the meaningful relations among the events. We first assume that Ariadne woke in a temper because of her bad dream, and that Leroy offered to take notes for her because she broke her ankle. But why did she fall? Perhaps because she saw Leroy? Does that suggest that her bad dream was about him? Was she, then, thinking about his dream-rejection as she broke her egg irritably on the edge of the frying pan? What is the effect of his offer? Is it a triumph or just another polite form of rejection when, really, he could have missed class once to drive her to the x-ray lab? All the emotional and dramatic significance of these ordinary events emerges in the relation of cause to effect, and where such relation can be shown, a possible plot comes into existence.

Ariadne's is a story you might very well choose to tell chronologically: it needs to cover only an hour or two, and that much can be handled in the compressed form of the short story. But such a choice of plot is not inevitable even in this short compass. Might it be more gripping to begin with the wince of pain as she stumbles? Leroy comes to help her up and the yolk yellow of his T-shirt fills her field of vision. In the shock of pain she is immediately back in her dream. . . .

When "nothing happens" in a story, it is because we fail to sense the causal relation between what happens first and what happens next. When something does "happen," it is because the resolution of a short story or a novel describes a change in the character's life, an effect of the events that have gone before. This is why Aristotle insisted with such apparent simplicity on "a beginning, a middle, and an end." A story is capable of many meanings, and it is first of all in the choice of structure—which portion of the story forms the plot—that you offer us the gratifying sense that we "understand."

The Short Story and the Novel

Many editors and writers insist on an essential disjunction between the form of the short story and that of the novel. It is my belief, however, that, like the distinction between story and plot, the distinction between the two forms is very simple, and the many and profound possibilities of difference proceed from that simple source: A short story is short, and a novel is long.

Because of this, a short story can waste no words. It can deal with only one or a very few consciousnesses. It may recount only one central action and one major change or effect in the life of the central character or characters. It can afford no digression that does not directly affect the action. A short story strives for a single emotional impact and imparts a single understanding, though both impact and understanding may be complex. The virtue of a short story is its density. If it is tight, sharp, economic, well knit, and charged, then it is a good short story because it has exploited a central attribute of the form—that it is short.

All of these qualities are praiseworthy in a novel, but a novel may also be comprehensive, vast, and panoramic. It may have power, not because of its economy but because of its scope, breadth, and sweep—the virtues of a medium that is long. Therefore, a novel may range through many consciousnesses, cover many years or generations, and travel the world. It may deal with a central line of action and one or several subplots. Many characters may change; many and various effects may constitute our final understanding. Many digressions may be tolerated and will not destroy the balance of the whole as long as they lead, finally, to some nuance of that understanding.

These differences in the possibilities of the novel and short-story forms may directly affect the relationship between story and plot. With the narrative leisure available to a novelist, it may very well be possible to begin with a character's birth, or even ancestry, even though the action culminates in middle or old age.

My own feeling as a writer is that in a novel I may allow myself, and ask the reader to share, an exploration of character, setting, and theme, letting these develop in the course of the narrative. When I am writing a short story, I must reject more, and I must select more rigorously.

One constant principle of artistic effectiveness is that you must discover what a medium cannot do and forget it; and discover what it can do and exploit it. Television is a good medium for domestic drama, but for a battle with a cast of thousands, you need a movie screen twelve feet high. For a woodland scene, water-color is fine; but for the agony of St. Sebastian, choose oil. If you are writing for radio, the conflict must be expressible in sound; if you are writing a mime, it must be expressible in movement.

This is not to say that one form is superior to another but simply that each is itself and that no medium and no form of that medium can do everything. The greater the limitation in time and space, the greater the necessity for pace, sharpness, and density. For this reason, it is a good idea to learn to write short stories before you attempt the scope of the novel, just as it is good to learn to write a lyric before you attempt an epic or to learn to draw an apple before you paint a god.

Nevertheless, the form of the novel is an expanded story form. It asks for a conflict, a crisis, and a resolution, and no technique described in this book is irrelevant to its effectiveness.

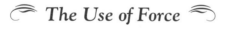

The Use of Force

WILLIAM CARLOS WILLIAMS

They were new patients to me, all I had was the name, Olson. Please come down as soon as you can, my daughter is very sick.

When I arrived I was met by the mother, a big startled looking woman, very clean and apologetic who merely said, Is this the doctor? and let me in. In the back, she added. You must excuse us, doctor, we have her in the kitchen where it is warm. It is very damp here sometimes.

The child was fully dressed and sitting on her father's lap near the kitchen table. He tried to get up, but I motioned for him not to bother, took off my overcoat and started to look things over. I could see that they were all very nervous, eyeing me up and down distrustfully. As often, in such cases, they weren't telling me more than they had to, it was up to me to tell them; that's why they were spending three dollars on me.

The child was fairly eating me up with her cold, steady eyes, and no expression to her face whatever. She did not move and seemed, inwardly, quiet; an unusually attractive little thing, and as strong as a heifer in appearance. But her face was flushed, she was breathing rapidly, and I realized that she had a high fever. She had magnificent blonde hair, in profusion. One of those picture children often reproduced in advertising leaflets and the photogravure sections of the Sunday papers.

She's had a fever for three days, began the father, and we don't know what it comes from. My wife has given her things, you know, like people do, but it don't do no good. And there's been a lot of sickness around. So we tho't you'd better look her over and tell us what is the matter.

As doctors often do I took a trial shot at it as a point of departure. Has she had a sore throat?

Both parents answered me together, No. . . No, she says her throat don't hurt her.

Does your throat hurt you? added the mother to the child. But the little girl's expression didn't change, nor did she move her eyes from my face.

Have you looked?

I tried to, said the mother, but I couldn't see.

As it happens, we had been having a number of cases of diphtheria in the school to which this child went during that month and we were all, quite apparently, thinking of that, though no one had as yet spoken of the thing.

Well, I said, suppose we take a look at the throat first. I smiled in my best professional manner and asking for the child's first name I said, come on, Mathilda, open your mouth and let's take a look at your throat.

Nothing doing.

Aw, come on, I coaxed, just open your mouth wide and let me take a look. Look, I said opening both hands wide, I haven't anything in my hands. Just open up and let me see.

Such a nice man, put in the mother. Look how kind he is to you. Come on, do what he tells you to. He won't hurt you.

At that I ground my teeth in disgust. If only they wouldn't use the word "hurt" I might be able to get somewhere. But I did not allow myself to be hurried or disturbed, but speaking quietly and slowly I approached the child again.

As I moved my chair a little nearer, suddenly with one catlike movement both her hands clawed instinctively for my eyes and she almost reached them too. In fact she knocked my glasses flying and they fell, though unbroken, several feet away from me on the kitchen floor.

Both the mother and father almost turned themselves inside out in embarrassment and apology. You bad girl, said the mother, taking her and shaking her by one arm. Look what you've done. The nice man.

For heaven's sake, I broke in. Don't call me a nice man to her. I'm here to look at her throat on the chance that she might have diphtheria and possibly die of it. But that's nothing to her. Look here, I said to the child, we're going to look at your throat. You're old enough to understand what I'm saying. Will you open it now by yourself or shall we have to open it for you?

Not a move. Even her expression hadn't changed. Her breaths however were coming faster and faster. Then the battle began. I had to do it. I had to have a throat culture for her own protection. But first I told the parents that it was entirely up to them. I explained the danger but said that I would not insist on a throat examination so long as they would take the responsibility.

If you don't do what the doctor says you'll have to go to the hospital, the mother admonished her severely.

Oh yeah? I had to smile to myself. After all, I had already fallen in love with the savage brat, the parents were contemptible to me. In the ensuing struggle they grew more and more abject, crushed, exhausted while she surely rose to magnificent heights of insane fury of effort bred of her terror of me.

The father tried his best, and he was a big man but the fact that she was his daughter, his shame at her behavior and his dread of hurting her made him release her just at the critical moment several times when I had almost achieved success, till I wanted to kill him. But his dread also that she might have diphtheria made him tell me to go on, go on though he himself was almost fainting, while the mother moved back and forth behind us raising and lowering her hands in an agony of apprehension.

Put her in front of you on your lap, I ordered, and hold both her wrists.

But as soon as he did the child let out a scream. Don't, you're hurting me. Let go of my hands. Let them go I tell you. Then she shrieked terrifyingly, hysterically. Stop it! Stop it! You're killing me!

Do you think she can stand it, doctor! said the mother.

You get out, said the husband to his wife. Do you want her to die of diphtheria?

Come on now, hold her, I said.

Then I grasped the child's head with my left hand and tried to get the wooden tongue depressor between her teeth. She fought, with clenched teeth, desperately! But now I also had grown furious—at a child. I tried to hold myself down but I couldn't. I know how to expose a throat for inspection. And I did my best. When finally I got the wooden spatula behind the last teeth and just the point of it into the mouth cavity, she opened up for an instant but before I could see anything she came down again and gripping the wooden blade between her molars she reduced it to splinters before I could get it out again.

Aren't you ashamed, the mother yelled at her. Aren't you ashamed to act like that in front of the doctor?

Get me a smooth-handled spoon of some sort, I told the mother. We're going through with this. The child's mouth was already bleeding. Her tongue was cut and she was screaming in wild hysterical shrieks. Perhaps I should have desisted and come back in an hour or more. No doubt it would have been better. But I have seen at least two children lying dead in bed of neglect in such cases, and feeling that I must get a diagnosis now or never I went at it again. But the worst of it was that I too had got beyond reason. I could have torn the child apart in my own fury and enjoyed it. It was a pleasure to attack her. My face was burning with it.

The damned little brat must be protected against her own idiocy, one says to one's self at such times. Others must be protected against her. It is social necessity. And all these things are true. But a blind fury, a feeling of adult shame, bred of a longing for muscular release are the operatives. One goes on to the end.

In a final unreasoning assault I overpowered the child's neck and jaws. I forced the heavy silver spoon back of her teeth and down her throat till she gagged. And there it was—both tonsils covered with membrane. She had fought valiantly to keep me from knowing her secret. She had been hiding that sore throat for three days at least and lying to her parents in order to escape just such an outcome as this.

Now truly she was furious. She had been on the defensive before but now she attacked. Tried to get off her father's lap and fly at me while tears of defeat blinded her eyes.

<hr />

Suggestions for Discussion

1. Identify the central conflict, the crisis, and the resolution in "The Use of Force."

2. This story has the feel of twentieth-century life, not at all the feel of a tale. Can it be positioned like "Cinderella" on the diagram?

3. How many power struggles are involved in this very short story? Identify the struggles between characters and within each character.

4. The doctor is clearly in a position of power with these poor people. Where and how is that power eroded?

5. What connects these characters? What separates them? What connections and disconnections occur?

6. How is the situation at the end of the story a reversal of that at the beginning? How is the doctor changed?

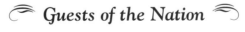

Guests of the Nation

FRANK O'CONNOR

I

At dusk the big Englishman, Belcher, would shift his long legs out of the ashes and say "Well, chums, what about it?" and Noble or me would say "All right, chum" (for we had picked up some of their curious expressions), and the little Englishman, Hawkins, would light the lamp and bring out the cards. Sometimes Jeremiah Donovan would come up and supervise the game and get excited over Hawkins's cards, which he always played badly, and shout at him as if he was one of our own "Ah, you divil, you, why didn't you play the tray?"

But ordinarily Jeremiah was a sober and contented poor devil like the big Englishman, Belcher, and was looked up to only because he was a fair hand at documents, though he was slow enough even with them. He wore a small cloth hat and big gaiters over his long pants, and you seldom saw him with his hands out of his pockets. He reddened when you talked to him, tilting from toe to heel and back, and looking down all the time at his big farmer's feet. Noble and me used to make fun of his broad accent, because we were from the town.

I couldn't at the time see the point of me and Noble guarding Belcher and Hawkins at all, for it was my belief that you could have planted that pair down anywhere from this to Claregalway and they'd have taken root there like a native weed. I never in my short experience seen two men to take to the country as they did.

They were handed on to us by the Second Battalion when the search for them became too hot, and Noble and myself, being young, took over with a natural feeling of responsibility, but Hawkins made us look like fools when he showed that he knew the country better than we did.

"You're the bloke they calls Bonaparte," he says to me. "Mary Brigid O'Connell told me to ask you what you done with the pair of her brother's socks you borrowed."

For it seemed, as they explained it, that the Second used to have little evenings, and some of the girls of the neighbourhood turned in, and, seeing they were such decent chaps, our fellows couldn't leave the two Englishmen out of them. Hawkins learned to dance "The Walls of Limerick," "The Siege of Ennis," and "The Waves of Tory" as well as any of them, though naturally, he couldn't return the compliment, because our lads at that time did not dance foreign dances on principle.

So whatever privileges Belcher and Hawkins had with the Second they just naturally took with us, and after the first day or two we gave up all pretence of keeping a close eye on them. Not that they could have got far, for they had accents you could cut with a knife and wore khaki tunics and overcoats with civilian pants and boots. But it's my belief that they never had any idea of escaping and were quite content to be where they were.

It was a treat to see how Belcher got off with the old woman of the house where we were staying. She was a great warrant to scold, and cranky even with us, but before ever she had a chance to giving our guests, as I may call them, a lick of her tongue, Belcher had made her his friend for life. She was breaking sticks, and Belcher, who hadn't been more than ten minutes in the house, jumped up from his seat and went over to her.

"Allow me, madam," he says, smiling his queer little smile, "please allow me"; and he takes the bloody hatchet. She was struck too paralytic to speak, and after that, Belcher would be at her heels, carrying a bucket, a basket, or a load of turf, as the case might be. As Noble said, he got into looking before she leapt, and hot water, or any little thing she wanted, Belcher would have it ready for her. For such a huge man (and though I am five foot ten myself I had to look up at him) he had an uncommon shortness—or should I say lack?—of speech. It took us some time to get used to him, walking in and out, like a ghost, without a word. Especially because Hawkins talked enough for a platoon, it was strange to hear big Belcher with his toes in the ashes come out with a solitary "Excuse me, chum," or "That's right, chum." His one and only passion was cards, and I will say for him that he was a good card-player. He could have fleeced myself and Noble, but whatever we lost to him Hawkins lost to us, and Hawkins played with the money Belcher gave him.

Hawkins lost to us because he had too much old gab, and we probably lost to Belcher for the same reason. Hawkins and Noble would spit at one another about religion into the early hours of the morning, and Hawkins worried the soul out of Noble, whose brother was a priest, with a string of questions that would puzzle a cardinal. To make it worse even in treating of holy subjects, Hawkins had a deplorable tongue. I never in all my career met a man who could mix such a variety of cursing and bad language into an argument. He was a terrible man, and a fright to argue. He never did a stroke of work, and when he had no one else to talk to, he got stuck in the old woman.

He met his match in her, for one day when he tried to get her to complain profanely of the drought, she gave him a great comedown by blaming it entirely on Jupiter Pluvius (a deity neither Hawkins nor I had ever heard of, though Noble said that among the pagans it was believed that he had something to do with the rain). Another day he was swearing at the capitalists for starting the German war when the old lady laid down her iron, puckered up her little crab's mouth, and said: "Mr. Hawkins, you can say what you like about the war, and think you'll deceive me because I'm only a simple poor countrywoman, but I know what started the war. It was the Italian Count that stole the heathen divinity out of the temple in Japan. Believe me, Mr. Hawkins, nothing but sorrow and want can follow the people that disturb the hidden powers."

A queer old girl, all right.

II

We had our tea one evening, and Hawkins lit the lamp and we all sat into cards. Jeremiah Donovan came in too, and sat down and watched us for a while, and it suddenly struck me that he had no great love for the two Englishmen. It came as a great surprise to me, because I hadn't noticed anything about him before.

Late in the evening a really terrible argument blew up between Hawkins and Noble, about capitalists and priests and love of your country.

"The capitalists," says Hawkins with an angry gulp, "pays the priests to tell you about the next world so as you won't notice what the bastards are up to in this."

"Nonsense, man!" says Noble, losing his temper. "Before ever a capitalist was thought of, people believed in the next world."

Hawkins stood up as though he was preaching a sermon.

"Oh, they did, did they?" he says with a sneer. "They believed all the things you believe, isn't that what you mean? And you believe that God created Adam, and Adam created Shem, and Shem created Jehoshophat. You believe all that silly old fairytale about Eve and Eden and the apple. Well, listen to me, chum. If you're entitled to hold a silly belief like that, I'm entitled to hold my silly belief—which is that the first thing your God created was a bleeding capitalist, with morality and Rolls-Royce complete. Am I right, chum?" he says to Belcher.

"You're right, chum," says Belcher with his amused smile, and got up from the table to stretch his long legs into the fire and stroke his moustache. So, seeing that Jeremiah Donovan was going, and that there was no knowing when the argument about religion would be over, I went out with him. We strolled down to the village together, and then he stopped and started blushing and mumbling and saying I ought to be behind, keeping guard on the prisoners. I didn't like the tone he took with me, and anyway I was bored with life in the cottage, so I replied by asking him what the hell we wanted guarding them at all for. I told him I'd talked it over with Noble, and that we'd both rather be out with a fighting column.

"What use are those fellows to us?" says I.

He looked at me in surprise and said: "I thought you knew we were keeping them as hostages."

"Hostages?" I said.

"The enemy have prisoners belonging to us," he says, "and now they're talking of shooting them. If they shoot our prisoners, we'll shoot theirs."

"Shoot them?" I said.

"What else did you think we were keeping them for?" he says.

"Wasn't it very unforeseen of you not to warn Noble and myself of that in the beginning?" I said.

"How was it?" says he. "You might have known it."

"We couldn't know it, Jeremiah Donovan," says I. "How could we when they were on our hands so long?"

"The enemy have our prisoners as long and longer," says he.

"That's not the same thing at all," says I.

"What difference is there?" says he.

I couldn't tell him, because I knew he wouldn't understand. If it was only an old dog that was going to the vet's, you'd try and not get too fond of him, but Jeremiah Donovan wasn't a man that would ever be in danger of that.

"And when is this thing going to be decided?" says I.

"We might hear tonight," he says. "Or tomorrow or the next day at latest. So if it's only hanging round here that's a trouble to you, you'll be free soon enough."

It wasn't the hanging round that was a trouble to me at all by this time. I had worse things to worry about. When I got back to the cottage the argument was still on. Hawkins was holding forth in his best style, maintaining that there was no next world, and Noble was maintaining that there was; but I could see that Hawkins had had the best of it.

"Do you know what, chum?" he was saying with a saucy smile. "I think you're just as big a bleeding unbeliever as I am. You say you believe in the next world, and you know just as much about the next world as I do, which is sweet damn-all. What's heaven? You don't know. Where's heaven? You don't know. You know sweet damn-all! I ask you again, do they wear wings?"

"Very well, then," says Noble, "they do. Is that enough for you? They do wear wings."

"Where do they get them, then? Who makes them? Have they a factory for wings? Have they a sort of store where you hands in your chit and takes your bleeding wings?"

"You're an impossible man to argue with," says Noble. "Now, listen to me—" And they were off again.

It was long after midnight when we locked up and went to bed. As I blew out the candle I told Noble what Jeremiah Donovan was after telling me. Noble took it very quietly. When we'd been in bed about an hour he asked me did I think we ought to tell the Englishmen. I didn't think we should, because it was more than likely that the English wouldn't shoot our men, and even if they did, the brigade officers, who were always up and down with the Second Battalion and knew the Englishmen well, wouldn't be likely to want them plugged. "I think so too," says Noble. "It would be great cruelty to put the wind to them now."

"It was very unforeseen of Jeremiah Donovan anyhow," says I.

It was next morning that we found it so hard to face Belcher and Hawkins. We went about the house all day scarcely saying a word. Belcher didn't seem to notice; he was stretched into the ashes as usual, with his look unusual of waiting in quietness for something unforeseen to happen, but Hawkins noticed and put it down to Noble's being beaten in the argument of the night before.

"Why can't you take a discussion in the proper spirit?" he says severely. "You and your Adam and Eve! I'm a Communist, that's what I am. Communist or anarchist, it all comes to much the same thing." And for hours he went round the house, muttering when the fit took him. "Adam and Eve! Adam and Eve! Nothing better to do with their time than picking bleeding apples!"

III

I don't know how we got through that day, but I was very glad when it was over, the tea things were cleared away, and Belcher said in his peaceable way: "Well, chums, what about it?" We sat round the table and Hawkins took out the cards, and just then I heard Jeremiah Donovan's footstep on the path and a dark presentiment crossed my mind. I rose from the table and caught him before he reached the door.

"What do you want?" I asked.

"I want those two soldier friends of yours," he says, getting red.

"Is that the way, Jeremiah Donovan?" I asked.

"That's the way. There were four of our lads shot this morning, one of them a boy of sixteen."

"That's bad," I said.

At that moment Noble followed me out, and the three of us walked down the path together, talking in whispers. Feeney, the local intelligence officer, was standing by the gate.

"What are you going to do about it?" I asked Jeremiah Donovan.

"I want you and Noble to get them out; tell them they're being shifted again; that'll be the quietest way."

"Leave me out of that," says Noble under his breath.

Jeremiah Donovan looks at him hard.

"All right," he says. "You and Feeney get a few tools from the shed and dig a hole by the far end of the bog. Bonaparte and myself will be after you. Don't let anyone see you with the tools. I wouldn't like it to go beyond ourselves."

We saw Feeney and Noble go round to the shed and went in ourselves. I left Jeremiah Donovan to do the explanations. He told them that he had orders to send them back to the Second Battalion. Hawkins let out a mouthful of curses, and you could see that though Belcher didn't say anything, he was a bit upset too. The old woman was for having them stay in spite of us, and she didn't stop advising them until Jeremiah Donovan lost his temper and turned on her. He had a nasty temper, I noticed. It was pitch-dark in the cottage by this time, but no one thought of lighting the lamp, and in the darkness the two Englishmen fetched their top-coats and said good-bye to the old woman.

"Just as a man makes a home of a bleeding place, some bastard at headquarters thinks you're too cushy and shunts you off," says Hawkins, shaking her hand.

"A thousand thanks, madam," says Belcher. "A thousand thanks for every-thing"—as though he'd made it up.

We went round to the back of the house and down towards the bog. It was only then that Jeremiah Donovan told them. He was shaking with excitement.

"There were four of our fellows shot in Cork this morning and now you're to be shot as a reprisal."

"What are you talking about?" snaps Hawkins. "It's bad enough being mucked about as we are without having to put up with your funny jokes."

"It isn't a joke," says Donovan. "I'm sorry, Hawkins, but it's true," and begins on the usual rigmarole about duty and how unpleasant it is.

I never noticed that people who talk a lot about duty find it much of a trouble to them.

"Oh, cut it out!" says Hawkins.

"Ask Bonaparte," says Donovan, seeing that Hawkins isn't taking him seriously. "Isn't it true, Bonaparte?"

"It is," I say, and Hawkins stops.

"Ah, for Christ's sake, chum!"

"You don't sound as if you meant it."

"If he doesn't mean it, I do," says Donovan, working himself up.

"What have you against me, Jeremiah Donovan?"

"I never said I had anything against you. But why did your people take out four of our prisoners and shoot them in cold blood?"

He took Hawkins by the arm and dragged him on, but it was impossible to make him understand that we were in earnest. I had the Smith and Wesson in my pocket and I kept fingering it and wondering what I'd do if they put up a fight for it or ran, and wishing to God they'd do one or the other. I knew if they did run for it, that I'd never fire on them. Hawkins wanted to know was Noble in it, and when we said yes, he asked us why Noble wanted to plug him. Why did any of us want to plug him? What had he done to us? Weren't we all chums? Didn't we understand him and didn't he understand us? Did we imagine for an instant that he'd shoot us for all the so-and-so officers in the so-and-so British Army?

By this time we'd reached the bog, and I was so sick I couldn't even answer him. We walked along the edge of it in the darkness, and every now and then Hawkins would call a halt and begin all over again, as if he was wound up, about our being chums, and I knew that nothing but the sight of the grave would convince him that we had to do it. And all the time I was hoping that something would happen; that they'd run for it or that Noble would take over the responsibility from me. I had the feeling that it was worse on Noble than on me.

IV

At last we saw the lantern in the distance and made towards it. Noble was carrying it, and Feeney was standing somewhere in the darkness behind him, and the picture of them so still and silent in the bogland brought it home to me that we were in earnest, and banished the last bit of hope I had.

Belcher, on recognizing Noble, said: "Hallo, chum," in his quiet way, but Hawkins flew at him at once, and the argument began all over again, only this time Noble had nothing to say for himself and stood with his head down, holding the lantern between his legs.

It was Jeremiah Donovan who did the answering. For the twentieth time, as though it was haunting his mind, Hawkins asked if anybody thought he'd shoot Noble.

"Yes, you would," says Jeremiah Donovan.

"No, I wouldn't, damn you!"

"You would, because you'd know you'd be shot for not doing it."

"I wouldn't, not if I was to be shot twenty times over. I wouldn't shoot a pal. And Belcher wouldn't—isn't that right, Belcher?"

"That's right, chum," Belcher said, but more by way of answering the question than of joining in the argument. Belcher sounded as though whatever unforeseen thing he'd always been waiting for had come at last.

"Anyway, who says Noble would be shot if I wasn't? What do you think I'd do if I was in his place, out in the middle of a blasted bog?"

"What would you do?" asks Donovan.

"I'd go with him wherever he was going, of course. Share my last bob with him and stick by him through thick and thin. No one can ever say of me that I let down a pal."

"We had enough of this," says Jeremiah Donovan, cocking his revolver. "Is there any message you want to send?"

"No, there isn't."

"Do you want to say your prayers?"

Hawkins came out with a cold-blooded remark that even shocked me and turned on Noble again.

"Listen to me, Noble," he says. "You and me are chums. You can't come over to my side, so I'll come over to your side. That show you I mean what I say? Give me a rifle and I'll go along with you and the other lads."

Nobody answered him. We knew that was no way out.

"Hear what I'm saying?" he says. "I'm through with it. I'm a deserter or anything else you like. I don't believe in your stuff, but it's no worse than mine. That satisfy you?"

Noble raised his head, but Donovan began to speak and he lowered it again without replying.

"For the last time, have you any messages to send?" says Donovan in a cold excited sort of voice.

"Shut up, Donovan! You don't understand me, but these lads do. They're not the sort to make a pal and kill a pal. They're not the tools of any capitalist."

I alone of the crowd saw Donovan raise his Webley to the back of Hawkins's neck, and as he did so I shut my eyes and tried to pray. Hawkins had begun to say something else when Donovan fired, and as I opened my eyes at the bang, I saw Hawkins stagger at the knees and lie out flat at Noble's feet, slowly and as quiet as a kid falling asleep, with the lantern-light on his lean legs and bright farmer's boots. We all stood very still, watching him settle out in the last agony.

Then Belcher took out a handkerchief and began to tie it about his own eyes (in our excitement we'd forgotten to do the same for Hawkins), and, seeing it wasn't big enough, turned and asked for the loan of mine. I gave it to him and he knotted the two together and pointed with his foot at Hawkins.

"He's not quite dead," he says. "Better give him another."

Sure enough, Hawkins's left knee is beginning to rise. I bend down and put my gun to his head; then, recollecting myself, I get up again. Belcher understands what's in my mind.

"Give him his first," he says. "I don't mind. Poor bastard, we don't know what's happening to him now."

I knelt and fired. By this time I didn't seem to know what I was doing. Belcher, who was fumbling a bit awkwardly with the handkerchiefs, came out with a laugh as he heard the shot. It was the first time I heard him laugh and it sent a shudder down my back; it sounded so unnatural.

"Poor bugger!" he said quietly. "And last night he was so curious about it all. It's very queer, chums, I always think. Now he knows as much about it as they'll ever let him know, and last night he was all in the dark."

Donovan helped him to tie the handkerchiefs about his eyes. "Thanks, chum," he said. Donovan asked if there were any messages he wanted sent.

"No, chum," he says. "Not for me. If any of you would like to write to Hawkins's mother, you'll find a letter from her in his pocket. He and his mother were great chums. But my missus left me eight years ago. Went away with another fellow and took the kid with her. I like the feeling of a home, as you may have noticed, but I couldn't start again after that."

It was an extraordinary thing, but in those few minutes Belcher said more than in all the weeks before. It was just as if the sound of the shot had started a flood of talk in him and he could go on the whole night like that, quite happily, talking about himself. We stood round like fools now that he couldn't see us any longer. Donovan looked at Noble, and Noble shook his head. Then Donovan raised his

Webley, and at that moment Belcher gives his queer laugh again. He may have thought we were talking about him, or perhaps he noticed the same thing I'd noticed and couldn't understand it.

"Excuse me, chums," he says. "I feel I'm talking the hell of a lot, and so silly, about my being so handy about a house and things like that. But this thing came on me suddenly. You'll forgive me, I'm sure."

"You don't want to say a prayer?" asks Donovan.

"No, chum," he says. "I don't think it would help. I'm ready, and you boys want to get it over."

"You understand that we're only doing our duty?" says Donovan.

Belcher's head was raised like a blind man's so that you could only see his chin and the tip of his nose in the lantern-light.

"I never could make out what duty was myself," he said. "I think you're all good lads, if that's what you mean. I'm not complaining."

Noble, just as if he couldn't bear any more of it, raised his fist at Donovan, and in a flash Donovan raised his gun and fired. The big man went over like a sack of meal, and this time there was no need for a second shot.

I don't remember much about the burying, but that it was worse than all the rest because we had to carry them to the grave. It was all mad lonely with nothing but a patch of lantern-light between ourselves and the dark, and birds hooting and screeching all round, disturbed by the guns. Noble went through Hawkins's belongings to find the letter from his mother, and then joined his hands together. He did the same with Belcher. Then, when we'd filled in the grave, we separated from Jeremiah Donovan and Feeney and took our tools back to the shed. All the way we didn't speak a word. The kitchen was dark and cold as we'd left it, and the old woman was sitting over the hearth, saying her beads. We walked past her into the room, and Noble struck a match to light the lamp. She rose quietly and came to the doorway with all her cantankerousness gone.

"What did ye do with them?" she asked in a whisper, and Noble started so that the match went out in his hand.

"What's that?" he asked without turning round.

"I heard ye," she said.

"What did you hear?" asked Noble.

"I heard ye. Do ye think I didn't hear ye, putting the spade back in the houseen?"

Noble struck another match and this time the lamp lit for him.

"Was that what ye did to them?" she asked.

Then, by God, in the very doorway, she fell on her knees and began praying, and after looking at her for a minute or two Noble did the same by the fireplace. I pushed my way out past her and left them at it. I stood at the door, watching the stars and listening to the shrieking of the birds dying out over the bogs. It is so strange what you feel at times like that that you can't describe it. Noble says he saw everything ten times the size, as though there were nothing in the whole world but that little patch of bog with the two Englishmen stiffening into it, but with me it was as if the patch of bog where the Englishmen were was a million miles away, and even Noble and the old woman, mumbling behind me, and the birds and the bloody stars were all far away, and I was somehow very small and very lost and lonely like a child astray in the snow. And anything that happened me afterwards, I never felt the same about again.

<hr />

Suggestions for Discussion

1. This story is literally about a war: Belcher and Hawkins are English soldiers captured by the Irish Republican Army during the 1922 battle for independence from Britain. Is the war itself the conflict of the story? What is the "territory" that is being fought over?

2. Which characters are connected in terms of politics, nationality, and religion on the one hand, and interests or personality on the other? How do these connections change during the course of the story? What disconnections occur?

3. What kinds of power can the prisoners of war be said to have?

4. How does the old woman function as a "complication" in the plot?

5. Identify three or four moments in the story where the power shifts from one character to another.

6. The narrator says very clearly that he has been changed: "And anything that happened me afterwards, I never felt the same about again." How has he changed? Describe his epiphany.

Writing Assignments

1. Write a scene placing two characters in this very fundamental conflict: One wants something that the other does not want to give. The something may be anything—money, respect, jewelry, sex, information, a match—but be sure to focus on the one desire.

2. A slightly more complicated variation on the same theme: Each of two characters has half of something that is no good without the other half. Neither wants to give up his or her half.

3. Write a scene in which a character changes from:
   > angry to ashamed
   > attracted to disgusted
   > exhausted to enthusiastic
   > or determined to uncertain

4. Write a short story on a postcard. Send it. Notice that if you're going to manage a conflict, crisis, and resolution in this small space, you'll have to introduce the conflict immediately.

5. Place a character in conflict with some aspect of nature. The character need not be fighting for survival; the danger may be as small as a mosquito. But balance the forces equally so that the reader is not sure who will "win" until the crisis action happens.

6. Write a short story, no longer than three pages, in which the protagonist does *not* get what s/he wants, but which nevertheless ends happily.

7. Write a scene involving two pairs of people. Introduce a conflict. Disconnect the pairs and reconnect them in some other pattern.

3

SEEING IS BELIEVING
Showing and Telling

- *Significant Detail*

- *The Active Voice*

- *Prose Rhythm*

- *Mechanics*

The purpose of all the arts, including literature, is to quell boredom. People recognize that it feels good to feel and that not to feel is unhealthy. "I don't feel anything" can be said in fear, defiance, or complaint. It is not a boast. The final absence of feeling is death.

But feeling is also dangerous, and it can be deadly. Both the body and the psyche numb themselves in the presence of pain too strong to bear. People often (healthily and unhealthily) avoid good feelings—intimacy, power, speed, drunkenness, possession—having learned that feelings have consequences and that powerful feelings have powerful consequences.

Literature offers feelings for which we do not have to pay. It allows us to love, condemn, condone, hope, dread, and hate without any of the risks those feelings ordinarily involve. Fiction must contain ideas, which give significance to characters and events. If the ideas are shallow or untrue, the fiction will be correspondingly shallow or untrue. But the ideas must be experienced through or with the characters; they must be felt or the fiction will fail also.

Much nonfiction writing, including literary criticism, also tries to persuade us to feel one way rather than another, and some—polemics and propaganda, for example—exhort us to feel strongly. But nonfiction works largely by means of reason and reasoning in order to appeal to and produce emotion. Fiction tries to reproduce the emotional impact of experience. And this is a more difficult task, because written words are symbols representing sounds, and the sounds themselves are symbols representing things, actions, qualities, spatial relationships, and so on. Written words are thus at two removes from experience. Unlike the images of film and drama, which directly strike the eye and ear, words are transmitted first to the mind, where they must be translated into images.

In order to move your reader, the standard advice runs, "Show, don't tell." This dictum can be confusing, considering that all a writer has to work with is words. What it means is that your job as a fiction writer is to focus attention not on the words, which are inert, nor on the thoughts these words produce, but through these to felt experience, where the vitality of understanding lies. There are techniques for accomplishing this—for making narrative vivid, moving, and resonant—which can be partly learned and can always be strengthened.

Significant Detail

In *The Elements of Style*, William Strunk, Jr., writes:

> If those who have studied the art of writing are in accord on any one point, it is on this: the surest way to arouse and hold the attention of the reader is by being specific, definite and concrete. The greatest writers ... are effective largely because they deal in particulars and report the details that matter.

Specific, definite, concrete, particular details—these are the life of fiction. Details (as every good liar knows) are the stuff of persuasiveness. Mary is sure that Ed forgot to go pay the gas bill last Tuesday, but Ed says, "I know I went, because this old guy in a knit vest was in front of me in the line, and went on and on about his twin granddaughters"—and it is hard to refute a knit vest and twins even if the furnace doesn't work. John Gardner in *The Art of Fiction* speaks of details as "proofs," rather like those in a geometric theorem or a statistical argument. The novelist, he says, "gives us such details about the streets, stores, weather, politics, and concerns of Cleveland (or wherever the setting is) and such details about the looks, gestures, and experiences of his characters that we cannot help believing that the story he tells us is true."

A detail is "definite" and "concrete" when it appeals to the senses. It should be seen, heard, smelled, tasted, or touched. The most superficial survey of any bookshelf of published fiction will turn up dozens of examples of this principle. Here is a fairly obvious one.

> It was a narrow room, with a rather high ceiling, and crowded from floor to ceiling with goodies. There were rows and rows of hams and sausages of all shapes and colors—white, yellow, red and black; fat and lean and round and long—rows of canned preserves, cocoa and tea, bright translucent glass bottles of honey, marmalade and jam.

I stood enchanted, straining my ears and breathing in the delightful atmosphere and the mixed fragrance of chocolate and smoked fish and earthy truffles. I spoke into the silence, saying: "Good day" in quite a loud voice; I can still remember how my strained, unnatural tones died away in the stillness. No one answered. And my mouth literally began to water like a spring. One quick, noiseless step and I was beside one of the laden tables. I made one rapturous grab into the nearest glass urn, filled as it chanced with chocolate creams, slipped a fistful into my coat pocket, then reached the door, and in the next second was safely round the corner.

Thomas Mann, *Confessions of Felix Krull, Confidence Man*

The shape of this passage is a tour through the five senses. Mann lets us see: *narrow room, high ceiling, hams, sausages, preserves, cocoa, tea, glass bottles, honey, marmalade, jam*. He lets us smell: *fragrance of chocolate, smoked fish, earthy truffles*. He lets us hear: *"Good day," unnatural tones, stillness*. He lets us taste: *mouth, water like a spring*. He lets us touch: *grab, chocolate creams, slipped, fistful into my coat pocket*. The writing is alive because we do in fact live through our sense percep-tions, and Mann takes us past words and through thought to let us perceive the scene in this way.

In this process, a number of ideas not stated reverberate off the sense images, so that we are also aware of a number of generalizations the author might have made but does not need to make: We will make them ourselves. Mann could have had his character "tell" us: *I was quite poor, and I was not used to seeing such a profusion of food, so that although I was very afraid there might be someone in the room and that I might be caught stealing, I couldn't resist taking the risk*.

This version would be very flat, and none of it is necessary. The character's rela-tive poverty is inherent in the tumble of images of sight and smell; if he were used to such displays, his eyes and nose would not dart about as they do. His fear is inherent in the "strained, unnatural tones" and their dying away in the stillness. His desire is in his watering mouth, his fear in the furtive speed of "quick" and "grab" and "slipped."

The points to be made here are two, and they are both important. The first is that the writer must deal in sense detail. The second is that these must be details "that matter." As a writer of fiction you are at constant pains not simply to say what you mean, but to mean more than you say. Much of what you mean will be an abstraction or a judgment. But if you write in abstractions or judgments, you are writing an essay, whereas if you let us use our senses and do our own generalizing and interpreting, we will be involved as participants in a real way. Much of the pleasure of reading comes from the egotistical sense that we are clever enough to understand. When the author explains to us or interprets for us, we suspect that he or she doesn't think us bright enough to do it for ourselves.

A detail is concrete if it appeals to one of the five senses; it is significant if it also conveys an idea or a judgment or both. *The windowsill was green* is concrete, because we can see it. *The windowsill was shedding flakes of fungus-green paint* is concrete, and also conveys the idea that the paint is old and suggests the judgment that the color is ugly. The second version can also be seen more vividly.

Here is a passage from a young writer, which fails through lack of appeal to the senses.

> Debbie was a very stubborn and completely independent person, and was always doing things her way despite her parents' efforts to get her to conform. Her father was an executive in a dress manufacturing company, and was able to afford his family all the luxuries and comforts of life. But Debbie was completely indifferent to her family's affluence.

This passage contains a number of judgments we might or might not share with the author, and she has not convinced us that we do. What constitutes stubbornness? Independence? Indifference? Affluence? Further, since the judgments are supported by generalizations, we have no sense of the individuality of the characters, which alone would bring them to life on the page. What things was she always doing? What efforts did her parents make to get her to conform? What level of executive? What dress manufacturing company? What luxuries and comforts?

> Debbie would wear a tank top to a tea party if she pleased, with fluorescent earrings and ankle-strap sandals.
> "Oh, sweetheart," Mrs. Chiddister would stand in the doorway wringing her hands. "It's not *nice*."
> "Not who?" Debbie would say, and add a fringed belt.
> Mr. Chiddister was Artistic Director of the Boston branch of Cardin, and had a high respect for what he called "elegant textures," which ranged from handwoven tweed to gold filigree, and which he willingly offered his daughter. Debbie preferred her laminated wrist bangles.

We have not passed a final judgment on the merits of these characters, but we know a good deal more about them, and we have drawn certain interim conclusions that are our own and not forced on us by the author. Debbie is independent of her parents' values, rather careless of their feelings, energetic, and possibly a tart. Mrs. Chiddister is quite ineffectual. Mr. Chiddister is a snob, though perhaps Debbie's taste is so bad we'll end up on his side.

But maybe that isn't at all what the author had in mind. The point is that we weren't allowed to know what the author did have in mind. Perhaps it was more like this version.

> One day Debbie brought home a copy of Ulysses. Mrs. Strum called it "filth" and threw it across the sunporch. Debbie knelt on the parquet and retrieved her bookmark, which she replaced. "No, it's not," she said.
> "You're not so old I can't take a strap to you!" Mr. Strum reminded her.
> Mr. Strum was controlling stockholder of Readywear Conglomerates, and was proud of treating his family, not only on his salary, but also on his

expense account. The summer before he had justified their company on a trip to Belgium, where they toured the American Cemetery and the torture chambers of Ghent Castle. Entirely ungrateful, Debbie had spent the rest of the trip curled up in the hotel with a shabby copy of some poet.

Now we have a much clearer understanding of *stubbornness, independence, indifference,* and *affluence,* both their natures and the value we are to place on them. This time our judgment is heavily weighed in Debbie's favor—partly because people who read books have a sentimental sympathy with people who read books—but also because we hear hysteria in "filth" and "take a strap to you," whereas Debbie's resistance is quiet and strong. Mr. Strum's attitude toward his expense account suggests that he's corrupt, and his choice of "luxuries" is morbid. The passage does contain two overt judgments, the first being that Debbie was "entirely ungrateful." Notice that by the time we get to this, we're aware that the judgment is Mr. Strum's and that Debbie has little enough to be grateful for. We understand not only what the author says but also that she means the opposite of what she says, and we feel doubly clever to get it; that is the pleasure of irony. Likewise, the judgment that the poet's book is "shabby" shows Mr. Strum's crass materialism toward what we know to be the finer things. At the very end of the passage, we are denied a detail that we might very well be given: *What* poet did Debbie curl up with? Again, by this time we understand that we are being given Mr. Strum's view of the situation and that it's Mr. Strum (not Debbie, not the author, and certainly not us) who wouldn't notice the difference between John Keats and Stanley Kunitz.

It may be objected that both rewrites of the passage are longer than the original. Doesn't "adding" so much detail make for long writing? The answer is yes and no. No because in the rewrites we know so much more about the values, activities, lifestyles, attitudes, and personalities of the characters that it would take many times the length of the original to "tell" it all in generalizations. Yes in the sense that detail requires words, and if you are to realize your characters through detail, then you must be careful to select the details that convey the characteristics essential to our understanding. You can't convey a whole person, or a whole action, or everything there is to be conveyed about a single moment of a single day. You must select the significant.

No amount of concrete detail will move us unless it also implicitly suggests meaning and value. Following is a passage that fails, not through lack of appeal to the senses, but through lack of significance.

Terry Landon, a handsome young man of twenty-two, was six foot four and broad shouldered. He had medium-length thick blond hair and a natural tan, which set off the blue of his intense and friendly long-lashed eyes.

Here we have a good deal of sensory information, but we still know very little about Terry. There are so many broad-shouldered twenty-two-year-olds in the world, so many blonds, and so on. This sort of cataloging of characteristics suggests an all-points bulletin: *Male Caucasian, medium height, dark hair, last seen wearing gray raincoat.* Such a description may help the police locate a suspect in a crowd, but the assumption is that the identity of the person is not known. As an author you want us to know the character individually and immediately.

The fact is that all our ideas and judgments are formed through our sense perceptions, and daily, moment by moment, we receive information that is not merely sensuous in this way. Four people at a cocktail party may *do* nothing but stand and nibble canapés and may *talk* nothing but politics and the latest films. But you feel perfectly certain that X is furious at Y, who is flirting with Z, who is wounding Q, who is trying to comfort X. You have only your senses to observe with. How do you reach these conclusions? By what gestures, glances, tones, touches, choices of words?

It may be that this constant emphasis on judgment makes the author, and the reader, seem opinionated or self-righteous. "I want to present my characters objectively/neutrally. I'm not making any value judgments. I want the reader to make up his or her own mind." This can be a legitimate position, and the whole school of experimental French fiction, the *nouveau roman*, strives to be wholly objective and to eschew the judgmental. But this is a highly sophisticated form, and writing such fiction entails a difficulty and a danger. The difficulty arises because human beings *are* constantly judging: *How was the film? He seemed friendly. What a boring class! Do you like it here? What did you think of them? That's kind of you. Which do you want? I'm not convinced. She's very thin. That's fascinating. I'm so clumsy. You're gorgeous tonight. Life is crazy, isn't it?*

The danger results from the fact that when we are not passing such judgments, it's because we aren't much interested. We are indifferent. Although you may not want to sanctify or damn your characters, you do want us to care about them, and if you refuse to direct our judgment, you may be inviting our indifference. Usually, when you "don't want us to judge," you mean that you want our feelings to be mixed, paradoxical, complex. *She's horribly irritating, but it's not her fault. He's sexy, but there's something cold about it underneath.* If this is what you mean, then you must direct our judgment in both or several directions, not in no direction.

Even a character who doesn't exist except as a type or function will come to life if presented through significant detail, as in this example from *The Right Stuff* by Tom Wolfe.

> The matter mustn't be bungled!—that's the idea. No, a man should bring the news when the time comes, a man with some official or moral authority, a clergyman or a comrade of the newly deceased. Furthermore, he should bring the bad news in person. He should turn up at the front door and ring the bell and be standing there like a pillar of coolness and competence, bearing the bad news on ice, like a fish.

For a character who is just "a man," we have a remarkably clear image of this personage! Notice how Wolfe moves us from generalization toward sharpness of image, gradually bringing the nonexistent character into focus. First he has only a gender, then a certain abstract quality, "authority"; then a distinct role, "a clergyman or a comrade." Then he appears "in person" at the front door, then acts, ringing the doorbell. Finally, his quality is presented to us in the sharp focus of similes that also suggest his deadly message: *pillar, ice, fish*.

John Gardner, in *The Art of Fiction*, points out that in addition to the faults of insufficient detail and the use of abstraction, there's a third failure.

> ...the needless filtering of the image through some observing consciousness. The amateur writes: "Turning, she noticed two snakes fighting in among the rocks." Compare: "She turned. In among the rocks, two snakes were fighting." (The improvement can of course be further improved. The phrase "two snakes were fighting" is more abstract than, say, "two snakes whipped and lashed, striking at each other"; and verbs with auxiliaries "were fighting" are never as sharp in focus as verbs without auxiliaries, since the former indicate indefinite time, whereas the latter e.g., "fought" suggest a given instant.) Generally speaking—though no laws are absolute in fiction— vividness urges that almost every occurrence of such phrases as "she noticed" and "she saw" be suppressed in favor of direct presentation of the thing seen.

In the following paragraph from Virginia Woolf's *Mrs. Dalloway*, we are introduced to an anonymous crowd and four other characters, none of whom we ever see again. Notice that although we observe the scene through the consciousness of the character, it is presented directly. We watch with her rather than watching her watch.

> The crush was terrific for the time of day. Lords, Ascot, Hurlingham, what was it? she wondered, for the street was blocked. The British middle classes sitting sideways on the tops of omnibuses with parcels and umbrellas, yes, even furs on a day like this, were, she thought, more ridiculous, more unlike anything there has ever been than one could conceive; and the Queen herself held up; the Queen herself unable to pass. Clarissa was suspended on one side of Brook Street; Sir John Buckhurst, the old Judge on the other, with the car between them (Sir John had laid down the law for years and liked a well-dressed woman) when the chauffeur, leaning over so slightly, said or showed something to the policeman, who saluted and raised his arm and jerked his head and moved the omnibus to the side and the car passed through.

The whole range of British class and class consciousness is conveyed in this brief passage through the use of significant detail. Clarissa's wry attitude toward the British middle classes is given credence by the fussiness of "parcels and umbrellas" and the pretension of "furs on a day like this." The judge's aristocratic hauteur is carried in the clichés he would use, "laid down the law" and "liked a well-dressed woman." That the Queen's chauffeur is described as leaning "ever so slightly" shows his consciousness of his own position's superiority to that of the policeman, who "saluted" him but then exercises his own brand of authority as he "jerked his head" to order the traffic about. Only the Queen is characterized by no detail of object or action, and that she is not emphasizes her royal remoteness: "the Queen herself, the Queen herself."

The point is not that an author must never express an idea, quality, or judgment. In the foregoing passages from Mann, Wolfe, and Woolf, each author uses several generalizations: *I stood enchanted, delightful atmosphere; the matter mustn't be bungled, coolness and competence; the crush was terrific, more unlike anything there has ever been than one could conceive.* The point is that in order to carry the felt weight of fiction, these abstractions must be realized through an appeal to the senses. It is in the details that they live.

The human brain has evolved in such a way that we have several distinct reactions to the information that we take in through our senses. The "highest" or neocortical portion of the brain sorts, compares, and makes predictions from the evidence of sight, sound, taste, smell and touch. The mammal brain or limbic system (literally below it) takes in the same information and produces in response physical reactions throughout the body. Here, for example, are two simultaneous responses you might have to a familiar situation: You break an egg on the edge of the skillet; the egg stinks and spreads. Your neocortex takes this information in through the senses of sight and smell, and then rapidly concludes, remembers, and predicts: "That egg is rotten. That's the third time I've bought rotten eggs from Pearson's Market; I won't buy them there again. This afternoon I'll be able to get back there between class and supper, and I'm sure the clerk will give me my money back because he was so embarrassed about that bad chicken last month." This is essentially an intellectual or abstract process. Meanwhile, the same information of sight and smell is being taken in by the mammalian brain, which reacts physically: Your stomach surges, a spasm grips the back of your throat, your tongue jerks forward, and you gasp, "Gyaagh!" This may be a particularly literal example of a "gut reaction," but the slang contains a scientific truth: The physical reaction of the body to sensory information *is what emotion is.*

Clearly, language and literature belong primarily to the human brain, with its computerlike possibilities of comparison and symbolic meaning. Yet if as a fiction writer you deal in abstraction and comparison only, if you name qualities rather than provide sense images, you will not penetrate to the layer of the brain where emotion lies. If, however, you provide concrete details that appeal to the senses, your reader will both think *and* feel.

The Active Voice

If your prose is to be vigorous as well as vivid, if your characters are to be people who do rather than people to whom things are done, if your descriptions are to "come to life," you must make use of the active voice.

The active voice occurs when the subject of a sentence performs the action described by the verb of that sentence: *She spilled the milk.* When the passive voice is used, the object of the active verb becomes the subject of the passive verb: *The milk was spilled by her.* The passive voice is more indirect than the active; the subject is acted upon rather than acting, and the effect is to weaken the prose and to distance the reader from the action.

The passive voice does have an important place in fiction, precisely because it expresses a sense that the character is being acted upon. If a prison guard is kicking the hero, then *I was slammed into the wall; I was struck blindingly from behind and forced to the floor* appropriately carries the sense of his helplessness.

In general, you should seek to use the active voice in all prose and use the passive only when the actor is unknown or insignificant or when you want to achieve special stylistic effects like the one above.

But there is one other common grammatical construction that is *in effect* passive and can distance the reader from a sense of immediate experience. The verbs that we learn in school to call *linking verbs* are effectively passive because they invite complements that tend to be generalized or judgmental: *Her hair was beautiful. He was very happy. The room seemed expensively furnished. They became morose.* Let her hair bounce, tumble, cascade, or swing; we'll see better. Let him laugh, leap, cry, or hug a tree; we'll experience his joy.

The following is a passage with very little action, nevertheless made vital by the use of active verbs:

> At Mixt she neither drinks nor eats. Each of the sisters furtively stares at her as she tranquilly sits in post-Communion meditation with her hands immersed in her habit. *Lectio* has been halted for the morning, so there is only the Great Silence and the tinks of cutlery, but handsigns are being traded as the sisters lard their hunks of bread or fold and ring their dinner napkins. When the prioress stands, all rise up with her for the blessing, and then Sister Aimee gives Mariette the handsigns. *You, infirmary.*
>
> Ron Hansen, *Mariette in Ecstasy*

Here, though the action is minimal, it would be inappropriate to suggest lifelessness or lack of will, so a number of the verbs suggest suppressed power: *stares, sits, lard, fold, ring, stands, rise, gives.*

Compare the first passage about Debbie on page 60 with the rewrite on page 60. In the generalized original we have, *was stubborn, was doing things, was executive, was able, was indifferent.* Apart from the compound verb *was doing*, all these are linking verbs. In the rewrite the characters *brought, called, threw, knelt, retrieved, replaced, said, reminded, justified, toured, spent,* and *curled up.* What energetic people! The rewrite contains two linking verbs: Mr. Strum *was stockholder* and *was proud*; these properly represent static states, a position and an attitude.

One beneficial side effect of active verbs is that they tend to call forth significant details. If you say "she was shocked," you are telling us; but if you are to show us that she was shocked through an action, you are likely to have to search for an image as well. "She clenched the arm of the chair so hard that her knuckles whitened." *Clenched* and *whitened* actively suggest shock, and at the same time we see her knuckles on the arm of the chair.

To be is the most common of the linking verbs and also the most overused, but all the linking verbs invite generalization and distance. *To feel, to seem, to look, to appear, to experience, to express, to show, to demonstrate, to convey, to display*—all these suggest in fiction that the character is being acted upon or observed by someone rather than doing something. She felt *happy/sad/amused/mortified* does not convince us. We want to see her and infer her emotion for ourselves. *He very clearly conveyed his displeasure*. It isn't clear to us. How did he convey it? To whom?

Most linking verbs have active as well as effectively passive senses, and it is important to distinguish between them. *She felt sad* is effectively passive, but *she felt his forehead* is an action. If *the magician appeared*, he is acting; but if *he appeared annoyed*, then the verb is a linking verb, and the only action implied is that of the observer who perceives this.

Linking verbs, like the passive voice, can appropriately convey a sense of passivity or helplessness when that is the desired effect. Notice that in the passage by Mann quoted earlier in this chapter, where Felix Krull is momentarily stunned by the sight of the food before him, linking verbs are used: *It was a narrow room, there were rows and rows*, while all the colors and shapes buffet his senses. Only as he gradually recovers can he *stand, breathe, speak*, and eventually *grab*.

In the following excerpt from Lawrence Durrell's *Justine*, Melissa is trapped into a ride she doesn't want, and we feel her passivity with her while the car and the headlights take all the power.

> Melissa was afraid now. She was aghast at what she had done. There was no way of refusing the invitation. She dressed in her shabby best and carrying her fatigue like a heavy pack, followed Selim to the great car which stood in deep shadow. She was helped in beside Nessim. They moved off slowly into the dense crepuscular evening of an Alexandria which, in her panic, she no longer recognized. They scouted a sea turned to sapphire and turned inland, folding up the slum, toward Mareotis and the bituminous slag-heaps of Mex where the pressure of the headlights now peeled off layer after layer of the darkness.

Was afraid, was aghast, was no way, was helped in—all imply Melissa's impotence. The active verbs that apply specifically to her either express weakness (*she followed*) or are negated (*no longer recognized*); the most active thing she can manage is to dress. In contrast, the "great car" *stands*, and it is inside and under the power of the car that they *move off, scout, turn*, and *fold up*; it is the headlights that *peel off*.

I don't mean to suggest either that Durrell is deliberately using a linking verb here, the passive or the active voice there, or that as an author you should analyze your grammar as you go along. Most word choice is instinctive, and instinct is often the best guide. I do mean to suggest that you should be aware of the vigor and variety of available verbs, and that if a passage lacks energy, it may be because your instinct has let you down. How often *are* things or are they acted *upon*, when they could more forcefully *do*?

A note of caution about active verbs: Make sparing use of what John Ruskin called the "pathetic fallacy"—the attributing of human emotions to natural and man-made objects. Even a description of a static scene can be invigorated if the houses *stand*, the streets *wander*, and the trees *bend*. But if the houses *frown*, the streets *stagger drunkenly*, and the trees *weep*, we will feel more strain than energy in the writing.

Prose Rhythm

Novelists and short-story writers are not under the same obligation as poets to reinforce sense with sound. In prose, on the whole, the rhythm is all right if it isn't clearly wrong. But it can be wrong if, for example, the cadence contradicts the meaning; on the other hand rhythm can greatly enhance the meaning if it is sensitively used.

> The river moved slowly. It seemed sluggish. The surface lay flat. Birds circled lazily overhead. Jon's boat slipped forward.

In this extreme example, the short, clipped sentences and their parallel structures—subject, verb, modifier—work against the sense of slow, flowing movement. The rhythm could be effective if the character whose eyes we're using is not appreciating or sharing the calm; otherwise it needs recasting.

> The surface lay flat on the sluggish, slow-moving river, and the birds circled lazily overhead as Jon's boat slipped forward.

There is nothing very striking about the rhythm of this version, but at least it moves forward without obstructing the flow of the river.

> The first impression I had as I stopped in the doorway of the immense City Room was of extreme rush and bustle, with the reporters moving rapidly back and forth in the long aisles in order to shove their copy at each other, or making frantic gestures as they shouted into their many telephones.

This long and leisurely sentence cannot possibly provide a sense of rush and bustle. The phrases need to move as fast as the reporters; the verbiage must be pared down because it slows them down.

> I stopped in the doorway. The City Room was immense, reporters rushing down the aisles, shoving copy at each other, bustling back again, flinging gestures, shouting into telephones.

> The poet Rolfe Humphries remarked that "*very* is the least very word in the language." It is frequently true that adverbs expressing emphasis or suddenness—*extremely, rapidly, suddenly, phenomenally, quickly, immediately, instantly, definitely, terribly, awfully*—slow the sentence down so as to dilute the force of the intended

meaning. "'It's a very nice day,'" said Humphries, "is not as nice a day as 'It's a day!'" Likewise, "They stopped very abruptly" is not as abrupt as "They stopped."

The rhythm of an action can be imitated by the rhythm of a sentence in a rich variety of ways. In this example, short sentences and phrases create a sense of a woman burdened with haste:

> . . . She slept late. The others went out for a walk. They'd left a note, a considerate note: 'Didn't wake you. You looked tired. Had a cold breakfast so as not to make too much mess. Leave everything 'til we get back.' But it was ten o'clock, and guests were coming at noon, so she cleared away the bread, the butter, the crumbs, the smears, the jam, the spoons, the spilt sugar, the cereal, the milk (sour by now) and the dirty plates, and swept the floors, and tidied up quickly, and grabbed a cup of coffee, and prepared to make a rice and fish dish and a chocolate mousse and sat down in the middle to eat a lot of bread and jam herself. Broad hips.

> Fay Weldon, *"Weekend"*

James Joyce, on the other hand, in the short story "The Dead," creates a similar domestic rush by structuring a long sentence with a number of prepositional phrases that carry us headlong.

> Lily, the caretaker's daughter, was literally run off her feet. Hardly had she brought one gentleman into the little pantry behind the office on the ground floor and helped him off with his overcoat than the wheezy hall-door bell clanged and she had to scamper along the bare hallway to let in another guest.

Lily's haste is largely created by beginning the sentence, "Hardly had she brought," so that we anticipate the clause that will finish the meaning, "than the bell clanged." Our anticipation forces us to scamper like Lily through the intervening actions.

Not only action but also character can be revealed and reinforced by sensitive use of rhythm. In Tillie Olsen's "Tell Me a Riddle," half a dozen grown children of a couple who have been married for forty-seven years ask each other what, after all this time, could be tearing their parents apart. The narrative answers:

> Something tangible enough.
>   Arthritic hands, and such work as he got, occasional. Poverty all his life, and there was little breath left for running. He could not, could not turn away from this desire: to have the troubling of responsibility, the fretting with money, over and done with; to be free, to be *care*free where success was not measured by accumulation, and there was use for the vitality still in him.

The old man's anguished irritability is conveyed by syncopation, the syntax wrenched, clauses and qualifiers erupting out of what would be their natural place in the sentence, just as they would erupt in the man's mind. Repetition conveys his frustration: "He could not, could not" and "to be free, to be *carefree*."

Just as action and character can find an echo in prose rhythm, so it is possible to help us experience a character's emotions and attitudes through control of the starts and stops of prose tempo. In the following passage from *Persuasion*, Jane Austen combines generalization, passive verbs, and a staccato speech pattern to produce a kind of breathless blindness in the heroine.

> . . . a thousand feelings rushed on Anne, of which this was the most consoling, that it would soon be over. And it was soon over. In two minutes after Charles's preparation, the others appeared; they were in the drawing room. Her eye half met Captain Wentworth's, a bow, a courtesy passed; she heard his voice; he talked to Mary, said all that was right, said something to the Miss Musgroves, enough to mark an easy footing; the room seemed full, full of persons and voices, but a few minutes ended it.

Sometimes a contrast in rhythm can help reinforce a contrast in characters, actions, attitudes, and emotions. In this passage from Frederick Busch's short story "Company," a woman whose movements are relatively confined watches her husband move, stop, and move again.

> Every day did not start with Vince awake that early, dressing in the dark, moving with whispery sounds down the stairs and through the kitchen, out into the autumn morning while groundfog lay on the milkweed burst open and on the stumps of harvested corn. But enough of them did.
>   I went to the bedroom window to watch him hunt in a business suit.
>   He moved with his feet in the slowly stirring fog, moving slowly himself with the rifle held across his body and his shoulders stiff. Then he stopped in a frozen watch for woodchucks. His stillness made the fog look faster as it blew across our field behind the barn. Vince stood. He waited for something to shoot. I went back to bed and lay between our covers again. I heard the bolt click. I heard the unemphatic shot, and then the second one, and after a while his feet on the porch, and soon the rush of water, the rattle of the pots on top of the stove, and later his feet again, and the car starting up as he left for work an hour before he had to.

The long opening sentence is arranged in a series of short phrases to move Vince forward. By contrast, "But enough of them did" comes abruptly, its abruptness as well as the sense of the words suggesting the woman's alienation. When Vince starts off again more slowly, the repetition of "moved, slowly stirring, moving slowly," slows down the sentence to match his strides. "Vince stood" again stills him, but the author also needs to convey that Vince stands for a long time, waiting, so we have the repetitions, "he stopped, his stillness, Vince stood. He waited." As his activity speeds up again, the tempo of the prose speeds up with another series of short phrases, of which only the last is drawn out with a dependent clause, "as he left for work an hour before he had to," so that we feel the retreat of the car in the distance. Notice that Busch chooses the phrase "the rush of water," not the flow or splash of water, as the sentence and Vince begin to rush. Here, meaning reinforces a tempo that, in turn, reinforces meaning.

Mechanics

Significant detail, the active voice, and prose rhythm are techniques for achieving the sensuous in fiction, means of taking the reader past the words and the thought to feeling and experience. None is of much use if the reader's eye is wrenched back to the surface; for that reason a word or two ought to be said here about the mechanics of the written language.

Spelling, grammar, and punctuation are a kind of magic; their purpose is to be invisible. If the sleight of hand works, we will not notice a comma or a quotation mark but will translate each instantly into a pause or an awareness of voice; we will not focus on the individual letters of a word but extract its sense whole. When the mechanics are incorrectly used, the trick is revealed and the magic fails; the reader's focus is shifted from the story to its surface. The reader is irritated at the author, and of all the emotions the reader is willing to experience, irritation at the author is not one.

There is no intrinsic virtue in standardized mechanics, and you can depart from them whenever you produce an effect that adequately compensates for the attention called to the surface. But only then. Unlike the techniques of narrative, the rules of spelling, grammar, and punctuation can be coldly learned anywhere in the English-speaking world—and they should be learned by anyone who aspires to write. Poor mechanics read instant amateurism to an editor. Perhaps a demonstrated genius can get away with sloppy mechanics, but in that case some other person must be hired to fill in. Since ghostwriters and editors are likely to be paid more per hour for their work than the author, this would constitute a heavy drain on the resources of those who publish fiction.

⤳ The Things They Carried ⤶

TIM O'BRIEN

First Lieutenant Jimmy Cross carried letters from a girl named Martha, a junior at Mount Sebastian College in New Jersey. They were not love letters, but Lieutenant Cross was hoping, so he kept them folded in plastic at the bottom of his rucksack. In the late afternoon, after a day's march, he would dig his foxhole, wash his hands under a canteen, unwrap the letters, hold them with the tips of his fingers, and spend the last hour of light pretending. He would imagine romantic camping trips into the White Mountains in New Hampshire. He would sometimes taste the envelope flaps, knowing her tongue had been there. More than anything, he wanted Martha to love him as he loved her, but the letters were mostly chatty, elusive on the matter of love. She was a virgin, he was almost sure. She was an English major at Mount Sebastian, and she wrote beautifully about her professors and roommates and midterm exams, about her respect for Chaucer and her great affection for Virginia Woolf. She often quoted lines of poetry; she never mentioned the war, except to say, Jimmy, take care of yourself. The letters weighed 10 ounces. They were signed Love, Martha, but Lieutenant Cross understood that Love was only a way of signing and did not mean what he sometimes pretended it meant. At dusk, he would carefully return the letters to his rucksack. Slowly, a bit distracted, he would get up and move among his men, checking the perimeter, then at full dark he would return to his hole and watch the night and wonder if Martha was a virgin.

The things they carried were largely determined by necessity. Among the necessities or near-necessities were P-38 can openers, pocket knives, heat tabs, wristwatches, dog tags, mosquito repellent, chewing gum, candy, cigarettes, salt tablets, packets of Kool-Aid, lighters, matches, sewing kits, Military Payment Certificates, C rations, and two or three canteens of water. Together, these items weighed between 15 and 20 pounds, depending upon a man's habits or rate of metabolism. Henry Dobbins, who was a big man, carried extra rations; he was especially fond of canned peaches in heavy syrup over pound cake. Dave Jensen, who practiced field hygiene, carried a toothbrush, dental floss, and several hotel-sized bars of soap he'd stolen on R&R in Sydney, Australia. Ted Lavender, who was scared, carried tranquilizers until he was shot in the head outside the village of Than Khe in mid-April. By necessity, and because it was SOP, they all carried steel helmets that weighed 5 pounds including the liner and camouflage cover. They carried the standard fatigue jackets and trousers. Very few carried underwear. On their feet they carried jungle boots—2.1 pounds—and Dave Jensen carried three pairs of socks and a can of Dr. Scholl's foot powder as a precaution against trench foot. Until he was shot, Ted Lavender carried six or seven ounces of premium dope, which for him was a necessity. Mitchell Sanders, the RTO, carried condoms. Norman Bowker carried a diary. Rat Kiley carried comic books. Kiowa, a devout Baptist, carried an illustrated New Testament that had been presented to him by his father, who taught Sunday school in Oklahoma City, Oklahoma. As a hedge against bad times, however, Kiowa also carried his grandmother's distrust of the white man, his grandfather's old hunting hatchet. Necessity dictated. Because the land was mined and booby-trapped, it was SOP for each man to carry a steel-centered, nylon-covered flak jacket, which weighed 6.7 pounds, but which on hot days seemed much heavier. Because you could die so quickly, each man carried at least one large compress bandage, usually in the helmet band for easy access. Because the nights were cold, and because the monsoons were wet, each carried a green plastic poncho that could be used as a raincoat or groundsheet or makeshift tent. With its quilted liner, the poncho weighed almost two pounds, but it was worth every ounce. In April, for instance, when Ted Lavender was shot, they used his poncho to wrap him up, then to carry him across the paddy, then to lift him into the chopper that took him away.

They were called legs or grunts.

To carry something was to hump it, as when Lieutenant Jimmy Cross humped his love for Martha up the hills and through the swamps. In its intransitive form, to hump meant to walk, or to march, but it implied burdens far beyond the intransitive.

Almost everyone humped photographs. In his wallet, Lieutenant Cross carried two photographs of Martha. The first was a Kodacolor snapshot signed Love, though he knew better. She stood against a brick wall. Her eyes were gray and neutral, her lips slightly open as she stared straight-on at the camera. At night, sometimes, Lieutenant Cross wondered who had taken the picture, because he knew she had boyfriends, because he loved her so much, and because he could see the shadow of the picture-taker spreading out against the brick wall. The second photograph had been clipped from the 1968 Mount Sebastian yearbook. It was an action shot— women's volleyball—and Martha was bent horizontal to the floor, reaching, the palms of her hands in sharp focus, the tongue taut, the expression frank and competitive. There was no visible sweat. She wore white gym shorts. Her legs, he thought, were almost certainly the legs of a virgin, dry and without hair, the left knee cocked and carrying her entire weight, which was just over one hundred pounds. Lieutenant Cross remembered touching that left knee. A dark theater, he remembered, and the movie was *Bonnie and Clyde*, and Martha wore a tweed skirt, and during the final scene, when he touched her knee, she turned and looked at him in a sad, sober way that made him pull his hand back, but he would always remember the feel of the tweed skirt and the knee beneath it and the sound of the gunfire that killed Bonnie and Clyde, how embarrassing it was, how slow and oppressive. He remembered kissing her good night at the dorm door. Right then, he thought, he should've done something brave. He should've carried her up the stairs to her room and tied her to the bed and touched that left knee all night long. He should've risked it. Whenever he looked at the photographs, he thought of new things he should've done.

What they carried was partly a function of rank, partly of field specialty.

As a first lieutenant and platoon leader, Jimmy Cross carried a compass, maps, code books, binoculars, and a .45-caliber pistol that weighed 2.9 pounds fully loaded. He carried a strobe light and the responsibility for the lives of his men.

As an RTO, Mitchell Sanders carried the PRC-25 radio, a killer, 26 pounds with its battery.

As a medic, Rat Kiley carried a canvas satchel filled with morphine and plasma and malaria tablets and surgical tape and comic books and all the things a medic must carry, including M&M's for especially bad wounds, for a total weight of nearly 20 pounds.

As a big man, therefore a machine gunner, Henry Dobbins carried the M-60, which weighed 23 pounds unloaded, but which was almost always loaded. In addition, Dobbins carried between 10 and 15 pounds of ammunition draped in belts across his chest and shoulders.

As PFCs or Spec 4s, most of them were common grunts and carried the standard M-16 gas-operated assault rifle. The weapon weighed 7.5 pounds unloaded, 8.2 pounds with its full 20-round magazine. Depending on numerous factors, such as topography and psychology, the riflemen carried anywhere from 12 to 20 magazines, usually in cloth bandoliers, adding on another 8.4 pounds at minimum, 14 pounds at maximum. When it was available, they also carried M-16 maintenance gear-rods and steel brushes and swabs and tubes of LSA oil—all of which weighed about a pound. Among the grunts, some carried the M-79 grenade launcher, 5.9 pounds unloaded, a reasonably light weapon except for the ammunition, which was heavy. A single round weighed 10 ounces. The typical load was 25 rounds. But Ted Lavender, who was scared, carried 34 rounds when he was shot and killed outside Than Khe, and he went down under an exceptional burden, more than 20 pounds of ammunition, plus the flak jacket and helmet and rations and water and toilet paper and tranquilizers and all the rest, plus the unweighed fear. He was dead weight. There was no twitching or flopping. Kiowa, who saw it happen, said it was like watching a rock fall, or a big sandbag or something—just boom, then down—not like the movies where the dead guy rolls around and does fancy spins and goes ass over teakettle—not like that, Kiowa said, the poor bastard just flat-fuck fell. Boom. Down. Nothing else. It was a bright morning in mid-April. Lieutenant Cross felt the pain. He blamed himself. They stripped off Lavender's canteens and ammo, all the heavy things, and Rat Kiley said the obvious, the guy's dead, and Mitchell Sanders used his radio to report one U.S. KIA and to request a chopper. Then they wrapped Lavender in his poncho. They carried him out to a dry paddy, established security, and sat smoking the dead man's dope until the chopper came. Lieutenant Cross kept to himself. He pictured Martha's smooth young face, thinking he loved her more than anything, more than his men, and now Ted Lavender was dead because he loved her so much and could not stop thinking about her. When the dustoff arrived, they carried Lavender aboard. Afterward they burned Than Khe. They marched until dusk, then dug their holes, and that night Kiowa kept explaining how you had to be there, how fast it was, how the poor guy just dropped like so much concrete. Boom-down, he said. Like cement.

In addition to the three standard weapons—the M-60, M-16, and M-79—they carried whatever presented itself, or whatever seemed appropriate as a means of killing or staying alive. They carried catch-as-catch-can. At various times, in various situations, they carried M-14s and CAR-15s and Swedish Ks and grease guns and captured AK-47s and Chi-Coms and RPGs and Simonov carbines and black market Uzis and .38-caliber Smith & Wesson handguns and 66 mm LAWs and shotguns and silencers and blackjacks and bayonets and C-4 plastic explosives. Lee Strunk carried a slingshot; a weapon of last resort, he called it. Mitchell Sanders carried brass knuckles. Kiowa carried his grandfather's feathered hatchet. Every third or fourth man carried a Claymore antipersonnel mine—3.5 pounds with its firing device. They all carried fragmentation grenades—14 ounces each. They all carried at least one M-18 colored smoke grenade—24 ounces. Some carried CS or tear gas grenades. Some carried white phosphorus grenades. They carried all they could bear, and then some, including a silent awe for the terrible power of the things they carried.

In the first week of April, before Lavender died, Lieutenant Jimmy Cross received a good-luck charm from Martha. It was a simple pebble, an ounce at most. Smooth to the touch, it was a milky white color with flecks of orange and violet, oval-shaped, like a miniature egg. In the accompanying letter, Martha wrote that she had found the pebble on the Jersey's shoreline, precisely where the land touched water at high tide, where things came together but also separated. It was this separate-but-together quality, she wrote, that had inspired her to pick up the pebble and to carry it in her breast pocket for several days, where it seemed weightless, and then to send it through the mail, by air, as a token of her truest feelings for him. Lieutenant Cross found this romantic. But he wondered what her truest feelings were, exactly, and what she meant by separate-but-together. He wondered how the tides and waves had come into play on that afternoon along the Jersey shoreline when Martha saw the pebble and bent down to rescue it from geology. He imagined bare feet. Martha was a poet, with the poet's sensibilities, and her feet would be brown and bare, the toenails unpainted, the eyes chilly and somber like the ocean in March, and though it was painful, he wondered who had been with her that afternoon. He imagined a pair of shadows moving along the strip of sand where things came together but also separated. It was phantom jealousy, he knew, but he couldn't help himself. He loved her so much. On the march, through the hot days of early April, he carried the pebble in his mouth, turning it with his tongue, tasting sea salt and moisture. His mind wandered. He had difficulty keeping his attention on the war. On occasion he would yell at his men to spread out the column, to keep their eyes open, but then he would slip away into daydreams, just pretending, walking barefoot along the Jersey shore, with Martha, carrying nothing. He would feel himself rising. Sun and waves and gentle winds, all love and lightness.

What they carried varied by mission.

When a mission took them to the mountains, they carried mosquito netting, machetes, canvas tarps, and extra bug juice.

If a mission seemed especially hazardous, or if it involved a place they knew to be bad, they carried everything they could. In certain heavily mined AOs, where the land was dense with Toe Poppers and Bouncing Betties, they took turns humping a 28-pound mine detector. With its headphones and big sensing plate, the equipment was a stress on the lower back and shoulders, awkward to handle, often useless because of the shrapnel in the earth, but they carried it anyway, partly for safety, partly for the illusion of safety.

On ambush, or other night missions, they carried peculiar little odds and ends. Kiowa always took along his New Testament and a pair of moccasins for silence. Dave Jensen carried night-sight vitamins high in carotene. Lee Strunk carried his slingshot; ammo, he claimed, would never be a problem. Rat Kiley carried brandy and M&M's candy. Until he was shot, Ted Lavender carried the starlight scope, which weighed 6.3 pounds with its aluminum carrying case. Henry Dobbins carried his girlfriend's pantyhose wrapped around his neck as a comforter. They all carried ghosts. When dark came, they would move out single file across the meadows and paddies to their ambush coordinates, where they would quietly set up the Claymores and lie down and spend the night waiting.

Other missions were more complicated and required special equipment. In mid-April, it was their mission to search out and destroy the elaborate tunnel complexes in the Than Khe area south of Chu Lai. To blow the tunnels, they carried one-pound blocks of pentrite high explosives, four blocks to a man, 68 pounds in all. They carried wiring, detonators, and battery-powered clackers. Dave Jensen carried earplugs. Most often, before blowing the tunnels, they were ordered by higher command to search them, which was considered bad news, but by and large they just shrugged and carried out orders. Because he was a big man, Henry Dobbins was excused from tunnel duty. The others would draw numbers. Before Lavender died there were 17 men in the platoon, and whoever drew the number 17 would strip off his gear and crawl in headfirst with a flashlight and Lieutenant Cross's .45-caliber pistol. The rest of them would fan out as security. They would sit down or kneel, not facing the hole, listening to the ground beneath them, imagining cobwebs and ghosts, whatever was down there—the tunnel walls squeezing in—how the flashlight seemed impossibly heavy in the hand and how it was tunnel vision in the very strictest sense, compression in all ways, even time, and how you had to wiggle in—ass and elbows—a swallowed-up feeling—and how you found yourself worrying about odd things: Will your flashlight go dead? Do rats carry rabies? If you screamed, how far would the sound carry? Would your buddies hear it? Would they have the courage to drag you out? In some respects, though not many, the waiting was worse than the tunnel itself. Imagination was a killer.

On April 16, when Lee Strunk drew the number 17, he laughed and muttered something and went down quickly. The morning was hot and very still. Not good, Kiowa said. He looked at the tunnel opening, then out across a dry paddy toward the village of Than Khe. Nothing moved. No clouds or birds or people. As they waited, the men smoked and drank Kool-Aid, not talking much, feeling sympathy for Lee Strunk but also feeling the luck of the draw. You win some, you lose some, said Mitchell Sanders, and sometimes you settle for a rain check. It was a tired line and no one laughed.

Henry Dobbins ate a tropical chocolate bar. Ted Lavender popped a tranquilizer and went off to pee.

After five minutes, Lieutenant Jimmy Cross moved to the tunnel, leaned down, and examined the darkness. Trouble, he thought—a cave-in maybe. And then suddenly, without willing it, he was thinking about Martha. The stresses and fractures, the quick collapse, the two of them buried alive under all that weight. Dense, crushing love. Kneeling, watching the hole, he tried to concentrate on Lee Strunk and the war, all the dangers, but his love was too much for him, he felt paralyzed, he wanted to sleep inside her lungs and breathe her blood and be smothered. He wanted her to be a virgin and not a virgin, all at once. He wanted to know her. Intimate secrets: Why poetry? Why so sad? Why that grayness in her eyes? Why so alone? Not lonely, just alone—riding her bike across campus or sitting off by herself in the cafeteria— even dancing, she danced alone—and it was the aloneness that filled him with love. He remembered telling her that one evening. How she nodded and looked away. And how, later, when he kissed her, she received the kiss without returning it, her eyes wide open, not afraid, not a virgin's eyes, just flat and uninvolved.

Lieutenant Cross gazed at the tunnel. But he was not there. He was buried with Martha under the white sand at the Jersey shore. They were pressed together, and the pebble in his mouth was her tongue. He was smiling. Vaguely, he was aware of how quiet the day was, the sullen paddies, yet he could not bring himself to worry about matters of security. He was beyond that. He was just a kid at war, in love. He was twenty-four years old. He couldn't help it.

A few moments later Lee Strunk crawled out of the tunnel. He came up grinning, filthy but alive. Lieutenant Cross nodded and closed his eyes while the others clapped Strunk on the back and made jokes about rising from the dead.

Worms, Rat Kiley said. Right out of the grave. Fuckin' zombie.

The men laughed. They all felt great relief.

Spook city, said Mitchell Sanders.

Lee Strunk made a funny ghost sound, a kind of moaning, yet very happy, and right then, when Strunk made that high happy moaning sound, when he went *Ahhooooo*, right then Ted Lavender was shot in the head on his way back from peeing. He lay with his mouth open. The teeth were broken. There was a swollen black bruise under his left eye. The cheekbone was gone. Oh shit, Rat Kiley said, the guy's dead. The guy's dead, he kept saying, which seemed profound—the guy's dead. I mean really.

The things they carried were determined to some extent by superstition. Lieutenant Cross carried his good-luck pebble. Dave Jensen carried a rabbit's foot. Norman Bowker, otherwise a very gentle person, carried a thumb that had been presented to him as as gift by Mitchell Sanders. The thumb was dark brown, rubbery to the touch, and weighed four ounces at most. It had been cut from a VC corpse, a boy of fifteen or sixteen. They'd found him at the bottom of an irrigation ditch, badly burned, flies in his mouth and eyes. The boy wore black shorts and sandals. At the time of his death he had been carrying a pouch of rice, a rifle, and three magazines of ammunition.

You want my opinion, Mitchell Sanders said, there's a definite moral here.

He put his hand on the dead boy's wrist. He was quiet for a time, as if counting a pulse, then he patted the stomach, almost affectionately, and used Kiowa's hunting hatchet to remove the thumb.

Henry Dobbins asked what the moral was.

Moral?

You know. *Moral*.

Sanders wrapped the thumb in toilet paper and handed it across to Norman Bowker. There was no blood. Smiling, he kicked the boy's head, watched the flies scatter, and said, It's like what that old TV show—Paladin. Have gun, will travel.

Henry Dobbins thought about it.

Yeah, well, he finally said. I don't see no moral.

There it is, man.

Fuck off.

They carried USO stationery and pencils and pens. They carried Sterno, safety pins, trip flares, signal flares, spools of wire, razor blades, chewing tobacco, liberated joss sticks and statuettes of the smiling Buddha, candles, grease pencils, *The Stars and Stripes,* fingernail clippers, Psy Ops leaflets, bush hats, bolos, and much more. Twice a week, when the resupply choppers came in, they carried hot chow in green mermite cans and large canvas bags filled with iced beer and soda pop. They carried plastic water containers, each with a two-gallon capacity. Mitchell Sanders carried a set of starched tiger fatigues for special occasions. Henry Dobbins carried Black Flag insecticide. Dave Jensen carried empty sandbags that could be filled at night for added protection. Lee Strunk carried tanning lotion. Some things they carried in common. Taking turns, they carried the big PRC–77 scrambler radio, which weighed 30 pounds with its battery. They shared the weight of memory. They took up what others could no longer bear. Often, they carried each other, the wounded or weak. They carried infections. They carried chess sets, basketballs, Vietnamese-English dictionaries, insignia of rank, Bronze Stars and Purple Hearts, plastic cards imprinted with the Code of Conduct. They carried diseases, among them malaria and dysentery. They carried lice and ringworm and leeches and paddy algae and various rots and molds. They carried the land itself—Vietnam, the place, the soil—a powdery orange-red dust that covered their boots and fatigues and faces. They carried the sky. The whole atmosphere, they carried it, the humidity, the monsoons, the stink of fungus and decay, all of it, they carried gravity. They moved like mules. By daylight they took sniper fire, at night they were mortared, but it was not battle, it was just the endless march, village to village, without purpose, nothing won or lost. They marched for the sake of the march. They plodded along slowly, dumbly, leaning forward against the heat, unthinking, all blood and bone, simple grunts, soldiering with their legs, toiling up the hills and down into the paddies and across the rivers and up again and down, just humping, one step and then the next and then another, but no volition, no will, because it was automatic, it was anatomy, and the war was entirely a matter of posture and carriage, the hump was everything, a kind of inertia, a kind of emptiness, a dullness of desire and intellect and conscience and hope and human sensibility. Their principles were in their feet. Their calculations were biological. They had no sense of strategy or mission. They searched the villages without knowing what to look for, not caring, kicking over jars of rice, frisking children and old men, blowing tunnels, sometimes setting fires and sometimes not, then forming up and moving on to the next village, then other villages, where it would always be the same. They carried their own lives. The pressures were enormous. In the heat of early afternoon, they would remove their helmets and flak jackets, walking bare, which was dangerous but which helped ease the strain. They would often discard things along the route of march. Purely for comfort, they would throw away rations, blow their Claymores and grenades, no matter, because by nightfall the resupply choppers would arrive with more of the same, then a day or two later still more, fresh watermelons and crates of ammunition and sunglasses and woolen sweaters—the resources were stunning-sparklers for the Fourth of July, colored eggs for Easter—it was the great American war chest—the fruits of science, the smokestacks, the canneries, the arsenals at Hartford, the Minnesota forests, the machine shops, the vast fields of corn and wheat—they carried like freight trains; they carried it on their backs and shoulders—and for all the ambiguities of Vietnam, all the mysteries and unknowns, there was at least the single abiding certainty that they would never be at a loss for things to carry.

After the chopper took Lavender away, Lieutenant Jimmy Cross led his men into the village of Than Khe. They burned everything. They shot chickens and dogs, they trashed the village well, they called in artillery and watched the wreckage, then they marched for several hours through the hot afternoon, and then at dusk, while Kiowa explained how Lavender died, Lieutenant Cross found himself trembling.

He tried not to cry. With his entrenching tool, which weighed five pounds, he began digging a hole in the earth.

He felt shame. He hated himself. He had loved Martha more than his men, and as a consequence Lavender was now dead, and this was something he would have to carry like a stone in his stomach for the rest of the war.

All he could do was dig. He used his entrenching tool like an ax, slashing, feeling both love and hate, and then later, when it was full dark, he sat at the bottom of his foxhole and wept. It went on for a long while. In part, he was grieving for Ted Lavender, but mostly it was for Martha, and for himself, because she belonged to another world, which was not quite real, and because she was a junior at Mount Sebastian College in New Jersey, a poet and a virgin and uninvolved, and because he realized she did not love him and never would.

Like cement, Kiowa whispered in the dark. I swear to God—boom, down. Not a word.

I've heard this, said Norman Bowker.

A pisser, you know? Still zipping himself up. Zapped while zipping.

All right, fine. That's enough.

Yeah, but you had to see it, the guy just—

I heard, man. Cement. So why not shut the fuck up?

Kiowa shook his head sadly and glanced over at the hole where Lieutenant Jimmy Cross sat watching the night. The air was thick and wet. A warm dense fog had settled over the paddies and there was the stillness that precedes rain.

After a time Kiowa sighed.

One thing for sure, he said. The lieutenant's in some deep hurt. I mean that crying jag—the way he was carrying on—it wasn't fake or anything, it was real heavy-duty hurt. The man cares.

Sure, Norman Bowker said.

Say what you want, the man does care.

We all got problems.

Not Lavender.

No, I guess not, Bowker said. Do me a favor, though.

Shut up?

That's a smart Indian. Shut up.

Shrugging, Kiowa pulled off his boots. He wanted to say more, just to lighten up his sleep, but instead he opened his New Testament and arranged it beneath his head as a pillow. The fog made things seem hollow and unattached. He tried not to think about Ted Lavender, but then he was thinking how fast it was, no drama, down and dead, and how it was hard to feel anything except surprise. It seemed unchristian. He wished he could find some great sadness, or even anger, but the emotion wasn't there and he couldn't make it happen. Mostly he felt pleased to be alive. He liked the smell of the New Testament under his cheek, the leather and ink and paper and glue, whatever the chemicals were. He liked hearing the sounds of night. Even his fatigue, it felt fine, the stiff muscles and the prickly awareness of his own body, a floating feeling. He enjoyed not being dead. Lying there, Kiowa admired Lieutenant Jimmy Cross's capacity for grief. He wanted to share the man's pain, he wanted to care as Jimmy Cross cared. And yet when he closed his eyes, all he could think was Boom-down, and all he could feel was the pleasure of having his boots off and the fog curling in around him and the damp soil and the Bible smells and the plush comfort of night.

After a moment Norman Bowker sat up in the dark.

What the hell, he said. You want to talk, *talk*. Tell it to me.

Forget it.

No, man, go on. One thing I hate, it's a silent Indian.

For the most part they carried themselves with poise, a kind of dignity. Now and then, however, there were times of panic, when they squealed or wanted to squeal but couldn't, when they twitched and made moaning sounds and covered their heads and said Dear Jesus and flopped around on the earth and fired their weapons blindly and cringed and sobbed and begged for the noise to stop and went wild and made stupid promises to themselves and to God and to their mothers and fathers, hoping not to die. In different ways, it happened to all of them. Afterward, when the firing ended, they would blink and peek up. They would touch their bodies, feeling shame, then quickly hiding it. They would force themselves to stand. As if in slow motion, frame by frame, the world would take on the old logic—absolute silence, then the wind, then sunlight, then voices. It was the burden of being alive. Awkwardly, the men would reassemble themselves, first in private, then in groups, becoming soldiers again. They would repair the leaks in their eyes. They would check for casualties, call in dustoffs, light cigarettes, try to smile, clear their throats and spit and begin cleaning their weapons. After a time someone would shake his head and say, No lie, I almost shit my pants, and someone else would laugh, which meant it was bad, yes, but the guy had obviously not shit his pants, it wasn't that bad, and in any case nobody would ever do such a thing and then go ahead and talk about it. They would squint into the dense, oppressive sunlight. For a few moments, perhaps, they would fall silent, lighting a joint and tracking its passage from man to man, inhaling, holding in the humiliation. Scary stuff, one of them might say. But then someone else would grin or flick his eyebrows and say, Roger-dodger, almost cut me a new asshole, *almost*.

There were numerous such poses. Some carried themselves with a sort of wistful resignation, others with pride or stiff soldierly discipline or good humor or macho zeal. They were afraid of dying but they were even more afraid to show it.

They found jokes to tell.

They used a hard vocabulary to contain the terrible softness. *Greased* they'd say. *Offed, lit up, zapped while zipping.* It wasn't cruelty, just stage presence. They were actors. When someone died, it wasn't quite dying, because in a curious way it seemed scripted, and because they had their lines mostly memorized, irony mixed with tragedy, and because they called it by other names, as if to encyst and destroy the reality of death itself. They kicked corpses. They cut off thumbs. They talked grunt lingo. They told stories about Ted Lavender's supply of tranquilizers, how the poor guy didn't feel a thing, how incredibly tranquil he was.

There's a moral here, said Mitchell Sanders.

They were waiting for Lavender's chopper, smoking the dead man's dope.

The moral's pretty obvious, Sanders said, and winked. Stay away from drugs. No joke, they'll ruin your day every time.

Cute, said Henry Dobbins.

Mind blower, get it? Talk about wiggy. Nothing left, just blood and brains.

They made themselves laugh.

There it is, they'd say. Over and over—there it is, my friend, there it is—as if the repetition itself were an act of poise, a balance between crazy and almost crazy, knowing without going, there it is, which meant be cool, let it ride, because Oh yeah, man, you can't change what can't be changed, there it is, there it absolutely and positively and fucking well is.

They were tough.

They carried all the emotional baggage of men who might die. Grief, terror, love, longing—these were intangibles, but the intangibles had their own mass and specific gravity, they had tangible weight. They carried shameful memories. They carried the common secret of cowardice barely restrained, the instinct to run or freeze or hide, and in many respects this was the heaviest burden of all, for it could never be put down, it required perfect balance and perfect posture. They carried their reputations. They carried the soldier's greatest fear, which was the fear of blushing. Men killed, and died, because they were embarrassed not to. It was what had brought them to the war in the first place, nothing positive, no dreams of glory or honor, just to avoid the blush of dishonor. They died so as not to die of embarrassment. They crawled into tunnels and walked point and advanced under fire. Each morning, despite the unknowns, they made their legs move. They endured. They kept humping, they did not submit to the obvious alternative, which was simply to close the eyes and fall. So easy, really. Go limp and tumble to the ground and let the muscles unwind and not speak and not budge until your buddies picked you up and lifted you into the chopper that would roar and dip its nose and carry you off to the world. A mere matter of falling, yet no one ever fell. It was not courage, exactly; the object was not valor. Rather, they were too frightened to be cowards.

By and large they carried these things inside, maintaining the masks of composure. They sneered at sick call. They spoke bitterly about guys who had found release by shooting off their own toes or fingers. Pussies, they'd say. Candy-asses. It was fierce, mocking talk, with only a trace of envy or awe, but even so the image played itself out behind their eyes.

They imagined the muzzle against flesh. So easy: squeeze the trigger and blow away a toe. They imagined it. They imagined the quick, sweet pain, then the evacuation to Japan, then a hospital with warm beds and cute geisha nurses.

And they dreamed of freedom birds.

At night, on guard, staring into the dark, they were carried away by jumbo jets. They felt the rush of takeoff. *Gone!* they yelled. And then velocity—wings and engines—a smiling stewardess—but it was more than a plane, it was a real bird, a big sleek silver bird with feathers and talons and high screeching. They were flying. The weights fell off; there was nothing to bear. They laughed and held on tight, feeling the cold slap of wind and altitude, soaring, thinking *It's over, I'm gone!*—they were naked, they were light and free—it was all lightness, bright and fast and buoyant, light as light, a helium buzz in the brain, a giddy bubbling in the lungs as they were taken up over the clouds and the war, beyond duty, beyond gravity and mortification and global entanglements—*Sin loi!* they yelled. *I'm sorry, motherfuckers, but I'm out of it, I'm goofed, I'm on a space cruise, I'm gone!*— and it was a restful, unencumbered sensation, just riding the light waves, sailing that big silver freedom bird over the mountains and oceans, over America, over the farms and great sleeping cities and cemeteries and highways and the golden arches of McDonald's, it was flight, a kind of fleeing, a kind of falling, falling higher and higher, spinning off the edge of the earth and beyond the sun and through the vast, silent vacuum where there were no burdens and where everything weighed exactly nothing—*Gone!* they screamed. *I'm sorry but I'm gone!*— and so at night, not quite dreaming, they gave themselves over to lightness, they were carried, they were purely borne.

On the morning after Ted Lavender died, First Lieutenant Jimmy Cross crouched at the bottom of his foxhole and burned Martha's letters. Then he burned the two photographs. There was a steady rain falling, which made it difficult, but he used heat tabs and Sterno to build a small fire, screening it with his body, holding the photographs over the tight blue flame with the tips of his fingers.

He realized it was only a gesture. Stupid, he thought. Sentimental, too, but mostly just stupid.

Lavender was dead. You couldn't burn the blame.

Besides, the letters were in his head. And even now, without photographs, Lieutenant Cross could see Martha playing volleyball in her white gym shorts and yellow T-shirt. He could see her moving in the rain.

When the fire died out, Lieutenant Cross pulled his poncho over his shoulders and ate breakfast from a can.

There was no great mystery, he decided.

In those burned letters Martha had never mentioned the war, except to say, Jimmy, take care of yourself. She wasn't involved. She signed the letters Love, but it wasn't love, and all the fine lines and technicalities did not matter. Virginity was no longer an issue. He hated her. Yes, he did. He hated her. Love, too, but it was a hard, hating kind of love.

The morning came up wet and blurry. Everything seemed part of everything else, the fog and Martha and the deepening rain.

He was a soldier, after all.

Half smiling, Lieutenant Jimmy Cross took out his maps. He shook his head hard, as if to clear it, then bent forward and began planning the day's march. In ten minutes, or maybe twenty, he would rouse the men and they would pack up and head west, where the maps showed the country to be green and inviting. They would do what they had always done. The rain might add some weight, but otherwise it would be one more day layered upon all the other days.

He was realistic about it. There was that new hardness in his stomach. He loved her but he hated her.

No more fantasies, he told himself.

Henceforth, when he thought about Martha, it would be only to think that she belonged elsewhere. He would shut down the daydreams. This was not Mount Sebastian, it was another world, where there were no pretty poems or mid-term exams, a place where men died because of carelessness and gross stupidity. Kiowa was right. Boom-down, and you were dead, never partly dead.

Briefly, in the rain, Lieutenant Cross saw Martha's gray eyes gazing back at him.

He understood.

It was very sad, he thought. The things men carried inside. The things men did or felt they had to do.

He almost nodded at her, but didn't.

Instead he went back to his maps. He was now determined to perform his duties firmly and without negligence. It wouldn't help Lavender, he knew that, but from this point on he would comport himself as an officer. He would dispose of his good-luck pebble. Swallow it, maybe, or use Lee Strunk's slingshot, or just drop it along the trail. On the march he would impose strict field discipline. He would be careful to send out flank security, to prevent straggling or bunching up, to keep his troops moving at the proper pace and at the proper interval. He would insist on clean weapons. He would confiscate the remainder of Lavender's dope. Later in the day, perhaps, he would call the men together and speak to them plainly. He would accept the blame for what had happened to Ted Lavender. He would be a man about it. He would look them in the eyes, keeping his chin level, and he would issue the new SOPs in a calm, impersonal tone of voice, a lieutenant's voice, leaving no room for argument or discussion. Commencing immediately, he'd tell them, they would no longer abandon equipment along the route of march. They would police up their acts. They would get their shit together, and keep it together, and maintain it neatly and in good working order.

He would not tolerate laxity. He would show strength, distancing himself.

Among the men there would be grumbling, of course, and maybe worse, because their days would seem longer and their loads heavier, but Lieutenant Jimmy Cross reminded himself that his obligation was not to be loved but to lead. He would dispense with love; it was not now a factor. And if anyone quarreled or complained, he would simply tighten his lips and arrange his shoulders in the correct command posture. He might give a curt little nod. Or he might not. He might just shrug and say, Carry on, then they would saddle up and form into a column and move out toward the villages west of Than Khe.

Suggestions for Discussion

1. For the most part, "The Things They Carried" uses a matter-of-fact tone listing an accumulation of concrete details. How do these details create the atmosphere of the Vietnam War and the feelings of the soldiers there?

2. What is the effect of insisting on the exact weight of things?

3. Lavender's death is reiterated several times as an incidental illustration of the worth or necessity of things—poncho, ammo, flashlight. What effect is achieved by this?

4. The story is structured around the verb "to carry." Note the frequency and variety of other active verbs.

5. How would you describe the overall rhythm of the story? How is it achieved?

6. At several points the soldiers carry, in addition to their gear, abstracts like *distrust of the white man, all they could bear, infections, grief, terror, love, fear*. How does O'Brien get away with using so many grand abstractions?

7. On page 76 we have a detailed description of Lavender after his death, and immediately thereafter a description of the thumb of a dead VC and of that corpse. What abstractions and judgments result from the juxtaposition?

8. How is Jimmy Cross's situation at the end of the story the opposite of that at the beginning? Why?

Where Are You Going, Where Have You Been?

JOYCE CAROL OATES

for Bob Dylan

Her name was Connie. She was fifteen and she had a quick nervous giggling habit of craning her neck to glance into mirrors, or checking other people's faces to make sure her own was all right. Her mother, who noticed everything and knew everything and who hadn't much reason any longer to look at her own face, always scolded Connie about it. "Stop gawking at yourself, who are you? You think you're so pretty?" she would say. Connie would raise her eyebrows at these familiar complaints and look right through her mother, into a shadowy vision of herself as she was right at that moment: she knew she was pretty and that was everything. Her mother had been pretty once too, if you could believe those old snapshots in the album, but now her looks were gone and that was why she was always after Connie.

"Why don't you keep your room clean like your sister? How've you got your hair fixed—what the hell stinks? Hair spray? You don't see your sister using that junk."

Her sister June was twenty-four and still lived at home. She was a secretary in the high school Connie attended, and if that wasn't bad enough—with her in the same building—she was so plain and chunky and steady that Connie had to hear her praised all the time by her mother and her mother's sisters. June did this, June did that, she saved money and helped clean the house and cooked and Connie couldn't do a thing, her mind was all filled with trashy daydreams. Their father was away at work most of the time and when he came home he wanted supper and he read the newspaper at supper and after supper he went to bed. He didn't bother talking much to them, but around his bent head Connie's mother kept picking at her until Connie wished her mother was dead and she herself was dead and it was all over. "She makes me want to throw up sometimes," she complained to her friends. She had a high, breathless, amused voice which made everything she said a little forced, whether it was sincere or not.

There was one good thing: June went places with girl friends of hers, girls who were just as plain and steady as she, and so when Connie wanted to do that her mother had no objections. The father of Connie's best girl friend drove the girls the three miles to town and left them off at a shopping plaza, so that they could walk through the stores or go to a movie, and when he came to pick them up again at eleven he never bothered to ask what they had done.

They must have been familiar sights, walking around that shopping plaza in their shorts and flat ballerina slippers that always scuffed the sidewalk, with charm bracelets jingling on their thin wrists; they would lean together to whisper and laugh secretly if someone passed by who amused or interested them. Connie had long dark blond hair that drew anyone's eye to it, and she wore part of it pulled up on her head and puffed out and the rest of it she let fall down her back. She wore a pullover jersey blouse that looked one way when she was at home and another way when she was away from home. Everything about her had two sides to it, one for home and one for anywhere that was not home: her walk that could be childlike and bobbing, or languid enough to make anyone think she was hearing music in her head, her mouth which was pale and smirking most of the time, but bright and pink on these evenings out, her laugh which was cynical and drawling at home— "Ha, ha, very funny"—but high-pitched and nervous anywhere else, like the jingling of the charms on her bracelet.

Sometimes they did go shopping or to a movie, but sometimes they went across the highway, ducking fast across the busy road, to a drive-in restaurant where older kids hung out. The restaurant was shaped like a big bottle, though squatter than a real bottle, and on its cap was a revolving figure of a grinning boy who held a hamburger aloft. One night in midsummer they ran across, breathless with daring, and right away someone leaned out a car window and invited them over, but it was just a boy from high school they didn't like. It made them feel good to be able to ignore him. They went up through the maze of parked and cruising cars to the bright-lit, fly-infested restaurant, their faces pleased and expectant as if they were entering a sacred building that loomed out of the night to give them what haven and what blessing they yearned for. They sat at the counter and crossed their legs at the ankles, their thin shoulders rigid with excitement and listened to the music that made everything so good: the music was always in the background like music at a church service, it was something to depend upon.

A boy named Eddie came in to talk with them. He sat backwards on his stool, turning himself jerkily around in semi-circles and then stopping and turning again, and after a while he asked Connie if she would like something to eat. She said she did and so she tapped her friend's arm on her way out—her friend pulled her face up into a brave droll look—and Connie said she would meet her at eleven, across the way. "I just hate to leave her like that," Connie said earnestly, but the boy said that she wouldn't be alone for long. So they went out to his car and on the way Connie couldn't help but let her eyes wander over the windshields and faces all around her, her face gleaming with the joy that had nothing to do with Eddie or even this place; it might have been the music. She drew her shoulders up and sucked in her breath with the pure pleasure of being alive, and just at that moment she happened to glance at a face just a few feet from hers. It was a boy with shaggy black hair, in a convertible jalopy painted gold. He stared at her and then his lips widened into a grin. Connie slit her eyes at him and turned away, but she couldn't help glancing back and there he was still watching her. He wagged a finger and laughed and said, "Gonna get you, baby," and Connie turned away again without Eddie noticing anything.

She spent three hours with him, at the restaurant where they ate hamburgers and drank Cokes in wax cups that were always sweating, and then down an alley a mile or so away, and when he left her off at five to eleven only the movie house was still open at the plaza. Her girl friend was there, talking with a boy. When Connie came up the two girls smiled at each other and Connie said, "How was the movie?" and the girl said, "*You* should know." They rode off with the girl's father, sleepy and pleased, and Connie couldn't help but look at the darkened shopping plaza with its big empty parking lot and its signs that were faded and ghostly now, and over at the drive-in restaurant where cars were still circling tirelessly. She couldn't hear the music at this distance.

Next morning June asked her how the movie was and Connie said, "So-so."

She and that girl and occasionally another girl went out several times a week that way, and the rest of the time Connie spent around the house—it was summer vacation—getting in her mother's way and thinking, dreaming, about the boys she met. But all the boys fell back and dissolved into a single face that was not even a face, but an idea, a feeling, mixed up with the urgent insistent pounding of the music and the humid night air of July. Connie's mother kept dragging her back to the daylight by finding things for her to do or saying suddenly, "What's this about the Pettinger girl?"

And Connie would say nervously, "Oh, her. That dope." She always drew thick clear lines between herself and such girls, and her mother was simple and kindly enough to believe her. Her mother was so simple, Connie thought, that it was maybe cruel to fool her so much. Her mother went scuffling around the house in old bedroom slippers and complained over the telephone to one sister about the other, then the other called up and the two of them complained about the third one. If June's name was mentioned her mother's tone was approving, and if Connie's name was mentioned it was disapproving. This did not really mean she disliked Connie and actually Connie thought that her mother preferred her to June because she was prettier, but the two of them kept up a pretense of exasperation, a sense that they were tugging and struggling over something of little value to either of them. Sometimes, over coffee, they were almost friends, but something would come up—some vexation that was like a fly buzzing suddenly around their heads—and their faces went hard with contempt.

One Sunday Connie got up at eleven—none of them bothered with church—and washed her hair so that it could dry all day long, in the sun. Her parents and sister were going to a barbecue at an aunt's house and Connie said no, she wasn't interested, rolling her eyes, to let mother know just what she thought of it. "Stay home alone then," her mother said sharply. Connie sat out back in a lawn chair and watched them drive away, her father quiet and bald, hunched around so that he could back the car out, her mother with a look that was still angry and not at all softened through the windshield, and in the back seat poor old June all dressed up as if she didn't know what a barbecue was, with all the running yelling kids and the flies. Connie sat with her eyes closed in the sun, dreaming and dazed with the warmth about her as if this were a kind of love, the caresses of love, and her mind slipped over onto thoughts of the boy she had been with the night before and how nice he had been, how sweet it always was, not the way someone like June would suppose but sweet, gentle, the way it was in movies and promised in songs; and when she opened her eyes she hardly knew where she was, the back yard ran off into weeds and a fenceline of trees and behind it the sky was perfectly blue and still. The asbestos "ranch house" that was now three years old startled her—it looked small. She shook her head as if to get awake.

It was too hot. She went inside the house and turned on the radio to drown out the quiet. She sat on the edge of her bed, barefoot, and listened for an hour and a half to a program called XYZ Sunday Jamboree, record after record of hard, fast, shrieking songs she sang along with, interspersed by exclamations from "Bobby King": "An' look here you girls at Napoleon's—Son and Charley want you to pay real close attention to this song coming up!"

And Connie paid close attention herself, bathed in a glow of slow-pulsed joy that seemed to rise mysteriously out of the music itself and lay languidly about the airless little room, breathed in and breathed out with each gentle rise and fall of her chest.

After a while she heard a car coming up the drive. She sat up at once, startled, because it couldn't be her father so soon. The gravel kept crunching all the way in from the road—the driveway was long—and Connie ran to the window. It was a car she didn't know. It was an open jalopy, painted a bright gold that caught the sun opaquely. Her heart began to pound and her fingers snatched at her hair, checking it, and she whispered "Christ. Christ," wondering how bad she looked. The car came to a stop at the side door and the horn sounded four short taps as if this were a signal Connie knew.

She went into the kitchen and approached the door slowly, then hung out the screen door, her bare toes curling down off the step. There were two boys in the car and now she recognized the driver: he had shaggy, shabby black hair that looked crazy as a wig and he was grinning at her.

"I ain't late, am I?" he said.

"Who the hell do you think you are?" Connie said.

"Toldja I'd be out, didn't I?"

"I don't even know who you are."

She spoke sullenly, careful to show no interest or pleasure, and he spoke in a fast bright monotone. Connie looked past him to the other boy, taking her time. He had fair brown hair, with a lock that fell onto his forehead. His sideburns gave him a fierce, embarrassed look, but so far he hadn't even bothered to glance at her. Both boys wore sunglasses. The driver's glasses were metallic and mirrored everything in miniature.

"You wanta come for a ride?" he said.

Connie smirked and let her hair fall loose over one shoulder.

"Don'tcha like my car? New paint job," he said. "Hey."

"What?"

"You're cute."

She pretended to fidget, chasing flies away from the door.

"Dont'cha believe me, or what?" he said.

"Look, I don't even know who you are," Connie said in disgust.

"Hey, Ellie's got a radio, see. Mine's broke down." He lifted his friend's arm and showed her the little transistor the boy was holding, and now Connie began to hear the music. It was the same program that was playing inside the house.

"Bobby King?" she said.

"I listen to him all the time. I think he's great."

"He's kind of great," Connie said reluctantly.

"Listen, that guy's *great*. He knows where the action is."

Connie blushed a little, because the glasses made it impossible for her to see just what this boy was looking at. She couldn't decide if she liked him or if he was just a jerk, and so she dawdled in the doorway and wouldn't come down or go back inside. She said, "What's all that stuff painted on your car?"

"Can'tcha read it?" He opened the door very carefully, as if he was afraid it might fall off. He slid out just as carefully, planting his feet firmly on the ground, the tiny metallic world in his glasses slowing down like gelatine hardening and in the midst of it Connie's bright green blouse. "This here is my name, to begin with," he said. ARNOLD FRIEND was written in tar-like black letters on the side, with a drawing of a round grinning face that reminded Connie of a pumpkin, except it wore sunglasses. "I wanta introduce myself, I'm Arnold Friend and that's my real name and I'm gonna be your friend, honey, and inside the car's Ellie Oscar, he's kinda shy." Ellie brought his transistor up to his shoulder and balanced it there. "Now these numbers are a secret code, honey," Arnold Friend explained. He read off the numbers 33, 19, 17 and raised his eyebrows at her to see what she thought of that, but she didn't think much of it. The left rear fender had been smashed and around it was written, on the gleaming gold background: DONE BY CRAZY WOMAN DRIVER. Connie had to laugh at that. Arnold Friend was pleased at her laughter and looked up at her. "Around the other side's a lot more—you wanta come and see them?"

"No."

"Why not?"

"Why should I?"

"Don'tcha wanta see what's on the car? Don'tcha wanta go for a ride?"

"I don't know."

"Why not?"

"I got things to do."

"Like what?"

"Things."

He laughed as if she had said something funny. He slapped his thighs. He was standing in a strange way, leaning back against the car as if he were balancing himself. He wasn't tall, only an inch or so taller than she would be if she came down to him. Connie liked the way he was dressed, which was the way all of them dressed: tight faded jeans stuffed into black, scuffed boots, a belt that pulled his waist in and showed how lean he was, and a white pull-over shirt that was a little soiled and showed the hard small muscles of his arms and shoulders. He looked as if he probably did hard work, lifting and carrying things. Even his neck looked muscular. And his face was a familiar face, somehow: the jaw and chin and cheeks slightly darkened, because he hadn't shaved for a day or two, and the nose long and hawk-like, sniffing as if she were a treat he was going to gobble up and it was all a joke.

"Connie, you ain't telling the truth. This is your day set aside for a ride with me and you know it," he said, still laughing. The way he straightened and recovered from his fit of laughing showed that it had been all fake.

"How do you know what my name is?" she said suspiciously.

"It's Connie."

"Maybe and maybe not."

"I know my Connie," he said, wagging his finger. Now she remembered him even better, back at the restaurant, and her cheeks warmed at the thought of how she sucked in her breath just at the moment she passed him—how she must have looked to him. And he had remembered her. "Ellie and I come out here especially for you," he said. "Ellie can sit in back. How about it?"

"Where?"

"Where what?"

"Where're we going?"

He looked at her. He took off the sunglasses and she saw how pale the skin around his eyes was, like holes that were not in shadow but instead in light. His eyes were like chips of broken glass that catch the light in an amiable way. He smiled. It was as if the idea of going for a ride somewhere, to some place, was a new idea to him.

"Just for a ride, Connie sweetheart."

"I never said my name was Connie," she said.

"But I know what it is. I know your name and all about you, lots of things," Arnold Friend said. He had not moved yet but stood still leaning back against the side of his jalopy. "I took a special interest in you, such a pretty girl, and found out all about you like I know your parents and sister are gone somewheres and I know where and how long they're going to be gone, and I know who you were with last night, and your best friend's name is Betty. Right?"

He spoke in a simple lilting voice, exactly as if he were reciting the words to a song. His smile assured her that everything was fine. In the car Ellie turned up the volume on his radio and did not bother to look around at them.

"Ellie can sit in the back seat," Arnold Friend said. He indicated his friend with a casual jerk of his chin, as if Ellie did not count and she should not bother with him.

"How'd you find out all that stuff?" Connie said.

"Listen: Betty Schultz and Tony Fitch and Jimmy Pettinger and Nancy Pettinger," he said, in a chant. "Raymond Stanley and Bob Hutter—"

"Do you know all those kids?"

"I know everybody."

"Look, you're kidding. You're not from around here."

"Sure."

"But—how come we never saw you before?"

"Sure you saw me before," he said. He looked down at his boots, as if he were a little offended. "You just don't remember."

"I guess I'd remember you," Connie said.

"Yeah?" He looked up at this, beaming. He was pleased. He began to mark time with the music from Ellie's radio, tapping his fists lightly together. Connie looked away from his smile to the car, which was painted so bright it almost hurt her eyes to look at it. She looked at that name, ARNOLD FRIEND. And up at the front fender was an expression that was familiar—MAN THE FLYING SAUCERS. It was an expression kids had used the year before, but didn't use this year. She looked at it for a while as if the words meant something to her that she did not yet know.

"What're you thinking about? Huh?" Arnold Friend demanded. "Not worried about your hair blowing around in the car, are you?"

"No."

"Think I maybe can't drive good?"

"How do I know?"

"You're a hard girl to handle. How come?" he said. "Don't you know I'm your friend? Didn't you see me put my sign in the air when you walked by?"

"What sign?"

"My sign." And he drew an X in the air, leaning out toward her. They were maybe ten feet apart. After his hand fell back to his side the X was still in the air, almost visible. Connie let the screen door close and stood perfectly still inside it, listening to the music from her radio and the boy's blend together. She stared at Arnold Friend. He stood there so stiffly relaxed, pretending to be relaxed, with one hand idly on the door handle as if he were keeping himself up that way and had no intention of ever moving again. She recognized most things about him, the tight jeans that showed his thighs and buttocks and the greasy leather boots and the tight shirt, and even that slippery friendly smile of his, that sleepy dreamy smile that all the boys used to get across ideas they didn't want to put into words. She recognized all this and also the singsong way he talked, slightly mocking, kidding, but serious and a little melancholy, and she recognized the way he tapped one fist against the other in homage to the perpetual music behind him. But all these things did not come together.

She said suddenly, "Hey, how old are you?"

His smile faded. She could see then that he wasn't a kid, he was much older— thirty, maybe more. At this knowledge her heart began to pound faster.

"That's a crazy thing to ask. Can'tcha see I'm your own age?"

"Like hell you are."

"Or maybe a coupla years older, I'm eighteen."

"Eighteen?" she said doubtfully.

He grinned to reassure her and lines appeared at the corners of his mouth. His teeth were big and white. He grinned so broadly his eyes became slits and she saw how thick the lashes were, thick and black as if painted with a black tar-like material. Then he seemed to become embarrassed, abruptly, and looked over his shoulder at Ellie. "*Him*, he's crazy," he said. "Ain't he a riot, he's a nut, a real character." Ellie was still listening to the music. His sunglasses told nothing about what he was thinking. He wore a bright orange shirt unbuttoned halfway to show his chest, which was a pale, bluish chest and not muscular like Arnold Friend's. His shirt collar was turned up all around and the very tips of the collar pointed out past his chin as if they were protecting him. He was pressing the transistor radio up against his ear and sat there in a kind of daze, right in the sun.

"He's kinda strange," Connie said.

"Hey, she says you're kinda strange! Kinda strange!" Arnold Friend cried. He pounded on the car to get Ellie's attention. Ellie turned for the first time and Connie saw with shock that he wasn't a kid either—he had a fair, hairless face, cheeks reddened slightly as if the veins grew too close to the surface of his skin, the face of a forty-year-old baby. Connie felt a wave of dizziness rise in her at this sight and she stared at him as if waiting for something to change the shock of the moment, make it all right again. Ellie's lips kept shaping words, mumbling along with the words blasting his ear.

"Maybe you two better go away," Connie said faintly.

"What? How come?" Arnold Friend cried. "We come out here to take you for a ride. It's Sunday." He had the voice of the man on the radio now. It was the same voice, Connie thought. "Don'tcha know it's Sunday all day and honey, no matter who you were with last night today you're with Arnold Friend and don't you forget it!—Maybe you better step out here," he said, and this last was in a different voice. It was a little flatter, as if the heat was finally getting to him.

"No. I got things to do."

"Hey."

"You two better leave."

"We ain't leaving until you come with us."

"Like hell I am—"

"Connie, don't fool around with me. I mean. I mean, don't fool *around*," he said, shaking his head. He laughed incredulously. He placed his sunglasses on top of his head, carefully, as if he were indeed wearing a wig, and brought the stems down behind his ears. Connie stared at him, another wave of dizziness and fear rising in her so that for a moment he wasn't even in focus but was just a blur, standing there against his gold car, and she had the idea that he had driven up the driveway all right but had come from nowhere before that and belonged nowhere and that everything about him and even the music that was so familiar to her was only half real.

"If my father comes and sees you—"

"He ain't coming. He's at a barbecue."

"How do you know that?"

"Aunt Tillie's. Right now they're—uh—they're drinking. Sitting around," he said vaguely, squinting as if he were staring all the way to town and over to Aunt Tillie's back yard. Then the vision seemed to clear and he nodded energetically. "Yeah. Sitting around. There's your sister in a blue dress, huh? And high heels, the poor sad bitch—nothing like you, sweetheart! And your mother's helping some fat woman with the corn, they're cleaning the corn—husking the corn—"

"What fat woman?" Connie cried.

"How do I know what fat woman. I don't know every goddam fat woman in the world!" Arnold Friend laughed.

"Oh, that's Mrs. Hornby. . . . Who invited her?" Connie said. She felt a little light-headed. Her breath was coming quickly.

"She's too fat. I don't like them fat. I like them the way you are, honey," he said, smiling sleepily at her. They stared at each other for a while, through the screen door. He said softly, "Now what you're going to do is this: you're going to come out that door. You're going to sit up front with me and Ellie's going to sit in the back, the hell with Ellie, right? This isn't Ellie's date. You're my date. I'm your lover, honey."

"What? You're crazy—"

"Yes, I'm your lover. You don't know what that is but you will," he said. "I know that too. I know all about you. But look: it's real nice and you couldn't ask for nobody better than me, or more polite. I always keep my word. I'll tell you how it is, I'm always nice at first, the first time. I'll hold you so tight you won't think you have to try to get away or pretend anything because you'll know you can't. And I'll come inside you where it's all secret and you'll give in to me and you'll love me—"

"Shut up! You're crazy!" Connie said. She backed away from the door. She put her hands against her ears as if she'd heard something terrible, something not meant for her. "People don't talk like that, you're crazy," she muttered. Her heart was almost too big now for her chest and its pumping made sweat break out all over her. She looked out to see Arnold Friend pause and then take a step toward the porch lurching. He almost fell. But, like a clever drunken man, he managed to catch his balance. He wobbled in his high boots and grabbed hold of one of the porch posts.

"Honey?" he said. "You still listening?"

"Get the hell out of here!"

"Be nice, honey. Listen."

"I'm going to call the police—"

He wobbled again and out of the side of his mouth came a fast spat curse, an aside not meant for her to hear. But even this "Christ!" sounded forced. Then he began to smile again. She watched this smile come, awkward as if he were smiling from inside a mask. His whole face was a mask, she thought wildly, tanned down onto his throat but then running out as if he had plastered make-up on his face but had forgotten about his throat.

"Honey—? Listen, here's how it is. I always tell the truth and I promise you this: I ain't coming in that house after you."

"You better not! I'm going to call the police if you—if you don't—"

"Honey," he said, talking right through her voice, "honey, I'm not coming in there but you are coming out here. You know why?"

She was panting. The kitchen looked like a place she had never seen before, some room she had run inside but which wasn't good enough, wasn't going to help her. The kitchen window had never had a curtain, after three years, and there were dishes in the sink for her to do—probably—and if you ran your hand across the table you'd probably feel something sticky there.

"You listening, honey? Hey?"

"—going to call the police—"

"Soon as you touch the phone I don't need to keep my promise and can come inside. You won't want that."

She rushed forward and tried to lock the door. Her fingers were shaking. "But why lock it," Arnold Friend said gently, talking right into her face. "It's just a screen door. It's just nothing." One of his boots was at a strange angle, as if his foot wasn't in it. It pointed out to the left, bent at the ankle. "I mean, anybody can break through a screen door and glass and wood and iron or anything else if he needs to, anybody at all and specially Arnold Friend. If the place got lit up with a fire, honey, you'd come running out into my arms, right into my arms and safe at home—like you knew I was your lover and'd stopped fooling around. I don't mind a nice shy girl but I don't like no fooling around." Part of those words were spoken with a slight rhythmic lilt, and Connie somehow recognized them—the echo of a song from last year, about a girl rushing into her boy friend's arms and coming home again—

Connie stood barefoot on the linoleum floor, staring at him. "What do you want?" she whispered.

"I want you," he said.

"What?"

"Seen you that night and thought, that's the one, yes sir. I never needed to look any more."

"But my father's coming back. He's coming to get me. I had to wash my hair first—" She spoke in a dry, rapid voice, hardly raising it for him to hear.

"No, your daddy is not coming and yes, you had to wash your hair and you washed it for me. It's nice and shining and all for me, I thank you, sweetheart," he said, with a mock bow, but again he almost lost his balance. He had to bend and adjust his boots. Evidently his feet did not go all the way down; the boots must have been stuffed with something so that he would seem taller. Connie stared out at him and behind him Ellie in the car, who seemed to be looking off toward Connie's right, into nothing. This Ellie said, pulling the words out of the air one after another as if he were just discovering them, "You want me to pull out the phone?"

"Shut your mouth and keep it shut," Arnold Friend said, his face red from bending over or maybe from embarrassment because Connie had seen his boots. "This ain't none of your business."

"What—what are you doing? What do you want?" Connie said. "If I call the police they'll get you, they'll arrest you—"

"Promise was not to come in unless you touch that phone, and I'll keep that promise," he said. He resumed his erect position and tried to force his shoulders back. He sounded like a hero in a movie, declaring something important. He spoke too loudly and it was as if he were speaking to someone behind Connie. "I ain't made plans for coming in that house where I don't belong but just for you to come out to me, the way you should. Don't you know who I am?"

"You're crazy," she whispered. She backed away from the door but did not want to go into another part of the house, as if this would give him permission to come through the door. "What do you. . . . You're crazy, you. . . ."

"Huh? What're you saying, honey?"

Her eyes darted everywhere in the kitchen. She could not remember what it was, this room.

"This is how it is, honey: you come out and we'll drive away, have a nice ride. But if you don't come out we're gonna wait till your people come home and then they're all going to get it."

"You want that telephone pulled out?" Ellie said. He held the radio away from his ear and grimaced, as if without the radio the air was too much for him.

"I toldja shut up, Ellie." Arnold Friend said, "You're deaf, get a hearing aid, right? Fix yourself up. This little girl's no trouble and's gonna be nice to me, so Ellie keep to yourself, this ain't your date—right? Don't hem in on me. Don't hog. Don't crush. Don't bird dog. Don't trail me," he said in a rapid meaningless voice, as if he were running through all the expressions he'd learned but was no longer sure which one of them was in style, then rushing on to new ones, making them up with his eyes closed, "Don't crawl under my fence, don't squeeze in my chipmunk hole, don't sniff my glue, suck my popsicle, keep your own greasy fingers on yourself!" He shaded his eyes and peered in at Connie, who was backed against the kitchen table. "Don't mind him, honey, he's just a creep. He's a dope. Right? I'm the boy for you and like I said you come out here nice like a lady and give me your hand, and nobody else gets hurt, I mean, your nice old bald-headed daddy and your mummy and your sister in her high heels. Because listen: why bring them in this?"

"Leave me alone," Connie whispered.

"Hey, you know that old woman down the road, the one with the chickens and stuff—you know her?"

"She's dead!"

"Dead? What? You know her?" Arnold Friend said.

"She's dead—"

"Don't you like her?"

"She's dead—she's—she isn't here any more—"

"But don't you like her, I mean, you got something against her? Some grudge or something?" Then his voice dipped as if he were conscious of rudeness. He touched the sunglasses on top of his head as if to make sure they were still there. "Now you be a good girl."

"What are you going to do?"

"Just two things, or maybe three," Arnold Friend said. "But I promise it won't last long and you'll like me that way you get to like people you're close to. You will. It's all over for you here, so come on out. You don't want your people in any trouble, do you?"

She turned and bumped against a chair or something, hurting her leg, but she ran into the back room and picked up the telephone. Something roared in her ear, a tiny roaring, and she was so sick with fear that she could do nothing but listen to it—the telephone was clammy and very heavy and her fingers groped down to the dial but were too weak to touch it. She began to scream into the phone, into the roaring. She cried out, she cried for her mother, she felt her breath start jerking back and forth in her lungs as if it were something Arnold Friend were stabbing her with again and again with no tenderness. A noisy sorrowful wailing rose all about her and she was locked inside it the way she was locked inside this house.

After a while she could hear again. She was sitting on the floor, with her wet back against the wall.

Arnold Friend was saying from the door, "That's a good girl. Put the phone back."

She kicked the phone away from her.

"No, honey. Pick it up. Put it back right."

She picked it up and put it back. The dial tone stopped.

"That's a good girl. Now you come outside."

She was hollow with what had been fear, but what was now just an emptiness. All that screaming had blasted it out of her. She sat, one leg cramped under her, and deep inside her brain was something like a pinpoint of light that kept going and would not let her relax. She thought, I'm not going to see my mother again. She thought, I'm not going to sleep in my bed again. Her bright green blouse was all wet.

Arnold Friend said, in a gentle-loud voice that was like a stage voice, "The place where you came from ain't there any more, and where you had in mind to go is cancelled out. This place you are now—inside your daddy's house—is nothing but a cardboard box I can knock down any time. You know that and always did know it. You hear me?"

She thought, I have got to think. I have to know what to do.

"We'll go out to a nice field, out in the country here where it smells so nice and it's sunny," Arnold Friend said. "I'll have my arms tight around you so you won't need to try to get away and I'll show you what love is like, what it does. The hell with this house! It looks solid all right," he said. He ran a fingernail down the screen and the noise did not make Connie shiver, as it would have the day before. "Now put your hand on your heart, honey. Feel that? That feels solid too but we know better, be nice to me, be sweet like you can because what else is there for a girl like you but to be sweet and pretty and give in?—and get away before her people come back?"

She felt her pounding heart. Her hands seemed to enclose it. She thought for the first time in her life that it was nothing that was hers, that belonged to her, but just a pounding, living thing inside this body that wasn't hers either.

"You don't want them to get hurt," Arnold Friend went on. "Now get up, honey. Get up all by yourself."

She stood.

"Now turn this way. That's right. Come over here to me—Ellie, put that away, didn't I tell you? You dope. You miserable creepy dope," Arnold Friend said. His words were not angry but only part of an incantation. The incantation was kindly. "Now come out through the kitchen to me honey and let's see a smile, try it, you're a brave sweet little girl and now they're eating corn and hotdogs cooked to bursting over an outdoor fire, and they don't know one thing about you and never did and honey you're better than them because not one of them would have done this for you."

Connie felt the linoleum under her feet; it was cool. She brushed her hair back out of her eyes. Arnold Friend let go of the post tentatively and opened his arms for her, his elbows pointing up toward each other and his wrists limp, to show that this was an embarrassed embrace and a little mocking, he didn't want to make her self-conscious.

She put out her hand against the screen. She watched herself push the door slowly open as if she were safe back somewhere in the other doorway, watching this body and this head of long hair moving out into the sunlight where Arnold Friend waited.

"My sweet little blue-eyed girl," he said, in a half-sung sigh that had nothing to do with her brown eyes but was taken up just the same by the vast sunlit reaches of the land behind him and on all sides of him, so much land that Connie had never seen before and did not recognize except to know that she was going to it.

Suggestions for Discussion

1. Analyze the first paragraph of "Where Are You Going, Where Have You Been?" for the contrast between generalities and concrete details. What are the functions of each?

2. Locate physical descriptions of Connie and show what abstractions about her are implied.

3. As the details that describe Arnold Friend change, how does our understanding of him change?

4. Take any long paragraph of this story and underline the active verbs. Try substituting them with passive constructions and linking verbs. What is the effect?

5. Note the rhythm of the paragraph beginning "And Connie paid close attention . . ." on page 86. Contrast the following paragraph. How do the two rhythms reinforce the meaning?

6. The changes in Connie over the course of the story are not explicitly stated, but they are many and profound. How would you describe them?

Retrospect

1. Examine the first page of the excerpt from Annie Dillard's *The Writing Life* on page 21 to see how she uses active verbs to describe the writing process.

2. Compare the conflicts in "Guests of the Nation" and "The Things They Carried." In what ways do they differ? How are they similar? What connections with the "enemy" are made in each?

Writing Assignments

1. The playwright Bertold Brecht had over his desk a sign that read, "The Truth is Concrete." You will notice, however, that this sentence is an abstraction (he didn't mean that the truth is cement.) In your journal, cluster the word "concrete." Write a passage about it. When you're finished, check whether you have used any abstractions or generalizations that could be effectively replaced by concrete details.

2. Paint a self-portrait in words. Prop a mirror in front of you and describe, in the most focused sight details you can manage, twenty or thirty things that you see. Then try to distance yourself from your portrait and choose the two or three details that most vividly and concisely convey the image you want to present. What attitude do you want the reader to have? Should we find you funny, intense, pitiable, vain, dedicated? Add a detail of sound, touch, smell, or taste that will help convey the image.

3. Write a passage using significant details and active verbs about a character who conveys one of the following:
     • belongs to another century
     • complete harmony
     • brains are fried
     • out of control
     • kittenish or puppy-like
     • the absolute boss

4. Write a description of a rural landscape, a city street, a room, or the desk in front of you. Use only active verbs to describe inanimate as well as animate things. Avoid the pathetic fallacy.

5. Write about a boring situation. Convince us that the situation is boring and that your characters are bored or boring or both. Fascinate us. Or make us laugh. Use no generalizations, no judgments, and no verbs in the passive voice.

6. Write about one of the following and suggest the rhythm of the subject in your prose: a machine, a vehicle, a piece of music, sex, something that goes in a circle, an avalanche.

7. Write about a character who begins at a standstill, works up to great speed, and comes to a halt again. The rush may be purely emotional, or it may represent the speed of the vehicle, of pursuit, of sport, or whatever you choose. The halt may be abrupt or gradual. In any case, let the prose rhythm reflect the changes.

8. Take any scene you have already written and "shrink for details." That is, imagine yourself from the vantage point of something *very* small—no bigger than a button, a cockroach, an earlobe, a baked bean—and write a paragraph or a page using the details you see from that perspective.

4

BOOK PEOPLE
Characterization, Part I

- *Credibility*

- *Purpose*

- *Complexity*

- *The Indirect Method of Character Presentation*

- *The Direct Methods of Character Presentation*

Human character is in the foreground of all fiction, however the humanity might be disguised. Anthropomorphism may be a scientific sin, but it is a literary necessity. Bugs Bunny isn't a rabbit; he's a plucky youth in ears. Peter Rabbit is a mischievous boy. Brer Rabbit is a sassy rebel. The romantic heroes of *Watership Down* are out of the Arthurian tradition, not out of the hutch. And that doesn't cover fictional *rabbits*.

Henri Bergson, in his essay "On Laughter," observes:

> . . . the comic does not exist outside the pale of what is strictly human. A landscape may be beautiful, charming or sublime, or insignificant and ugly; it will never be laughable.

Bergson is right, but it is just as true that only the human is tragic. We may describe a landscape as "tragic" because nature has been devastated by industry, but the tragedy lies in the cupidity of those who wrought the havoc, in the dreariness, poverty, or disease of those who must live there. A conservationist or ecologist (or a novelist) may care passionately about nature and dislike people because they pollute oceans and cut down trees. Then we say he or she "identifies" with nature (a wholly human capacity) or "respects the natural unity" (of which humanity is a part) or wants to keep the earth habitable (for whom?) or "values nature for its own sake" (using standards of value that nature does not share). By all available evidence, the universe is indifferent to the destruction of trees, property, peoples, and planets. Only people care.

If this is so, then your fiction can be only as successful as the characters who move it and move within it. Whether they are drawn from life or are pure fantasy—and all fictional characters lie somewhere between the two—we must find them interesting, we must find them believable, and we must care about what happens to them.

As a writer you may have the lucky, facile sort of imagination to which characters spring full-blown, complete with gestures, histories, and passions. Or it may be that you need to explore in order to exploit, to draw your characters out gradually and coax them into being. That can be lucky, too.

For either kind of writer, but especially the latter, the journal is an invaluable help. A journal lets you coax and explore without committing yourself to anything or anyone. It allows you to know everything about your character whether you use it or not. Before you put a character in a story, know how well that character sleeps. Know what the character eats for lunch and how much it matters, what he buys and how the bills get paid, how she spends what we call working hours. Know how your character would prefer to spend evenings and weekends and why such plans get thwarted. Know what memories the character has of pets and parents, cities, snow, or school. You may end up using none of this information in the brief segment of your character's life that is your plot, but knowing it may teach you how your bookperson taps a pencil or twists a lock of hair, and when and why. When you know these things, you will have taken a step past invention toward the moment of imagination in which you become your character, live in his or her skin, and produce an action that, for the reader, rings universally true.

Use the journal to note your observations of people. Try clustering your impressions of the library assistant who annoys you or the loner at the bar who intrigues you. Try to capture a gesture or the messages that physical features and clothing send. Invent a reason for that harshness or that loneliness; invent a past. Then try taking the character out of context and setting her or him in another. Get your character in trouble, and you may be on your way to a short story.

It is interesting and relevant that actors schooled in what is called the Stanislavski Method write biographies of the characters they must play. Adherents of "The Method" believe that in the process of inventing a dramatic character's past, the actor will find points of emotional contact with that role and so know how to make the motives and actions prescribed by the script natural and genuine. As a writer you can also use "The Method", imagining much that you will not bring specifically to "the script" but that will enrich your sense of that character until you know with absolute certainty how he or she will move, act, react, and speak.

In any case, the key to rich characterization is the same as that outlined in the preceding chapter, an attention to detail that is significant. Though critics often praise literature for exhibiting characteristics of the *individual*, the *typical*, and the *universal* all at the same time, I don't think this is of much use to the practicing writer. For though you may labor to create an individual character, and you may make that character a credible example of type, I don't think you can *set out to be* "universal."

It is true, I believe, that if literature has any social justification or use it is that readers can identify the common humanity in, and can therefore identify with, characters vastly different from themselves in century, geography, gender, culture, and beliefs; and that this enhances the scope of the reader's sympathy. It is also true that if the fiction does not have this universal quality—if a middle-class American male author creates as protagonist a middle-class American male with whom only middle-class American male readers can sympathize—then the fiction is thin and small. William Sloane voices the "frightening" demand of the reader in his book *The Craft of Writing*: "Tell me about me. I want to be more alive. Give me me." But unfortunately, the capacity for universality, like talent, is a trick of the genes or a miracle of the soul, and if you aim for the universal, you're likely to achieve the pompous, whereas if you aim for the individual, you're likely to achieve the typical, and the universal can't be forced.

Imagine this scene: The child chases a ball into the street. The tires screech, the bumper thuds, the blood geysers into the air, the pulp of the small body lies inert on the asphalt. How would a bystander react? (Is it universal?) How would a passing doctor react? (Is it typical?) How would Dr. Henry Lowes, just coming from the maternity ward of his own hospital, where his wife has had her fourth miscarriage, react? (Is it individual?) Each question narrows the range of convincing reaction, and as a writer you want to convince in each range. If you succeed in the third, you are likely to have succeeded in the other two.

My advice then is to labor in the range of the particular. If you aim for a universal character you may end up with a vague or dull or windy one. On the other hand, if you set out to write a typical character you're likely to produce a caricature, because people are typical only in the generalized qualities that lump them together. *Typical* is the most provincial adjective in a writer's vocabulary, signaling that you're writing only for those who share your assumptions. A "typical" schoolgirl in Dar es Salaam is a very different type from one in San Francisco. Furthermore, every person is typical of many things successively or simultaneously. She may be in turn a "typical" schoolgirl, bride, divorcée, and feminist. He may be at one and the same time a "typical" New Yorker, math professor, doting father, and adulterer. It is in the confrontation and convolution of types that much of our individuality is produced.

Writing in generalities and typicalities is akin to bigotry—we only see what's alike about people, not what's unique. When effective, a description of type blames the character for the failure to individualize, and if an author sets out deliberately to produce types rather than individuals, then that author invariably wants to condemn or ridicule those types. Joyce Carol Oates illustrates the technique in "How I Contemplated the World from the Detroit House of Correction and Began My Life Over Again."

George, Clyde G. 240 Sioux. A manufacturer's representative; children, a dog, a wife. Georgian with the usual columns. You think of the White House, then of Thomas Jefferson, then your mind goes blank on the white pillars and you think of nothing.

Mark Helprin, in "The Schreuderspitze", takes the ridicule of type to comic extreme.

In Munich are many men who look like weasels. Whether by genetic accident, meticulous crossbreeding, an early and puzzling migration, coincidence, or a reason that we do not know, they exist in great numbers. Remarkably, they accentuate this unfortunate tendency by wearing mustaches, Alpine hats, and tweed. A man who resembles a rodent should never wear tweed.

This is not to say that all characters must be fully drawn or *"round."* Flat characters—who exist only to exhibit a function or a single characteristic—are useful and necessary. Eric Bentley suggests in *The Life of the Drama* that if a messenger's function in a play is to deliver his message, it would be very tedious to stop and learn about his psychology. The same is true in fiction; the Queen's chauffeur in the passage from *Mrs. Dalloway* (see chapter 3) exists for no purpose but leaning "ever so slightly", and we do not want to hear about his children or his hernia. Nevertheless, onstage even a flat character has a face and a costume, and in fiction detail can give even a flat character a few angles and contours. The servant classes in the novels of Henry James are notoriously absent as individuals because they exist only in their functions (*that excellent creature had already assembled the baggage,* etc.), whereas Charles Dickens, who peoples his novels with dozens of flat characters, brings even these alive in detail.

And Mrs. Miff, the wheezy little pew opener—a mighty dry old lady, sparely dressed, with not an inch of fullness anywhere about her—is also here.

Dombey and Son

To borrow a notion from George Orwell's *Animal Farm*, all good characters are created round, but some are created rounder than others.

Credibility

Though you aim at individuality and not typicality in characters, your characters will exhibit typicality in the sense of "appropriateness". A Baptist Texan behaves differently from an Italian nun; a rural schoolboy behaves differently from a professor emeritus at Harvard. If you are to succeed in creating an individual character, particular and alive, you will also inevitably know what is appropriate to that sort of person and will let us know as much as we need to know to feel the appropriateness of the behavior.

We need to know soon, for instance, preferably in the first paragraph, the character's gender, age, and race or nationality. We need to know something of his or her class, period, and region. A profession (or the clear lack of it) and a marital status help, too. Almost any reader can identify with almost any character; what no reader can identify with is confusion. When some or several of the fundamentals of type are withheld from us—when we don't know whether we're dealing with a man or a woman, an adult or a child—the process of identifying cannot begin, and the story is slow to move us.

None of the information need come as information; it can be implied by appearance, tone, action, or detail. In the next example William Melvin Kelley pitches his protagonist straight into the conflict. Only the character's gender is given us directly, but by the end of the story's opening paragraph, we know a lot about his life and type.

> To find this Cooley, the Black baby's father, he knew he would have to contact Opal Simmons. After dressing, he began to search for her address and number. Tam, very organized for a woman, saved everything. Among the envelopes containing the sports-clothes receipts, a letter from her dressmaker asking for payment, old airline tickets, the nursery school bill, the canceled checks and deposit slips, he finally found Opal's address.
>
> "Passing"

We know from the apparently "irrelevant" collection of bills that the protagonist is middle class, married, a father, affluent, and perhaps (that letter from the dressmaker) living at the edge of his income. Because he specifies a "Black baby", we know that he is white. We also know something about his attitudes toward both blacks ("this Cooley") and women ("very organized for a woman"). With an absolute minimum of exposition, letting us share the search for the address, Kelley has drawn clear boundaries of what we may expect from a character whose name we don't yet know.

The following passage is an even more striking example of indirect information.

> Every time the same story. Your Barbie is roommates with my Barbie, and my Barbie's boyfriend comes over and your Barbie steals him, okay? Kiss kiss kiss. Then the two Barbies fight. You dumbbell! He's mine. Oh no he's not, you stinky! Only Ken's invisible, right? Because we don't have money for a stupid-looking boy doll when we'd both rather ask for a new Barbie outfit next Christmas. We have to make do with your mean-eyed Barbie and my bubblehead Barbie and our one outfit apiece not including the sock dress.
>
> Sandra Cisneros, "Barbie-Q"

Here there is no description whatever of the characters, and no direct reference to them except for the designations *you* and *I*. What do we nevertheless know about their gender, their age, their financial status, the period in which they live, their personalities, their attitudes, their relationship, the narrator's emotions?

Students of writing are sometimes daunted by the need to give so much information immediately. The thing to remember is that credibility consists in the combination of appropriateness and specificity. The trick is to find telling details that will convey the information indirectly while our attention remains on the desire or emotion of the character. Nobody wants to read a story that begins:

> She was a twenty-eight-year-old suburban American woman, relatively affluent, who was extremely distressed when her husband Peter left her.

But most of that, and much more besides, could be contained in a few details.

> After Peter left with the VCR, the microwave, and the key to the garage, she went down to the kitchen and ate three jars of peanut butter without tasting a single spoonful.

I don't mean to imply that it is necessarily easy to signal the essentials of type immediately. It would be truer to say that it is necessary and hard. The opening paragraph of a story is its second strongest statement (the final paragraph is the strongest) and sets the tone for all that follows. If the right words don't come to you as a gift, you may have to sit sifting and discarding the inadequate ones for a long time before you achieve both clarity and interest.

Purpose

Your character's purpose—that is, the desire that impels her or him to action—will determine our degree of identification and sympathy on the one hand, or judgment on the other.

Aristotle, in *The Poetics*, says that "there will be an element of character if what a person says or does reveals a certain moral purpose; and a good element of character, if the purpose so revealed is good." It might seem that the antiheroes, brutes, hoods, whores, perverts, and bums who people modern literature do very little in the way of revealing good moral purpose. The history of Western literature shows a movement downward and inward: downward through society from royalty to gentry to the middle classes to the lower classes to the dropouts; inward from heroic action to social drama to individual consciousness to the subconscious to the unconscious. What has remained consistent is that, for the time spent in an author's world, we understand and identify with the protagonist or protagonists, we "see their point of view"; and the fiction succeeds largely because we are willing to grant them a goodness that we would not grant them in life. Aristotle goes on to explain that "such goodness is possible in every type of personage, even in a woman or a slave, though the one is perhaps an inferior, and the other a wholly worthless being"—and the sentence strikes us as both offensive and funny. But in Aristotle's society, women and slaves were legally designated inferior and worthless, and what Aristotle is saying is precisely what Ken Kesey acknowledges when he picks the inmates of an "Institute of Psychology" as his heroes: that the external status granted by society is not an accurate measure of good moral purpose.

> This new redheaded admission, McMurphy, knows right away he's not a Chronic. . . The Acutes look spooked and uneasy when he laughs, the way kids look in a schoolroom when one ornery kid is raising too much hell. . .
> . . . "Which one of you claims to be the craziest? Which one is the biggest looney? Who runs these card games? It's my first day, and what I like to do is make a good impression straight off on the right man if he can prove to me he is the right man. Who's the bull goose looney here?"

> *One Flew Over the Cuckoo's Nest*

If you met McMurphy in real life, you'd probably say he was crazy and you'd hope he would be locked up. If you encountered the Neanderthals of William Golding's *The Inheritors* on your evening walk, you'd run. If you were forced to live with the visionaries of Doris Lessing's *Four-Gated City* or the prisoners of Jean Genet's *Our Lady of the Flowers*, you would live in skepticism and fear. But while you read you expand your mental scope by identifying with, temporarily "becoming," a character who convinces you that the inmates of the asylum are saner than the staff, that the apemen are more human than *Homo sapiens*, that mental breakdown is mental breakthrough, that perversion is purer than the sexual code by which you live. For the drama audiences of fourth-century B.C. Athens, it was easier to see human nobility embodied in the heroic external actions of those designated by class as noble. It is largely because literature has moved inward, within the mind, that it is possible to move downward in social status—even to women and slaves!—and maintain this sympathy. In our own minds each of us is fundamentally justified, however conscious we are of our flaws—indeed, the more conscious of our flaws, the more commendable we are. As readers we are allowed to borrow a different mind. Fiction, as critic Laurence Gonzales said of rock music, "lets you wander around in someone else's hell for a while and see how similar it is to your own."

Obviously we don't identify with all characters, and those whose purpose is revealed as ambiguous or evil will invite varying degrees of judgment. When on pages 89–90 of the story "Where Are You Going, Where Have You Been?" Arnold Friend is described as "stiffly relaxed," with a "slippery friendly smile" and a series of familiar styles that "did not come together," we are immediately skeptical of him; because we suspect his purpose toward Connie we pass judgment on his fundamental character.

Complexity

If the characters of your story are credible through being appropriate and individual, and if they invite identification or judgment through a sense of their purpose, they also need to be complex. They need to exhibit enough conflict and contradiction that we can recognize them as belonging to the contradictory human race; and they should exhibit a range of possibility so that a shift of power in the plot can also produce a shift of purpose or morality. That is, they need to be capable of change.

Conflict is at the core of character as it is of plot. If plot begins with trouble, then character begins with a person in trouble; and trouble most dramatically occurs because we all have traits, tendencies, and desires that are at war, not simply with the world and other people, but with other of our own traits, tendencies, and desires. All of us probably know a woman of the strong, striding, independent sort, attractive only to men who like a strong and striding woman. And when she falls in love? She becomes a clinging sentimentalist. All of us know a father who is generous, patient, and dependable. And when the children cross the line? He smashes crockery and wields a strap. All of us are gentle, violent; logical, schmaltzy; tough, squeamish; lusty, prudish; sloppy, meticulous; energetic, apathetic; manic, depressive. Perhaps you don't fit that particular list of contradictions, but you are sufficiently in conflict with yourself that as an author you have characters enough in your own psyche to people the work of a lifetime if you will identify, heighten, and dramatize these conflicts within character, which Aristotle called "consistent inconsistencies."

If you think of the great characters of literature, you can see how consistent inconsistency brings each to a crucial dilemma. Hamlet is a strong and decisive man who procrastinates. Dorothea Brooke of *Middlemarch* is an idealistic and intellectual young woman, a total fool in matters of the heart. Ernest Hemingway's Francis Macomber wants to test his manhood against a lion and cannot face the test. Here, in a moment of crisis from *Mom Kills Self and Kids*, Alan Saperstein reveals with great economy the consistent inconsistency of his protagonist, a man who hadn't much time for his family until their absence makes clear how dependent he has been on them.

> When I arrived home from work I found my wife had killed our two sons and taken her own life.
>
> I uncovered a blast of foul, black steam from the pot on the stove and said, "Hi, hon, what's for dinner?" But she did not laugh. She did not bounce to her feet and pirouette into the kitchen to greet me. My little one didn't race into my legs and ask what I brought him. The seven-year-old didn't automatically beg me to play a game knowing my answer would be a tired, "Maybe later."

It is, of course, impossible to know to what degree Shakespeare, Eliot, Hemingway, or Saperstein used consistent inconsistencies of which they were aware in themselves to build and dramatize their characters. An author works not only from his or her own personality but also from observation and imagination, and I fully believe that you are working at full stretch only when all three are involved. The question of autobiography is a complicated one, and as writer you frequently won't know yourself how much you have experienced, how much you have observed, and how much you have invented. Actress Mildred Dunnock once observed that drama is possible "because people can feel what they haven't experienced"; if this is true of audiences and readers, I see no reason the capacity should be denied to writers. A vast proportion of our experience is mental, and it is safe to say that all your writing is autobiographical in the sense that it must have passed through your mind.

The Indirect Method of Character Presentation: Authorial Interpretation

In the writing itself, there are five basic *methods of character presentation*, of which the indirect method, *authorial interpretation*, and two of the four direct methods, *appearance* and *action*, will be discussed in this chapter. Two further direct methods, *speech* and *thought*, will be discussed in chapter 5. Employing a variety of these methods can help you draw a full character. If you produce a conflict among the methods, it can also help you create a three-dimensional character.

The indirect method of presenting a character is authorial interpretation— "telling" us the character's background, motives, values, virtues, and the like. The advantages of the indirect method are enormous, for its use leaves you free to move in time and space; to know anything you choose to know whether the character knows it or not; and godlike, to tell us what we are to feel. The indirect method allows you to convey a great deal of information in a short time.

> The most excellent Marquis of Lumbria lived with his two daughters, Caroline, the elder, and Luisa; and his second wife, Doa Vicenta, a woman with a dull brain, who, when she was not sleeping, was complaining of everything, especially the noise. . .
>
> The Marquis of Lumbria had no male children, and this was the most painful thorn in his existence. Shortly after having become a widower, he had married Doa Vicenta, his present wife, in order to have a son, but she proved sterile.
>
> The Marquis' life was as monotonous and as quotidian, as unchanging and regular, as the murmur of the river below the cliff or as the liturgic services in the cathedral.
>
> Miguel De Unamuno, *The Marquis of Lumbria*

The disadvantages of this indirect method are outlined in chapter 3. Indeed, in the passage above, it may well be part of Unamuno's purpose to convey the "monotonous and quotidian" quality of the Marquis's life by this summarized and distanced rehearsal of facts, motives, and judgments. Nearly every author will use the indirect method occasionally, and you may find it useful when you want to cover the exposition quickly. Occasionally you may convince us that you are so much more knowledgeable about a character than we can be, and so much more subtle at analyzing him or her, that we will accept your explanations. Very occasionally an author will get away with explaining the characters as much as, or more than, they are directly presented. Henry James is such an author; he is not an author I would advise anyone to imitate.

> Mrs. Touchett was certainly a person of many oddities, of which her behavior on returning to her husband's house after many months was a noticeable specimen. She had her own way of doing all that she did, and this is the simplest description of a character which, although it was by no means without benevolence, rarely succeeded in giving an impression of softness. Mrs. Touchett might do a great deal of good, but she never pleased.
>
> *Portrait of a Lady*

The very clear presence of the author in this passage, commenting, guiding our reactions, is the hallmark of James's prose, and (although it is by no means without benevolence) the technique is a difficult one to sustain. Direct presentation of the characters is much more likely to please the modern reader.

The Direct Methods of Character Presentation

The four methods of direct presentation are *appearance, action, speech,* and *thought.* A character may also be presented through the opinions of other characters, which may be considered a second indirect method. When this method is employed, however, the second character must give his or her opinions in speech, action, or thought. In the process, the character is inevitably also characterized. Whether we accept the opinion depends on what we think of that character as he or she is thus directly characterized. In this scene from Jane Austen's *Mansfield Park*, for example, the busybody Mrs. Norris gives her opinion of the heroine.

> ". . . there is something about Fanny, I have often observed it before,—she likes to go her own way to work; she does not like to be dictated to; she takes her own independent walk whenever she can; she certainly has a little spirit of secrecy, and independence, and nonsense, about her, which I would advise her to get the better of."
> As a general reflection on Fanny, Sir Thomas thought nothing could be more unjust, though he had been so lately expressing the same sentiments himself, and he tried to turn the conversation, tried repeatedly before he could succeed.

Here Mrs. Norris's opinion is directly presented in her speech and Sir Thomas's in his thoughts, each of them being characterized in the process. It is left to the reader to decide (without much difficulty) whose view of Fanny is the more reliable.

APPEARANCE

Of the four methods of direct presentation, appearance is especially important because our eyes are our most highly developed means of perception, and we therefore receive more non-sensuous information by sight than by any other sense. Beauty is only skin deep, but people are embodied, and whatever beauty—or ugliness—there is in them must somehow surface in order for us to perceive it. Such surfacing involves speech and action as well as appearance, but it is appearance that prompts our first reaction to people, and everything they wear and own bodies forth some aspect of their inner selves.

Writers are sometimes inclined to neglect or even deny this power of the visible. The choice of writing as a profession or avocation usually contains an implicit rejection of materialism (an English degree won't get you a job; your folks wish you'd major in business; starving in a gloomy basement is a likely option), and writers are concerned to see beyond mere appearances.

In fact, much of the tension and conflict in character does proceed from the truth that appearance is not reality. But in order to know this, we must see the appearance, and it is often in the contradiction between appearance and reality that the truth comes out. Features, shape, style, clothing, and objects can make statements of internal values that are political, religious, social, intellectual, and essential. The man in the Ultrasuede jacket is making a different statement from the one in the holely sweatshirt. The woman with the cigarette holder is telling us something different from the one with the the palmed joint. Even a person who has forsaken our materialistic society altogether, sworn off supermarkets, and gone to the country to grow organic potatoes has a special relationship with his or her hoe. However indifferent we may be to our looks, that indifference is the result of experiences with our bodies. A twenty-two-year-old Apollo who has been handsome since he was six is a very different person from the man who spent his childhood cocooned in fat and burst the chrysalis at age sixteen.

Following are four very brief portraits of women. Each is mainly characterized by such trivialities as fabric, hairdo, and cosmetics. It would nevertheless be impossible to mistake the essential nature of any one of them for that of any of the others.

Mrs. Withers, the dietician, marched in through the back door, drew up, and scanned the room. She wore her usual Betty Grable hairdo and open-toed pumps, and her shoulders had an aura of shoulder pads even in a sleeveless dress.

Margaret Atwood, *The Edible Woman*

My grandmother had on not just one skirt, but four, one over the other. It should not be supposed that she wore one skirt and three petticoats; no, she wore four skirts; one supported the next, and she wore the lot of them in accordance with a definite system, that is, the order of the skirts was changed from day to day. . . The one that was closest to her yesterday clearly disclosed its pattern today, or rather its lack of pattern: all my grandmother Anna Bronski's skirts favored the same potato color. It must have been becoming to her.

Gunter Grass, *The Tin Drum*

How beautiful Helen is, how elegant, how timeless: how she charms Esther Songford and how she flirts with Edwin, laying a scarlet fingernail on his dusty lapel, mesmerizing.

She comes in a chauffered car. She is all cream and roses. Her stockings are purest silk; her underskirt, just briefly showing, is lined with lace.

Fay Weldon, *Female Friends*

As soon as I entered the room, a pungent odor of phosphorus told me she'd taken rat poison. She lay groaning between the quilts. The tatami by the bed was splashed with blood, her waved hair was matted like rope waste, and a bandage tied round her throat showed up unnaturally white. . . The painted mouth in her waxen face created a ghastly effect, as though her lips were a gash open to the ears.

Masuji Ibuse, *"Tajinko Village"*

Vividness and richness of character are created in these four passages, which use nothing more than appearance to characterize.

ACTION

The significant characters of a fiction must be both capable of causing an action and capable of being changed by it.

It is important to understand the difference between action and movement, terms that are not synonymous. Physical movement is generally necessary to the action, but it is not adequate to ensure that there will be an action. Much movement in a story—the way he crosses his legs, the way she charges down the hall—is actually part of appearance and characterizes without necessarily moving the plot forward. When a book or film is advertised as "action-packed," it is also likely that what is being touted is movement rather than action—lots of sword fights, karate chops, or bombs away—but not necessarily that meaningful arrangement of events in which a character is convincingly compelled to pursue a goal, to make decisions along the way, and to undergo a subtle or dramatic alteration in the process. The words "motive," "motion," and "emotion" have the same root, and this is neither accidental nor irrelevant to the way the human drama unfolds.

Here is a passage from Zora Neale Hurston's "The Gilded Six-Bits" in which the amount of movement is very small, but the tension is high, the two characters' motives and emotions are richly apparent, and both are immediately characterized:

> Missie May was sobbing. Wails of weeping without words. Joe stood, and after a while he found out that he had something in his hand. And then he stood and felt without thinking and without seeing with his natural eyes. Missie May kept on crying and Joe kept on feeling so much, and not knowing what to do with all his feelings, he put Slemmon's watch charm in his pants pocket and took a good laugh and went to bed.

Playwrights are good people to ask about action, since plays depend on the externalized, rather than on interior thought. Sam Smiley, in *Playwrighting: The Structure of Action*, defines action simply as "human change." Change occurs with a dramatic event, an event that makes a difference.

Claudia Johnson agrees that each drama (or for our purposes each story), is *a pattern of change*. Scenes are built around dramatic events, Johnson says, and she thinks of the scene as an oyster, the dramatic event as the pearl. Building a story is stringing the pearls. She finds that *decision* and *discovery* are the agents of real change—and goes so far as to say that all human turning points are moments of either discovery or decision. Deeds and accidents are necessary to both drama and fiction, but the moment of change for the characters involved is the moment at which she decides to do something, or he discovers that the accident has occurred. (No doubt this is why, when a hero is hit, he so often calls attention to the fact. Once he is dead no further action can occur that will change him, and the drama shifts to the friend who discovers him.) Likewise, revelation is a stunning moment of drama, but the change in the characters occurs when one decides to reveal and the other discovers whatever has been revealed. Here is a passage in which mere events are followed by a moment of discovery that changes the character's mood and situation—and involves us in immediate suspense.

> I turned on a light in the living room and looked at Rachel's books. I chose one by an author named Lin Yutang and sat down on a sofa under a lamp. Our living room is comfortable. The book seemed interesting. I was in a neighborhood where most of the front doors were unlocked, and on a street that is very quiet on a summer night. All the animals are domesticated, and the only night birds that I've ever heard are some owls way down by the railroad track. So it was very quiet. I heard the Barstows' dog bark, briefly, as if he had been waked by a nightmare, and then the barking stopped. Everything was quiet again. Then I heard, very close to me, a footstep and a cough.
>
> I felt my flesh get hard—you know that feeling—but I didn't look up from my book, although I felt that I was being watched.

> John Cheever, *"The Cure"*

Here is another passage, where the character's insistence that there is no discovery to be made—the disease is no mystery, she knows how a virus works—throws into dramatic relief her discovery that her perception has changed.

> I wonder if it is possible to prepare yourself for anything. Of course I lay there, saying, This is the flu, it isn't supposed to last more than two or three days, I should find the Tylenol. In the moment I didn't feel bad, really, a little queasy, a degree feverish. The disease wasn't a mystery to me. I know what a virus looks like, how it works. I could imagine the invasion and the resistance. In fact, imagining the invasion and the resistance took my attention off the queasiness and the feverishness. But when I opened my eyes and my gaze fell upon the bookcases looming above me in the half-light, I shuddered reflexively, because the books seemed to swell outward from the wall and threaten to drop on me, and my thoughts about the next few days had exactly that quality as well. I did not see how we would endure, how I would endure.

> Jane Smiley, *"The Age of Grief"*

You don't want your technique to show, and once you're sure of your structure, you need to bury it. In the next example, from Raymond Carver's "Neighbors," the pattern of change—Bill Miller's gradual intrusion into his neighbor's house—is based on a series of decisions that Carver does not explicitly state. The passage ends with a turning point, a moment of discovery.

> When he returned to the kitchen the cat was scratching in her box. She looked at him steadily for a minute before she turned back to the litter. He opened all the cupboards and examined the canned goods, the cereals, the packaged foods, the cocktail and wine glasses, the china, the pots and pans. He opened the refrigerator. He sniffed some celery, took two bites of cheddar cheese, and chewed on an apple as he walked into the bedroom. The bed seemed enormous, with a fluffy white bedspread draped to the floor. He pulled out a nightstand drawer, found a half-empty package of cigarettes and stuffed them into his pocket. Then he stepped to the closet and was opening it when the knock sounded at the front door.

There is hardly grand larceny being committed here, but the actions build toward tension through two distinct techniques. The first is that they do actually "build": At first Bill only "examines." The celery he only sniffs, whereas he takes two bites of the cheese, then a whole apple, then half a pack of cigarettes. He moves from the kitchen to the bedroom, which is a clearer invasion of privacy, and from cupboard to refrigerator to nightstand to closet, each a more intimate intrusion than the last.

The second technique is that the narrative subtly hints at Bill's own sense of stealth. It would be easy to imagine a vandal who performed the same actions with complete indifference. But Bill thinks the cat looks "steadily" at him, which is hardly of any importance except that he feels it to be. His awareness of the enormous white bed hints at sexual guilt. When the knock at the front door sounds, we start, as he must, in a clear sense of getting caught.

Thus it turns out that the internal or mental moment of change is where the action lies. Much movement in a story is mere event, and this is why descriptions of actions, like stage directions in a dull play, sometimes add little or nothing. When the wife picks up a cup of coffee, that is mere event. If she finds that the lipstick on the cup is not her shade, that is a dramatic event, a discovery; it makes a difference. She makes a decision to fling it at the woman wearing the Cherry Ice mouth. Flinging it is an action, but the dramatic change occurs with the second character's realization (discovery) that she has been hit—and so on.

Every story is a pattern of change (events connected, as Forster observed, primarily by cause and effect) in which small and large changes are made through decision and discovery.

☞ The Tambourine Lady ☜

JOHN EDGAR WIDEMAN

Now I lay me down to sleep. . . there will be new shoes in the morning. New shoes and an old dress white as new. Starched white and stiff with petticoats whispering like angel wings and hair perfect as heat and grease can press it. There will be hands to shake as she rises from the curb onto the one broad step that took you off Homewood Avenue, which was nowhere, to the red doors of the church that were wide enough to let the whole world in but narrow too, narrower than your narrow hips, child, eye of the needle straight and narrow, don't make no mistake. Hands to help her across the threshold, through the tall red doors, from hard pavement that burned in summer, froze in winter, to the deep cushion of God's crimson carpet. She's unsteady as she passes to His world. Like that first step from moving stairs downtown in Kaufmann's Department Store when you always think you're falling pitched down and about to be cracked to pieces on the shiny checkerboard floor rushing up to mire your feet. At the church door her mother's hand, the gloved hand of Miss Payton to help her through. Miss Payton all in white, white veil, white gloves, white box tied over her hair with a silky white bandage. Breath might catch in her throat, her heart stutter but she wouldn't fall. She'd catch hold to old Miss Payton's hand, soft and white as a baby rabbit. Miss Payton smelling like Johnson's baby powder, who'd say, Bless you, sweet darling daughter, so the step up did not trip you, the wide doors slam in your face.

New shoes pinched your feet. Too big, too small, too much money, too ugly for anybody to be caught dead in. The white ladies who sold them would stick any old thing on your feet and smile at your mama and say, Just right. But sometimes when her feet in new shoes she'd forget how they felt, and she'd float. Couldn't take her eyes off them, stepping where she stepped, she follows them everywhere they go, click-clack cleats on the bottoms to save the heels and soles. They are new and shiny and for a while she's brand-new and shiny in them. Now she's nobody, nowhere, kneeled down beside her bed, remembering into the silence of God's ear a little girl in new shoes that didn't belong to her, that wouldn't fit. Her toes are drawn up curly, black against pink underskin. She dreams white anklets with a lacy band around the top. Dreams meat on her bones so socks don't slip down to her shoe tops.

If you polished old shoes, you could see your face inside. New ones come with your face in them. In the morning she'd take them out the box polish them anyway and then wash and dry her face and clean her hands and tug the purple Buds of Promise sash straight. Make sure of everyting in the mirror. On the threshold of the African Methodist Episcopal Zion Church there will be a mirror in the gray sky, a mirror in the brick walls, a mirror in her mother's eyes and in the hand of Miss Payton reaching for hers, patting her ashy skin, promising she will not fall.

She closes her eyes and hears tambourines. Crashing like a pocketful of silver in her daddy's pants when he stuck in his hand and rummaged round, teasing out a piece of change for her. Like somebody saying dish dish dish dish and every dish piled high with something good to eat.

Dish. Dish.

And if I die. . . before I wake. You walk funny because more crack then sidewalk some places on the way home from school. You sneak out into Hamilton Avenue to get past the real bad busted-up part where sidewalk's in little pieces like a broken jar.

You looked both ways up and down Hamilton Avenue but you know you might die. *A thousand times, I've told you a thousand times to stay out of Hamilton Avenue, girl.* But if the sidewalk looked like a witch's face you'd rather get runned over than step on a crack and break your mama's back. So you looked both ways up and down the street like Mama always said. You looked and listened and hoped you wouldn't get hit like little fat Angela everybody called Jelly who was playing in Cassina Way and the car mashed her up against the fence where you can still see the spot to this day.

She feels mashed like Jelly when Tommy Bonds pushes her down. He laughs and calls her crybaby. Says, You ain't hurt and runs away. But she ain't no crybaby over no little blood snot on her knee. She cries cause he hurt her mama. Pushed her into the spider web cracks cause he knew what she was playing. She'd told him her secert because she thought they were friends. But he never really was. He hates her and pushes her right dead down in a whole mess of snakes. She cries cause she's trapped, can't get out without stepping on more. Every crack a bone in her mama's back. He hates her. He follows her after school and calls her nasty stuck-up bitch till she stops, hands on hips, and hollers, Boy, I ain't studying you. You ain't nothing, Tommy Bonds, and wiggles her butt at him, then she is running, tearing down the sidewalk, scared and happy to have him after her again no matter what he wants to do. She would forgive him. Forgive his bad words, forgive his lies, forgive him for telling her secrets to everybody. She is forgiving, forgetting everything as he flies down Hamilton after her. She knows he can't catch her if she doesn't want to be caught. Says to herself, See what he wants now. Stops, hands on hips, at the edge of the worst busted-up place. *Girl, don't you dare set foot in that traffic on Hamilton Avenue.* And all he wants is to shove her down. Kill her mama.

She'd told Tommy Bonds her secret. He'd sneaked out into the street with her. Played her game and the cars whipping past on Hamilton Avenue had never been louder, closer, their wind up under her clothes as they ran the twenty steps past Wicked Witch Face City. And never had she cared less about getting mashed because who ever heard of a car killing two at a time.

Tommy, Tommy, Tommy *Bonds*. If she didn't duck just in time the rope would cut off her neck. If she didn't bounce high enough there go her cut-off feet hopping down the street all by they ownselves. Say it, girl. Say it. *Bonds* was when the rope popped the ground. *Tommy* three fast times while the loop turned lazy in the air.

Shake it to the east, Shake it to the west. Now tell the one you love the best. Say it loud and proud, girl. We ain't turning for nothing.

Tommy-Tommy-Tommy *Bonds*.

She is not crying because it hurts. A little snotty-looking blood. Scab on her knee next day. That's all. That's not why I'm crying, Mister Smarty-pants. Mister Know-it-all. But she can't say his name, can't say what she's thinking because the tears in her nose and ears and mouth might come crashing down and she'd be a puddle. Nasty brown puddle in the middle of the street.

Pray the Lord my soul to take.

The lady who beat the tambourine and sang in church was a Russell. Tomorrow was church so she'd see the Russells, the Strothers, Bells, Frenches, Pattersons, Whites, Bonds. Tomorrow was church so this was Saturday night and her mama ironing white things in the kitchen and her daddy away so long he mize well be dead and the new patent-leather shoes in their box beneath her side of the bed be worn out before he sees them. She thinks about how long it takes to get to the end of your prayers, how the world might be over and gone while you still saying the words to yourself. Words her mama taught her, words her mama said her mother had taught her so somebody would always be saying them world without end amen. So God would not forget His children. Saying the words this Saturday night, saying them tomorrow morning so He would not forget. Tommy Tommy Tommy Bonds. Words like doors. You open one wide and peek inside and everybody in there, strolling up and down the red aisles, singing, shaking hands. People she wanted to see and people she didn't know and the ones she'd been seeing all her life. People she hates. *God bless. . .* Words like the rope right on time slapping the pavement, snapping her heart. Her feet in new shoes she knows better than to be wearing outside playing in the street girl and they break and she falls and falls and if she had one wish it would be let me hear the lady sing her tambourine song tomorrow morning in church.

Suggestions for Discussion

1. List the details that lend credibility to the child heroine of "The Tambourine Lady." How much information is given through these details?

2. How would you describe her "purpose"?

3. This is a very young person to be so complex! Identify elements of her complexity. Does she exhibit consistent inconsistencies?

4. How does action contribute to character in this story, and how does the use of active verbs contribute to action?

5. There is no authorial interpretation in this story. Or is there?

 **Yours**

MARY ROBISON

Allison struggled away from her white Renault, limping with the weight of the last of the pumpkins. She found Clark in the twilight on the twig-and leaf-littered porch, behind the house. He wore a tan wool shawl. He was moving up and back in a cushioned glider, pushed by the ball of his slippered foot.

Allison lowered a big pumpkin and let it rest on the porch floor.

Clark was much older than she—seventy-eight to Allison's thirty-five. They had been married for four months. They were both quite tall, with long hands, and their faces looked something alike. Allison wore a natural-hair wig. It was a thick blond hood around her face. She was dressed in bright-dyed denims today. She wore durable clothes, usually, for she volunteered afternoons at a children's daycare center.

She put one of the smaller pumpkins on Clark's long lap. "Now, nothing surreal," she told him. "Carve just a *regular* face. These are for kids."

In the foyer, on the Hepplewhite desk, Allison found the maid's chore list, with its cross-offs, which included Clark's supper. Allison went quickly through the day's mail: a garish coupon packet, a flyer advertising white wines at Jamestown Liquors, November's pay-TV program guide, and—the worst thing, the funniest—an already opened, extremely unkind letter from Clark's married daughter, up North. "You're an old fool," Allison read, and "You're being cruelly deceived." There was a gift check for twenty-five dollars, made out to Clark, enclosed—his birthday had just passed—but it was uncashable. It was signed "Jesus H. Christ."

Late, late into this night, Allison and Clark gutted and carved the pumpkins together, at an old table set out on the back porch. They worked over newspaper after soggy newspaper, using paring knives and spoons and a Swiss Army knife Clark liked for the exact shaping of teeth and eyes and nostrils. Clark had been a doctor—an internist—but he was also a Sunday watercolor painter. His four pumpkins were expressive and artful. Their carved features were suited to the sizes and shapes of the pumpkins. Two looked ferocious and jagged. One registered surprise. The last was serene and beaming.

Allison's four faces were less deftly drawn, with slits and areas of distortion. She had cut triangles for noses and eyes. The mouths she had made were all just wedges—two turned up and two turned down.

By 1 A.M., they were finished. Clark, who had bent his long torso forward to work, moved over to the glider again and looked out sleepily at nothing. All the neighbors' lights were out across the ravine. For the season and time, the Virginia night was warm. Most of the leaves had fallen and blown away already, and the trees stood unbothered. The moon was round, above them.

Allison cleaned up the mess.

"Your jack-'o-lanterns are much much better than mine," Clark said to her.

"Like hell," Allison said.

"Look at me," Clark said, and Allison did. She was holding a squishy bundle of newspapers. The papers reeked sweetly with the smell of pumpkin innards. "Yours are *far* better," he said.

"You're wrong. You'll see when they're lit," Allison said.

She went inside, came back with yellow vigil candles. It took her a while to get each candle settled into a pool of its own melted wax inside the jack-o'-lanterns, which were lined up in a row on the porch railing. Allison went along and relit each candle and fixed the pumpkin lids over the little flames. "See?" she said. They sat together a moment and looked at the orange faces.

"We're exhausted. It's good-night time," Allison said. "Don't blow out the candles. I'll put in new ones tomorrow."

In her bedroom, a few weeks earlier in her life than had been predicted, she began to die. "Don't look at me if my wig comes off," she told Clark. "Please." Her pulse cords were fluttering under his fingers. She raised her knees and kicked away the comforter. She said something to Clark about the garage being locked.

At the telephone, Clark had a clear view out back and down to the porch. He wanted to get drunk with his wife once more. He wanted to tell her, from the greater perspective he had, that to own only a little talent, like his, was an awful, plaguing thing; that being only a little special meant you expected too much, most of the time, and liked yourself too little. He wanted to assure her that she had missed nothing.

Clark was speaking into the phone now. He watched the jack-o'-lanterns. The jack-o'-lanterns watched him.

≈≈≈≈≈≈≈≈≈≈≈

Suggestions for Discussion

1. The author is very modest about interpreting characters' actions. Yet some information is "told" us by the indirect method rather than coming to us directly. Identify such information.

2. What details of appearance operate as immediate clues to character and to the characters' situation? What actions?

3. How do the pumpkin faces reveal character?

4. This is a very short story. Are the characters made complex? If so, how? How do the actions of the characters as they unfold reveal *unexpected* traits of character?

5. The most violent action in the story involves an offstage character—the daughter who sends the "extremely unkind" letter and the uncashable check. What does this action, and the way it is received, reveal about the daughter? About the relationship between Allison and Clark? The plot?

6. How would you describe the characters' purpose(s)? How are these revealed? What judgment is invited?

The Point

CHARLES D'AMBROSIO

I had been lying awake after my nightmare, a nightmare in which Father and I bought helium balloons at a circus. I tied mine around my finger and Father tied his around a stringbean and lost it. After that, I lay in the dark, tossing and turning, sleepless from all the sand in my sheets and all the uproar out in the living room. Then the door opened, and for a moment the blade of bright light blinded me. The party was still going full blast, and now with the door ajar and my eyes adjusting I glimpsed the silver smoke swirling in the light and all the people suspended in it, hovering around as if they were angels in heaven—some kind of heaven where the host serves highballs and the men smoke cigars and the women all smell like rotting fruit. Everything was hysterical out there—the men laughing, the ice clinking, the women shrieking. A woman crossed over and sat on the edge of my bed, bending over me. It was Mother. She was backlit, a vague, looming silhouette, but I could smell lily of the valley and something else—lemon rind from the bitter twist she always chewed when she reached the watery bottom of her vodka-and-tonic. When Father was alive, she rarely drank, but after he shot himself you could say she really let herself go.

"Dearest?" she said.

"Hi, Mom," I said.

"Your old mother's bombed, dearest—flat-out bombed."

"That's O.K.," I said. She liked to confess these things to me, although it was always obvious how tanked she was, and I never cared. I considered myself a pro at this business. "It's a party," I said, casually. "Live it up."

"Oh, God," she laughed. "I don't know how I got this way."

"What do you want, Mom?"

"Yes, dear," she said. "There was something I wanted."

She looked out the window—at the sail-white moon beyond the black branches of the apple tree—and then she looked into my eyes. "What was it I wanted?" Her eyes were moist, and mapped with red veins. "I came here for a reason," she said, "but I've forgotten it now."

"Maybe if you go back you'll remember," I suggested.

Just then, Mrs. Gurney leaned through the doorway. "Well?" she said, slumping down on the floor. Mrs. Gurney had bright-silver hair and a dark tan—the sort of tan that women around here get when their marriages start busting up. I could see the gaudy gold chains looped around Mrs. Gurney's dark-brown neck winking in the half-light before they plunged from sight into the darker gulf between her breasts.

"That's it," Mother said. "Mrs. Gurney. She's worse off than me. She's really blitzo. Blotto? Blitzed?"

"Hand me my jams," I said.

I slipped my swim trunks on underneath the covers.

For years I'd been escorting these old inebriates over the sandy playfield and along the winding boardwalks and up the salt-whitened steps of their homes, brewing coffee, fixing a little toast or heating leftovers, searching the medicine cabinets for aspirin and Vitamin B, setting a glass of water on the nightstand, or the coffee table if they'd collapsed on the couch—and even, once, tucking some old fart snugly into bed between purple silk sheets. I'd guide these drunks home and hear stories about the alma matter, Theta Xi, Boeing stock splits, Cadillacs, divorce, Nembutal, infidelity, and often the people I helped home gave me three or four bucks for listening to all their sad business. I suppose it was better than a paper route. Father, who'd been a medic in Vietnam, made it my job when I was ten, and at thirteen I considered myself a hard-core veteran, treating every trip like a mission.

"O.K., Mrs. Gurney," I said. "Upsy-daisy."

She held her hand out, and I grabbed it, leaned back, and hoisted her to her feet. She stood there a minute, listing this way, that way, like a sailor who hadn't been to port in a while.

Mother kissed her wetly on the lips and then said to me, "Hurry home."

"I'm toasted," Mrs. Gurney explained. "Just toasted."

"Let's go out the back way," I said. It would only take longer if we had to navigate our way through the party, offering excuses and making those ridiculous promises adults always make to one another when the party's over. "Hey, we'll do it again," they assure each other, as if that needed to be said. And I'd noticed how, with the summer ending and Labor Day approaching, all the adults would acquire a sort of desperate, clinging manner, as if this were all going to end forever, and the good times would never be seen again. Of course I now realize that the end was just an excuse to party like maniacs. The softball tournament, the salmon derby, the cocktails, the clambakes, the barbecues, would all happen again. They always had and they always would.

Anyway, out the back door and down the steps.

Once I'd made a big mistake with a retired account executive, a friend of Father's. Fred was already falling-down drunk, so it didn't help at all that he had two more drinks on the way out the door, apologizing for his condition, which no one noticed, and boisterously offering bad stock tips. I finally got Fred going and dragged him partway home in a wagon, dumping his fat ass in front of his house—close enough, I figured—wedged in against some driftwood so the tide wouldn't wash him out to sea. He didn't get taken out to sea, but the sea did come to him, as the tide rose, and when he woke he was lassoed in green kelp. Fortunately, he'd forgotten the whole thing—how he'd got where he was, where he'd been before that—but it scared me that a more or less right-hearted attempt on my part might end in such an ugly mess.

By now, though, I'd worked this job so long I knew all the tricks.

The moon was full and immaculately white in a blue-black sky.

The wind funneled down Saratoga Passage, blowing hard, blowing south, and Mrs. Gurney and I were struggling against it, tacking back and forth across the playfield. Mrs. Gurney strangled her arm around my neck and we wobbled along. Bits of sand shot in our eyes and blinded us.

"Keep your head down, Mrs. Gurney! I'll guide you!"

She plopped herself down in the sand, nesting there as if she were going to lay an egg. She unbuckled her sandals and tossed them behind her. I ran back and fetched them from the sand. Her skirt fluttered in the wind and flew up in her face. Her silver hair, which was usually shellacked with spray and coiffed to resemble a crash helmet, cracked and blew apart, splintering like a clutch of straw.

"Why'd I drink so damned much?" she screamed. "I'm toasted—really, Kurt, I'm totally toasted. I shouldn't have drunk so damned much."

"Well, you did, Mrs. Gurney," I said, bending toward her. "That's not the problem now. The problem now is how to get you home."

"Why, God damn it!"

"Trust me, Mrs. Gurney. Home is where you want to be."

One tip about these drunks: My opinion is that it pays in the long run to stick as close as possible to the task at hand. We're just going home, you assure them, and tomorrow it will all be different. I've found if you stray too far from the simple goal of getting home and going to sleep, you let yourself in for a lot of unnecessary hell. You start hearing about their whole miserable existence, and suddenly it's the most important thing in the world to fix it all up, right then. Certain things in life can't be repaired, as in Father's situation, and that's always sad, but I believe there's nothing in life that can be remedied under the influence of half a dozen planter's punches.

Now, not everyone on the Point was a crazed rumhound, but the ones that weren't, the people who accurately assessed their capacities and balanced their intake accordingly, the people who never got lost, who never passed out in flower beds or, adrift in the maze of narrow boardwalks, gave up the search for home altogether and walked into any old house that was nearby—they, the people who never did these things and knew what they were about, never needed my help. They also weren't too friendly with my mother and didn't participate in her weekly bashes. The Point was kind of divided that way—between the upright, seaworthy residents and the easily overturned friends of my mother's.

Mrs. Gurney lived about a half-mile up the beach in a bungalow with a lot of Gothic additions. The scuttlebutt on Mrs. Gurney was that while she wasn't divorced, her husband didn't love her. This kind of knowledge was part of my job, something I didn't relish but accepted as an occupational hazard. I knew all the gossip, the rumors, the rising and falling fortunes of my mother's friends. After a summer, I'd have the dirt on everyone, whether I wanted it or not. But I had developed a priestly sense of my position, and whatever anyone told me in a plastered, blathering confessional fit was as safe and privileged as if it had been spoken in a private audience with the Pope. Still, I hoped Mrs. Gurney would stick to the immediate goal and not start talking about how sad and lonely she was, or how cruel her husband was, or what was going to become of us all, etc.

The wind rattled the swings back and forth, chains creaking, and whipped the ragged flag, which flew at half-mast. Earlier that summer, Mr. Crutchfield, the insurance lawyer, had fallen overboard and drowned while hauling in his crab trap. He always smeared his bait box with Mentholatum, which is illegal, and the crabs went crazy for it, and I imagined that in his greed, catching over the limit, he couldn't haul the trap up but wouldn't let go, either, and the weight pulled him into the sea, and he had a heart attack and drowned. The current floated him all the way to Everett before he was found, white and bloated as soggy bread.

Mrs. Gurney was squatting on the ground, lifting fistfuls of sand and letting them course through her fingers, the grains falling away as through an hourglass.

"Mrs. Gurney? We're not making much progress."

She rose to her feet, gripping my pant leg, my shirt, my sleeve, then my neck. We started walking again. The sand was deep and loose, and with every step we sank down through the soft layers until a solid purchase was gained in the hard-packed sand below, and we could push off in baby steps. The night was sharp, and alive with shadows—everything, even the tiny tufted weeds that sprouted through the sand, had a shadow—and this deepened the world, made it seem thicker, with layers, and more layers, and then a darkness into which I couldn't see.

"You know," Mrs. Gurney said, "the thing about these parties is, the thing about drinking is—you know, getting so damnably blasted is . . ." She stopped, and tried to mash her wild hair back down into place, and, no longer holding on to anything other than her head, fell back on her ass into the sand.

I waited for her to finish her sentence, then gave up, knowing it was gone forever. Her lipstick, I noticed, was smeared clownishly around her mouth, fixing her lips into a frown, or maybe a smirk. She smelled different from my mother—like pepper, I thought, and bananas. She was taller than me, and a little plump, with a nose shaped exactly like her head, like a miniature replica of it right in the middle of her face.

We finally got off the playfield and onto the boardwalk that fronted the seawall. A wooden wagon leaned over in the sand. I tipped it upright.

"Here you go, Mrs. Gurney," I said, pointing to the wagon. "Hop aboard."

"I'm O.K.," she protested. "I'm fine. Fine and dandy."

"You're not fine, Mrs. Gurney."

The caretaker built these wagons out of old hatches from P.T. boats. They were heavy, monstrous, and made to last. Once you got them rolling, they cruised.

Mrs. Gurney got in, not without a good deal of operatics, and when I finally got her to shut up and sit down I started pulling. I'd never taken her home before, but on a scale of one to ten, ten being the most obstreperous, I was rating her about a six at this point.

She stretched out like Cleopatra floating down the Nile in her barge. "Stop the world," she sang, "I want to get off."

I vaguely recalled that as a song from my parents' generation. It reminded me of my father, who shot himself in the head one morning—did I already say this? He was sitting in the grass parking lot above the Point. Officially, his death was ruled an accident, a "death by misadventure," and everyone believed that he had in fact been cleaning his gun, but Mother told me otherwise one night. Mother had a batch of lame excuses she tried on me, but it only made me sad to see her groping for an answer and falling way short. I wished she'd come up with something, just for herself. Father used to say that everyone up here was *dinky dow*, which is Vietnamese patois for "crazy." At times, after Father died, I thought Mother was going a little *dinky dow* herself.

I leaned forward, my head bent against the wind. Off to starboard, the sea was black, with a line of moonlit white waves continually crashing on the shore. Far off, I could see the dark headlands of Hat Island, the island itself rising from the water like a breaching whale, and then, beyond, the soft, blue, irresolute lights of Everett, on the distant mainland.

I stopped for a breather, and Mrs. Gurney was gone. She was sitting on the boardwalk, a few houses back.

"Look at all these houses," Mrs. Gurney said, swinging her arms around.

"Let's go, Mrs. Gurney."

"Another fucking great summer at the Point."

The wind seemed to be refreshing Mrs. Gurney, but that was a hard one to call. Often drunks seemed on the verge of sobering up, and then, just as soon as they got themselves nicely balanced, they plunged off the other side, into depression.

"Poor Crutchfield," Mrs. Gurney said. We stood in front of Mr. Crutchfield's house. An upstairs light—in the bedroom, I knew—was on, although the lower stories were dark and empty. "And Lucy—God, such grief. They loved each other, Kurt." Mrs. Gurney frowned. "They loved each other. And now?"

Actually, the Crutchfields hadn't loved each other—information I alone was privy to. Lucy's grief, I was sure, had to do with the fact that her husband died in a state of absolute misery, and now she would never be able to change things. In Lucy's mind, he would be forever screwing around, and she would be forever waiting for him to cut it out and come home. After he died, she spread the myth of their reconciliation, and everyone believed it, but I knew it to be a lie. Mr. Crutchfield's sense of failure over the marriage was enormous. He blamed himself, as perhaps he should have. But I remember, one night earlier in the summer, telling him it was O.K., that if he was unhappy with Lucy, it was fine to fuck around. He said, You think so? I said, Sure, go for it.

Of course, you might ask, what did I know? At thirteen, I'd never even smooched with a girl, but I had nothing to lose by encouraging him. He was drunk, he was miserable, and I had a job, and that job was to get him home and try to prevent him from dwelling too much on himself.

It was that night, the night I took Mr. Crutchfield home, as I walked back to our house, that I developed the theory of the black hole, and it helped me immeasurably in conducting this business of steering drunks around the Point. The idea was this— that at a certain age, a black hole emerged in the middle of your life, and everything got sucked into it, and you knew, forever afterward, that it was there, this dense negative space, and yet you went on, you struggled, you made your money, you had some babies, you got wasted, and you pretended it wasn't there and never looked directly at it, if you could manage the trick. I imagined that this black hole existed somewhere just behind you and also somewhere just in front of you, so that you were always leaving it behind and entering it at the same time. I hadn't worked out the spatial thing too carefully, but that's what I imagined. Sometimes the hole was only a pinprick in the mind, often it was vast, frequently it fluctuated, beating like a heart, but it was always there, and when you got drunk, thinking to escape, you only noticed it more. Anyway, when I discovered this, much like an astronomer gazing out at the universe, I thought I had the key—and it became a policy with me never to let one of my drunks think too much and fall backward or forward into the black hole. We're going home, I would say to them—we're just going home.

I wondered how old Mrs. Gurney was, and guessed thirty-seven. I imagined her black hole was about the size of a sewer cap.

Mrs. Gurney sat down on the hull of an overturned life raft. She reached up under her skirt and pulled her nylons off, rolling them down her legs, tossing the little black doughnuts into the wind. I fetched them, too, and stuffed them into the straps of her sandals.

"Much better," she said.

"We're not far now, Mrs. Gurney. We'll have you home in no time."

She managed to stand up on her own. She floated past me, heading toward the sea. A tangle of ghostly gray driftwood—old tree stumps, logs loosed from booms, planks—barred the way, being too treacherous for her to climb in such a drunken state, I thought, but Mrs. Gurney just kept going, her hair exploding in the wind, her skirt billowing like a sail, her arms wavering like a trapeze artist's high up on the wire.

"Mrs. Gurney?" I called.

"I want—" she started, but the wind tore her words away. Then she sat down on a log, and when I got there, she was holding her head in her hands and vomiting between her legs. Vomit, and the spectacle of adults vomiting, was one of the unpleasant aspects of this job. I hated to see these people in such an abject position. Still, after three years, I knew in which closets the mops and sponges and cleansers were kept in quite a few houses on the Point.

I patted Mrs. Gurney's shoulder and said, "That's O.K., that's O.K., just go right ahead. You'll feel much better when it's all out."

She choked and spat, and a trail of silver hung from her lip down to the sand. "Oh, damn it all, Kurt. Just damn it all to hell." She raised her head. "Look at me, just look at me, will you?"

She looked a little wretched, but all right. I'd seen worse.

"Have a cigarette, Mrs. Gurney," I said. "Calm down."

I didn't smoke, myself—thinking it was a disgusting habit—but I'd observed from past experience that a cigarette must taste good to a person who has just thrown up. A cigarette or two seemed to calm people right down, giving them something simple to concentrate on.

Mrs. Gurney handed me her cigarettes. I shook one from the pack and stuck it in my mouth. I struck half a dozen matches before I got one going, cupping the flame against the wind in the style of old war movies. I puffed the smoke. I passed Mrs. Gurney the cigarette, and she dragged on it, abstracted, gazing off. I waited, and let her smoke in peace.

"I feel god-awful," Mrs. Gurney groaned.

"It'll go away, Mrs. Gurney. You're drunk. We just have to get you home."

"Look at my skirt," she said.

True, she'd messed it up a little, barfing on herself, but it was nothing a little soap and water couldn't fix. I told her that.

"How old am I, Kurt?" she retorted.

I pretended to think it over, then aimed low.

"Twenty-nine? Good God!" Mrs. Gurney stared out across the water, at the deep, black shadow of Hat Island, and I looked, too, and it was remarkable, the way that darkness carved itself out of the darkness all around. But I could marvel over this when I was off duty.

"I'm thirty-eight, Kurt," she screamed. "Thirty-eight, thirty-eight, thirty-eight!"

I was losing her. She was heading for ten on a scale of ten.

"On a dark night, bumping around," she said, "you can't tell the difference between thirty-eight and forty. Fifty! Sixty!" She pitched her cigarette in a high, looping arc that exploded against a log in a spray of gold sparks. "Where am I going, God damn it?"

"You're going home, Mrs. Gurney. Hang tough."

"I want to die."

A few boats rocked in the wind, and a seal moaned out on the diving raft, the cries carrying away from us, south, downwind. A red warning beacon flashed out on the sandbar. Mrs. Gurney clambered over the driftwood and weaved across the wet sand toward the sea. She stood by the shoreline, and for a moment I thought she might hurl herself into the breach, but she didn't. She stood on the shore's edge, the white waves swirling at her feet, and dropped her skirt around her ankles. She was wearing a silky white slip underneath, the sheen like a bike reflector in the moonlight. She waded out into the water and squatted down, scrubbing her skirt. Then she walked out of the water and stretched herself on the sand.

"Mrs. Gurney?"

"I've got the fucking spins."

Her eyes were closed. I suggested that she open them. "It makes a difference," I said. "And sit up, Mrs. Gurney. That makes a difference, too."

"You've had the spins?" Mrs. Gurney asked. "Don't tell me you sneak into your mother's liquor cabinet, Kurt Pittman. Don't tell me that. Please, just please spare me that. Jesus Christ, I couldn't take it. Really, I couldn't take it, Kurt. Just shut the fuck up about that, all right?"

I'd never taken a drink in my life. "I don't drink, Mrs. Gurney."

"I don't drink, Mrs. Gurney," she repeated. "You prig."

I wondered what time it was, and how long we'd been gone.

"Do you know how suddenly life can turn?" Mrs. Gurney asked. "How bad it can get?"

At first I didn't say anything. This kind of conversation didn't lead anywhere. Mrs. Gurney was drunk and belligerent. She was looking for an enemy. "We need to get you home, Mrs. Gurney," I said. "That's my only concern."

"Your only concern," Mrs. Gurney said, imitating me again. "Lucky you."

I stood there, slightly behind Mrs. Gurney. I was getting tired, but sitting down in the sand might indicate to her that where we were was O.K., and it wasn't. We needed to get beyond this stage, this tricky stage of groveling in the sand and feeling depressed, and go to sleep.

"We're not getting anywhere like this," I said.

"I've got cottonmouth," Mrs. Gurney said. She made fish movements with her mouth. She was shivering, too. She clasped her knees and tucked her head between her legs, trying to ball herself up like a potato bug.

"Kurt," Mrs. Gurney said, looking up at me, "do you think I'm beautiful?"

I switched the sandals I was holding to the other hand. First I'll tell you what I said, and then I'll tell you what I was thinking. I said yes, and I said it immediately. And why? Because I sensed that questions that didn't receive an immediate response fell away into silence and were never answered. They got sucked into the black hole. I'd observed this, and I knew the trick was to close the gap in Mrs. Gurney's mind, to bridge that spooky silence between the question and the answer. There she was, drunk, sick, shivering, loveless, sitting in the sand and asking me, a mere boy, if I thought she was beautiful. I said yes, because I knew it wouldn't hurt, or cost me anything but one measly breath, though that wasn't really my answer. The answer was in the immediacy, the swiftness of my response, stripped of all uncertainty and hesitation.

"Yes," I said.

Mrs. Gurney lay down again in the sand. She unbuttoned her blouse and unfastened her brassiere.

I scanned the dark, and fixed my eyes on a tug hauling a barge north through the Passage, up to the San Juans.

Mrs. Gurney sat up. She shrugged out of her blouse and slipped her bra off and threw them into the wind. Again I fetched her things from where they fell, and held the bundle at my side, waiting.

"That's better," Mrs. Gurney said, arching her back and stretching her hands in the air, waggling them as if she were some kind of dignitary in a parade. "The wind blowing, it's like a spirit washing over you."

"We should go, Mrs. Gurney."

"Sit, Kurt, sit," she said, patting the wet sand. The imprint of her hand remained there a few seconds, then flattened and vanished. The tide was coming in fast, and it would be high tonight, with the moon full.

I crouched down, a few feet away.

"So you think I'm beautiful?" Mrs. Gurney said. She stared ahead, not looking at me, letting the words drift in the wind.

"This really isn't a question of beauty or not beauty, Mrs. Gurney."

"No?"

"No," I said. "I know your husband doesn't love you, Mrs. Gurney. That's the problem here."

"Beauty," she sang.

"No. Like they say, beauty is in the eye of the beholder. You don't have a beholder anymore, Mrs. Gurney."

"The moon and the stars," she said, "the wind and the sea."

Wind, sea, stars, moon: we were in uncharted territory, and it was my fault. I'd let us stray from the goal, and now it was nowhere in sight. I had to steer this thing back on course, or we'd end up talking about God.

"Get dressed, Mrs. Gurney; it's cold. This isn't good. We're going home."

She clasped her knees, and rocked back and forth. She moaned, "It's so far."

"It's not far," I said. "We can see it from here."

"Someday I'm leaving all this to you," Mrs. Gurney said, waving her hands around in circles, pointing at just about everything in the world. "When I get it from my husband, after the divorce, I'm leaving it to you. That's a promise, Kurt. I mean that. It'll be in my will. You'll get a call. You'll get a call and you'll know I'm dead. But you'll be happy, you'll be very happy, because all of this will belong to you."

Her house was only a hundred yards away. A wind sock, full of the air that passed through it, whipped back and forth on a tall white pole. Her two kids had been staying in town most of that summer. I wasn't sure if they were up this weekend. She'd left the porch light on for herself.

"You'd like all this, right?" Mrs. Gurney asked.

"Now is not the time to discuss it," I said.

Mrs. Gurney lay back down in the sand. "The stars have tails," she said. "When they spin."

I looked up; they seemed fixed in place to me.

"The first time I fell in love I was fourteen. I fell in love when I was fifteen, I fell in love when I was sixteen, seventeen, eighteen. I just kept falling, over and over," Mrs. Gurney said. "This eventually led to marriage." She packed a lump of wet sand on her chest. "It's so stupid—you know where I met him?"

I assumed she was referring to Jack, to Mr. Gurney. "No," I said.

"On a golf course, can you believe it?"

"Do you golf, Mrs. Gurney?"

"No! Hell no."

"Does Jack?"

"No."

I couldn't help her—it's the stories that don't make sense that drunks like to repeat. From some people, I'd been hearing the same stories every summer for the last three years—the kind everyone thinks is special, never realizing how everyone tells pretty much the same one, never realizing how all those stories blend, one to the next, and bleed into each other.

"I'm thirsty," Mrs. Gurney said. "I'm so homesick."

"We're close now," I said.

"That's not what I mean," she said. "You don't know what I mean."

"Maybe not," I said. "Please put your shirt on, Mrs. Gurney."

"I'll kill myself," Mrs. Gurney said. "I'll go home and I'll kill myself."

"That won't get you anywhere."

"It'll show them."

"You'd just be dead, Mrs. Gurney. Then you'd be forgotten."

"Crutchfield isn't forgotten. Poor Crutchfield. The flag's at half-mast."

"This year," I said. "Next year it'll be back where it always is."

"My boys wouldn't forget."

That was certainly true, I thought, but I didn't want to get into it.

Mrs. Gurney sat up. She shook her head back and forth, wildly, and sand flew from it. Then she stood, wobbling. I held the shirt out to her, looking down. She wiggled her toes, burrowing them into the sand.

"Look at me," Mrs. Gurney said.

"I'd rather not, Mrs. Gurney," I said. "Tomorrow you'll be glad I didn't."

For a moment we didn't speak, and into that empty space rushed the wind, the waves, the moaning seal out on the diving raft. I looked up, into Mrs. Gurney's eyes, which were dark green and floating in tears. She stared back, but kind of vaguely, and I wondered what she saw.

I had the feeling that the first to flinch would lose.

She took the shirt from my hand.

I looked.

In this I had no experience, but I knew what I saw was not young flesh. Her breasts sagged away like sacks of wet sand, slumping off to either side. They were quite enormous, I thought, although I had nothing to compare them with. There were long whitish scars on them, as if a wild man or a bear had clawed her. The nipples were purple in the moonlight, and they puckered in the cold wind. The gold, squiggling loops of chain shone against the dark of her neck, and the V of her tan line made everything else seem astonishingly white. The tan skin of her chest looked like parchment, like the yellowed, crinkled page of some ancient text, maybe the Bible, or the Constitution, the original copy, or even the rough draft.

Mrs. Gurney slipped the shirt over her shoulders and let it flap there in the wind. It blew off and tumbled down the beach. She sighed. Then she stepped closer and leaned toward me. I could smell her—the pepper, the bananas.

"Mrs. Gurney," I said, "let's go home now." The tide was high enough for us to feel the first foamy white reaches of the waves wash around our feet. The receding waves dragged her shirt into the sea, and then the incoming waves flung it back. It hung there in the margin, agitated. We were looking into each other's eyes. Up so close, there was nothing familiar in hers; they were just glassy and dark and expressionless.

It was then, I was sure, that her hand brushed the front of my trunks. I don't remember too much of what I was thinking, if I was, and this, this not thinking too clearly, might have been my downfall. What is it out there that indicates the right way? I might have gone down all the way. I might have sunk right there. I knew all the words for it, and they were all short and brutal. Fuck, poke, screw. A voice told me I could get away with it. Who will know the difference, the voice asked. It said, Go for it. And I knew the voice, knew it was the same voice that told Mr. Crutchfield to go ahead, fuck around. We were alone—nothing out there but the moon and the sea. I looked at Mrs. Gurney, looked into her eyes, and saw two black lines pouring out of them and running in crazy patterns down her cheeks.

I felt I should be gallant, or tender, and kiss Mrs. Gurney. I felt I should say something, then I felt I should be quiet. It seemed as if the moment were poised, as if everything were fragile, and held together with silence.

We moved up the beach, away from the shore and the incoming tide, and the sand beneath the surface still held some of the day's warmth.

I took off my T-shirt. "Put this on," I said.

She tugged it on, inside out, and I gathered up her sandals and stockings and her bra. We kept silent. We worked our way over the sand, over the tangle of drift-wood, the wind heaving at us from the north.

We crossed the boardwalk, and I held Mrs. Gurney's elbow as we went up the steps of her house. Inside, I found the aspirin and poured a glass of apple cider, and brought these to her in bed, where she'd already curled up beneath a heavy Mexican blanket. She looked like she was sleeping underneath a rug. "I'm thirsty," she said, and drank down the aspirin with the juice. A lamp was on. Mrs. Gurney's silver hair splayed out against the pillow, poking like bike spokes, every which way. I knelt beside the bed, and she touched my hand and parted her lips to speak, but I squeezed her hand and her eyes closed. Soon she was asleep.

As I was going downstairs, her two boys, Mark and Timmy, came out of their bedroom and stared at me from the landing.

"Mommy home?" asked Timmy, who was three.

"Yeah," I said. "She's in bed, she's sleeping."

They stood there on the lighted landing, blinking and rubbing knuckles in their eyes, and I stood below them on the steps in the dark.

"Where's the sitter?" I asked.

"She fell asleep," Timmy said.

"You guys should be asleep, too."

"I can't sleep," Timmy said. "Tell a bedtime story."

"I don't know any bedtime stories," I said.

Back home, inside our house, the bright light and smoke stung my eyes. The living room was crowded, but I knew everybody—the Potters, the Shanks, the Capstands, etc. It was noisy and shrill, and someone had cranked up the Victrola, and one of my grandfather's old records was sending a sea of hissing static through the room. I could see on the mantel, through the curling smoke, the shrine Mother had made for Father: his Silver Star and Purple Heart, which he got in Lao Bao, up near Khe Sanh, near the DMZ when he was a medic. His diploma from medical school angled cockeyed off a cut nail. A foul ball he'd caught at a baseball game, his reading glasses, a pocketknife, a stethoscope, a framed Hippocratic oath with snakes wreathed around what looked like a barber pole. I saw Mother flit through the kitchen with a silver cocktail shaker, jerking it like a percussion instrument. She just kept pacing like a caged animal, rattling cracked ice in the shaker. I couldn't hear any distinct voices above the party noise. I stood there awhile. No one seemed to notice me until Fred, three sheets to the wind, as they say, hoisted his empty glass in the air and said, "Hey, Captain!"

I went into the kitchen. Mother set down the shaker and looked at me. I gave her a hug. "I'm back," I said.

Then I crossed into my room and stripped the sheets from my bed. I hung them out the window and shook the sand away. I tossed the sheets back on the bed and stretched out, but I couldn't get to sleep. I got up and pulled one of Father's old letters out from under my mattress. I went out the back door. It was one of those nights on the Point when the blowing wind, the waves breaking in crushed white lines against the shore, the grinding sand, the moon-washed silhouettes of the huddled houses, the slapping of buoys offshore—when all of this seems to have been going on for a long, long time, and you feel eternity looking down on you. I sat on the swing. The letter was torn at the creases, and I opened it carefully, tilting it into the moonlight. It was dated 1966, and written to Mother. The print was smudged and hard to see.

First, the old news: thank you for the necktie. I'm not sure when I'll get a chance to wear it, but thanks. Now for my news. I've been wounded, but don't worry. I'm O.K.

For several days a company had been deployed on the perimeter of this village—the rumor was that somehow the fields had been planted with VC mines. The men work with tanks—picture tanks moving back and forth over a field like huge lawnmowers. They clear the way by exploding the mines. Generally VC mines are antipersonnel, and the idea is that the tanks are supposed to set off the mines and absorb the explosions. Tanks can easily sustain the blows, and the men inside are safe. A textbook operation. Simple. Yesterday they set off twelve mines. Who knows how they got there?

Clearing the perimeter took several days. Last night they thought they were done. But as the men were jumping off the tanks, one of them landed right on a mine. I was the first medic to reach him. His feet and legs were blown off, blown away up to his groin. I've never seen anything so terrible, but here's what I remember most clearly: a piece of shrapnel had penetrated his can of shaving cream, and it was shooting a stream of white foam about five feet in the air. Blood spilling everywhere, and then this fountain of white arcing out of his back. The pressure inside the can kept hissing. The kid was maybe nineteen. "Doc, I'm a mess," he said. I called in a medevac. I started packing dressings, then saw his eyes lock up, and tried to revive him with heart massage. The kid died before the shaving cream was done spraying.

Everything became weirdly quiet, considering the havoc, and then suddenly the LZ got hot and we took fire—fifteen minutes of artillery and incoming mortar fire, then quiet again. Nothing, absolutely nothing. I took a piece of shrapnel in my back, but don't worry. I'm all right, though I won't have occasion to wear that tie soon. I didn't even know I was wounded until I felt the blood, and even then I thought it was someone else's.

Strange, during that fifteen minutes of action I felt no fear. But there's usually not much contact with the enemy. Often you don't see a single VC the whole time. Days pass without any contact. They're out there, you know, yet you never see them. Just mines, booby traps. I'm only a medic, and my contact with the enemy is rarely direct—what I see are the wounded men and the dead, the bodies. I see the destruction, and I have begun to both fear and hate the Vietnamese—even here in South Vietnam, I can't tell whose side they're on. Every day I visit a nearby village and help a local doctor vaccinate children. The morning after the attack I felt the people in the village were laughing at me because they knew an American had died. Yesterday I returned to the same village. Everything quiet, business as usual, but I stood there, surrounded by hooches, thinking of that dead kid, and for a moment I felt the urge to even the score somehow.

What am I saying, sweetie? I'm a medic, trained to save lives. Every day I'm closer to death than most people ever get, except in their final second on earth. It's a world of hurt—that's the phrase we use—and things happen over here, things you just can't keep to yourself. I've seen what happens to men who try. They're consumed by what they've seen and done, they grow obsessive, and slowly they lose sight of the job they're supposed to be doing. I have no hard proof of this, but I think in this condition men open themselves up to attack. You've got to talk things out, get everything very clear in your mind. Lucky for me I've got a buddy over here who's been under fire too, and can understand what I'm feeling. That helps.

I'm sorry to write like this, but in your letter you said you wanted to know everything. It's not in my power to say what this war means to you or anyone back home, but I can describe what happens, and if you want, I'll continue doing that. For me, at least, it's a comfort to know someone's out there, far away, who can't really understand, and I hope is never able to. I'll write again soon.

All love,
Henry

I'd snagged this letter from a box Mother kept in her room, under the bed. There were other kinds of letters in the box, letters about love and family and work, but I didn't think Mother would miss this one, which was just about war. Father never talked much about his tours in Vietnam, but he would if I asked. Out of respect, I learned not to ask too much, but I knew about Zippo raids, trip flares, bouncing bettys, hand frags, satchel charges, and such, and when he was angry, or sad, Father often peppered his speech with slang he'd picked up, like *lili*, which means "little," and *didi mow*, which means "go quickly," and *xin loi*, meaning "sorry about that."

I tucked the letter away. I got the swing going real good, and I rose up, then fell, rose and fell, seeing, then not seeing. When the swing was going high enough I let go and sailed through the open air, landing in an explosion of soft sand. I wiped the grains out of my eyes. My eyes watered, and everything was unclear. Things toppled and blew in the wind. A striped beach umbrella rolled across the playfield, twirling like a pinwheel. A sheet from someone's clothesline flapped loose and sailed away. I thought of my nightmare, of Father's balloon tied to a stringbean. I looked up at the sky, and it was black, with some light. There were stars, millions of them like tiny holes in something, and the moon, like a bigger hole in the same thing. White holes. I thought of Mrs. Gurney and her blank eyes and the black pouring out of them. Was it the wind, a sudden gust kicking up and brushing my trunks? It happened so quickly. Had she tried to touch me? Had she? I stretched out in the sand. The wind gave me goose bumps. Shivering, I listened. From inside the house, I heard the men laughing, the ice clinking, the women shrieking. Everything in there was still hysterical. I'd never get to sleep. I decided to stay awake. They would all be going home, but until then I'd wait outside.

I lay there, very quietly. I brushed some sand off me. I waited.

It was me who found Father, that morning. I'd gone up to get some creosote out of the trunk of his car. It was a cold, gray, misty morning, the usual kind we have, and in the grass field above the parking lot there was a family of deer, chewing away, looking around, all innocent. And there he was, sitting in the car. I opened the passenger door. At first my eyes kind of separated from my brain, and I saw everything real slow, like you might see a movie, or something far away that wasn't happening to you. Some of his face was gone. One of his eyes was staring out. He was still breathing, but his lungs worked like he'd swallowed a yard of chunk gravel or sand. He was twitching. I touched his hand and the fingers curled around mine, gripping, but it was just nerves, an old reaction or something, because he was brain-dead already. My imagination jumped right out of its box when he grabbed me. I knew right away I was being grabbed by a dead man. I got away. I ran away. In our house I tried to speak, but there were no words. I started pounding the walls and kicking over the furniture and breaking stuff. I couldn't see, I heard falling. I ran around the house holding and ripping at my head. Eventually Mother caught me. I just pointed up to the car. You understand, I miss Father, miss having him around to tell me what's right and what's wrong, or to talk about *boom-boom*, which is sex, or just to go salmon fishing out by Hat Island and not worry about things, either way, but I also have to say, never again do I want to see anything like what I saw that morning. I never, as long as I live, want to find another dead person. He wasn't even a person then, just a blown-up thing, just crushed-up garbage. Part of his head, was blasted away, and there was blood and hair and bone splattered on the windshield. It looked like he'd just driven the car through something awful, like he needed to use the windshield wipers, needed to switch the blades on high and clear the way, except that the wipers wouldn't do him any good, because the mess was all on the inside.

~~~~~~~~~~

Suggestions for Discussion

1. Examine the details of appearance that introduce Kurt's mother on page 118 and Mrs. Gurney on pages 118-119. How are the women differentiated and how are they made to belong to a type? To what extent does typing invite judgment?

2. How is the character of Mrs. Gurney made more complex through details of appearance and action as the story progresses?

3. Kurt has a fairly blasé attitude toward the parties of the Point, and some cynical views of the inhabitants, yet he doggedly carries on with his escort service. How do you account for this contradiction? How does it reveal "moral purpose"?

4. What moments of decision and discovery change the course of the action?

5. The father's letter describes characters and actions far from the scene of the story in both place and time. How do they nevertheless reveal information about Kurt?

6. The description of Kurt's dead father, and Kurt's reaction, reveal still further information crucial to our understanding of his character. Why does the author keep this scene for the end of the story?

Retrospect

1. Show how elements of type are revealed in four of the characters in "Where Are You Going, Where Have You Been?"

2. Contrast the description of Jeremiah Donovan in the second paragraph of "Guests of the Nation", with that of Belcher on p. 47. What methods of characterization are used in each? Which dominate? What essentials of character are revealed in which concrete details? How much do you know about the narrator? How?

3. What is the function of the "flat" characters in "The Things They Carried"?

Writing Assignments

1. Each day for two weeks, cluster and write a paragraph in your journal about a character drawn from memory, observation, or invention. Each day, also go back and add to a former characterization. Focus on details of appearance and action.

2. Below is a list of familiar types, each of them comic or unsympathetic to the degree that they have become clichés. Write a short character sketch

of one or two of them, but individualizing the character through particular details that will make us sympathize and/or identify with him or her.

- an absent-minded professor
- a lazy laborer
- an aging film star
- a domineering wife
- her timid husband
- a tyrannical boss
- a staggering drunk

3. In the sociological science of garbology, human habits are assessed by studying what people throw away. Write a character sketch by describing the contents of a wastebasket or garbage can.

4. For an exercise (only), try writing a character sketch without any of the elements of type. We shouldn't be able to tell the age, race, gender, nationality, or class of your character. Can you do it? Is it satisfying?

5. Pick two contrasting or contradictory qualities of your own personality (consistent inconsistencies). Create a character that embodies each, and set them in conflict with each other. Since you are not writing about yourself but aiming at heightening and dramatizing these qualities, make each character radically different from yourself in at least one fundamental aspect of type: age, race, gender, nationality, or class.

6. Write a scene from your own life in which a discovery led to a quick decision. Rewrite it changing the character to someone significantly different from yourself.

7. Take an earlier assignment you have written and sharpen characterization by clarifying (especially for yourself) the protagonist's central desire, and by introducing an element of "consistent inconsistency" in him or her.

5

THE FLESH MADE WORD
Characterization, Part II

- *The Direct Methods of Character Presentation (Cont'd)*

- *Character: A Summary*

Appearance and action reveal, which is one thing meant by *showing* rather than telling in fiction. But characters also reveal themselves in the way they speak and think, and the revelation is more profound when they are also shown in these ways.

Note that sense impressions other than sight are still a part of the way a character "appears." A limp handshake or a soft cheek; an odor of Chanel, oregano, or decay—if we are allowed to taste, smell, or touch a character through the narrative, then these sense impressions characterize much the way looks do.

The sound and associations of a character's name, too, can give a clue to personality: The affluent Mr. Chiddister in chapter 3 is automatically a more elegant sort than the affluent Mr. Strum; Huck Finn must have a different life from that of the Marquis of Lumbria. Although names with a blatant meaning—Joseph Surface, Billy Pilgrim, Martha Quest—tend to stylize a character and should be used sparingly, if at all, ordinary names can hint at traits you mean to heighten, and it is worth combing any list of names, including the telephone book, to find suggestive sounds. My own telephone book yields, at a glance this morning, Linda Holladay, Marvin Entzminger, and Melba Peebles, any one of which might set me to speculating on a character.

Sound also characterizes as a part of "appearance" insofar as sound represents timbre, tenor, or quality of noise and speech, the characterizing reediness or gruffness of a voice, the lift of laughter or stiffness of delivery.

SPEECH

Speech, however, characterizes in a way that is different from appearance, because speech represents an effort, mainly voluntary, to externalize the internal and to manifest not merely taste or preference but also deliberated thought. Like fiction itself, human dialogue attempts to marry logic to emotion.

We have many means of communicating that are direct expressions of emotion: laughing, leering, shaking hands, screaming, shouting, shooting, making love. We have many means of communicating that are symbolic and emotionless: mathematical equations, maps, checkbooks, credit cards, and chemical formulas. Between body language and pure math lies language, in which judgments and feelings take the form of structured logic: in vows, laws, news, notes, essays, letters, and talk; and the greatest of these is talk.

Speech can be conveyed in fiction with varying degrees of directness. It can be summarized as part of the narrative so that a good deal of conversation is condensed:

> At home in the first few months, he and Maizie had talked brightly about changes that would make the company more profitable and more attractive to a prospective buyer: new cuts, new packaging, new advertising, new incentives to make supermarkets carry the brand.
>
> Joan Wickersham, *"The Commuter Marriage"*

It can be reported in the third person as indirect speech so that it carries, without actual quotation, the feel of the exchange:

> Had he brought the coffee? She had been waiting all day long for coffee. They had forgot it when they ordered at the store the first day.
> Gosh, no, he hadn't. Lord, now he'd have to go back. Yes, he would if it killed him. He thought, though, he had everything else. She reminded him it was only because he didn't drink coffee himself. If he did he would remember it quick enough.
>
> Katherine Anne Porter, *"Rope"*

But usually when the exchange is vital and represents dramatic action, it will be presented in direct quotation:

> "But I thought you hardly knew her, Mr. Morning."
> He picked up a pencil and began to doodle on a notebook page. "Did I tell you that?"
> "Yes, you did."
> "It's true. I didn't know her well."
> "What is it you're after, then? Who was this person you're investigating?"
> "I would like to know that too."
>
> Siri Hustvedt, *"Mr. Morning"*

These three methods of presenting speech can be used in combination to take advantage of the virtues of each:

> They differed on the issue of the holiday, and couldn't seem to find a common ground. (Summary.) She had an idea: why not some Caribbean island over Christmas? Well, but his mother expected them for turkey. (Indirect.)
>   "Oh, lord, yes, I wouldn't want to go without a yuletide gizzard." (Direct.)

Summary and indirect speech are often useful, to get us quickly to the core of the scene; or when, for example, one character has to inform another of events that we already know, or when the emotional point of a conversation is that it has become tedious.

> Carefully, playing down the danger, Len filled her in on the events of the long night.

> Samantha claimed to be devastated. It was all very well if the Seversons wanted to let their cats run loose, but she certainly wasn't responsible for Lisbeth's parakeets, now was she?

But nothing is more frustrating to a reader than to be told that significant events are taking place in talk and to be denied the drama of the dialogue.

> They whispered to each other all night long, and as he told her all about his past, she began to realize that she was falling in love with him.

Such a summary—it's *telling*—is a stingy way of treating the reader, who wants the chance to fall in love, too: Give me me!

Because direct dialogue has a dual nature—emotion within a logical structure—its purpose in fiction is never merely to convey information. Dialogue may do that, but it needs simultaneously to characterize, provide exposition, set the scene, advance the action, foreshadow, and/or remind. William Sloane, in *The Craft of Writing*, says:

> There is a tentative rule that pertains to all fiction dialogue. It must do more than one thing at a time or it is too inert for the purposes of fiction. This may sound harsh, but I consider it an essential discipline.

In considering Sloane's "tentative rule," I place the emphasis on rule. With dialogue as with significant detail, when you write you are constantly at pains to mean more than you say. If a significant detail must both call up a sense image and *mean*, then the character's words, which presumably mean something, should simultaneously suggest image, personality, or emotion. Even rote exchanges can call up images. A character who says, "It is indeed a pleasure to meet you," carries his back at a different angle, dresses differently, from a character who says, "Hey, man, what it is?"

In the three very brief speeches that follow are three fictional men, sharply differentiated from each other not only by what they say, but also by how they say it. How much do you know about each? How does each look?

"I had a female cousin one time—a Rockefeller, as it happened—" said the Senator, "and she confessed to me that she spent the fifteenth, sixteenth and seventeenth years of her life saying nothing but, No, thank you. Which is all very well for a girl of that age and station. But it would have been a damned unattractive trait in a male Rockefeller."

Kurt Vonnegut, *God Bless You, Mr. Rosewater*

"Hey, that's nice, Grandma," says Phantom as he motions me to come in the circle with him. "I'll tell you what. You can have a contest too. Sure. I got a special one for you. A sweater contest. You get all the grannies out on the porch some night when you could catch a death a chill, and see which one can wear the most sweaters. I got an aunt who can wear fourteen. You top that?"

Robert Ward, *Shedding Skin*

The Knight looked surprised at the question. "What does it matter where my body happens to be?" he said. "My mind goes on working all the same. In fact, the more head downward I am, the more I keep inventing new things.

"Now, the cleverest thing of the sort that I ever did," he went on after a pause, "was inventing a new pudding during the meat course."

Lewis Carroll, *Through the Looking-Glass*

There are forms of insanity that condemn people to hear voices against their will, but as writers we invite ourselves to hear voices without relinquishing our hold on reality or our right to control. The trick to writing good dialogue is hearing voice. The question is, What would he or she say? The answer is entirely in language. The choice of language reveals content, character, and conflict, as well as type.

It's logical that if you must develop voices in order to develop dialogue, you'd do well to start with monologue and develop voices one by one. Use your journal to experiment with speech patterns that will characterize. Some people speak in telegraphically short sentences missing various parts of speech. Some speak in convoluted eloquence or in rhythms tedious with qualifying phrases. Some rush headlong without a pause for breath until they're breathless; others are measured or terse or begrudge even forming a sentence. Trust your "inner ear" and use your journal to practice catching voices. Freewriting is invaluable to dialogue writing because it is the manner of composition closest to speech. There is no time to mull or edit. Any qualifications, corrections, and disavowals must be made part of the process and the text.

When you hear a passage of speech that interests you, next time you sit down at your journal freedraft a monologue passage of that speech. Don't look for words that seem right; just listen to the voice and let it flow. The principle is the same as keeping your eye on the ball. If you feel you're going wrong, let yourself go wrong, and keep going. You're allowed to fail. And the process has two productive outcomes in any case: You begin to develop your own range of voices whether you catch a particular voice or not, and you develop your ear by the very process of "hearing" it go wrong.

You can also limber up in your journal by setting yourself deliberate exercises in making dialogue—or monologue—do more than one thing at a time. In addition to revealing character, dialogue can *set the scene*.

> "We didn't know no one was here. We thought hit a summer camp all closed up. Curtains all closed up. Nothing here. No cars or gear nor nothing. Looks closed to me, don't hit to you, J.J.?"
>
> Joy Williams, *"Woods"*

Dialogue can *set the mood*.

> "I have a lousy trip to Philadelphia, lousy flight back, I watch my own plane blow a tire on closed-circuit TV, I go to my office, I find Suzy in tears because Warren's camped in her one-room apartment. I come home and I find my wife hasn't gotten dressed in two days."
>
> Joan Didion, *Book of Common Prayer*

Dialogue can *reveal the theme* because, as William Sloane says, the characters talk about what the story is about.

> "You feel trapped, don't you?"
> Jane looks at her.
> "Don't you?"
> "No."
> "O.K.—You just have a headache."
> "I do.". . .
> Milly waits a moment and then clears her throat and says, "You know, for a while there after Wally and I were married, I thought maybe I'd made a mistake. I remember realizing that I didn't like the way he laughed. I mean, let's face it, Wally laughs like a hyena. . . "
>
> Richard Bausch, *"The Fireman's Wife"*

Dialogue is also one of the simplest ways to reveal the past (a fundamental play-wrighting device is to have a character who knows tell a character who doesn't know); and it is one of the most effective, because we get both the drama of the memory and the drama of the telling. Here is a passage from Toni Morrison's *The Bluest Eye* in which the past is evoked, the speaker characterized, the scene and mood set, and the theme revealed, all at the same time and in less than a dozen lines.

"The onliest time I be happy seem like was when I was in the picture show. Every time I got, I went. I'd go early, before the show started. They'd cut off the lights, and everything be black. Then the screen would light up, and I'd move right on in them pictures. White men taking such good care of they women, and they all dressed up in big clean houses with the bathtubs right in the same room with the toilet. Them pictures gave me a lot of pleasure, but it made coming home hard, and looking at Cholly hard. I don't know."

If the telling of a memory *changes the relationship* between the teller and the lis-tener (what is in theater called an emotional recall), then you have a scene of high drama, and the dialogue can *advance the action*.

This is an important device, because dialogue is the most valuable to fiction when it is indivisible from the story itself.

A crucial (and sometimes difficult) distinction to make is between speech that is mere discussion or debate and speech that is drama or action. If in doubt, ask yourself: Can this conversation between characters really change anything? Dialogue is action when it contains the possibility of change. Doubt (internal con-flict) is more dramatic than certainty; *to discuss* is not of itself a dramatic action; *to realize* is. If your characters are set in their ideas, more committed to their points of view than to each other, we're likely to find them wooden and uninteresting, mere spokespersons, no matter how significant their topic:

"This has been the traditional fishing spot of the river people for a
thousand years, and your rigs will destroy the whole ecology system."
"Join the real world, Sybil. We're talking a thousand gallons a day here."

Ho-hum. In order to engage us emotionally in a disagreement, the characters must have an emotional stake in the outcome; we need to feel that, even if it's unlikely they would change their minds, they might change their lives.

"If you sink that drill tomorrow morning, I'll be gone by noon."
"Sybil, I have no choice."

Often the most forceful dialogue can be achieved by *not* having the characters say what they mean. People in extreme emotional states—whether of fear, pain, anger, or love—are at their least articulate. There is more narrative tension in a love scene where the lovers make anxious small talk, terrified of revealing their feelings, than in one where they hop into bed. A character who is able to say "I hate you!" hates less than one who bottles the fury and pretends to submit, unwilling to expose the truth. Dialogue often fails if it is too eloquent. The characters debate ideas with great accuracy or define their feelings precisely and honestly. But often the purpose of human exchange is to conceal as well as to reveal; to impress, hurt, protect, seduce, or reject.

In this rather extreme example from Kazuo Ishiguro's *The Remains of the Day*, a British lord and his butler, early in the Second World War, discuss a staff matter. How much concealed emotion can you identify? What information is given without being stated? What are the political sympathies of each character? What lies are told?

> 'I've been doing a great deal of thinking, Stevens. A great deal of thinking. And I've reached my conclusion. We cannot have Jews on the staff here at Darlington Hall.'
>
> 'Sir?'
>
> 'It's for the good of this house, Stevens. In the interests of the guests we have staying here. I've looked into this carefully, Stevens, and I'm letting you know my conclusion.'
>
> 'Very well, sir.'
>
> 'Tell me, Stevens, we have a few on the staff at the moment, don't we? Jews, I mean.'
>
> 'I believe two of the present staff members would fall into that category, sir.'
>
> 'Ah. His lordship paused for a moment, staring out of his window. Of course, you'll have to let them go.'
>
> 'I beg your pardon, sir?'
>
> 'It's regrettable, Stevens, but we have no choice. There's the safety and well-being of my guests to consider. Let me assure you, I've looked into this matter and thought it through thoroughly. It's in all our best interests.'

Listen to the patterns of speech you hear and try to catch differences of character through syntax—the arrangement of words within a sentence. Then put two or more of these characters in a scene; try giving them a strong emotional connection with strongly different ideas, and see if their speech can amount to dramatic action.

Here is an exchange among three members of a Chinese-American family in which the subject is political but much more than politics is conveyed.

> In fact, he hardly ever stopped talking, and we kids watched the spit foam at the corners of his mouth. . . It was more like a lecture than a conversation.
>
> "Actually these aren't dreams or plans," Uncle Bun said. "I'm making predictions about ineluctabilities. This Beautiful Nation, this Gold Mountain, this America will end as we know it. There will be one nation,

and it will be a world nation. A united planet. Not just Russian
Communism. Not just Chinese Communism. World Communism."

He said, "When we don't need to break our bodies earning our daily living
any more, and we have time to think, we'll write poems, sing songs, develop
religions, invest customs, build statues, plant gardens and make a perfect
world." He paused to contemplate the wonders.

"Isn't that great?" I said after he left.

"Don't get brainwashed," said my mother. "He's going to get in trouble for
talking like that."

Maxine Hong Kingston, China Men

Uncle Bun is richly characterized by his idealistic eloquence, but so are the narrator and her mother in their brief reactions. The contrast between Uncle Bun's
"predictions about ineluctabilities" and the narrator's "Isn't that great?" makes her
both a teenager and Americanized, whereas the mother's hostile practicality comes
out in her blunt imperative.

This passage also illustrates an essential element of conflict in dialogue: tension
and drama are heightened when characters are constantly (in one form or another)
saying no to each other. Here the mother is saying a distinct *no* to both Uncle Bun
and her daughter. In the following exchange from Ernest Hemingway's *The Old
Man and the Sea*, the old man feels only love for his young protégé, and their conversation is a pledge of affection. Nevertheless, it is the old man's steady denial
that lends the scene tension.

"Can I go out and get sardines for you tomorrow?"

"No. Go and play baseball. I can still row and Rogelio will throw the net."

"I would like to go. If I cannot fish with you, I would like to serve in some way."

"You brought me a beer," the old man said. "You are already a man."

"How old was I when you first took me in a boat?"

"Five and you were nearly killed when I brought the fish in too green and
he nearly tore the boat to pieces. Can you remember?"

"I can remember the tail slapping and banging and the thwart breaking
and the noise of the clubbing. I can remember you throwing me into the bow
where the wet coiled lines were and feeling the whole boat shiver and the
noise of you clubbing him like chopping a tree down and the sweet blood
smell all over me."

"Can you really remember that or did I just tell it to you?"

"I remember everything from when we first went together."

The old man looked at him with his sunburned, confident loving eyes.

"If you were my boy I'd take you out and gamble," he said. "But you are
your father's and mother's and you are in a lucky boat."

Neither of these characters is consciously eloquent, and the dialogue is extremely
simple. But look how much more it does than "one thing at a time"! It provides

exposition on the beginning of the relationship, and it conveys the mutual affection of the two and the conflict within the old man between his love for the boy and his loyalty to the parents. It conveys the boy's eagerness to persuade and carries him into the emotion he had as a small child while the fish was clubbed. The dialogue represents a constant shift of power back and forth between the boy and the old man, as the boy, whatever else he is saying, continues to say *please*, and the old man, whatever else he is saying, continues to say *no*.

The same law of plausibility operates in dialogue as in narrative. We will tend to believe a character who speaks in concrete details and to be skeptical of one who generalizes or who delivers judgments unsupported by example. Uncle Bun is eloquent and attractive, but he hardly convinces us he has the formula for a perfect world. When the boy in the Hemingway passage protests, "I remember everything," however, we believe him because of the vivid details in his memory of the fish. If one character says, "It's perfectly clear from all his actions that he adores me and would do anything for me," and another says, "I had my hands all covered with the clay slick, and he just reached over to lift a lock of hair out of my eyes and tuck it behind my ear," which character do you believe is the more loved?

It's interesting to observe that, whereas in narrative you will demonstrate control if you state the facts and let the emotional value rise off of them, in dialogue you will convey information more naturally if the emphasis is on the speaker's feelings. "My brother is due to arrive at midafternoon and is bringing his four children with him" reads as bald exposition; whereas, "That idiot brother of mine thinks he can walk in in the middle of the afternoon and plunk his four kids in my lap!" or, "I can't wait till my brother gets here at three! You'll see—those are the four sweetest kids this side of the planet."—will sound like talk and will slip us the information sideways.

Examine your dialogue to see if it does more than one thing at a time. Do the sound and syntax characterize by region, education, attitude? Do the choice of words and their syntax reveal that the character is stiff, outgoing, stifling anger, ignorant of the facts, perceptive, bigoted, afraid? Is the conflict advanced by "*no-dialogue*," in which the characters say no to each other? Is the drama heightened by the characters' inability or unwillingness to tell the whole truth?

Once you are comfortable with the voice of your character, it is well to acknowledge that everyone has many voices and that what that character says will be, within his or her verbal range, determined by the character *to whom* it is said. All of us have one sort of speech for the vicar and another for the man who pumps the gas. Huck Finn, whose voice is idiosyncratically his own, says, "Yes, sir," to the judge, and "Maybe I am, maybe I ain't," to his degenerate dad.

Dialect is a tempting, and can be an excellent, means of characterizing, but it is difficult to do well and easy to overdo. Dialect should always be achieved by word choice and syntax, and misspellings kept to a minimum. They distract and slow the reader, and worse, they tend to make the character seem stupid rather than regional. There is no point in spelling phonetically any word as it is ordinarily pronounced: almost all of us say things like "fur" for *for*, "uv" for *of*, "wuz" for *was*, "an" for *and*, "sez" for *says*. Nearly everyone drops the g in words ending in *ing*, at least now and then. When you misspell these words in dialogue, you indicate that the speaker is ignorant enough to spell them that way when writing. Even if you want to indicate ignorance, you may alienate the reader by the means you choose to do so.

These rules for dialect have changed in the past fifty years or so, largely for political reasons. Nineteenth-century authors felt free to misspell the dialogue of foreigners, the lower classes, and racial, regional, and ethnic groups. This literary habit persisted into the first decades of the twentieth century. But the world is considerably smaller now, and its consciousness has been raised. Dialect, after all, is entirely relative, and an author who seems unaware of this may sound like a bigot. The word *bath* pronounced by an Englishman may sound like "bahth" to an American, and pronounced by an American may sound like "banth" to an Englishman, but both know how the word is spelled and resent the implied mockery. Liverpudlians have been knighted; the White House has housed the accents of the Deep South and the Far West; and we resent the implication that regionality is ignorance. Ignorance itself is a charged issue. If you misspell a foreign accent or black English, the reader is likely to have a political rather than a literary reaction. A line of dialogue that runs "Doan rush me nun, Ah be gwine" reads as caricature, whereas "Don't rush me none, I be going" makes legitimate use of black English syntax and lets us concentrate on the meaning and emotion.

It's tricky catching the voice of a foreigner with imperfect English, and you need either a sensitive ear and a good deal of experience with the relevant speakers, or to be an accomplished linguist. This is because everyone has a native language, and when someone whose native language is French or Ibu starts to learn English, the grammatical mistakes they make will be based on the grammatical structure of the native language. Unless you know French or Ibu, you will make mistaken mistakes, and your dialogue is likely to sound as if it came from second-rate sitcoms. We're all tired of German characters who say "Ve vant you should feel goot," and Native Americans who—whether Sioux, Crow or Navaho— can't tell the difference between "I" and "Me"—as in "Me no want paleface wampum." If you seem to be indicating ignorance in a character of whose native language you are ignorant, your reader instinctively mistrusts you.

In dialect or standard English, the bottom-line rule is that dialogue must be speakable. If it isn't speakable, it isn't dialogue.

> "Certainly I had had a fright I wouldn't soon forget," Reese would say later, "and as I slipped into bed fully dressed except for my shoes, which I flung God-knows-where, I wondered why I had subjected myself to a danger only a fool would fail to foresee for the dubious pleasure of spending one evening in the company of a somewhat less than brilliant coed."

Nobody would say this because it can't be said. It is not only convoluted beyond reason but it also stumbles over its alliteration, "only a fool would fail to foresee for," and takes more breath than the human lungs can hold. Read your dialogue aloud and make sure it is comfortable to the mouth, the breath, and the ear. If not, then it won't ring true as talk.

Identifying dialogue sometimes presents more of a problem than it needs to. The purpose of a ~~dialogue tag~~ is to make clear who is speaking, and it usually needs to do nothing else. *Said* is quite adequate to the purpose. People also *ask* and *reply* and occasionally *add, recall, remember,* or *remind.* But sometimes an unsure writer will strain for emphatic synonyms: *She gasped, he whined, they chorused, John snarled, Mary spat.* This is unnecessary and obtrusive, because although unintentional repetition usually makes for awkward style, the word *said* is as invisible as punctuation. When reading we're scarcely aware of it, whereas we are forced to be aware of *she wailed.* If it's clear who is speaking without any dialogue tag at all, don't use one. Usually an identification at the beginning of a dialogue passage and an occasional reminder are sufficient. If the speaker is inherently identified in the speech pattern, so much the better.

Similarly, tonal dialogue tags should be used sparingly: *he said with relish; she added limply.* Such phrases are blatant "telling," and the chances are that good dialogue will convey its own tone. *"Get off my case!" she said angrily.* We do not need to be told that she said this angrily. If she said it sweetly, then we would probably need to be told. If the dialogue does not give us a clue to the manner in which it is said, an action will often do so better than an adverb. *"I'll have a word with Mr. Ritter about it," he said with finality,* is weaker than *"I'll have a word with Mr. Ritter about it," he said, and picked up his hat.*

THOUGHT

Fiction has a flexibility denied to film and drama, where everything the spectator knows must be externally manifested. In fiction you have the privilege of entering a character's mind, sharing at its source internal conflict, reflection, and the crucial processes of decision and discovery. Like speech, a character's thought can be offered in summary (*He hated the way she ate.*), or as indirect thought (*Why did she hold her fork straight up like that?*) or directly, as if we are overhearing the character's own mind (*My God, she's going to drop the yolk!*) As with speech, the three methods can be alternated in the same paragraph to achieve at once immediacy and pace.

Methods of presenting a character's thought will be more fully discussed in Chapters 7 and 8 on Point of View. What's most important to characterization is that thought, like speech, reveals more than information. It can also set mood, reveal or betray desires, develop theme, and so forth.

The territory of a character's mind is above all likely to be the center of the action. Aristotle says, as we have seen, that a man "is his desire," that is, his character is defined by his ultimate purpose, good or bad. *Thought,* says Aristotle, is the process by which a person works backward in his mind from his goal to determine what action he can take toward that goal at a given moment.

It is not, for example, your ultimate desire to read this book. Very likely you don't even "want" to read it; you'd rather be asleep or jogging or making love. But your ultimate goal is, say, to be a rich, respected, and famous writer. In order to attain this goal, you reason, you must know as much about the craft as you can learn. To do this, you would like to take a graduate degree at the Writer's

Workshop in Iowa. To do that, you must take an undergraduate degree in _____, where you now find yourself, and must get an A in Ms. or Mr. _____'s creative writing course. To do that, you must produce a character sketch from one of the assignments at the end of this chapter by a week from Tuesday. To do so, you must sit here reading this chapter now instead of sleeping, jogging, or making love. Your ultimate motive has led you logically backward to a deliberate "moral" decision on the action you can take at this minor crossroad. In fact, it turns out that you want to be reading after all.

The relation that Aristotle perceives among desire, thought, and action seems to me a very useful one for an author, both in structuring plot and in creating character. What does this protagonist want to happen in the last paragraph of this story? What is the particular thought process by which this person works backward to determine what she or he will do now, in the situation that presents itself in the first paragraph on page one?

The action, of course, may be the wrong one. Thought thwarts us, because it leads to a wrong choice (if only you'd gone to sleep, you would now be having a dream that would give you the most brilliant idea for a short story you've ever had), or because thought is full of conflicting desires and consistent inconsistencies (actually you are no longer reading this paragraph; someone knocked on your door and suggested a pizza and you couldn't resist), or because there is enormous human tension between suppressed thought and expressed thought (you didn't want a pizza, and certainly not in the company of that bore, but you'd turned him down twice this week already).

In "Where Are You Going, Where Have You Been?" at the end of Chapter 3, Connie wants to get away every chance she can from a family she despises. She devises a number of schemes and subterfuges to avoid their company. At the end of the story her success is probably permanent, at a cost she had not figured into her plan. Through the story she is richly characterized, inventing two personalities in order single-mindedly to pursue her freedom, finally caught between conflicting and paralyzing desires.

A person, a character, can't do much about what he or she wants; it just is (which is another way of saying that character is desire). What we can deliberately choose is our behavior, the action we take in a given situation. Achievement of our desire would be easy if the thought process between desire and act were not so faulty and so wayward, or if there were not such an abyss between the thoughts we think and those which we are willing and able to express.

CONFLICT BETWEEN METHODS OF PRESENTATION

The conflict that is the essence of character can be effectively (and, if it doesn't come automatically, quite consciously) achieved in fiction by producing a conflict between methods of presentation. A character can be directly revealed to us through *appearance, speech, action, and thought*. If you set one of these methods (in narrative practice most frequently *thought*) at odds with the others, then dramatic tension will be produced. Imagine, for example, a character who is impeccable and expensively dressed, who speaks eloquently, who acts decisively, and whose mind is revealed to us as full of order and determination. He is inevitably a flat character. But suppose that he is impeccable, eloquent, decisive, and that his mind is a mess of wounds and panic. He is at once interesting.

Here is the opening passage of Saul Bellow's *Seize the Day*, in which appearance and action are blatantly at odds with thought. Notice that it is the tension between suppressed thought and what is expressed through appearance and action that produces the rich character conflict.

> When it came to concealing his troubles, Tommy Wilhelm was not less capable than the next fellow. So at least he thought, and there was a certain amount of evidence to back him up. He had once been an actor— no, not quite, an extra—and he knew what acting should be. Also, he was smoking a cigar, and when a man is smoking a cigar, wearing a hat, he has an advantage: it is harder to find out how he feels. He came from the twenty-third floor down to the lobby on the mezzanine to collect his mail before breakfast, and he believed—he hoped—he looked passably well: doing all right.

Tommy Wilhelm is externally composed but mentally anxious, mainly anxious about looking externally composed. By contrast, in the next passage, from Samuel Beckett's *Murphy*, the landlady, Miss Carridge, who has just discovered a suicide in one of her rooms, is anxious in speech and action but is mentally composed.

> She came speeding down the stairs one step at a time, her feet going so fast that she seemed on little caterpillar wheels, her forefinger sawing horribly at her craw for Celia's benefit. She slithered to a stop on the steps of the house and screeched for the police. She capered in the street like a consternated ostrich, with strangled distracted rushes towards the York and Caledonian Roads in turn, embarrassingly equidistant from the tragedy, tossing up her arms, undoing the good work of the samples, screeching for police aid. Her mind was so collected that she saw clearly the impropriety of letting it appear so.

I have said that thought is most frequently at odds with one or more of the other three methods of direct presentation—reflecting the difficulty we have expressing ourselves openly or accurately—but this is by no means always the case. A character may be successfully, calmly, even eloquently expressing fine opinions while betraying himself by pulling at his ear, or herself by crushing her skirt. Captain Queeg of Herman Wouk's *The Caine Mutiny* is a memorable example of this, maniacally clicking the steel balls in his hand as he defends his disciplinary code. Often we are not privy to the thoughts of a character at all, so that the conflicts must be expressed in a contradiction between the external methods of direct presentation, appearance, speech, and action. Character A may be speaking floods of friendly welcome, betraying his real feeling by backing steadily away. Character B, dressed in taffeta ruffles and ostrich plumes, may wail pityingly over the miseries of the poor. Notice that the notion of "betraying oneself" is important here: We're more likely to believe the evidence unintentionally given than deliberate expression.

A classic example of such self-betrayal is found in Leo Tolstoy's *The Death of Ivan Ilyich*, where the widow confronts her husband's colleague at the funeral.

> . . . Noticing that the table was endangered by his cigarette ash, she immediately passed him an ashtray, saying as she did so: "I consider it an affectation to say that my grief prevents my attending to practical affairs. On the contrary, if anything can—I won't say console me, but—distract me, it is seeing to everything concerning him." She again took out her handkerchief as if preparing to cry, but suddenly, as if mastering her feeling, she shook herself and began to speak calmly. "But there is something I want to talk to you about."

It is no surprise either to the colleague or to us that Praskovya Federovna wants to talk about getting money.

Finally, character conflict can be expressed by creating a tension between the direct and the indirect methods of presentation, and this is a source of much irony. The author presents us with a judgment of the character and then lets him or her speak, appear, act, and/or think in contradiction of this judgment.

> Sixty years had not dulled his responses; his physical reactions, like his moral ones, were guided by his will and strong character, and these could be seen plainly in his features. He had a long tube-like face with a long rounded open jaw and a long depressed nose.
>
> Flannery O'Connor, *"The Artificial Nigger"*

What we see here in the details of Mr. Head's features are not will and strong character but grimly unlikable qualities. "Tube-like" is an ugly image; an "open jaw" suggests stupidity; and "depressed" connotes more than shape, while the dogged repetition of "long" stretches the face grotesquely.

Jane Austen is a master of this ironic method, the authorial voice often having a naive goodwill toward the characters while the characters themselves prevent the reader from sharing it.

> Mr. Woodhouse was fond of society in his own way. He liked very much to have his friends come and see him; and from various united causes, from his long residence at Hartfield, and his good nature, from his fortune, his house, and his daughter, he could command the visits of his own little circle in a great measure as he liked. He had not much intercourse with any families beyond that circle; his horror of late hours and large dinner parties made him unfit for any acquaintance but such as would visit him on his own terms. Upon such occasions poor Mr. Woodhouse's feelings were in sad warfare. He

loved to have the cloth laid, because it had been the fashion of his youth; but his conviction of suppers being very unwholesome made him rather sorry to see anything put on it; and while his hospitality would have welcomed his visitors to everything, his care for their health made him grieve that they would eat.

Emma

Here all the authorial generalizations about Mr. Woodhouse are generous and positive, whereas his actions and the "sad warfare" of his mind lead us to the conviction that we would just as soon not sup with this good-natured and generous man.

In addition to providing tension between methods of presentation, you can try a few other ways of making a character fresh and forceful in your mind before you start writing.

If the character is based on you or on someone you know, drastically alter the model in some external way: Change blond to dark or thin to thick; imagine the character as the opposite gender or radically alter the setting in which the character must act. Part of the trouble with writing directly from experience is that you know too much about it—what "they" did, how you felt. Under such circumstances it's hard to know whether everything in your mind is getting onto the page. An external alteration forces you to re-see, and so to see more clearly, and so to convey more clearly what you see.

On the other hand, if the character is created primarily out of your observation or invention and is unlike yourself, try to find an internal area that you have in common with the character. If you are a blond, slender young woman and the character is a fat, balding man, do you nevertheless have in common a love of French *haute cuisine*? Are you haunted by the same sort of dream? Do you share a fear of public performance or a susceptibility to fine weather?

I can illustrate these techniques only from my own writing, because I am the only author whose self I can identify with any certainty in fictional characters. In a recent novel, I wanted to open with a scene in which the heroine buries a dog in her backyard. I had recently buried a dog in my backyard. I wanted to capture the look and feel of red Georgia earth at sunrise, the tangle of roots, and the smell of decay. But I knew that I was likely to make the experience too much my own, too little my character's. I set about to make her not-me. I have long dark hair and an ordinary figure, and I tend to live in Levi's. I made Shaara Soole

> . . . big boned, lanky, melon-breasted, her best feature was a head of rusty barbed-wire hair that she tried to control with a wardrobe of scarves and headband things. Like most costume designers, she dressed with more originality than taste, usually on the Oriental or Polynesian side, sometimes with voluminous loops of thong and matte metal over an ordinary shirt. This was somewhat eccentric in Hubbard, Georgia, but Shaara may have been oblivious to her eccentricity, being so concerned to keep her essential foolishness in check.

Having thus separated Shaara from myself, I was able to bury the dog with her arms and through her eyes rather than my own. On the other hand, a few pages later I was faced with the problem of introducing her ex-husband, Boyd Soole. I had voluminous notes on this character, and I knew that he was almost totally unlike me. A man, to begin with, and a huge man, a theater director with a natural air of power and authority and very little interest in domestic affairs. I sat at my desk for several days, unable to make him move convincingly. My desk oppressed me, and I felt trapped and uncomfortable, my work thwarted, it seemed, by the very chair and typewriter. Then it occurred to me that Boyd was *also* sitting at a desk trying to work.

> The dresser at the Travelodge was some four inches too narrow and three inches too low. If he set his feet on the floor his knees would sit free of the drawer but would be awkwardly constricted left and right. If he crossed his legs, he could hook his right foot comfortably outside the left of the kneehole but would bruise his thigh at the drawer. If he shifted back he was placed at an awkward distance from his script. And in this position he could not work.

This passage did not instantly allow me to live inside Boyd Soole's skin, nor did it solve all my problems with his characterization. But it did let me get on with the story, and it gave me a flash of sympathy for him that later grew much more profound than I had foreseen.

Often, identifying what you have in common with the feelings of your character will also clarify what is important about her or him to the story—why, in fact, you chose to write about such a person at all. Even if the character is presented as a villain, you have something in common, and I don't mean something forgivable. If he or she is intolerably vain, watch your own private gestures in front of the mirror and borrow them. If he or she is cruel, remember how you enjoyed hooking the worm.

There is no absolute requirement that a writer need behave honestly in life; there is absolutely no such requirement. Great writers have been public hams, domestic dictators, emotional con artists, and Nazis. What is required for fine writing is honesty on the page—not how the characters *should* react at the funeral, the surprise party, in bed, but how they *would*. In order to develop such honesty of observation on the page, you must begin with a willing honesty of observation (though mercifully not of behavior) in yourself.

Character: A Summary

It may be helpful to summarize such practical advice on character as this chapter and the previous chapter contain.

1. Keep a journal and use it to explore and build ideas for characters.
2. Know all the influences that go into the making of your character's type: age, gender, race, nationality, marital status, region, education, religion, profession.

3. Know the details of your character's life: what he or she does during every part of the day, thinks about, remembers, wants, likes and dislikes, eats, says, means.

4. Identify, heighten, and dramatize consistent inconsistencies. What does your character want that is at odds with whatever else the character wants? What patterns of thought and behavior work against the primary goal?

5. Focus sharply on how the character looks, on what she or he wears and owns, and on how she or he moves. Let us focus on it, too.

6. Examine the character's speech to make sure it does more than convey information. Does it characterize, accomplish exposition, and reveal emotion, intent, or change? Does it advance the conflict through "no"-dialogue? Speak it aloud: Does it "say"?

7. Build action by making your characters discover and decide. Make sure that what happens is action and not mere event or movement, that is, that it contains the possibility for human change.

8. Know what your character wants, both generally out of life, and specifically in the context of the story. Keeping that desire in mind, "think backward" with the character to decide what he or she would do in any situation presented.

9. Be aware of the five methods of character presentation: authorial interpretation, appearance, speech, action, and thought. Reveal the character's conflicts by presenting attributes in at least one of these methods that contrast with attributes you present in the others.

10. If the character is based on a real model, including yourself, make a dramatic external alteration.

11. If the character is imaginary or alien to you, identify a mental or emotional point of contact.

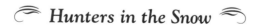 Hunters in the Snow

TOBIAS WOLFF

Tub had been waiting for an hour in the falling snow. He paced the sidewalk to keep warm and stuck his head out over the curb whenever he saw lights approaching. One driver stopped for him but before Tub could wave the man on he saw the rifle on Tub's back and hit the gas. The tires spun on the ice.

The fall of snow thickened. Tub stood below the overhang of a building. Across the road the clouds whitened just above the rooftops, and the street lights went out. He shifted the rifle strap to his other shoulder. The whiteness seeped up the sky.

A truck slid around the corner, horn blaring, rear end sashaying. Tub moved to the sidewalk and held up his hand. The truck jumped the curb and kept coming, half on the street and half on the sidewalk. It wasn't slowing down at all. Tub stood for a moment, still holding up his hand, then jumped back. His rifle slipped off his shoulder and clattered on the ice, a sandwich fell out of his pocket. He ran for the steps of the building. Another sandwich and a package of cookies tumbled onto the new snow. He made the steps and looked back.

The truck had stopped several feet beyond where Tub had been standing. He picked up his sandwiches and his cookies and slung the rifle and went up to the driver's window. The driver was bent against the steering wheel, slapping his knees and drumming his feet on the floorboards. He looked like a cartoon of a person laughing, except that his eyes watched the man on the seat beside him. "You ought to see yourself," the driver said. "He looks just like a beach ball with a hat on, doesn't he? Doesn't he, Frank?"

The man beside him smiled and looked off.

"You almost ran me down," Tub said. "You could've killed me."

"Come on, Tub," said the man beside the driver. "Be mellow. Kenny was just messing around." He opened the door and slid over to the middle of the seat.

Tub took the bolt out of his rifle and climbed in beside him. "I waited an hour," he said. "If you meant ten o'clock why didn't you say ten o'clock?"

"Tub, you haven't done anything but complain since we got here," said the man in the middle. "If you want to piss and moan all day you might as well go home and bitch at your kids. Take your pick." When Tub didn't say anything he turned to the driver. "Okay, Kenny, let's hit the road."

Some juvenile delinquents had heaved a brick through the windshield on the driver's side, so the cold and snow tunneled right into the cab. The heater didn't work. They covered themselves with a couple of blankets Kenny had brought along and pulled down the muffs on their caps. Tub tried to keep his hands warm by rubbing them under the blanket but Frank made him stop.

They left Spokane and drove deep into the country, running along black lines of fences. The snow let up, but still there was no edge to the land where it met the sky. Nothing moved in the chalky fields. The cold bleached their faces and made the stubble stand out on their cheeks and along their upper lips. They stopped twice for coffee before they got to the woods where Kenny wanted to hunt.

Tub was for trying someplace different; two years in a row they'd been up and down this land and hadn't seen a thing. Frank didn't care one way or the other, he just wanted to get out of the goddamned truck. "Feel that," Frank said, slamming the door. He spread his feet and closed his eyes and leaned his head way back and breathed deeply. "Tune in on that energy."

"Another thing," Kenny said. "This is open land. Most of the land around here is posted."

"I'm cold," Tub said.

Frank breathed out. "Stop bitching, Tub. Get centered."

"I wasn't bitching."

"Centered," Kenny said. "Next thing you'll be wearing a nightgown, Frank. Selling flowers out at the airport."

"Kenny," Frank said, "you talk too much."

"Okay," Kenny said. "I won't say a word. Like I won't say anything about a certain babysitter."

"What babysitter?" Tub asked.

"That's between us," Frank said, looking at Kenny. "That's confidential. You keep your mouth shut."

Kenny laughed.

"You're asking for it," Frank said.

"Asking for what?"

"You'll see."

"Hey," Tub said, "are we hunting or what?"

They started off across the field. Tub had trouble getting through the fences. Frank and Kenny could have helped him; they could have lifted up on the top wire and stepped on the bottom wire, but they didn't. They stood and watched him. There were a lot of fences and Tub was puffing when they reached the woods.

They hunted for over two hours and saw no deer, no tracks, no sign. Finally they stopped by the creek to eat. Kenny had several slices of pizza and a couple of candy bars: Frank had a sandwich, an apple, two carrots, and a square of chocolate; Tub ate one hard-boiled egg and a stick of celery.

"You ask me how I want to die today," Kenny said, "I'll tell you burn me at the stake." He turned to Tub. "You still on that diet?" He winked at Frank.

"What do you think? You think I like hard-boiled eggs?"

"All I can say is, it's the first diet I ever heard of where you gained weight from it."

"Who said I gained weight?"

"Oh, pardon me. I take it back. You're just wasting away before my very eyes. Isn't he, Frank?"

Frank had his fingers fanned out, tips against the bark of the stump where he'd laid his food. His knuckles were hairy. He wore a heavy wedding band and on his right pinky another gold ring with a flat face and an "F" in what looked like diamonds. He turned the ring this way and that. "Tub," he said, "you haven't seen your own balls in ten years."

Kenny doubled over laughing. He took off his hat and slapped his leg with it.

"What am I supposed to do?" Tub said. "It's my glands."

They left the woods and hunted along the creek. Frank and Kenny worked one bank and Tub worked the other, moving upstream. The snow was light but the drifts were deep and hard to move through. Wherever Tub looked the surface was smooth, undisturbed, and after a time he lost interest. He stopped looking for tracks and just tried to keep up with Frank and Kenny on the other side. A moment came when he realized he hadn't seen them in a long time. The breeze was moving from him to them; when it stilled he could sometimes hear Kenny laughing but that was all. He quickened his pace, breasting hard into the drifts, fighting away the snow with his knees and elbows. He heard his heart and felt the flush on his face but he never once stopped.

Tub caught up with Frank and Kenny at a bend of the creek. They were standing on a log that stretched from their bank to his. Ice had backed up behind the log. Frozen reeds stuck out, barely nodding when the air moved.

"See anything?" Frank asked.

Tub shook his head.

There wasn't much daylight left and they decided to head back toward the road. Frank and Kenny crossed the log and they started downstream, using the trail Tub had broken. Before they had gone very far Kenny stopped. "Look at that," he said, and pointed to some tracks going from the creek back into the woods. Tub's footprints crossed right over them. There on the bank, plain as day, were several mounds of deer sign. "What do you think that is, Tub?" Kenny kicked at it. "Walnuts on vanilla icing?"

"I guess I didn't notice."

Kenny looked at Frank.

"I was lost."

"You were lost. Big deal."

They followed the tracks into the woods. The deer had gone over a fence half buried in drifting snow. A no hunting sign was nailed to the top of one of the posts. Frank laughed and said the son of a bitch could read. Kenny wanted to go after him but Frank said no way, the people out here didn't mess around. He thought maybe the farmer who owned the land would let them use it if they asked. Kenny wasn't so sure. Anyway, he figured that by the time they walked to the truck and drove up the road and doubled back it would be almost dark.

"Relax," Frank said. "You can't hurry nature. If we're meant to get that deer, we'll get it. If we're not, we won't."

They started back toward the truck. This part of the woods was mainly pine. The snow was shaded and had a glaze on it. It held up Kenny and Frank but Tub kept falling through. As he kicked forward, the edge of the crust bruised his shins. Kenny and Frank pulled ahead of him, to where he couldn't even hear their voices any more. He sat down on a stump and wiped his face. He ate both the sandwiches and half the cookies, taking his own sweet time. It was dead quiet.

When Tub crossed the last fence into the road the truck started moving. Tub had to run for it and just managed to grab hold of the tailgate and hoist himself into the bed. He lay there, panting. Kenny looked out the rear window and grinned. Tub crawled into the lee of the cab to get out of the freezing wind. He pulled his earflaps low and pushed his chin into the collar of his coat. Someone rapped on the window but Tub would not turn around.

He and Frank waited outside while Kenny went into the farmhouse to ask permission. The house was old and paint was curling off the sides. The smoke streamed westward off the top of the chimney, fanning away into a thin gray plume. Above the ridge of the hills another ridge of blue clouds was rising.

"You've got a short memory," Tub said.

"What?" Frank said. He had been staring off.

"I used to stick up for you."

"Okay, so you used to stick up for me. What's eating you?"

"You shouldn't have just left me back there like that."

"You're a grown-up, Tub. You can take care of yourself. Anyway, if you think you're the only person with problems I can tell you that you're not."

"Is something bothering you, Frank?"

Frank kicked at a branch poking out of the snow. "Never mind," he said.

"What did Kenny mean about the babysitter?"

"Kenny talks too much," Frank said. "You just mind your own business."

Kenny came out of the farmhouse and gave the thumbs-up and they began walking back toward the woods. As they passed the barn a large black hound with a grizzled snout ran out and barked at them. Every time he barked he slid backwards a bit, like a cannon recoiling. Kenny got down on all fours and snarled and barked back at him, and the dog slunk away into the barn, looking over his shoulder and peeing a little as he went.

"That's an old-timer," Frank said. "A real graybeard. Fifteen years if he's a day."

"Too old," Kenny said.

Past the barn they cut off through the fields. The land was unfenced and the crust was freezing up thick and they made good time. They kept to the edge of the field until they picked up the tracks again and followed them into the woods, farther and farther back toward the hills. The trees started to blur with the shadows and the wind rose and needled their faces with the crystals it swept off the glaze. Finally they lost the tracks.

Kenny swore and threw down his hat. "This is the worst day of hunting I ever had, bar none." He picked up his hat and brushed off the snow. "This will be the first season since I was fifteen I haven't got my deer."

"It isn't the deer," Frank said. "It's the hunting. There are all these forces out here and you just have to go with them."

"You go with them," Kenny said. "I came out here to get me a deer, not listen to a bunch of hippie bullshit. And if it hadn't been for dimples here I would have, too."

"That's enough," Frank said.

"And you—you're so busy thinking about that little jailbait of yours you wouldn't know a deer if you saw one."

"Drop dead," Frank said, and turned away.

Kenny and Tub followed him back across the fields. When they were coming up to the barn Kenny stopped and pointed. "I hate that post," he said. He raised his rifle and fired. It sounded like a dry branch cracking. The post splintered along its right side, up towards the top. "There," Kenny said. "It's dead."

"Knock it off," Frank said, walking ahead.

Kenny looked at Tub. He smiled. "I hate that tree," he said, and fired again. Tub hurried to catch up with Frank. He started to speak but just then the dog ran out of the barn and barked at them. "Easy, boy," Frank said.

"I hate that dog." Kenny was behind them.

"That's enough," Frank said. "You put that gun down."

Kenny fired. The bullet went in between the dog's eyes. He sank right down into the snow, his legs splayed out on each side, his yellow eyes open and staring.

Except for the blood he looked like a small bearskin rug. The blood ran down the dog's muzzle into the snow.

They all looked at the dog lying there.

"What did he ever do to you?" Tub asked. "He was just barking."

Kenny turned to Tub. "I hate you."

Tub shot from the waist. Kenny jerked backward against the fence and buckled to his knees. He folded his hands across his stomach. "Look," he said. His hands were covered with blood. In the dusk his blood was more blue than red. It seemed to belong to the shadows. It didn't seem out of place. Kenny eased himself onto his back. He sighed several times, deeply. "You shot me," he said.

"I had to," Tub said. He knelt beside Kenny. "Oh God," he said. "Frank. Frank."

Frank hadn't moved since Kenny killed the dog.

"Frank!" Tub shouted.

"I was just kidding around," Kenny said. "It was a joke. Oh!" he said, and arched his back suddenly. "Oh!" he said again, and dug his heels into the snow and pushed himself along on his head for several feet. Then he stopped and lay there, rocking back and forth on his heels and head like a wrestler doing warm-up exercises.

Frank roused himself. "Kenny," he said. He bent down and put his gloved hand on Kenny's brow. "You shot him," he said to Tub.

"He made me," Tub said.

"No no no," Kenny said.

Tub was weeping from the eyes and nostrils. His whole face was wet. Frank closed his eyes, then looked down at Kenny again. "Where does it hurt?"

"Everywhere," Kenny said, "just everywhere."

"Oh God," Tub said.

"I mean where did it go in?" Frank said.

"Here." Kenny pointed at the wound in his stomach. It was welling slowly with blood.

"You're lucky," Frank said. "It's on the left side. It missed your appendix. If it had hit your appendix you'd really be in the soup." He turned and threw up onto the snow, holding his sides as if to keep warm.

"Are you all right?" Tub said.

"There's some aspirin in the truck," Kenny said.

"I'm all right," Frank said.

"We'd better call an ambulance," Tub said.

"Jesus," Frank said. "What are we going to say?"

"Exactly what happened," Tub said. "He was going to shoot me but I shot him first."

"No sir!" Kenny said. "I wasn't either!"

Frank patted Kenny on the arm. "Easy does it, partner." He stood. "Let's go."

Tub picked up Kenny's rifle as they walked down toward the farmhouse. "No sense leaving this around," he said. "Kenny might get ideas."

"I can tell you one thing," Frank said. "You've really done it this time. This definitely takes the cake."

They had to knock on the door twice before it was opened by a thin man with lank hair. The room behind him was filled with smoke. He squinted at them. "You get anything?" he asked.

"No," Frank said.

"I knew you wouldn't. That's what I told the other fellow."

"We've had an accident."

The man looked past Frank and Tub into the gloom. "Shoot your friend, did you?"

Frank nodded.

"I did," Tub said.

"I suppose you want to use the phone."

"If it's okay."

The man in the door looked behind him, then stepped back. Frank and Tub followed him into the house. There was a woman sitting by the stove in the middle of the room. The stove was smoking badly. She looked up and then down again at the child asleep in her lap. Her face was white and damp; strands of hair were pasted across her forehead. Tub warmed his hands over the stove while Frank went into the kitchen to call. The man who had let them in stood at the window, his hands in his pockets.

"My friend shot your dog," Tub said.

The man nodded without turning around. "I should have done it myself. I just couldn't."

"He loved that dog so much," the woman said. The child squirmed and she rocked it.

"You asked him to?" Tub said. "You asked him to shoot your dog?"

"He was old and sick. Couldn't chew his food any more. I would have done it myself but I don't have a gun."

"You couldn't have anyway," the woman said. "Never in a million years."

The man shrugged.

Frank came out of the kitchen. "We'll have to take him ourselves. The nearest hospital is fifty miles from here and all their ambulances are out anyway."

The woman knew a shortcut but the directions were complicated and Tub had to write them down. The man told them where they could find some boards to carry Kenny on. He didn't have a flashlight but he said he would leave the porch light on.

It was dark outside. The clouds were low and heavy-looking and the wind blew in shrill gusts. There was a screen loose on the house and it banged slowly and then quickly as the wind rose again. They could hear it all the way to the barn. Frank went for the boards while Tub looked for Kenny, who was not where they had left him. Tub found him farther up the drive, lying on his stomach. "You okay?" Tub said.

"It hurts."

"Frank says it missed your appendix."

"I already had my appendix out."

"All right," Frank said, coming up to them. "We'll have you in a nice warm bed before you can say Jack Robinson." He put the two boards on Kenny's right side.

"Just as long as I don't have one of those male nurses," Kenny said.

"Ha ha," Frank said. "That's the spirit. Get ready, set, *over you go*," and he rolled Kenny onto the boards. Kenny screamed and kicked his legs in the air. When he quieted down Frank and Tub lifted the boards and carried him down the drive. Tub had the back end, and with the snow blowing into his face he had trouble with his footing. Also he was tired and the man inside had forgotten to turn the porch light on. Just past the house Tub slipped and threw out his hands to catch himself. The boards fell and Kenny tumbled out and rolled to the bottom of the drive, yelling all the way. He came to rest against the right front wheel of the truck.

"You fat moron," Frank said. "You aren't good for diddly."

Tub grabbed Frank by the collar and backed him hard up against the fence. Frank tried to pull his hands away but Tub shook him and snapped his head back and forth and finally Frank gave up.

"What do you know about fat," Tub said. "What do you know about glands." As he spoke he kept shaking Frank. "What do you know about me."

"All right," Frank said.

"No more," Tub said.

"All right."

"No more talking to me like that. No more watching. No more laughing."

"Okay, Tub. I promise."

Tub let go of Frank and leaned his forehead against the fence. His arms hung straight at his sides.

"I'm sorry, Tub." Frank touched him on the shoulder. "I'll be down at the truck."

Tub stood by the fence for a while and then got the rifles off the porch. Frank had rolled Kenny back onto the boards and they lifted him into the bed of the truck. Frank spread the seat blankets over him. "Warm enough?" he asked.

Kenny nodded.

"Okay. Now how does reverse work on this thing?"

"All the way to the left and up." Kenny sat up as Frank started forward to the cab. "Frank!"

"What?"

"If it sticks don't force it."

The truck started right away. "One thing," Frank said, "you've got to hand it to the Japanese. A very ancient, very spiritual culture and they can still make a hell out of a truck." He glanced over at Tub. "Look, I'm sorry. I didn't know you felt that way, honest to God I didn't. You should have said something."

"I did."

"When? Name one time."

"A couple of hours ago."

"I guess I wasn't paying attention."

"That's true, Frank," Tub said. "You don't pay attention very much."

"Tub," Frank said, "what happened back there, I should have been more sympathetic. I realize that. You were going through a lot. I just want you to know it wasn't your fault. He was asking for it."

"You think so?"

"Absolutely. It was him or you. I would have done the same thing in your shoes, no question."

The wind was blowing into their faces. The snow was a moving white wall in front of their lights; it swirled into the cab through the hole in the windshield and settled on them. Tub clapped his hands and shifted around to stay warm, but it didn't work.

"I'm going to have to stop," Frank said. "I can't feel my fingers."

Up ahead they saw some lights off the road. It was a tavern. Outside in the parking lot there were several jeeps and trucks. A couple of them had deer strapped across their hoods. Frank parked and they went back to Kenny. "How you doing, partner," Frank said.

"I'm cold."

"Well, don't feel like the Lone Ranger. It's worse inside, take my word for it. You should get that windshield fixed."

"Look," Tub said, "he threw the blankets off." They were lying in a heap against the tailgate.

"Now look, Kenny," Frank said, "it's no use whining about being cold if you're not going to try and keep warm. You've got to do your share." He spread the blankets over Kenny and tucked them in at the corners.

"They blew off."

"Hold on to them then."

"Why are we stopping, Frank?"

"Because if me and Tub don't get warmed up we're going to freeze solid and then where will you be?" He punched Kenny lightly in the arm. "So just hold your horses."

The bar was full of men in colored jackets, mostly orange. The waitress brought coffee. "Just what the doctor ordered," Frank said, cradling the steaming cup in his hand. His skin was bone white. "Tub, I've been thinking. What you said about me not paying attention, that's true."

"It's okay."

"No. I really had that coming. I guess I've just been a little too interested in old number one. I've had a lot on my mind. Not that that's any excuse."

"Forget it, Frank. I sort of lost my temper back there. I guess we're all a little on edge."

Frank shook his head. "It isn't just that."

"You want to talk about it?"

"Just between us, Tub?"

"Sure, Frank. Just between us."

"Tub, I think I'm going to be leaving Nancy."

"Oh, Frank. Oh, Frank." Tub sat back and shook his head.

Frank reached out and laid his hand on Tub's arm. "Tub, have you ever been really in love?"

"Well—"

"I mean *really* in love." He squeezed Tub's wrist. "With your whole being."

"I don't know. When you put it like that, I don't know."

"You haven't then. Nothing against you, but you'd know it if you had." Frank let go of Tub's arm. "This isn't just some bit of fluff I'm talking about."

"Who is she, Frank?"

Frank paused. He looked into his empty cup. "Roxanne Brewer."

"Cliff Brewer's kid? The babysitter?"

"You can't just put people into categories like that, Tub. That's why the whole system is wrong. And that's why this country is going to hell in a rowboat."

"But she can't be more than—" Tub shook his head.

"Fifteen. She'll be sixteen in May." Frank smiled. "May fourth, three twenty-seven p.m. Hell, Tub, a hundred years ago she'd have been an old maid by that age. Juliet was only thirteen."

"Juliet? Juliet Miller? Jesus, Frank, she doesn't even have breasts. She doesn't even wear a top to her bathing suit. She's still collecting frogs."

"Not Juliet Miller. The real Juliet. Tub, don't you see how you're dividing people up into categories? He's an executive, she's a secretary, he's a truck driver, she's fifteen years old. Tub, this so-called babysitter, this so-called fifteen-year-old has more in her little finger than most of us have in our entire bodies. I can tell you this little lady is something special."

Tub nodded. "I know the kids like her."

"She's opened up whole worlds to me that I never knew were there."

"What does Nancy think about all of this?"

"She doesn't know."

"You haven't told her?"

"Not yet. It's not so easy. She's been damned good to me all these years. Then there's the kids to consider." The brightness in Frank's eyes trembled and he wiped quickly at them with the back of his hand. "I guess you think I'm a complete bastard."

"No, Frank. I don't think that."

"Well, you *ought* to."

"Frank, when you've got a friend it means you've always got someone on your side, no matter what. That's the way I feel about it, anyway."

"You mean that, Tub?"

"Sure I do."

Frank smiled. "You don't know how good it feels to hear you say that."

Kenny had tried to get out of the truck but he hadn't made it. He was jack-knifed over the tailgate, his head hanging above the bumper. They lifted him back into the bed and covered him again. He was sweating and his teeth chattered. "It hurts, Frank."

"It wouldn't hurt so much if you just stayed put. Now we're going to the hospital. Got that? Say it—I'm going to the hospital."

"I'm going to the hospital."

"Again."

"I'm going to the hospital."

"Now just keep saying that to yourself and before you know it we'll be there."

After they had gone a few miles Tub turned to Frank. "I just pulled a real boner," he said.

"What's that?"

"I left the directions on the table back there."

"That's okay. I remember them pretty well."

The snowfall lightened and the clouds began to roll back off the fields, but it was no warmer and after a time both Frank and Tub were bitten through and shaking. Frank almost didn't make it around a curve, and they decided to stop at the next roadhouse.

There was an automatic hand-dryer in the bathroom and they took turns standing in front of it, opening their jackets and shirts and letting the jet of hot air breathe across their faces and chests.

"You know," Tub said, "what you told me back there, I appreciate it. Trusting me."

Frank opened and closed his fingers in front of the nozzle. "The way I look at it, Tub, no man is an island. You've got to trust someone."

"Frank—"

Frank waited.

"When I said that about my glands, that wasn't true. The truth is I just shovel it in."

"Well, Tub—"

"Day and night, Frank. In the shower. On the freeway." He turned and let the air play over his back. "I've even got stuff in the paper towel machine at work."

"There's nothing wrong with your glands at all?" Frank had taken his boots and socks off. He held first his right, then his left foot up to the nozzle.

"No. There never was."

"Does Alice know?" The machine went off and Frank started lacing up his boots.

"Nobody knows. That's the worst of it, Frank. Not the being fat, I never got any big kick out of being thin, but the lying. Having to lead a double life like a spy or a hit man. This sounds strange but I feel sorry for those guys, I really do. I know what they go through. Always having to think about what you say and do. Always feeling like people are watching you, trying to catch you at something. Never able to just be yourself. Like when I make a big deal about only having an orange for breakfast and then scarf all the way to work. Oreos, Mars Bars, Twinkies. Sugar Babies. Snickers." Tub glanced at Frank and looked quickly away. "Pretty disgusting, isn't it?"

"Tub. Tub." Frank shook his head. "Come on." He took Tub's arm and led him into the restaurant half of the bar. "My friend is hungry," he told the waitress. "Bring four orders of pancakes, plenty of butter and syrup."

"Frank—"

"Sit down."

When the dishes came Frank carved out slabs of butter and just laid them on the pancakes. Then he emptied the bottle of syrup, moving it back and forth over the plates. He leaned forward on his elbows and rested his chin in one hand. "Go on, Tub."

Tub ate several mouthfuls, then started to wipe his lips. Frank took the napkin away from him. "No wiping," he said. Tub kept at it. The syrup covered his chin; it dripped to a point like a goatee. "Weigh in, Tub," Frank said, pushing another fork across the table. "Get down to business." Tub took the fork in his left hand and lowered his head and started really chowing down. "Clean your plate," Frank said when the pancakes were gone, and Tub lifted each of the four plates and licked it clean. He sat back, trying to catch his breath.

"Beautiful," Frank said. "Are you full?"

"I'm full," Tub said. "I've never been so full."

Kenny's blankets were bunched up against the tailgate again.

"They must have blown off," Tub said.

"They're not doing him any good," Frank said. "We might as well get some use out of them."

Kenny mumbled. Tub bent over him. "What? Speak up."

"I'm going to the hospital," Kenny said.

"Attaboy," Frank said.

The blankets helped. The wind still got their faces and Frank's hands but it was much better. The fresh snow on the road and the trees sparkled under the beam of the headlight. Squares of light from farmhouse windows fell onto the blue snow in the fields.

"Frank," Tub said after a time, "you know that farmer? He told Kenny to kill the dog."

"You're kidding!" Frank leaned forward, considering. "That Kenny. What a card." He laughed and so did Tub. Tub smiled out the back window. Kenny lay with his arms folded over his stomach, moving his lips at the stars. Right overhead was the Big Dipper, and behind, hanging between Kenny's toes in the direction of the hospital, was the North Star, Pole Star, Help to Sailors. As the truck twisted through the gentle hills the star went back and forth between Kenny's boots, staying always in his sight. "I'm going to the hospital," Kenny said. But he was wrong. They had taken a different turn a long way back.

Suggestions for Discussion

1. What details of appearance, what habits of speech, reveal these characters as typical, and of what? How important is Tub's appearance to his character and to his relations with the others?

2. The opening scene is full of action in the sense of movement. Analyze it in terms of discovery and decision.

3. Find several examples of *no-dialogue*. What is being conveyed besides information? Where can the dialogue be considered dramatic action?

4. Identify several scenes where what the characters say is in conflict with what they do. What is the effect in each case?

5. What does each of the three hunters want? How does that desire lead backward to an example of behavior for each?

6. Like chapter 5 of this book, Frank lectures against dividing people into types (page 160). How does this lecture reveal his moral purpose? What judgments does our awareness of purpose invite toward the characters?

7. Character is revealed in this story almost entirely by direct methods. But the last sentence is suddenly in the mode of authorial interpretation. Why do you think the author chose this effect?

My Man Bovanne

TONI CADE BAMBARA

Blind people got a hummin jones if you notice. Which is understandable completely once you been around one and notice what no eyes will force you into to see people, and you get past the first time, which seems to come out of nowhere, and it's like you in church again with fat-chest ladies and old gents gruntin a hum low in the throat to whatever the preacher be saying. Shakey Bee bottom lip all swole up with Sweet Peach and me explainin how come the sweet-potato bread was a dollar–quarter this time stead of dollar regular and he say uh hunh he understand, then he break into this thizzin kind of hum which is quiet, but fiercesome just the same, if you ain't ready for it. Which I wasn't. But I got used to it and the onliest time I had to say somethin bout it was when he was playin checkers on the stoop one time and he commenst to hummin quite churchy seem to me. So I says, "Look here Shakey Bee, I can't beat you and Jesus too." He stop.

So that's how come I asked My Man Bovanne to dance. He ain't my man mind you, just a nice ole gent from the block that we all know cause he fixes things and the kids like him. Or used to fore Black Power got hold their minds and mess em around till they can't be civil to ole folks. So we at this benefit for my niece's cousin who's runnin for somethin with this Black party somethin or other behind her. And I press up close to dance with Bovanne who blind and I'm hummin and he hummin, chest to chest like talkin. Not jammin my breasts into the man. Wasn't bout tits. Was about vibrations. And he dug it and asked me what color dress I had on and how my hair was fixed and how I was doin without a man, not nosy but nice-like, and who was at this affair and was the canaps dainty-stingy or healthy enough to get hold of proper. Comfy and cheery is what I'm tryin to get across. Touch talkin like the heel of the hand on the tambourine or on a drum.

But right away Joe Lee come up on us and frown for dancin so close to the man. My own son who knows what kind of warm I am about; and don't grown men all call me long distance and in the middle of the night for a little Mama comfort? But he frown. Which ain't right since Bovanne can't see and defend himself. Just a nice old man who fixes toasters and busted irons and bicycles and things and changes the lock on my door when my men friends get messy. Nice man. Which is not why they invited him. Grass roots you see. Me and Sister Taylor and the woman who does heads at Mamies and the man from the barber shop, we all there on account of we grass roots. And I ain't never been souther than Brooklyn Battery and no more country than the window box on my fire escape. And just yesterday my kids tellin me to take them countrified rags off my head and be cool. And now can't get Black enough to suit 'em. So everybody passin sayin My Man Bovanne. Big deal, keep steppin and don't even stop a minute to get the man a drink or one of them cute sandwiches or tell him what's goin on. And him standin there with a smile ready case someone do speak he want to be ready. So that's how come I pull him on the dance floor and we dance squeezin past the tables and chairs and all them coats and people standin round up in each other face talkin bout this and that but got no use for this blind man who mostly fixed skates and skooters for all these folks when they were just kids. So I'm pressed up close and we touch talkin with the hum. And here come my daughter cuttin her eye at me like she do when she tell me about my "apolitical" self like I got hoof and mouf disease and there ain't no hope at all. And I don't pay her no mind and just look up in Bovanne shadow face and tell him his stomach like a drum and he laugh. Laugh real loud. And here come my youngest, Task, with a tap on my elbow like he the third grade monitor and I'm cuttin up on the line to assembly.

"I was just talkin on the drums," I explained when they hauled me into the kitchen. I figured drums was my best defense. They can get ready for drums what with all this heritage business. And Bovanne stomach just like that drum Task give me when he come back from Africa. You just touch it and it hum thizzm, thizzm. So I stuck to the drum story. "Just drummin that's all."

"Mama, what are you talkin about?

"She had too much to drink," say Elo to Task cause she don't hardly say nuthin to me direct no more since that ugly argument about my wigs.

"Look here Mama," say Task, the gentle one. "We just trying to pull your coat. You were makin a spectacle of yourself out there dancing like that."

"Dancin like what?"

Task run a hand over his left ear like his father for the world and his father before that.

"Like a bitch in heat," say Elo.

"Well uhh, I was goin to say like one of them sex-starved ladies gettin on in years and not too discriminating. Know what I mean?"

I don't answer cause I'll cry. Terrible thing when your own children talk to you like that. Pullin me out the party and hustlin me into some stranger's kitchen in the back of a bar just like the damn police. And ain't like I'm old old. I can still wear me some sleeveless dresses without the meat hangin off my arm. And I keep up with some thangs through my kids. Who ain't kids no more. To hear them tell it. So I don't say nuthin.

"Dancin with that tom," say Elo to Joe Lee, who leanin on the folks' freezer. "His feet can smell a cracker a mile away and go into their shuffle number post haste. And them eyes. He could be a little considerate and put on some shades. Who wants to look into them blown-out fuses that—"

"Is this what they call the generation gap?" I say.

"Generation gap," spits Elo, like I suggested castor oil and fricassee possum in the milk-shakes or somethin. "That's a white concept for a white phenomenon. There's no generation gap among Black people. We are a col—"

"Yeh, well never mind," says Joe Lee. "The point is Mama well, it's pride. You embarrass yourself and us too dancin like that."

"I wasn't shame." Then nobody say nuthin. Them standin there in they pretty clothes with drinks in they hands and gangin up on me, and me in the third-degree chair and nary a olive to my name. Felt just like the police got hold to me.

"First of all," Task say, holdin up his hand and tickin off the offenses, "the dress. Now that dress is too short, Mama, and too low-cut for a woman your age. And Tamu's going to make a speech tonight to kick off the campaign and will be introducin you and expecting you to organize the council of elders—"

"Me? Didn nobody ask me nuthin. You mean Nisi? She change her name?"

"Well, Norton was supposed to tell you about it. Nisi wants to introduce you and then encourage the older folks to form a Council of the Elders to act as an advisory—"

"And you going to be standing there with your boobs out and that wig on your head and that hem up to your ass. And people'll say, 'Ain't that the horny bitch that was grindin with the blind dude?'"

"Elo, be cool a minute," say Task, gettin to the next finger. "And then there's the drinkin. Mama, you know you can't drink cause next thing you know you be laughin loud and carryin on," and he grab another finger for the loudness. "And then there's the dancin. You been tattooed on the man for four records straight and slow draggin even on the fast numbers. How you think that look for a woman your age?"

"What's my age?"

"What?"

"I'm axin you all a simple question. You keep talkin bout what's proper for a woman my age. How old am I anyhow?" And Joe Lee slams his eyes shut and squinches up his face to figure. And Task run a hand over his ear and stare into his glass like the ice cubes goin calculate for him. And Elo just starin at the top of my head like she goin rip the wig off any minute now.

"Is your hair braided up under that thing? If so, why don't you take it off? You always did do a neat cornroll."

"Uh huh," cause I'm thinkin how she couldn't undo her hair fast enough talking bout cornroll so countrified. None of which was the subject. "How old, I say?"

"Sixtee-one or—"

"You a damn lie Joe Lee Peoples."

"And that's another thing," say Task on the fingers.

"You know what you all can kiss," I say, gettin up and brushin the wrinkles out my lap.

"Oh, Mama," Elo say, puttin a hand on my shoulder like she hasn't done since she left home and the hand landin light and not sure it supposed to be there. Which hurt me to my heart. Cause this was the child in our happiness fore Mr. Peoples die. And I carried that child strapped to my chest till she was nearly two. We was close is what I'm tryin to tell you. Cause it was more me in the child than the others. And even after Task it was the girlchild I covered in the night and wept over for no reason at all less it was she was a chub-chub like me and not very pretty, but a warm child. And how did things get to this, that she can't put a sure hand on me and say Mama we love you and care about you and you entitled to enjoy yourself cause you a good woman?

"And then there's Reverend Trent," say Task, glancin from left to right like they hatchin a plot and just now lettin me in on it. "You were suppose to be talking with him tonight, Mama, about giving us his basement for campaign headquarters and—"

"Didn nobody tell me nuthin. If grass roots mean you kept in the dark I can't use it. I really can't. And Reven Trent a fool anyway the way he tore into the widow man up there on Edgecomb cause he wouldn't take in three of them foster children and the woman not even comfy in the ground yet and the man's mind messed up and—"

"Look here," say Task. "What we need is a family conference so we can get all this stuff cleared up and laid out on the table. In the meantime I think we better get back into the other room and tend to business. And in the meantime, Mama, see if you can't get to Reverend Trent and—"

"You want me to belly rub with the Reven, that it?"

"Oh, damn," Elo say and go through the swingin door.

"We'll talk about all this at dinner. How's tomorrow night, Joe Lee?" While Joe Lee being self-important I'm wonderin who's doin the cookin and how come no body ax me if I'm free and do I get a corsage and things like that. Then Joe nod that it's O.K. and he go through the swingin door and just a little hubbub come through from the other room. Then Task smile his smile, lookin just like his daddy, and he leave. And it just me and this stranger's kitchen, which was a mess I wouldn't never let my kitchen look like. Poison you just to look at the pots. Then the door swing the other way and it's My Man Bovanne standin there sayin Miss Hazel but lookin at the deep fry and then at the steam table, and most surprised when I come up on him from the other direction and take him on out of there. Pass the folks pushin up towards the stage where Nisi and some other people settin and ready to talk, and folks gettin to the last of the sandwiches and the booze fore they settle down in one spot and listen serious. And I'm thinkin bout tellin Bovanne what a lovely long dress Nisi got on and the earrings and her hair piled up in a cone and the people bout to hear how we all gettin screwed and gotta form our own party and everybody there listenin and lookin. But instead I just haul the man on out of there, and Joe Lee and his wife look at me like I'm terrible, but they ain't said boo to the man yet. Cause he blind and old and don't nobody there need him since they grown up and don't need they skates fixed no more.

"Where we goin, Miss Hazel?" Him knowin all the time.

"First we gonna buy you some dark sunglasses. Then you comin with me to the supermarket so I can pick up tomorrow's dinner, which is goin to be a grand thing proper and you invited. Then we goin to my house."

"That be fine. I surely would like to rest my feet." Bein cute, but you got to let men play out they little show, blind or not. So he chat on bout how tired he is and how he appreciate me takin him in hand this way. And I'm thinkin I'll have him change the lock on my door first thing. Then I'll give the man a nice warm bath with jasmine leaves in the water and a little Epsom salt on the sponge to do his back. And then a good rubdown with rose water and olive oil. Then a cup of lemon tea with a taste in it. And a little talcum, some of that fancy stuff Nisi mother sent over last Christmas. And then a massage, a good face massage round the forehead which is the worryin part. Cause you gots to take care of the older folks. And let them know they still needed to run the mimeo machine and keep the spark plugs clean and fix the mailboxes for folks who might help us get the breakfast program goin, and the school for the little kids and the campaign and all. Cause old folks in the nation. That what Nisi was sayin and I mean to do my part.

"I imagine you are a very pretty woman, Miss Hazel."

"I surely am," I say just like the hussy my daughter always say I was.

Suggestions for Discussion

1. Bambara makes use of some dialect misspellings (including the dropping of *g*'s I've advised against), but the voice of her narrator is fundamentally achieved by other means. How is Hazel characterized by her syntax? Her vocabulary? Her imagery?

2. How does the dialogue of the children differentiate them from Hazel? From each other?

3. One of the difficulties of a story told in the first person is that the narrator can't describe herself from the outside. How does Hazel let us know what she looks like?

4. Take any passage of dialogue between mother and children and observe how consistently the characters are saying "no" to each other.

5. Identify moments of decision and discovery in the pattern of changes. How does Hazel change?

6. Where are Hazel's thoughts in contrast to her speech, action, and/or appearance?

Retrospect

1. Arnold Friend is characterized in "Where Are You Going, Where Have You Been?" pages 87-88 by appearance, action and speech. Identify each. Is there a conflict employed between the methods?

2. How do the speech and actions of the doctor in "The Use of Force" contrast with his thoughts? What would be lost in this story if we did not know his thoughts?

3. How does what's going on in Kurt's mind in "The Point" contradict both his speech and his behavior? Could this story be told without this contrast?

4. Frank O'Connor was very much concerned with the voices of his characters. Between the first publication of "Guests of the Nation" in 1931 and the final version of 1954, he did away with the phonetic misspellings of his Cockney characters' dialect. Here is a sample of the early version:

> "Well, Bonaparte, Mary Brigid Ho'Connell was arskin' about you and said 'ow you'd a pair of socks belonging to 'er young brother.

Compare this to the final version on page 47. How is the character of Hawkins altered even in this very brief passage?

Writing Assignments

1. Write a scene in which a character speaks politely or enthusiastically but whose thoughts run in strong contradiction. Characterize the listener by appearance, action, and dialogue.

2. Write a scene in which the central character does something palpably outrageous—violent, cruel, foolhardy, obscene. Let us, because we see into his or her mind, know that the character is behaving justly, kindly, or reasonably.

3. Write a character sketch describing the character both in generalizations (authorial interpretation) and in specific details. Let the details contradict the generalizations. ("Larry was the friendliest kid on the block. He had a collection of brass knucks he would let you see for fifty cents, and he would let you cock his BB gun for him as long as you were willing to hold the target.")

4. Write a scene in which a man (or boy) questions a woman (or girl) about her mother. Characterize all three.

5. Two friends are in love with the same person. One describes his or her feelings honestly and well; the other is unwilling or unable to do so, but betrays his or her feelings through appearance and action. Write the scene.

6. A class assignment. Each person folds a sheet of paper in four. Hold it so that one fold is down the center of the nose, the other across the middle of the eye. Grasp it in front of the eye, then tear out a small hole at that spot. Unfold the paper and draw a mask. Exchange them. Name the character you now have, and on the reverse side of the paper write a brief description of the character behind the mask. Go round the room, each person asking a question that can be answered for each character. (*Where was s/he born? How does s/he feel about rain? What is her/his first*

memory/favorite food, and so forth.) Write the answers on the mask. Discuss what happened in the process.

7. Nearly every writer under pressure of a deadline at some point succumbs to the temptation of writing a story about writing a story. These stories are rarely successful because they offer so few possibilities of external conflict and lively characterization. So write this story: You must write a short story, and you must therefore get your major character to do whatever he or she is to do in the story. But the character is too lazy, irritable, sick, suicidal, cruel, stupid, frivolous, or having too good a time. You must trick, cajole, or force the character into the story. Do you succeed?

6

LONG AGO AND FAR AWAY
Fictional Place and Time

- *Setting and Atmosphere*
- *Some Aspects of Narrative Time*

Our relation to place, time, and weather, like our relation to clothes and other objects, is charged with emotion more or less subtle, more or less profound. It is filled with judgment mellow or harsh. And it alters according to what happens to us. In some rooms you are always trapped; you enter them with grim purpose and escape them as soon as you can. Others invite you to settle in, to nestle or carouse. Some landscapes lift your spirits; others depress you. Cold weather gives you energy and bounce, or else it clogs your head and makes you huddle, struggling. You describe yourself as a night person or a morning person. The house you loved as a child now makes you, precisely because you were once happy there, think of loss and death.

All such emotion can be used or heightened (or invented) to dramatic effect in fiction. Just as significant detail calls up a sense impression and also an abstraction, so the setting and atmosphere of a story impart both information and emotion. Likewise, just as the rhythm of your prose must work with and not against your intention, so the use of narrative place and time must work with and not against your ultimate meaning.

As I write, part of me is impatient with these speculations. Dully aware that every discussion of the elements of fiction includes of necessity the notions of atmosphere, setting, flashback and so on, I have an impulse to deal with the matter summarily and get on to the next chapter. Events occur in time and through time; people move in space and through space. Therefore, let your story occur during some time and in some place, and take some attitude or other.

But part of me is aware of a dull March day outside my window, a stubbled field of muddy snow, the students' heels sucked by the thawing path, the rubble of win-

171

ter without any sign that the contract for spring is in the mail. The river is frozen to the bridge and breaking up fitfully below; ice fidgets at the bank. This morning, stretching too far in a series of sit-ups, I pulled my back out of joint, and now my movements are confined; my spine reaches cautiously for the back of the chair, and my hand moves gingerly toward my tea. The dullness in myself looks for dullness in the day, finds it, and creates it there.

And so, observing this, part of me is impelled toward awe at the boundaries of time and space imposed on human beings and on their fictions, and yet always pulling them toward a wider context. Why must a story be set during some time and in some place, and why does the choice inevitably matter? Psychologists have determined that one of the earliest processes of a child's mental development is the differentiation between self and other. Until the infant discovers that its mother is not itself, it has no sense of self as we know it. Yet even before this discovery it has instinctive reactions to the elements, to warmth, cold, damp. As the mind develops it becomes aware of its environment, both social and physical, and hard on the heels of this awareness comes the attempt to control and manipulate: crying for mama, grasping the bars of the crib.

Biologists point out that the cells of our blood and bodies change according to the season, like the sap of trees, so that spring fever is a physical fact. The blood will thin and thicken in response to climate on the zones of the globe. The pupils of our eyes expand at night, contract by day.

Some linguists posit the theory that language itself originates in prepositions— that is, that spatial and temporal relationships are the primary function of the mind, and our perceptions of *above, below, before, after, toward, beyond* precede any other element in the structure of logical expression. If this is so, then it would suggest that our need to know and express *where* and *when* are at the core of our humanity, the form of communication that differentiates us from all other species. If this seems far-fetched, take this paragraph or any other and try making sense of it without the prepositional phrases.

Setting and Atmosphere

Your fiction must have an *atmosphere* because without it your characters will be unable to breathe.

Part of the atmosphere of a scene or story is its setting, including the locale, period, weather, time of day. Part of the atmosphere is its *tone*, an attitude taken by the narrative voice that can be described in terms of a quality—sinister, facetious, formal, solemn, wry. The two facets of atmosphere, setting and tone, are often inextricably mixed in the ultimate effect: a sinister atmosphere might be achieved partly by syntax, rhythm, and word choice; partly by night, dampness and a desolated landscape.

You can orient your reader in place and time with straight information (*"On the southern bank of the Bayou Teche in the fall of '69 . . . "*), but as with the revelation of character, you may more effectively reveal place and time through concrete detail (*"The bugs hung over the black water in clusters of a steady hum."*) Here the information is indirect and we may have to wait for some of it, but the experience is direct. This technique of dropping us immediately into the scene (famously parodied by Snoopy in *Peanuts* as "It was a dark and stormy night") inevitably reveals an attitude toward the setting and produces an atmosphere.

HARMONY AND CONFLICT
BETWEEN CHARACTER AND BACKGROUND

If character is the foreground of fiction, setting is the background, and as in a painting's composition, the foreground may be in harmony or in conflict with the background. If we think of the Impressionist paintings of the late nineteenth century, we think of the harmony of, say, women with light-scattering parasols strolling against summer landscapes of light-scattering trees. By contrast, the Spanish painter Jose Cortijo has a portrait of a girl on her Communion day; she sits curled and ruffled, in a lace mantilla, on an ornately carved Mediterranean throne against a backdrop of stark, harshly lit, poverty-stricken shacks.

Likewise the setting and characters of a story may be in harmony:

> The Bus to St. James's—a Protestant Episcopal school for boys and girls—started its round at eight o'clock in the morning, from a corner of Park Avenue in the Sixties. The earliness of the hour meant that some of the parents who took their children there were sleepy and still without coffee, but with a clear sky the light struck the city at an extreme angle, the air was fresh, and it was an exceptionally cheerful time of day. It was the hour when cooks and door men walk dogs, and when porters scrub the lobby floor mats with soap and water.
>
> -John Cheever, *"The Bus to St. James's"*

Or there can be a inherent conflict between the background and foreground:

> . . . He opened the door himself and started down the walk to get her going. The sky was a dying violet and the houses stood out darkly against it, bulbous liver-colored monstrosities of a uniform ugliness though no two were alike. Since this had been a fashionable neighborhood forty years ago, his mother persisted in thinking they did well to have an apartment in it. Each house had a narrow collar of dirt around it in which sat, usually, a grubby child. Julian walked with his hands in his pockets, his head down and thrust forward and his eyes glazed with the determination to make himself completely numb during the time he would be sacrificed to her pleasure.
>
> -Flannery O'Connor, *"Everything That Rises Must Converge"*

Notice how images of the time of day work with concrete details of place to create very different atmospheres—on the one hand *morning, Park Avenue, earliness, clear sky, light, extreme angle, air, fresh, cheerful, dogs, scrub, soap, water;* and on the other *dying violet, darkly, bulbous liver-colored monstrosities, uniform ugliness, narrow, dirt, grubby child.* Notice also that where conflict occurs, there is already "narrative content," or the makings of a story. We might reasonably expect that in the Cheever story, where the characters are in apparent harmony with their background, there is or will be conflict between or among those children, parents, and perhaps the servitors who keep their lives so well scrubbed. It won't surprise us, toward the end of the story, to see this contrast between weather and narrative mood: ". . . Mr. Bruce led her out the door into the freshness of a winter evening, holding her, supporting her really, for she might have fallen."

SYMBOLIC AND SUGGESTIVE SETTING

Whether there is conflict between character and setting or the conflict takes place entirely in the foreground, within, between, or among the characters, the setting is important to our understanding of character type and of what to expect, as well as to the emotional value that arises from the conflict. As we need to know a character's gender, race, and age, we need to know in what atmosphere she or he operates to understand the significance of the action.

Since the rosy-fingered dawn came over the battlefield of Homer's *Iliad* (and no doubt well before that), poets and writers have used the context of history, night, storm, stars, sea, city, and plain to give their stories a sense of reaching out toward the universe. Sometimes the universe resonates with an answer. In his plays Shakespeare consistently drew parallels between the conflicts of the heavenly bodies and the conflicts of nations and characters. Whether or not an author deliberately uses this correspondence to suggest the influence of the macrocosm on the microcosm, a story's setting can give the significant sense of other without which, as in an infant's consciousness, there is no valid sense of self.

In "The Life You Save May Be Your Own," Flannery O'Connor uses the elements in a conscious Shakespearian way, letting the setting reflect and effect the theme.

> The old woman and her daughter were sitting on their own porch when Mr. Shiflet came up their road for the first time. The old woman slid to the edge of her chair and leaned forward, shading her eyes from the piercing sunset with her hand. The daughter could not see far in front of her and continued to play with her fingers. Although the old woman lived in this desolate spot with only her daughter, and she had never seen Mr. Shiflet before, she could tell, even from a distance, that he was a tramp and no one to be afraid of. His left coat sleeve was folded up to show there was only half an arm in it and his gaunt figure listed lightly to the side as if the breeze were pushing him. He had on a black town suit and a brown felt hat that was turned up in the front and down in the back and he carried a tin tool box by a handle. He came on at an amble, up her road, his face turned toward the sun which appeared to be balancing itself on the peak of a small mountain.

The focus in this opening paragraph of the story is on the characters and their actions, and the setting is economically, almost incidentally established: *porch, road, sunset, breeze, peak, small mountain.* What the passage gives us is a type of landscape, rural and harsh; the only adjectives in the description of the setting are *piercing, desolate,* and *small.* But this general background works together with details of action, thought, and appearance to establish a great deal more that is both informational and emotional. The old woman's peering suggests that people on the road are not only unusual but suspicious. On the other hand, that she is reassured to see a tramp suggests both a period and a set of assumptions about country life. That Mr. Shiflet wears a town suit establishes him as a stranger to this set of assumptions. That the sun appeared to be balancing itself (we are not sure whether it is the old woman's observation or the author's) leaves us, at the end of the paragraph, with a sense of anticipation and tension.

Now, what happens in the story is this: Mr. Shiflet repairs the old woman's car and (in order to get the car) marries her retarded daughter. He abandons the daughter on their honeymoon and picks up a hitchhiker who insults both Mr. Shiflet and the memory of his mother. The hitchhiker jumps out. Mr. Shiflet curses and drives on.

Throughout the story, as in the first paragraph, the focus remains on the characters and their actions. Yet the landscape and the weather make their presence felt, subtly commenting on attitudes and actions. As Mr. Shiflet's fortunes wax promising and he expresses satisfaction with his own morality, "A fat yellow moon appeared in the branches of the fig tree as if it were going to roost there with the chickens." When, hatching his plot, he sits on the steps with the mother and daughter, "The old woman's three mountains were black against the sky." Once he has abandoned the girl, the weather grows "hot and sultry, and the country had flattened out. Deep in the sky a storm was preparing very slowly and without thunder." Once more there is a sunset, but this time the sun "was a reddening ball that through his windshield was slightly flat on the bottom and top," and this deflated sun reminds us of the "balanced" one about to be punctured by the peak in its inevitable decline. When the hitchhiker has left him, a cloud covers the sun, and Mr. Shiflet in his fury prays for the Lord to "break forth and wash the slime from this earth!" His prayer is apparently answered.

> After a few minutes there was a guffawing peal of thunder from behind and fantastic raindrops, like tin-can tops, crashed over the rear of Mr. Shiflet's car. Very quickly he stepped on the gas and with his stump sticking out the window he raced the galloping shower to Mobile.

The setting in this story, as this bald summary emphasizes, is deliberately used as a comment on the actions. The behavior of the elements, in ironic juxtaposition to the title, "The Life You Save May Be Your Own", makes clear that the "slime" Mr. Shiflet has damned may be himself. Yet the reader is never aware of this as a symbolic intrusion. The setting remains natural and realistically convincing, an incidental backdrop, until the heavens are ready to make their guffawing comment.

Robert Coover's settings rarely present a symbolic or sentient universe, but they produce in us an emotionally charged expectation of what is likely to happen here. The following passages are the opening paragraphs of three short stories from a single collection, *Pricksongs and Descants*. Notice how the three different settings are achieved not only by imagery and content, but also by the very different rhythms of the sentence structure.

A pine forest in the midafternoon. Two children follow an old man, dropping breadcrumbs, singing nursery tunes. Dense earthy greens seep into the darkening distance, flecked and streaked with filtered sunlight. Spots of red, violet, pale blue, gold, burnt orange. The girl carries a basket for gathering flowers. The boy is occupied with the crumbs. Their song tells of God's care for little ones.

"The Gingerbread House"

Situation: television panel game, live audience. Stage strobelit and cameras insecting about. Moderator, bag shape corseted and black suited behind desk/rostrum, blinking mockmodesty at lens and lamps, practised pucker on his soft mouth and brows arched in mild goodguy astonishment. Opposite him, the panel: Aged Clown, Lovely Lady and Mr. America, fat as the continent and bald as an eagle. There is an empty chair between Lady and Mr. A, which is now filled, to the delighted squeals of all, by a spectator dragged protesting from the Audience, nondescript introduced as Unwilling Participant, or more simply, Bad Sport. Audience: same as ever, docile, responsive, good-natured, terrifying. And the Bad Sport, you ask, who is he? fool! thou art!

"Panel Game"

She arrives at 7:40, ten minutes late, but the children, Jimmy and Bitsy, are still eating supper, and their parents are not ready to go yet. From the other rooms come the sounds of a baby screaming, water running, a television musical (no words: probably a dance number—patterns of gliding figures come to mind). Mrs. Tucker sweeps into the kitchen, fussing with her hair, and snatches a baby bottle full of milk out of a pan of warm water, rushes out again. Harry! she calls. The babysitter's here already!

"The Babysitter"

Here are three quite familiar places: a fairy-tale forest, a television studio, and a suburban house. In at least the first two selections, the locale is more consciously and insistently set than in the O'Connor opening, yet all three remain suggestive backdrops rather than active participants. Coover directs our attitude toward these places through imagery and tone. The forest is a neverland, and the time is once upon a time, though there are grimmer than Grimm hints of violence about it. The television studio is a place of hysteria, chaos, and hypocrisy, whereas the American suburbia, where presumably such television shows are received, is boring rather than chaotic, not hysterical but merely hassled in a predictable sort of way.

In "The Gingerbread House," simple sentence structure helps establish the childlike quality appropriate to a fairy tale. But a more complex sentence intervenes, with surprising intensity of imagery: *dense, earthy, seep, darkening, flecked, streaked, filtered.* Because of this, the innocence of the tone is set askew, so that by the time we hear of God's care for little ones, we fully and accurately expect a brutal disillusionment.

Note that although all fiction is bounded by place and time, the place and time may perfectly well be no place and outside time. The failure to create an atmosphere, to establish a sense of where or when the story takes place, always leaves us bored or confused. But an intensely created fantasy world makes new boundaries for the mind. *Once upon a time, long ago and far away, a dream, hell, heaven, time warp, black hole,* and *the subconscious* all have been the settings of excellent fiction. Outer space is an exciting setting precisely because its physical boundary is the outer edge of our familiar world. Obviously this does not absolve the writer from the necessity of giving outer space its own characteristics, atmosphere, and logic. If anything, these must be more intensely realized within the fiction, since we have less to borrow from in our own experience.

Setting can often, and in a variety of ways, arouse reader expectation and foreshadow events to come. In "The Gingerbread House," there is an implied conflict between character and setting, between the sentimentality of the children's flowers and nursery tunes and the threatening forest, so that we are immediately aware of the central conflict of the story: innocence versus violence.

But as in the Cheever passage quoted earlier, anticipation can also be aroused by an insistent single attitude toward setting, and in this case the reader, being a contrary sort of person, is likely to anticipate a change or paradox. The opening pages of E. M. Forster's *A Passage to India,* for instance, create an unrelenting portrait of the muddy dreariness of Chadrapore: *nothing extraordinary, rubbish, mean, ineffective, alleys, filth, made of mud, mud moving, abased, monotonous, rotting, swelling, shrinking, low but indestructible form of life.* The images are a little too one-sided, and as we might protest in life against a too fanatical condemnation of a place—isn't there anything good about it?—so we are led to expect (accurately again) that in the pages that follow, somehow beauty and mystery will break forth from the dross. Likewise but in the opposite way the opening pages of Woolf's *Mrs. Dalloway* burst with affirmation, the beauty of London and spring, love of life and love of life and love of life again! We suspect (accurately once more) that death and hatred lurk.

Where conflict between character and setting is immediately introduced, as it is in both "The Gingerbread House" and "Panel Game," it is usually because the character is unfamiliar with, or uncomfortable in, the setting. In "Panel Game" it's both. The television studio, which is in fact a familiar and unthreatening place to most of us, has been made mad. This is achieved partly by violating expected grammar. The sentences are not sentences. They are missing vital verbs and logical connectives, so that the images are squashed against each other. The prose is cluttered, effortful, negative; as a result, as reader you know the delighted squeals of all do not include your own, and you're ready to sympathize with the unwilling central character (you!).

ALIEN AND FAMILIAR SETTING

Many poets and novelists have observed that the function of literature is to make the ordinary fresh and strange. F. Scott Fitzgerald, on the other hand, advised a young writer that reporting extreme things as if they were ordinary was the starting point of fiction. Both of these views are true, and they are particularly true of setting. Whether a place is familiar or unfamiliar, comfortable or discomfiting in fiction has nothing to do with whether the reader actually knows the place and feels good there. It is an attitude taken, an assumption made. In his detective novels, Ross MacDonald assumes a familiarity toward California that is perfectly translatable into Japanese ("I turned left off the highway and down an old switchback blacktop to a dead end"), whereas even the natives of North Hollywood must feel alien on Tom Wolfe's version of their streets.

> . . . endless scorched boulevards lined with one-story stores, shops, bowling alleys, skating rinks, taco drive-ins, all of them shaped not like rectangles but like trapezoids, from the way the roofs slant up from the back and the plate-glass fronts slant out as if they're going to pitch forward on the sidewalk and throw up.

> *The Kandy-Kolored Tangerine-Flake Streamline Baby*

The prose of Tom Wolfe, whether about rural North Carolina, Fifth Avenue, or Cape Kennedy, lives in a tone of constant astonishment. Ray Bradbury's outer space is pure down-home.

> It was quiet in the deep morning of Mars, as quiet as a cool black well, with stars shining in the canal waters, and, breathing in every room, the children curled with their spiders in closed hands.

> Martian Chronicles

The setting of the passage from Coover's "The Babysitter" is ordinary and is presented as ordinary. The sentences have standard and rather leisurely syntax; neither form nor image startles. In fact, there are few details of the sort that produce interesting individuality: The house is presented without a style; the children are named but not seen; Mrs. Tucker behaves in a way predictable and familiar to anyone in late-twentieth-century America. What Coover has in fact done is to present us with a setting so usual that we begin to suspect that something unusual is afoot.

I have said of characterization that if the character is presented as typical, we would judge that character to be stupid or evil. The same is true of setting, but with results more varied and fruitful for an author's ultimate purpose. At the center of a fiction is a consciousness, one as individual and vital as the author can produce. If the setting remains dull and damnable, then there is conflict between character and setting, and this conflict can throw that individuality and vitality into relief. Many great stories and novels have relied on setting as a means of showing the intensity and variety of human consciousness by contrasting consciousness with a social or physical world that is rule-hampered, insincere, and routine. Gustave Flaubert's *Madame Bovary* comes instantly to mind: the fullness and exactitude of the portrait is partly achieved by the provinciality of the background. This provinciality, which is French and nineteenth century, remains typical to American readers of the 1990s, who are much more likely to have grown up in Coover's suburban house. It is Flaubert's tone that creates a sense of the familiar and the typical.

Much the same thing happens in "The Babysitter." The Tuckers, their house, their children, their car, their night out, and their babysitter remain unvaryingly typical through all the external actions in the course of the evening. Against this backdrop play the individual fantasies of the characters—brilliant, brutal, sexual, dangerous, and violent—which provides the conflict of the story.

One great advantage of being a writer is that you may create the world. Places and the elements have the significance and the emotional effect you give them in language. As a person you may be depressed by rain, but as an author you are free to make rain mean freshness, growth, bounty, and God. You may choose; the only thing you are not free to do is not to choose.

As with character, the first requisite of effective setting is to know it fully, to experience it mentally, and the second is to create it through significant detail. What sort of place is this, and what are its peculiarities? What is the weather like, the light, the season, the time of day? What are the contours of the land and architecture? What are the social assumptions of the inhabitants, and how familiar and comfortable are the characters with this place and its life-style? These things are not less important in fiction than in life, but more, since their selection inevitably takes on significance.

AN EXERCISE IN SETTING

Here are a series of passages about war, set in various periods and places. The first is in Russia during the campaign of Napoleon, the second in Italy during World War I, the third on the island of Pianosa during World War II, the fourth during the Vietnam War, the fifth in a post-holocaust future.

Compare the settings. How do climate, period, imagery, and language contribute to each? To what degree is setting a sentient force? Is there conflict between character and setting? How does setting affect and/or reveal the attitude taken toward the war?

Several tens of thousands of the slain lay in diverse postures and various uniforms. Over the whole field, previously so gaily beautiful with the glitter of bayonets and cloudlets of smoke in the morning sun, there now spread a mist of damp and smoke and a strange acid smell of saltpeter and blood. Clouds gathered and drops of rain began to fall on the dead and wounded, on the frightened, exhausted, and hesitating men, as if to say: Enough, men! Enough! Cease! Bethink yourselves! What are you doing?

Leo Tolstoy, *War and Peace*

In the late summer of that year we lived in a house in a village that looked across the river and plain to the mountains. In the bed of the river there were pebbles and boulders, dry and white in the sun, and the water was clear and swiftly moving and blue in the channels. Troops went by the house and down the road and the dust they raised powdered the leaves of the trees. The trunks of the trees too were dusty and the leaves fell early that year and we saw the troops marching along the road and the dust rising and leaves, stirred by the breeze, falling and the soldiers marching and afterward the road bare and white except for the leaves.

Ernest Hemingway, A *Farewell to Arms*

Their only hope was that it would never stop raining, and they had no hope because they all knew it would. When it did stop raining in Pianosa, it rained in Bologna. When it stopped raining in Bologna, it began again in Pianosa. If there was no rain at all, there were freakish, inexplicable phenomena like the epidemic of diarrhea or the bomb line that moved. Four times during the first six days they were assembled and briefed and then sent back. Once, they took off and were flying in formation when the control tower summoned them down. The more it rained, the worse they suffered. The worse they suffered, the more they prayed that it would continue raining.

Joseph Heller, *Catch-22*

The rain fed fungus that grew in the men's boots and socks, and their socks rotted, and their feet turned white and soft so that the skin could be scraped off with a fingernail, and Stink Harris woke up screaming one night with a leech on his tongue. When it was not raining, a low mist moved across the paddies, blending the elements into a single gray element, and the war was cold and pasty and rotten. Lieutenant Corson, who came to replace Lieutenant Sidney Martin, contracted the dysentery. The trip-flares were useless. The ammunition corroded and the foxholes filled with mud and water during the nights, and in the mornings there was always the next village and the war was the same.

Tim O'Brien, *Going After Cacciato*

She liked the wild, quatrosyllabic lilt of the word, Barbarian. Then, looking beyond the wooden fence, she saw a trace of movement in the fields beyond. It was not the wind among the young corn; or, if it was wind among the young corn, it carried her the whinny of a raucous horse. It was too early for poppies but she saw a flare of scarlet. She ceased to watch the Soldiers; instead she watched the movement flow to the fences and crash through them and across the tender wheat. Bursting from the undergrowth came horseman after horseman. They flashed with curious curved plates of metal dredged up from the ruins. Their horses were bizarrely caparisoned with rags, small knives, bells and chains dangling from manes and tails, and man and horse together, unholy centaurs crudely daubed with paint, looked twice as large as life. They fired long guns. Confronted with the terrors of the night in the freshest hours of the morning, the gentle crowd scattered, wailing.

Angela Carter, *Heroes and Villains*

Some Aspects of Narrative Time

Literature is, by virtue of its nature and subject matter, tied to time in a way the other arts are not. A painting represents a frozen instant in time, and the viewing time is a matter of the viewer's choice; no external limits are imposed in order to say that you have seen the painting. Music takes a certain time to hear, and the timing of the various parts is of utmost importance, but the time scheme is self-enclosed and makes no reference to time in the world outside itself. A book takes time to read, but the reader chooses his or her rate and may put it down and take it up at will. In narrative, the vital relationship to time is content time, the period covered in the story. It is quite possible to write a story that takes about twenty minutes to read and covers about twenty minutes of action (Jean-Paul Sartre performed experiments in this durational realism), but no one has suggested such a correspondence as a fictional requirement. Sometimes the period covered is telescoped, sometimes stretched. The history of the world up until now can be covered in a sentence; four seconds of crisis may take a chapter. It's even possible to do both at once: William Golding's entire novel *Pincher Martin* takes place between the time the drowning protagonist begins to take off his boots and the moment he dies with his boots still on. But when asked by a student, "How long does it really take?" Golding replied, "Eternity."

SUMMARY AND SCENE

Summary and *scene* are methods of treating time in fiction. A summary covers a relatively long period of time in relatively short compass; a scene deals at length with a relatively short period of time.

Summary is a useful and often necessary device: to give information, fill in a character's background, let us understand a motive, alter pace, create a transition, leap moments or years.

Scene is *always* necessary to fiction. Scene is to time what concrete detail is to the senses; that is, it is the crucial means of allowing your reader to experience the story with the characters. A confrontation, a turning point, or a crisis occurs at given moments that take on significance as moments and cannot be summarized. The form of a story requires confrontation, turning points, and crises, and therefore requires scenes.

It is quite possible to write a short story in a single scene, without any summary at all. It is not possible to write a successful story entirely in summary. One of the most common errors beginning fiction writers make is to summarize events rather than to realize them as moments.

In the following paragraph from Margaret Atwood's *Lady Oracle*, the narrator has been walking home from her Brownie troop with older girls who tease and terrify her with threats of a bad man.

> The snow finally changed to slush and then to water, which trickled down the hill of the bridge in two rivulets, one on either side of the path; the path itself turned to mud. The bridge was damp, it smelled rotten, the willow branches turned yellow, the skipping ropes came out. It was light again in the afternoons, and on one of them, when for a change Elizabeth hadn't run off but was merely discussing the possibilities with the others, a real man actually appeared.
>
> He was standing at the far side of the bridge, a little off the path, holding a bunch of daffodils in front of him. He was a nice-looking man, neither old nor young, wearing a good tweed coat, not at all shabby or disreputable. He didn't have a hat on, his taffy-colored hair was receding and the sunlight gleamed on his high forehead.

The first paragraph of this quotation covers the way things were over a period of a few months and then makes a transition to one of the afternoons; the second paragraph specifies a particular moment. Notice that although summary sets us at a distance from the action, sense details remain necessary to its life: *snow, path, bridge, willow branches, skipping ropes*. These become more sharply focused as we concentrate on the particular moment. More important, the scene is introduced when an element of conflict and confrontation occurs. That the threatened bad man does appear and that he is surprisingly innocuous promises a turn of events and a change in the relationship among the girls. We need to see the moment when this change occurs.

Throughout *Lady Oracle*, which is by no means unusual in this respect, the pattern recurs: a summary leading up to, and followed by, a scene that represents a turning point.

> My own job was fairly simple. I stood at the back of the archery range, wearing a red leather change apron, and rented out the arrows. When the

barrels of arrows were almost used up, I'd go down to the straw targets. The difficulty was that we couldn't make sure all the arrows had actually been shot before we went down to clear the targets. Rob would shout, Bows DOWN, please, arrows OFF the string, but occasionally someone would let an arrow go, on purpose or by accident. This was how I got shot. We'd pulled the arrows and the men were carrying the barrels back to the line; I was replacing a target face, and I'd just bent over.

The summaries in these two passages are of the two most common types, which I would call *sequential* and *circumstantial*, respectively. The summary in the first passage is sequential; it relates events in their sequence but compresses them: *snow finally changed to slush and then to water, willow branches turned yellow, and then skipping ropes came out;* the transition from winter to spring is made in a paragraph. The summary in the second excerpt is circumstantial because it describes the general circumstances during a period of time: This is how things were, this is what usually or frequently happened. The narrator in the second passage describes her job in such a way: *I stood at the back of the archery range. I'd go down to the straw targets. Rob would shout.* Again, when the narrator arrives at an event that changes her circumstance (*I got shot*), she focuses on a particular moment: *I was replacing a target face, and I'd just bent over.*

These two types of summary accurately represent two methods of the memory, which also drastically condenses. You might think of your past as a movement through time: *I was born in Arizona and lived there with my parents until I was eighteen; then I spent three years in New York before going on to England.* Or you might remember the way things were during a period of that time: *In New York we used to go down Broadway for a midnight snack, and Judy would always dare us to some nonsense or other before we got back.* But when you think of the events that significantly altered either the sequence or the circumstances of your life, your mind will present you with a scene: *Then one afternoon Professor Bovie stopped me in the hall after class and wagged his glasses at me. Had you thought about studying in England?*

Jerome Stern, in *Making Shapely Fiction*, astutely observes that like a child in a tantrum, when you want everyone's full attention you "make a scene," using the writer's full complement of "dialogue, physical reactions, gestures, smells, sounds, and thoughts."

Frequently, the function of summary is precisely to heighten scene. It is in the scene, the "present" of the story that the drama, the discovery, the decision, the potential for change, engage our attention. But summary may be used within such a scene to suggest contrast with the past, to intensify mood, to delay while augmenting our anticipation of what will happen next. This example from Rosellen Brown's *Before and After*—in which a father disturbed by reports of a young girl's murder is checking out his son's car in a dark garage—does all three.

The snow was lavendar where the light came down on it, like the weird illumination you see in planetariums that changes every color and makes white electric blue. Jacob and I loved to go to the science museum in Boston—not that long ago he had been at that age when the noisy saga of whirling planets and inexplicable anti-gravitational feats, narrated by a man with a deep official-facts voice, was thrilling. He was easily, unstintingly thrilled, or used to be. Not now, though.

Notice how Brown uses brief summaries both of the way things used to be and the way things have changed over time (both circumstantial and sequential summary), as well as images of time, weather, and even the whirling cosmos, to rouse our fear toward the "instant" in which major change occurs:

> At the last instant I thought I'd look at the trunk. I was beginning to feel relief wash over me like that moon-white air outside—a mystery still, where he might be, but nothing suspicious. The trunk snapped open and rose with the slow deliberation of a drawbridge, and then I thought I'd fall over for lack of breath. Because I knew I was looking at blood.

Examining your own mind for the three kinds of memory—sequential summary, circumstantial summary, and scene—will help make evident the necessity of scene in fiction. The moments that altered your life you remember at length and in detail; your memory tells you your story, and it is a great natural storyteller.

FLASHBACK

Flashback is one of the most magical of fiction's contrivances, easier and more effective in this medium than in any other, because the reader's mind is a swifter mechanism for getting into the past than anything that has been devised for stage or even film. All you must do is to give the reader smooth passage into the past, and the force of the story will be time warped to whenever and wherever you want it.

Nevertheless, many beginning writers use unnecessary flashbacks. This happens because flashback can be a useful way to provide background to character or events, and is often seen as the easiest or only way. It isn't. Dialogue, brief summary, a reference or detail can often tell us all we need to know, and when that is the case, a flashback becomes cumbersome and overlong, taking us from the present where the story and our interest lie. Furthermore, these intrusive passages of childhood, motivation, and explanation tend to come early in the story, before we are caught up in the action. Then we wonder whether there is any story on its way.

If you are tempted to use flashback to fill in the whole past, try using your journal for exploring background. Write down everything, fast. Then take a hard look at it to decide just how little of it you can use, how much of it the reader can infer, how you can sharpen an image to imply a past incident or condense a grief into a line of dialogue. Trust the reader's experience of life to understand events from attitudes. And keep the present of the story moving.

Flashback is effectively used in fiction to *reveal* at the *right time*. It does not so much take us from, as contribute to, the central action of the story, so that as readers we suspend the forward motion of the narrative in our minds as our understanding of it deepens. David Madden, in A *Primer of the Novel for Readers and Writers*, says that such time shifts are most effective if the very fact of their occurrence contributes to the revelation of character and theme.

If you find that you need an excursion into the past to reveal, at some point, why the character reacts as she does, or how totally he is misunderstood by those around him, or some other point of emotional significance, then there are several ways to get the reader to cooperate.

Provide some sort of transition. A connection between what's happening in the present and what happened in the past will often best transport the reader, just as it does the character.

Avoid blatant transitions, such as "Henry thought back to the time" and "I drifted back in memory." Assume the reader's intelligence and ability to follow a leap back.

> The kid in the Converse high-tops lifted off on the tips of his toes and slam-dunked it in.
> Joe'd done that once, in the lot off Seymour Street, when he was still four inches shorter than Ruppert and had already started getting zits. It was early fall, and. . .

A graceful transition to the past allows you to summarize necessary background quickly, as in this example from James W. Hall's *Under Cover of Daylight*.

> Thorn watched as Sugarman made a quick inspection of the gallery. Thorn sat on the couch where he'd done his homework as a boy, the one that looked out across the seawall toward Carysfort light.
> That was how his nights had been once, read a little Thoreau, do some algebra, and look up, shifting his body so he could see through the louvers the fragile pulse of that marker light, and let his mind roam, first out the twelve miles to the reef and then pushing farther, out past the shipping lanes into a world he pictured as gaudy and loud, chaotic. Bright colors and horns honking, exotic vegetables and market stalls, and water, clear and deep and shadowy, an ocean of fish, larger and more powerful than those he had hauled to light. Beyond the reef.

If you are writing in the past tense, begin the flashback in the past perfect and use the construction "had (verb)" two or three times. Then switch to the simple past; the reader will be with you. If you are writing in the present tense, you may want to keep the whole flashback in the past.

Try to avoid a flashback within a flashback. If you find yourself tempted by this awkward shape, it probably means you're trying to let flashback carry too much of the story.

When the flashback ends, be very clear that you are catching up to the present again. Repeat an action or image that the reader will remember belongs to the basic time period of the story. Often simply beginning the paragraph with "Now . . ." will accomplish the reorientation.

SLOW MOTION

Flashback is a term borrowed from film, and I want to borrow another—*slow motion*—to point out a correlation between narrative time and significant detail.

When people experience moments of great intensity, their senses become especially alert and they register, literally, more than usual. In extreme crisis people have the odd sensation that time is slowing down, and they see, hear, smell, remember ordinary sensations with extraordinary clarity. This psychological fact can work artistically in reverse: If you record detail with special focus and precision, it will create the effect of intensity. The phenomenon is so universal that it has become a film cliché to register a physical blow, gunshot, sexual passion, or extreme fear in slow motion. The technique works forcefully in fiction. Note in the quotation from Rosellen Brown above, how the trunk "snapped open and rose with the slow deliberation of a drawbridge."

Ian McEwan, in *A Child in Time*, demonstrates the technique in an extended passage:

> . . . He was preparing to overtake when something happened—he did not quite see what—in the region of the lorry's wheels, a hiatus, a cloud of dust, and then something black and long snaked through a hundred feet towards him. It slapped the windscreen, clung there a moment and was whisked away before he had time to understand what it was. And then—or did this happen in the same moment?—the rear of the lorry made a complicated set of movements, a bouncing and swaying, and slewed in a wide spray of sparks, bright even in sunshine. Something curved and metallic flew off to one side. So far Stephen had had time to move his foot towards the brake, time to notice a padlock swinging on a loose flange, and 'Wash me please' scrawled in grime. There was a whinnying of scraped metal and new sparks, dense enough to form a white flame which seemed to propel the rear of the lorry into the air. He was applying first pressure to the brake as he saw the dusty, spinning wheels, the oily bulge of the differential, the camshaft, and now, at eye level, the base of the gear box. The upended lorry bounced on its nose once, perhaps twice, then lazily, tentatively, began to complete the somersault, bringing Stephen the inverted radiator grill, the downward flash of windscreen and a deep boom as the roof hit the road, rose again several feet, fell back, and surged along before him on a bed of flame. Then it swung its length round to block the road, fell on to its side and stopped abruptly as Stephen headed into it from a distance of less than a hundred feet and at a speed which he estimated, in a detached kind of way, to be forty-five miles an hour.
>
> Now, in this slowing of time, there was a sense of a fresh beginning. He had entered a much later period in which all the terms and conditions had

changed. So these were the new rules, and he experienced something like awe, as though he were walking alone into a great city on a newly discovered planet. There was space too for a little touch of regret, genuine nostalgia for the old days of spectacle, back then when a lorry used to catapult so impressively before the impassive witness. Now was a more demanding time of effort and concentration. He was pointing the car towards a six-foot gap formed between a road sign and the front bumper of the motionless lorry. He had removed his foot from the brakes, reasoning—and it was as if he had just completed a monograph on the subject—that they were pulling the car to one side, interfering with his aim. Instead he was changing down through the gears and steering with both hands firmly, but not too tightly, on the wheel, ready to bring them up to cover his head if he missed. He beamed messages, or rather messages sprang from him, to Julie and Kate, nothing more distinct than pulses of alarm and love. There were others he should send to, he knew, but time was short, less than half a second, and fortunately they did not come to mind to confuse him. As he shifted to second and the small car gave out a protesting roar, it was clear that he must not think too hard, that he had to trust to a relaxed and dissociated thinking, that he must imagine himself into the gap. On the sound of this very word, which he must have spoken aloud, there was a brisk crunch of metal and glass and he was through and coming to a halt, with his door handle and wing mirror scattered across the road fifty feet behind.

Before the relief, before the shock, came an intense hope that the driver of the lorry had witnessed this feat of driving.

In this passage, McEwan consciously records the psychological phenomenon traced above, so that in effect he is announcing his slow-motion device even as he describes the action. On the psychological level, anyone old enough to be reading the novel can almost inevitably identify with the experience of sensual slow-down. At the same time, part of our enjoyment is following the brilliance of the technique and knowing we're clever enough to get it.

It's also evident that the author is having a wonderful time. Beginning writers often rush through or skimp on the elements of setting and time, probably out of dreary memories of long descriptions they have read.

But when atmosphere is well created we do not experience it as description; we experience it. We yawn over passages in which authors have indulged themselves in plum-colored homilies on the beauties of nature or the wealth of decor. But just as dialogue that only offers information is too inert for the purposes of fiction, so too is description that only describes. The full realization of locale and period, the revelation of a character through architecture or of emotion through weather, the advancement of plot through changes in season and history, are among the pleasures of both writer and reader. Once you become adept at the skill of manipulating atmosphere, you will find that the necessity of setting your story some place and some time is a liberating opportunity.

A Very Old Man With Enormous Wings

GABRIEL GARCIA MARQUEZ

translated by Gregory Rabassa

On the third day of rain they had killed so many crabs inside the house that Pelayo had to cross his drenched courtyard and throw them into the sea, because the new-born child had a temperature all night and they thought it was due to the stench. The world had been sad since Tuesday. Sea and sky were a single ash-gray thing and the sands of the beach, which on March nights glimmered like powdered light, had become a stew of mud and rotten shellfish. The light was so weak at noon that when Pelayo was coming back to the house after throwing away the crabs, it was hard for him to see what it was that was moving and groaning in the rear of the courtyard. He had to go very close to see that it was an old man, a very old man, lying face down in the mud, who, in spite of his tremendous efforts, couldn't get up, impeded by his enormous wings.

Frightened by that nightmare, Pelayo ran to get Elisenda, his wife, who was putting compresses on the sick child, and he took her to the rear of the courtyard. They both looked at the fallen body with mute stupor. He was dressed like a rag-picker. There were only a few faded hairs left on his bald skull and very few teeth in his mouth, and his pitiful condition of a drenched great-grandfather had taken away any sense of grandeur he might have had. His huge buzzard wings, dirty and half-plucked, were forever entangled in the mud. They looked at him so long and so closely that Pelayo and Elisenda very soon overcame their surprise and in the end found him familiar. Then they dared speak to him, and he answered in an incomprehensible dialect with a strong sailor's voice. That was how they skipped over the inconvenience of the wings and quite intelligently concluded that he was a lonely castaway from some foreign ship wrecked by the storm. And yet, they called in a neighbor woman who knew everything about life and death to see him, and all she needed was one look to show them their mistake.

"He's an angel," she told them. "He must have been coming for the child, but the poor fellow is so old that the rain knocked him down."

On the following day everyone knew that a flesh-and-blood angel was held captive in Pelayo's house. Against the judgment of the wise neighbor woman, for whom angels in those times were the fugitive survivors of a celestial conspiracy, they did not have the heart to club him to death. Pelayo watched over him all afternoon from the kitchen, armed with his bailiff's club, and before going to bed he dragged him out of the mud and locked him up with the hens in the wire chicken coop. In the middle of the night, when the rain stopped, Pelayo and Elisenda were still killing crabs. A short time afterward the child woke up without a fever and with a desire to eat. Then they felt magnanimous and decided to put the angel on a raft with fresh water and provisions for three days and leave him to his fate on the high seas. But when they went out into the courtyard with the first light of dawn, they found the whole neighborhood in front of the chicken coop having fun with the angel, without the slightest reverence, tossing him things to eat through the openings in the wire as if he weren't a supernatural creature but a circus animal.

Father Gonzaga arrived before seven o'clock, alarmed at the strange news. By that time onlookers less frivolous than those at dawn had already arrived and they were making all kinds of conjectures concerning the captive's future. The simplest among them thought that he should be named mayor of the world. Others of sterner mind felt that he should be promoted to the rank of five-star general in order to win all wars. Some visionaries hoped that he could be put to stud in order to implant on earth a race of winged wise men who could take charge of the universe. But Father Gonzaga, before becoming a priest, had been a robust woodcutter. Standing by the wire, he reviewed his catechism in an instant and asked them to open the door so that he could take a close look at that pitiful man who looked more like a huge decrepit hen among the fascinated chickens. He was lying in a corner drying his open wings in the sunlight among the fruit peels and breakfast leftovers that the early risers had thrown him. Alien to the impertinences of the world, he only lifted his antiquarian eyes and murmured something in his dialect when Father Gonzaga went into the chicken coop and said good morning to him in Latin. The parish priest had his first suspicion of an impostor when he saw that he did not understand the language of God or know how to greet His ministers. Then he noticed that seen close up he was much too human: he had an unbearable smell of the outdoors, the back side of his wings was strewn with parasites and his main feathers had been mistreated by terrestrial winds, and nothing about him measured up to the proud dignity of angels. Then he came out of the chicken coop and in a brief sermon warned the curious against the risks of being ingenuous. He reminded them that the devil had the bad habit of making use of carnival tricks in order to confuse the unwary. He argued that if wings were not the essential element in determining the difference between a hawk and an airplane, they were even less so in the recognition of angels. Nevertheless, he promised to write a letter to his bishop so that the latter would write to his primate so that the latter would write to the Supreme Pontiff in order to get the final verdict from the highest courts.

His prudence fell on sterile hearts. The news of the captive angel spread with such rapidity that after a few hours the courtyard had the bustle of a marketplace and they had to call in troops with fixed bayonets to disperse the mob that was about to knock the house down. Elisenda, her spine all twisted from sweeping up so much marketplace trash, then got the idea of fencing in the yard and charging five cents admission to see the angel.

The curious came from far away. A traveling carnival arrived with a flying acrobat who buzzed over the crowd several times, but no one paid any attention to him because his wings were not those of an angel but, rather, those of a sidereal bat. The most unfortunate invalids on earth came in search of health: a poor woman who since childhood had been counting her heartbeats and had run out of numbers; a Portuguese man who couldn't sleep because the noise of the stars disturbed him; a sleepwalker who got up at night to undo the things he had done while awake; and many others with less serious ailments. In the midst of that shipwreck disorder that made the earth tremble, Pelayo and Elisenda were happy with fatigue, for in less than a week they had crammed their rooms with money and the line of pilgrims waiting their turn to enter still reached beyond the horizon.

The angel was the only one who took no part in his own act. He spent his time trying to get comfortable in his borrowed nest, befuddled by the hellish heat of the oil lamps and sacramental candles that had been placed along the wire. At first they tried to make him eat some mothballs, which, according to the wisdom of the wise neighbor woman, were the food prescribed for angels. But he turned them down, just as he turned down the papal lunches that the penitents brought him, and they never found out whether it was because he was an angel or because he was an old man that in the end he ate nothing but eggplant mush. His only super-natural virtue seemed to be patience. Especially during the first days, when the hens pecked at him, searching for the stellar parasites that proliferated in his wings, and the cripples pulled out feathers to touch their defective parts with, and even the most merciful threw stones at him, trying to get him to rise so they could see him standing. The only time they succeeded in arousing him was when they burned his side with an iron for branding steers, for he had been motionless for so many hours that they thought he was dead. He awoke with a start, ranting in his hermetic language and with tears in his eyes, and he flapped his wings a couple of times, which brought on a whirlwind of chicken dung and lunar dust and a gale of panic that did not seem to be of this world. Although many thought that his reac-tion had been one not of rage but of pain, from then on they were careful not to annoy him, because the majority understood that his passivity was not that of a hero taking his ease but that of a cataclysm in repose.

Father Gonzaga held back the crowd's frivolity with formulas of maidservant inspiration while awaiting the arrival of a final judgment on the nature of the cap-tive. But the mail from Rome showed no sense of urgency. They spent their time finding out if the prisoner had a navel, if his dialect had any connection with Aramaic, how many times he could fit on the head of a pin, or whether he wasn't just a Norwegian with wings. Those meager letters might have come and gone until the end of time if a providential event had not put an end to the priest's tribulations.

It so happened that during those days, among so many other carnival attrac-tions, there arrived in town the traveling show of the woman who had been changed into a spider for having disobeyed her parents. The admission to see her was not only less than the admission to see the angel, but people were permitted to ask her all manner of questions about her absurd state and to examine her up and down so that no one would ever doubt the truth of her horror. She was a frightful tarantula the size of a ram and with the head of a sad maiden. What was most heart-rending, however, was not her outlandish shape but the sincere affliction with which she recounted the details of her misfortune. While still practically a child she had sneaked out of her parents' house to go to a dance, and while she was coming back through the woods after having danced all night without permission, a fearful thunderclap rent the sky in two and through the crack came the lightning bolt of brimstone that changed her into a spider. Her only nourishment came from the meatballs that charitable souls chose to toss into her mouth. A spectacle like that, full of so much human truth and with such a fearful lesson, was bound to defeat without even trying that of a haughty angel who scarcely deigned to look at mortals. Besides, the few miracles attributed to the angel showed a certain mental disorder, like the blind man who didn't recover his sight but grew three new teeth, or the paralytic who didn't get to walk but almost won the lottery, and the leper whose sores sprouted sunflowers. Those consolation miracles, which were more like mocking fun, had already ruined the angel's reputation when the woman who had been changed into a spider finally crushed him completely. That was how Father Gonzaga was cured forever of his insomnia and Pelayo's courtyard went back to being as empty as during the time it had rained for three days and crabs walked through the bedrooms.

The owners of the house had no reason to lament. With the money they saved they built a two-story mansion with balconies and gardens and high netting so that crabs wouldn't get in during the winter, and with iron bars on the windows so that angels wouldn't get in. Pelayo also set up a rabbit warren close to town and gave up his job as bailiff for good, and Elisenda bought some satin pumps with high heels and many dresses of iridescent silk, the kind worn on Sunday by the most desirable women in those times. The chicken coop was the only thing that didn't receive any attention. If they washed it down with creolin and burned tears of myrrh inside it every so often, it was not in homage to the angel but to drive away the dungheap stench that still hung everywhere like a ghost and was turning the new house into an old one. At first, when the child learned to walk, they were careful that he not get too close to the chicken coop. But then they began to lose their fears and got used to the smell, and before the child got his second teeth he'd gone inside the chicken coop to play, where the wires were falling apart. The angel was no less standoffish with him than with other mortals, but he tolerated the most ingenious infamies with the patience of a dog who had no illusions. They both came down with chicken pox at the same time. The doctor who took care of the child couldn't resist the temptation to listen to the angel's heart, and he found so much whistling in the heart and so many sounds in his kidneys that it seemed impossible for him to be alive. What surprised him most, however, was the logic of his wings. They seemed so natural on that completely human organism that he couldn't understand why other men didn't have them too.

When the child began school it had been some time since the sun and rain had caused the collapse of the chicken coop. The angel went dragging himself about here and there like a stray dying man. They would drive him out of the bedroom with a broom and a moment later find him in the kitchen. He seemed to be in so many places at the same time that they grew to think that he'd been duplicated, that he was reproducing himself all through the house, and the exasperated and unhinged Elisenda shouted that it was awful living in that hell full of angels. He could scarcely eat and his antiquarian eyes had also become so foggy that he went about bumping into posts. All he had left were the bare cannulae of his last feathers. Pelayo threw a blanket over him and extended him the charity of letting him sleep in the shed, and only then did they notice that he had a temperature at night, and was delirious with the tongue twisters of an old Norwegian. That was one of the few times they became alarmed, for they thought he was going to die and not even the wise neighbor woman had been able to tell them what to do with dead angels.

And yet he not only survived his worst winter, but seemed improved with the first sunny days. He remained motionless for several days in the farthest corner of the courtyard, where no one would see him, and at the beginning of December some large, stiff feathers began to grow on his wings, the feathers of a scarecrow, which looked more like another misfortune of decrepitude. But he must have known the reason for those changes, for he was quite careful that no one should notice them, that no one should hear the sea chanteys that he sometimes sang under the stars. One morning Elisenda was cutting some bunches of onions for lunch when a wind that seemed to come from the high seas blew into the kitchen. Then she went to the window and caught the angel in his first attempts at flight. They were so clumsy that his fingernails opened a furrow in the vegetable patch and he was on the point of knocking the shed down with the ungainly flapping that slipped on the light and couldn't get a grip on the air. But he did manage to gain altitude. Elisenda let out a sigh of relief, for herself and for him, when she saw him pass over the last houses, holding himself up in some way with the risky flapping of a senile vulture. She kept watching him even when she was through cutting the onions and she kept on watching until it was no longer possible for her to see him, because then he was no longer an annoyance in her life but an imaginary dot on the horizon of the sea.

∽∽∽∽∽∽∽∽∽∽

Suggestions for Discussion

1. Garcia Marquez frequently specifies the time in this story (*On the third day; On the following day; before seven o'clock; When the child began school; at the beginning of December; one morning . . .*) Besides keeping us oriented in time, what function does this serve?

2. Garcia Marquez is a major practitioner of "magic realism," a form in which fabulous events are told in the most detailed and matter-of-fact way. Where and how does he create a sense of the familiar in this unlikely chain of events?

3. How do references to seasons and weather reach toward a larger significance in this story?

4. Where is there harmony between characters and background? Where is there conflict? How do these help reveal the conflicts of the story as a whole?

5. Much of the plot is told in summary form. Why? What tone results? Identify circumstantial and sequential summaries, and scenes. What change does each of the scenes signal?

6. Where is flashback used, and to what purpose?

Car Crash While Hitchhiking

DENIS JOHNSON

A salesman who shared his liquor and steered while sleeping. . . A Cherokee filled with bourbon. . . A VW no more than a bubble of hashish fumes, captained by a college student. . .

And a family from Marshalltown who head-onned and killed forever a man driving west out of Bethany, Missouri. . .

. . . I rose up sopping wet from sleeping under the pouring rain, and something less than conscious, thanks to the first three of the people I've already named—the salesman and the Indian and the student—all of whom had given me drugs. At the head of the entrance ramp I waited without hope of a ride. What was the point, even, of rolling up my sleeping bag when I was too wet to be let into anybody's car? I draped it around me like a cape. The downpour raked the asphalt and gurgled in the ruts. My thoughts zoomed pitifully. The traveling salesman had fed me pills that made the linings of my veins feel scraped out. My jaw ached. I knew every raindrop by its name. I sensed everything before it happened. I knew a certain Oldsmobile would stop for me even before it slowed, and by the sweet voices of the family inside it I knew we'd have an accident in the storm.

I didn't care. They said they'd take me all the way.

The man and the wife put the little girl up front with them, and left the baby in back with me and my dripping bedroll. "I'm not taking you anywhere very fast," the man said. "I've got my wife and babies here, that's why."

You are the ones, I thought. And I piled my sleeping bag against the left-hand door and slept across it, not caring whether I lived or died. The baby slept free on the seat beside me. He was about nine months old.

. . . But before any of this, that afternoon, the salesman and I had swept down into Kansas City in his luxury car. We'd developed a dangerous cynical camaraderie beginning in Texas, where he'd taken me on. We ate up his bottle of amphetamines, and every so often we pulled off the interstate and bought another pint of Canadian Club and a sack of ice. His car had cylindrical glass holders attached to either door and a white, leathery interior. He said he'd take me home to stay overnight with his family, but first he wanted to stop and see a woman he knew.

Under midwestern clouds like great gray brains we left the superhighway with a drifting sensation and entered Kansas City's rush hour with a sensation of running aground. As soon as we slowed down, all the magic of traveling together burned away. He went on and on about his girlfriend. "I like this girl, I think I love this girl—but I've got two kids and a wife, and there's certain obligations there. And on top of everything else, I love my wife. I'm gifted with love. I love my kids. I love all my relatives." As he kept on, I felt jilted and sad: "I have a boat, a little sixteen-footer. I have two cars. There's room in the back yard for a swimming pool." He found his girlfriend at work. She ran a furniture store, and I lost him there.

The clouds stayed the same until night. Then, in the dark, I didn't see the storm gathering. The driver of the Volkswagen, a college man, the one who stoked my head with all the hashish, let me out beyond the city limits just as it began to rain.

Never mind the speed I'd been taking, I was too overcome to stand up. I lay out in the grass off the exit ramp and woke in the middle of a puddle that had filled up around me.

And later, as I've said, I slept in the back seat while the Oldsmobile—the family from Marshalltown—splashed along through the rain. And yet I dreamed I was looking right through my eyelids, and my pulse marked off the seconds of time. The Interstate through western Missouri was, in that era, nothing more than a two-way road, most of it. When a semi truck came toward us and passed going the other way, we were lost in a blinding spray and a warfare of noises such as you get being towed through an automatic car wash. The wipers stood up and lay down across the windshield without much effect. I was exhausted, and after an hour I slept more deeply.

I'd known all along exactly what was going to happen. But the man and his wife woke me up later, denying it viciously.

"Oh—*no!*"

"NO!"

I was thrown against the back of their seat so hard that it broke. I commenced bouncing back and forth. A liquid which I knew right away was human blood flew around the car and rained down on my head. When it was over I was in the back seat again, just as I had been. I rose up and looked around. Our headlights had gone out. The radiator was hissing steadily. Beyond that, I didn't hear a thing. As far as I cound tell, I was the only one conscious. As my eyes adjusted I saw that the baby was lying on its back beside me as if nothing had happened. Its eyes were open and it was feeling its cheeks with its little hands.

In a minute the driver, who'd been slumped over the wheel, sat up and peered at us. His face was smashed and dark with blood. It made my teeth hurt to look at him—but when he spoke, it didn't sound as if any of his teeth were broken.

"What happened?"

"We had a wreck," he said.

"The baby's okay," I said, although I had no idea how the baby was.

He turned to his wife.

"Janice," he said. "Janice, Janice!"

"Is she okay?"

"She's dead!" he said, shaking her angrily.

"No, she's not." I was ready to deny everything myself now.

Their little girl was alive, but knocked out. She whimpered in her sleep. But the man went on shaking his wife.

"Janice!" he hollered.

His wife moaned.

"She's not dead," I said, clambering from the car and running away.

"She won't wake up," I heard him say.

I was standing out here in the night, with the baby, for some reason, in my arms. It must have still been raining, but I remember nothing about the weather. We'd collided with another car on what I now perceived was a two-lane bridge. The water beneath us was invisible in the dark.

Moving toward the other car I began to hear rasping, metallic snores. Somebody was flung halfway out the passenger door, which was open, in the posture of one hanging from a trapeze by his ankles. The car had been broadsided, smashed so flat that no room was left inside of it even for this person's legs, to say nothing of a driver or any other passengers. I just walked right on past.

Headlights were coming from far off. I made for the head of the bridge, waving them to stop with one arm, and clutching the baby to my shoulder with the other.

It was a big semi, grinding its gears as it decelerated. The driver rolled down his window and I shouted up at him. "There's a wreck. Go for help."

"I can't turn around here," he said.

He let me and the baby up on the passenger side, and we just sat there in the cab, looking at the wreckage in his headlights.

"Is everybody dead?" he asked.

"I can't tell who is and who isn't," I admitted.

He poured himself a cup of coffee from a thermos and switched off all but his parking lights.

"What time is it?"

"Oh, it's around quarter after three," he said.

By his manner he seemed to endorse the idea of not doing anything about this. I was relieved and tearful. I'd thought something was required of me, but I hadn't wanted to find out what it was.

When another car showed, coming the opposite direction, I thought I should talk to them. "Can you keep the baby?" I asked the truck driver.

"You'd better hang on to him," the driver said. "It's a boy, isn't it?"

"Well, I think so," I said.

The man hanging out of the wrecked car was still alive as I passed, and I stopped, grown a little more used to the idea now of how really badly broken he was, and made sure there was nothing I could do. He was snoring loudly and rudely. His blood bubbled out of his mouth with every breath. He wouldn't be taking many more. I knew that, but he didn't, and therefore I looked down into the great pity of a person's life on this earth. I don't mean that we all end up dead, that's not the great pity. I mean that he couldn't tell me what he was dreaming, and I couldn't tell him what was real.

Before too long there were cars backed up for a ways at either end of the bridge, and headlights giving a night-game atmosphere in the steaming rubble, and ambulances and cop cars nudging through so that the air pulsed with color. I didn't talk to anyone. My secret was that in this short while I had gone from being the president of this tragedy to being a faceless onlooker at a gory wreck. At some point an officer learned that I was one of the passengers, and took my statement. I don't remember any of this, except that he told me, "Put out your cigarette." We paused in our conversation to watch the dying man being loaded into the ambulance. He was still alive, still dreaming obscenely. The blood ran off of him in strings. His knees jerked and his head rattled.

There was nothing wrong with me, and I hadn't seen anything, but the policeman had to question me and take me to the hospital anyway. The word came over his car radio that the man was now dead, just as we came under the awning of the emergency-room entrance.

I stood in a tiled corridor with my wet sleeping bag bunched against the wall beside me, talking to a man from the local funeral home.

The doctor stopped to tell me I'd better have an x-ray.

"No."

"Now would be the time. If something turns up later . . . "

"There's nothing wrong with me."

Down the hall came the wife. She was glorious, burning. She didn't know yet that her husband was dead. We knew. That's what gave her such power over us. The doctor took her into a room with a desk at the end of the hall, and from under the closed door a slab of brilliance radiated as if, by some stupendous process, diamonds were being incinerated in there. What a pair of lungs! She shrieked as I imagined an eagle would shriek. It felt wonderful to be alive to hear it! I've gone looking for that feeling everywhere.

"There's nothing wrong with me"—I'm surprised I let those words out. But it's always been my tendency to lie to doctors, as if good health consisted only of the ability to fool them.

Some years later, one time when I was admitted to the detox at Seattle General Hospital, I took the same tack.

"Are you hearing unusual sounds or voices?" the doctor asked.

"Help us, oh God, it hurts," the boxes of cotton screamed.

"Not exactly," I said.

"Not exactly," he said. "Now what does that mean."

"I'm not ready to go into all that," I said. A yellow bird fluttered close to my face, and my muscles grabbed. Now I was flopping like a fish. When I squeezed shut my eyes, hot tears exploded from the sockets. When I opened them, I was on my stomach.

"How did the room get so white?" I asked.

A beautiful nurse was touching my skin. "These are vitamins," she said, and drove the needle in.

It was raining. Gigantic ferns leaned over us. The forest drifted down a hill. I could hear a creek rushing down among rocks. And you, you ridiculous people, you expect me to help you.

<center>~~~~~~~~~~~</center>

Suggestions for Discussion

1. This story begins with a quick elliptical summary, backtracks to rehearse part of it more fully, then flashes back to an earlier part. Why does Johnson play with time in this way? How does it effect the story's atmosphere?

2. How do changing light and weather contribute to the telling of the story?

3. When is the setting familiar and when alien? How do the changes from one to the other advance the story? What is the purpose of the ferns and forest in the final paragraph?

4. What images suggest the effect of drugs on the narrator's perception? How does this effect the atmosphere? How is it integrated into the plot?

5. The accident in this piece is not detailed at the length of the passage quoted above from *A Child In Time*, but the technique of slow motion is used in other ways and places. Where and how?

6. This is a story of crisis; what do you consider the crisis action of the story? How is the narrator changed?

Retrospect

1. Find examples of "slow motion" in Joyce Carol Oates' "Where Are You Going, Where Have You Been?" How does the technique function in the story?

2. On page 72 of "The Things They Carried," there is a flashback to the time Jimmy Cross touched Martha's knee in a movie theater. How is the flashback introduced? Speculate on how much background is implied in this short passage and how much the author knew that he left out.

3. Consider the function of each of these in "Hunters in the Snow" by Tobias Wolff: the weather; flashback; alternating sequential summary and scene.

Writing Assignments

1. Write a scene, involving only one character, who is uncomfortable in his or her surroundings: socially inadequate, frightened, revolted, painfully nostalgic, or the like. Using active verbs in your description of the setting, build forceful conflict between the person and the place.

2. Write a scene with two characters in conflict over the setting: One wants to go, and one wants to stay. The more interesting the setting you choose, the more interesting the conflict will inevitably be.

3. Write a scene in a setting that is likely to be quite familiar to your readers (supermarket, dormitory, classroom, movie theater, suburban house, etc.) but that is unfamiliar, strange, outlandish, or outrageous to the central character. Let us feel the strangeness through the character's eyes.

4. Write a scene set in a strange, exotic place or a time far distant either in the past or the future, in which the setting is quite familiar to the central character. Convince us of the ordinariness of the place.

5. Write a scene in which the character's mood is at odds with the weather and make the weather nevertheless express her or his mood: The rain is

joyful, the clear skies are threatening, the snow is comforting, the summer beach is chilling.

6. Write a scene containing a flashback in which the information about the past is crucial to an understanding of the present.

7. Write a scene that begins with a circumstantial summary and then moves to a scene in slow motion.

7

CALL ME ISHMAEL

Point of View, Part I

- *Who Speaks?*

- *To Whom?*

- *In What Form?*

Point of view is the most complex element of fiction. Although it lends itself to analysis, it is finally a question of relationship among writer, characters, and reader—subject like any relationship to organic subtleties. We can discuss person, omniscience, narrative voice, tone, authorial distance, and reliability; but none of these things will ever pigeonhole a work in such a way that any other work may be placed in the exact same pigeonhole.

The first thing to do is to set aside the common use of the phrase "point of view" as synonymous with "opinion", as in *It's my point of view that they all ought to be shot.* An author's view of the world as it is and as it ought to be will ultimately be revealed by his or her manipulation of the technique of point of view, but not vice versa—identifying the author's beliefs will not describe the point of view of the work. Rather than thinking of point of view as an opinion or belief, begin with the more literal synonym of "vantage point." *Who* is standing *where* to watch the scene?

Better, since we are dealing with a verbal medium, these questions might be translated: *Who speaks? To whom? In what form? At what distance from the action? With what limitations?* All these issues go into the determination of the point of view. Because the author *inevitably wants to convince us to share the same perspective,* the answers will also help reveal her or his final opinion, judgment, attitude, or message.

This chapter deals with the first three questions: Who speaks? To whom? In what form? Distance and limitations are considered in chapter 8.

Point of View

Who Speaks?

The Author	The Author	A Character
In: Third Person	In: Second Person	In: First Person
Editorial Omniscient	You as character	Central Narrator
Limited Omniscient	You as reader-turned-	Peripheral narrator
Objective	character	

To Whom?

The Reader	Another Character or Characters	The Self
Characterized or Uncharacterized		

In What Form?

Written Story, Spoken Story, Reportage, Oratory, Monologue, Confessional, Journal, Diary, Interior Monologue, Stream of Consciousness, etc.

At What Distance?

Reader and Author↔Narrator↔Characters

Complete Identification↔Complete Opposition

Temporal, Spatial, Moral, Intellectual, Aesthetic, Physical, Educational, Experiential

With What Limitations?

Reliable Narrator (or Author)↔Unreliable Narrator (or Author) on any of values listed above

Who Speaks?

The primary point-of-view decision that you as author must make before you can set down the first sentence of the story is *person*. This is the simplest and crudest subdivision that must be made in deciding who speaks. The story can be told in the third person (*She walked out into the harsh sunlight*), the second person (*You walked out into the harsh sunlight*), or the first person (*I walked out into the harsh sunlight*). Third- and second-person stories are told by an author; first-person stories, by a character.

THIRD PERSON

Third person, in which the author is telling the story, can be subdivided again according to the degree of knowledge, or *omniscience*, the author assumes. Notice that since this is a matter of degree, the subdivisions are again only a crude indication of the variations possible. As an author you are free to decide how much you know. You may know every universal and eternal truth; you may know what is in the mind of one character but not what is in the mind of another; or you may know only what can be externally observed. You decide, and very early in the story you signal to the reader what degree of omniscience you have chosen. Once given, this signal constitutes a "contract" between author and reader, and it will be difficult to break the contract gracefully. If you have restricted yourself to the mind of James Lordly for five pages, as he observes the actions of Mrs. Grumms and her cats, you will violate the contract by suddenly dipping into Mrs. Grumms's mind to let us know what she thinks of James Lordly. We are likely to feel misused, and likely to cancel the contract altogether, if you suddenly give us the thoughts of the cats.

The *omniscient author*, sometimes referred to as the *editorial omniscient author* because she or he tells us directly what we are supposed to think, has total knowledge. As omniscient author you are God. You can:

1. Objectively report what is happening;
2. Go into the mind of any character;
3. Interpret for us that character's appearance, speech, actions, and thoughts, even if the character cannot do so;
4. Move freely in time or space to give us a panoramic, telescopic, microscopic, or historical view; tell us what has happened elsewhere or in the past or what will happen in the future; and
5. Provide general reflections, judgments, and truths.

In all these aspects, we will accept what the omniscient author tells us. If you tell us that Ruth is a good woman, that Jeremy doesn't really understand his own motives, that the moon is going to explode in four hours, and that everybody will be better off for it, we will believe you. Here is a paragraph that blatantly exhibits all five of these areas of knowledge.

(1) Joe glared at the screaming baby. (2) Frightened by his scowl, the baby gulped and screamed louder. I hate that thing, Joe thought. (3) But it was not really hatred that he felt. (4) Only two years ago he himself had screamed like that. (5) Children can't tell hatred from fear.

This illustration is awkwardly compressed, but authors well in control of their craft can move easily from one area of knowledge to another. In the first scene of *War and Peace*, Tolstoy describes Anna Scherer.

To be an enthusiast had become her social vocation, and sometimes even when she did not feel like it, she became enthusiastic in order not to disappoint the expectations of those who knew her. The subdued smile which, though it did not suit her faded features, always played around her lips, expressed as in a spoiled child, a continual consciousness of her charming defect, which she neither wished, nor could, nor considered it necessary to correct.

In two sentences Tolstoy tells us what is in Anna's mind, what the expectations of her acquaintances are, what she looks like, what suits her, what she can and cannot do; and he offers a general reflection on spoiled children.

The omniscient voice is the voice of the classical epic (*And Meleager, far-off, knew nothing of this, but felt his vitals burning with fever*), of the Bible (*So the Lord sent a pestilence upon Israel; and there fell seventy thousand men*), and of most nineteenth-century novels (*Tito put out his hand to help him, and so strangely quick are men's souls that in this moment, when he began to feel that his atonement was accepted, he had a darting thought of the irksome efforts it entailed*). But it is one of the manifestations of literature's movement downward in class from heroic to common characters, inward from action to the mind, that authors of the twentieth century have largely avoided the godlike stance of the omniscient author and have chosen to restrict themselves to fewer areas of knowledge.

The *limited omniscient* viewpoint is one in which the author may move with some, but not all, of the omniscient author's freedom. You may grant yourself the right, for example, to know what the characters in a scene are thinking but not to interpret their thoughts. You may interpret one character's thoughts and actions but see the others only externally. You may see with microscopic accuracy but not presume to reach any universal truths. The most commonly used form of the limited omniscient point of view is one in which the author can see events objectively and also grants himself or herself access to the mind of one character, but not to the minds of the others, nor to any explicit powers of judgment. This point of view is particularly useful for the short story because it very quickly establishes the point of view character or *means of perception*. The short story is so compressed a form that there is rarely time or space to develop more than one consciousness. Staying with external observation and one character's thoughts helps control the focus and avoid awkward point-of-view shifts.

But the form is also frequently used for the novel, as in Gail Godwin's *The Odd Woman*.

> It was ten o'clock on the evening of the same day, and the permanent residents of the household on the mountain were restored to routines and sobriety. Jane, on the other hand, sat by herself in the kitchen, a glass of Scotch before her on the cleanly wiped table, going deeper and deeper into a mood she could recognize only as unfamiliar. She could not describe it; it was both frightening and satisfying. It was like letting go and being taken somewhere. She tried to trace it back. When, exactly, had it started?

It is clear here that the author has limited her omniscience. She is not going to tell us the ultimate truth about Jane's soul, nor is she going to define for us the unfamiliar mood that the character herself cannot define. The author has the facts at her disposal, and she has Jane's thoughts, and that is all.

The advantage of the limited omniscient over the omniscient voice is immediacy. Here, because we are not allowed to know more than Jane does about her own thoughts and feelings, we grope *with* her toward understanding. In the process, a contract has been made between the author and the reader, and this contract must not now be broken. If at this point the author should step in and answer Jane's question, "When, exactly, had it started?" with, "Jane was never to remember this, but in fact it had started one afternoon when she was two years old," we would feel it as an abrupt and uncalled-for *authorial intrusion*.

Nevertheless, within the limits the author has set herself, there is fluidity and a range of possibilities. Notice that the passage begins with a panoramic observation (*ten o'clock, permanent residents, routines*) and moves to the tighter focus of a view, still external, of Jane (*sat by herself in the kitchen*), before moving into her mind. The sentence "She tried to trace it back" is a relatively factual account of her mental process, whereas in the next sentence, "When, exactly, had it started?" we are in Jane's mind, overhearing her question to herself.

Although this common form of the limited omniscient (objective reporting plus one mind) may seem very restricted, given all the possibilities of omniscience, it has a freedom that no human being has. In life you have full access to only one mind, your own; and you are also the one person you may not externally observe. As a fiction writer you can do what no human being can do, be simultaneously inside and outside a given character; it is this that E. M. Forster describes in *Aspects of the Novel* as the fundamental difference between people in daily life and people in books.

In daily life we never understand each other, neither complete clairvoyance nor complete confessional exists. We know each other approximately, by external signs, and these serve well enough as a basis for society and even for intimacy. But people in a novel can be understood completely by the reader, if the novelist wishes; their inner as well as their outer life can be exposed. And this is why they often seem more definite than characters in history, or even our own friends.

The *objective author* is not omniscient but impersonal. As an objective author, you restrict your knowledge to the external facts that might be observed by a human being; to the senses of sight, sound, smell, taste, and touch. In the story "Hills Like White Elephants", Ernest Hemingway reports what is said and done by a quarreling couple, both without any direct revelation of the characters' thoughts and without comment.

The American and the girl with him sat at a table in the shade, outside the building. It was very hot and the express from Barcelona would come in forty minutes. It stopped at this junction for two minutes and went on to Madrid.

"What should we drink?" the girl asked. She had taken off her hat and put it on the table.

"It's pretty hot," the man said.

"Let's drink beer."

"Dos cervezas," the man said into the curtain.

"Big ones?" a woman asked from the doorway.

"Yes. Two big ones."

The woman brought two glasses of beer and two felt pads. She put the felt pads and the beer glasses on the table and looked at the man and the girl.

The girl was looking off at the line of hills. They were white in the sun and the country was brown and dry.

In the course of this story we learn, entirely by inference, that the girl is pregnant and that she feels herself coerced by the man into having an abortion. Neither pregnancy nor abortion is ever mentioned. The narrative remains clipped, austere, and external. What does Hemingway gain by this pretense of objective reporting? The reader is allowed to discover what is really happening. The characters avoid the subject, prevaricate, and pretend, but they betray their real meanings and feelings through gestures, repetitions, and slips of the tongue. The reader, focus directed by the author, learns by inference, as in life, so that we finally have the pleasure of knowing the characters better than they know themselves.

For the sake of clarity, the possibilities of third-person narration have been divided into the editorial omniscient, limited omniscient, and objective authors, but between the extreme stances of the editorial omniscient (total knowledge) and the objective author (external observation only), the powers of the limited omniscient are immensely variable. Because you are most likely to choose your authorial voice in this range, you need to be aware that you make your own rules and that having made them, you must stick to them. Your position as a writer is analogous to that of a poet who may choose whether to write free verse or a ballad stanza. If the poet chooses the stanza, then he or she is obliged to rhyme. Beginning writers of prose fiction are often tempted to shift viewpoint when it is both unnecessary and disturbing.

> Leo's neck flushed against the prickly weave of his uniform collar. He concentrated on his buttons and tried not to look into the face of the bandmaster, who, however, was more amused than angry.

This is an awkward point-of-view shift because, having felt Leo's embarrassment with him, we are suddenly asked to leap into the bandmaster's feelings. The shift can be corrected by moving instead from Leo's mind to an observation that he might make.

> Leo's neck flushed against the prickly weave of his uniform collar. He concentrated on his buttons and tried not to look into the face of the bandmaster, who, however, was astonishingly smiling.

The rewrite is easier to follow because we remain with Leo's mind as he observes that the bandmaster is not angry. It further serves the purpose of implying that Leo fails to concentrate on his buttons, and so intensifies his confusion.

SECOND PERSON

First and third persons are most common in literature; the second person remains an idiosyncratic and experimental form, but it is worth mentioning because several twentieth-century authors have been attracted to its possibilities.

Person refers to the basic mode of a piece of fiction. In the third person, all the characters will be referred to as *he, she, or they*. In the first person, the character telling the story will refer to himself or herself as *I* and to other characters as *he, she,* or *they*. The second person is the basic mode of the story *only when a character* is referred to as *you*. When an omniscient author addresses the reader as *you* (*You will remember that John Doderring was left dangling on the cliff at Dover*), this does not alter the basic mode of the piece from third to second person. Only when "you" become an actor in the drama is the story or novel written in second person.

In *Even Cowgirls Get the Blues*, Tom Robbins exhibits both of these uses of the second person.

> If you could buckle your Bugs Bunny wristwatch to a ray of light, your watch would continue ticking but its hands wouldn't move.

The *you* involved here is a generalized reader, and the passage is written in the stance of an omniscient author delivering a general "truth".

But when the author turns to address his central character, Sissy Hankshaw, the basic mode of the narration becomes that of the second person.

> You hitchhike. Timidly at first, barely flashing your fist, leaning almost imperceptibly in the direction of your imaginary destination. A squirrel runs along a tree limb. You hitchhike the squirrel. A blue jay flies by. You flag it down.

The effect of this second-person narration is odd and original; the author observes Sissy Hankshaw, and yet his direct address implies an intimate and affectionate relationship that makes it easy to move further into her mind.

> Your thumbs separate you from other humans. You begin to sense a presence about your thumbs. You wonder if there is not magic there.

In this example it is a character clearly delineated and distinguished from the reader who is the you of the narrative. But the second person can also be used as a means of making the reader into a character, as in Lorrie Moore's "How to Become a Writer":

First, try to be something, anything, else. A movie star/astronaut. A movie star/missionary. A movie star/kindergarten teacher. President of the World. Fail miserably. It is best if you fail at an early age—say, fourteen. Early, critical disillusionment is necessary so that at fifteen you can write long haiku sentences about thwarted desire. It is a pond, a cherry blossom, a wind brushing against sparrow wing leaving for mountain. Count the syllables. Show it to your mom.

Here again the effect of the second person is unusual and complex. The author assigns you, the reader, specific characteristics and reactions, and thereby—assuming that you go along with her characterization of you—pulls you deeper and more intimately into the story.

It is unlikely that the second person will ever become a major mode of narration as the first and third are, but for precisely that reason you may find it an attractive experiment.

FIRST PERSON

A story is told in the first person when it is a character who speaks. The term "narrator" is sometimes loosely used to refer to any teller of a tale, but strictly speaking a story has a narrator only when it is told in the first person by one of the characters. This character may be the protagonist, the *I* telling *my* story, in which case that character is a *central narrator*; or the character may be telling a story about someone else, in which case he or she is a *peripheral narrator*.

In either case it's important to indicate early which kind of narrator we have so that we know who the story's protagonist is, as in the first paragraph of Alan Sillitoe's "The Loneliness of the Long-Distance Runner."

> As soon as I got to Borstal they made me a long-distance cross-country runner. I suppose they thought I was just the build for it because I was long and skinny for my age (and still am) and in any case I didn't mind it much, to tell you the truth, because running had always been made much of in our family, especially running away from the police.

The focus here is immediately thrown on the *I* of the story, and we expect that *I* to be the central character whose desires and decisions impel the action. But from the opening lines of R. Bruce Moody's *The Decline and Fall of Daphne Finn*, it is Daphne who is brought alive by attention and detail, while the narrator is established as an observer and recorder of his subject.

> "Is it really you?"
> Melodious and high, this voice descended to me from behind and above—as it seemed it was always to do—indistinct as bells in another country.
> Unable to answer in the negative, I turned from my desk, looked up, and smiled sourly.

"Yes," I said, startling a face which had been peering over my shoulder, a face whose beauty it was apparent at the outset had made no concession to convention. It retreated as her feet staggered back.

The central narrator is always, as the term implies, at the center of the action; the peripheral narrator may be in virtually any position that is not the center. He or she may be the second most important character in the story, or may not be involved in the action at all but merely placed in a position to observe. The narrator may characterize himself or herself in detail or may remain detached and scarcely identifiable. It is even possible to make the first-person narrator plural, as William Faulkner does in "A Rose for Emily," where the story is told by a narrator identified only as one of *us*, the people of the town in which the action has taken place.

That a narrator may be either central or peripheral, that a character may tell either his own story or someone else's, is both commonly assumed and obviously logical. But the author and editor Rust Hills, in his book *Writing in General and the Short Story in Particular*, takes interesting and persuasive exception to this idea. When point of view fails, Hills argues, it is always because the perception we are using for the course of the story is different from that of the character who is moved or changed by the action. Even when a narrator seems to be a peripheral observer and the story is "about" someone else, in fact it is the narrator who is changed, and must be, in order for us to be satisfied by our emotional identification with him or her.

This, I believe, is what will always be the case in successful fiction: that either the character moved by the action will be the point-of-view character, or else the point of view character will *become* the character moved by the action. Call it Hills' Law.

Obviously, this view does not mean that we have to throw out the useful fictional device of the peripheral narrator. Hills uses the familiar examples of *The Great Gatsby* and *Heart of Darkness* to illustrate his meaning. In the former, Nick Carroway as a peripheral narrator observes and tells the story of Jay Gatsby, but by the end of the book it is Nick's life that has been changed by what he has observed. In the latter, Marlow purports to tell the tale of the ivory hunter Kurtz, even protesting that "I don't want to bother you much with what happened to me personally." By the end of the story, Kurtz (like Gatsby) is dead, but it is not the death that moves us so much as what, "personally," Marlow has learned through Kurtz and his death. The same can be said of *The Decline and Fall of Daphne Finn*; the focus of the action is on Daphne, but the pain, the passion, and the loss are those of her biographer. Even in "A Rose for Emily," where the narrator is a collective "we," it is the implied effect of Miss Emily on the town that moves us, the emotions of the townspeople that we share. Because we tend to identify with the means of perception in a story, we are moved with that perception; even when the overt action of the story is elsewhere, it is often the act of observation itself that provides the epiphany.

The thing to recognize about a first-person narrator is that because she or he is a character, she or he has all the limitations of a human being and cannot be omniscient. The narrator is confined to reporting what she or he could realistically know. More than that, although the narrator may certainly interpret actions, deliver dictums, and predict the future, these remain the fallible opinions of a human being; we are not bound to accept them as we are bound to accept the interpretations, truths, and predictions of the omniscient author. You may want us to accept the narrator's word, and then the most difficult part of your task, and the touchstone of your story's success, will be to convince us to trust and believe the narrator. On the other hand, it may be an important part of your purpose that we should reject the narrator's opinions and form our own. In the latter case, the narrator is "unreliable," a phenomenon that will be taken up in chapter 8.

To Whom?

In choosing a point of view, the author implies an identity not only for the teller of the tale, but also for the audience.

THE READER

Most fiction is addressed to a literary convention, "the reader." When we open a book, we tacitly accept our role as a member of this unspecified audience. If the story begins, "I was born of a drunken father and an illiterate mother in the peat bogs of Galway during the Great Potato Famine," we are not, on the whole, alarmed. We do not face this clearly deceased Irishman who has crossed the Atlantic to take us into his confidence and demand, "Why are you telling me all this?"

Notice that the tradition of "the reader" assumes the universality of the audience. Most stories do not specifically address themselves to a segment or period of humanity, and they make no concessions to such difference as might exist between reader and author; they assume that anyone who reads the story can be brought around to the same understanding of it the author has. In practice most writers, though they do not acknowledge it in the text and may not admit it to themselves, are addressing someone *who can* be brought around to the same understanding as themselves. The author of a "Harlequin Romance" addresses the story to a generalized "reader" but knows that his or her likely audience is trained by repetition of the formula to expect certain Gothic features—rich lover, virtuous heroine, threatening house, colorful costume. Slightly less formulaic is the notion of "a *New Yorker* story," which is presumably what the author perceives that the editors perceive will be pleasing to the people who buy *The New Yorker*. Anyone who pens or types what he or she hopes is "literature" is assuming that his or her audience is literate, which leaves out better than half the world. My mother, distressed at the difficulty of my fictional style, used to urge me to write for "the masses," by which she meant subscribers to *Reader's Digest*, whom she thought to be in need of cheering and escape. I considered this a very narrow goal until I realized that my own ambition to be "universal" was more exclusive still: I envisioned my audience as made up of people who would *not* subscribe to the *Reader's Digest*.

Nevertheless, the most common assumption of the tale-teller, whether omniscient author or narrating character, is that the reader is an amenable and persuasible Everyman, and that the telling needs no justification.

But there are various exceptions to this tendency which can be used to dramatic effect and which always involve a more definite characterizing of the receiver of the story. The author may address "the reader" but assign that reader specific traits that we, the actual readers, must then accept as our own if we are to accept the fiction. Nineteenth-century novelists had a tradition of addressing "You, gentle reader," "Dear reader," and the like, and this minimal characterization was a technique for implying mutual understanding. In "The Loneliness of the Long-Distance Runner," by Alan Sillitoe, on the other hand, the narrator divides the world into "us" and "you." *We*, the narrator and his kind, are the outlaws, all those who live by their illegal wits; *you*, the readers, are by contrast law-abiding, prosperous, educated, and rather dull. To quote again from "The Loneliness of the Long-Distance Runner":

> I suppose you'll laugh at this, me saying the governor's a stupid bastard when I
> know hardly how to write and he can read and write and add-up like a
> professor. But what I say is true right enough. He's stupid and I'm not, because
> I can see further into the likes of him than he can see into the likes of me.

The clear implication here is that the narrator can see further into the likes of us readers than we can see into the likes of him, and much of the effective irony of the story rests in the fact that the more we applaud and identify with the narrator, the more we must accept his condemning characterization of "us."

ANOTHER CHARACTER

More specifically still, the story may be told to *another character*, or *characters*, in which case we as readers "overhear" it; the teller of the tale does not acknowledge us even by implication. Just as the third-person author telling "her story" is theoretically more impersonal than the first-person character telling "my story," so "the reader" is theoretically a more impersonal receiver of the tale than another character. I insert the word "theoretically" because, with regard to point of view more than any other element of fiction, any rule laid down seems to be an invitation to rule breaking by some original and inventive author.

In the *epistolary* novel or story, the narrative consists entirely of letters written from one character to another, or between characters.

> I, Mukhail Ivanokov, stone mason in the village of Ilba in the Ukranian
> Soviet Socialist Republic, greet you and pity you, Charles Ashland,
> petroleum merchant in Titusville, Florida, in the United States of America. I
> grasp your hand.
>
> Kurt Vonnegut, *"The Manned Missiles"*

Or the convention of the story may be that of a monologue, spoken aloud by one character to another.

> May I, *monsieur*, offer my services without running the risk of intruding? I fear you may not be able to make yourself understood by the worthy ape who presides over the fate of this establishment. In fact, he speaks nothing but Dutch. Unless you authorize me to plead your case, he will not guess that you want gin.
>
> Albert Camus, *The Fall*

Again, the possible variations are infinite; the narrator may speak in intimate confessional to a friend or lover, or may present his case to a jury or a mob; she may be writing a highly technical report of the welfare situation, designed to hide her emotions; he may be pouring out his heart in a love letter he knows (and we know) he will never send.

In any of these cases, the convention employed is the opposite of that employed in a story told to "the reader." The listener as well as the teller is involved in the action; the assumption is not that we readers are there but that we are not. We are eavesdroppers, with all the ambiguous intimacy that position implies.

THE SELF

An even greater intimacy is implied if the character's story is as secret as a diary or as private as a mind, addressed to *the self* and not intended to be heard by anyone inside or outside the action.

In a *diary* or *journal*, the convention is that the thoughts are written but not expected to be read by anyone except the writer.

> November 6
>
> Something has got into the Chief of my Division. When I arrived at the office he called me and began as follows: "Now then, tell me. What's the matter with you? . . . I know you're trailing after the Director's daughter. Just look at yourself—what are you? Just nothing. You haven't a penny to your name. Look in the mirror. How can you even think of such things?" The hell with him! Just because he's got a face like a druggist's bottle and that quiff of hair on his head all curled and pomaded.
>
> Nikolai Gogol, *The Diary of a Madman*

The protagonist here is clearly using his diary to vent his feelings and does not intend it to be read by anyone else. Still, he has deliberately externalized his secret thoughts in a journal. Because the author has the power to enter a character's mind, the reader also has the power to eavesdrop on thoughts, read what is not written, hear what is not spoken, and share what cannot be shared.

Overheard thoughts are generally of two kinds, of which the more common is *interior monologue*, the convention being that we follow that character's thoughts in their sequence, though in fact the author, for our convenience, sets out those thoughts with a coherence and logic that no human mind ever possessed.

> I must organize myself. I must, as they say, pull myself together, dump this cat from my lap, stir—yes, resolve, move, do. But do what? My will is like the rosy dustlike light in this room: soft, diffuse, and gently comforting. It lets me do. . . anything. . . nothing. My ears hear what they happen to; I eat what's put before me; my eyes see what blunders into them; my thoughts are not thoughts, they are dreams. I'm empty or I'm full. . . depending; and I cannot choose. I sink my claws in Tick's fur and scratch the bones of his back until his rear rises amorously. Mr. Tick, I murmur, I must organize myself, I must pull myself together. And Mr. Tick rolls over on his belly, all ooze.

> William H. Gass, *"In the Heart of the Heart of the Country"*

This interior monologue ranges, as human thoughts do, from sense impression to self-admonishment, from cat to light to eyes and ears, from specific to general and back again. But the logical connections between these things are all provided; the mind "thinks" logically and grammatically as if the character were trying to express himself.

Stream of consciousness acknowledges the fact that the human mind does not operate with the order and clarity of the monologue just quoted. Even what little we know of its operations makes clear that it skips, elides, makes and breaks images, leaps faster and further than any mere sentence can suggest. Any mind at any moment is simultaneously accomplishing dozens of tasks that cannot be conveyed simultaneously. As you read this sentence, part of your mind is following the sense of it; part of your mind is directing your hand to hold the book open; part of it is twisting your spine into a more comfortable position; part of it is still lingering on the last interesting image of this text, Mr. Tick rolling over on his belly, which reminds you of a cat you had once that was also *all ooze*, which reminds you that you're nearly out of milk and have to finish this chapter before the store closes—and so forth.

In *Ulysses*, James Joyce tried to catch the speed and multiplicity of the mind with the technique that has come to be known as stream of consciousness. The device is difficult and in many ways thankless: Since the speed of thought is so much faster than that of writing or speaking, and stream of consciousness tries to suggest the process as well as the content of the mind, it requires a more, not less, rigorous selection and arrangement than ordinary grammar requires. But Joyce and a very few other writers have handled stream of consciousness as an ebullient and exciting way of capturing the mind.

> Yes because he never did a thing like that before as ask to get his breakfast in bed with a couple of eggs since the City Arms hotel when he used to be pretending to be laid up with a sick voice doing his highness to make himself

interesting to that old faggot Mrs. Riordan that he thought he had a great leg of and she never left us a farthing for all masses for herself and her soul greatest miser ever was actually afraid to lay out 4d for her methylated spirit telling me all her ailments she had too much old chat in her about politics and earthquakes and the end of the world let us have a bit of fun first God help the world if all the women were her sort. . .

James Joyce, *Ulysses*

The preceding two examples, of interior monologue and stream of consciousness, respectively, are written in the first person, so that we overhear the minds of narrator characters. Through the omniscient and limited omniscient authors we may also overhear the thoughts of the characters, and when this is the case there is a curious doubling or crossing of literary conventions. Say that the story is told by a limited omniscient author, who is therefore speaking to "the reader." But this author may also enter the mind of a character, who is speaking to himself or herself. The passage from *The Odd Woman* on page 202 is of this sort. Here is a still more striking example:

Dusk was slowly deepening. Somewhere, he could not tell exactly where, a cricket took up a fitful song. The air was growing soft and heavy. He looked over the fields, longing for Bobo. . .
He shifted his body to ease the cold damp of the ground, and thought back over the day. Yeah, hed been dam right erbout not wantin t go swimmin. N ef hed followed his right min hed neverve gone n got inter all this trouble.

Richard Wright, *"Big Boy Leaves Home"*

Though this story, first published in 1938, makes use of an old style of dialect misspelling, Wright moves gracefully between the two voices. An authorial voice—educated, eloquent, and mature—tells us what is in Big Boy's mind: *he could not tell exactly where, longing for Bobo*; and a dialect voice lets us overhear Big Boy's thoughts, adolescent and uneducated: *Yeah, hed been dam right*. If either of these voices were absent, the passage would be impoverished; it needs the scope of the author and the immediacy of the character to achieve its effect.

In What Form?

The form of the story, like the teller and the listener, can be more or less specified as part of the total point of view. The form may announce itself without justification as a generalized *story*, either *written* or *spoken*; or it may suggest *reportage, confessional, interior monologue,* or *stream of consciousness*; or it may be overtly identified as *monologue, oratory, journal,* or *diary*. The relationship between the teller of a tale and its receiver often automatically implies a form for the telling, so that most of the forms above have already been mentioned. The list is not exhaustive; you can tell your story in the form of a catalogue or a television commercial as long as you can also contrive to give it the form of a story.

Form is important to point of view because the form in which a story is told indicates the degree of self-consciousness on the part of the teller; this will in turn affect the language chosen, the intimacy of the relationship, and the honesty of the telling. A written account will imply less spontaneity, on the whole, than one that appears to be spoken aloud, which suggests less spontaneity than thought. A narrator writing a letter to his grandmother may be less honest than he is when he tells the same facts aloud to his friend.

Certain relationships established by the narrative between teller and audience make certain forms more likely than others, but almost any combination of answers is possible to the questions: *Who speaks? To whom? In what form?* If you are speaking as an omniscient author to the literary convention of "the reader," we may assume that you are using the convention of "written story" as your form. But you might say:

Wait, step over here a minute. What's this in the corner, stuffed down
between the bedpost and the wall?

If you do this, you slip at least momentarily into the different convention of the spoken word—the effect is that we are drawn more immediately into the scene—and the point of view of the whole is slightly altered. A central narrator might be thinking, and therefore "talking to herself," while actually angrily addressing her thoughts to another character. Conversely, one character might be writing a letter to another but letting the conscious act of writing deteriorate into a betrayal of his own secret thoughts. Any complexities such as these will alter and inform the total point of view.

Here are the opening passages from a student short story in which the point of view is extremely complex. An adequate analysis of it will require more than a definition or a diagram, a series of *yes but*'s and *but also*'s.

Report: He is the light-bringer, the peerless one. She is the dark-water
creature, the Queen of Fishes. I don't know why I say that except sometimes
I get desperate for sheer sound. You would too if you went to St. Katherine's
Day Academy where the D. H. Lawrence is in a locked cabinet in the library.
I used to wonder why Tom sends me there except now I know it's his notion
of a finishing school. "It's what your mother would have wanted," he says,
tragic-eyed. But I know he's thinking about Vivian.
    I started my journal to show you what she's doing to him. He doesn't
know. He wouldn't. But I sit in on the seminar. I read the Eliot, the Rhys,
the Muir, the MacDiarmid with them. They think I'm amusing, these long
tall girls in Rive Gauche jeans and velour with Parker chrome mechanical
pencils—engraved initials—and notebooks written all over: "Bring *The
Green Helmet* to class Tues." and "talk to Dr. Johnson about Parents' Day

Brunch" and phone numbers everywhere. I am a sort of mascot. They'd be surprised to know that I, their Tom's daughter, knows what they are at when they talk of regional sensibility in Muir and the mythic fallacy. Especially Vivian who comes to class early and stays late and comes for dinner and once "took Elaine shopping, isn't that nice?" God, I hated it. "Look, Elaine, that grey would just match your eyes. I'll bet Tom, I mean your father, would like that." I went home that day and cast a Mars number square against her for discord, discord, discord. But still she came back—back for Tom.

Diane Roberts, "Lamia"

Who speaks? The passage is written in the first person—that much is easy. So it is a narrator who speaks, and this narrator tells us that she is peripheral: "I started my journal to show you what she's doing to him." But against this statement of the narrator's intention, we feel so much personal grief and bottled fury, and the focus of the narrative returns so insistently to what the I of the story is doing and feeling, that we are inclined to believe the real subject is not "what she's doing to him" but *what they're doing to me* and, therefore, to feel that we're dealing with a central narrator.

To whom? The narrator addresses a you who is clearly the convention of "the reader." Yet on several counts this notion doesn't bear pursuing. She is revealing bitter attitudes that couldn't be confessed to her father, so the you to whom she reveals them can scarcely include a reader sitting with printed pages. The reader who is the you of the narrative becomes so abstract that it might be the spirit of justice she addresses, or God. Yet the narrator makes little attempt to present a coherent account of background facts, which come out obliquely, subsidiary to the pent-up emotion—*I am a sort of mascot; They'd be surprised to know*—which suggests that she's really talking to herself.

In what form? She tells us twice: this is "a report" and "my journal." Neither is quite possible. The opening word "Report" is immediately contradicted by the dramatic imagery of "light-bringer" and "dark-water creature," so that we understand the word itself is an ironic attempt to claim logic and objectivity for an emotion that admits of neither. It's a journal, then, a diary of great intimacy. That's what it feels like; but how can a diary be addressed to a reader?

The amazing thing about all this is that we are not in the least confused! The paradoxes and contradictions of the narrative do not make us feel that the author is inept but, on the contrary, that she has captured with great precision the paradoxes and contradictions of the narrator's emotional state. We feel no awkward point-of-view shift because all the terms of the contract—those same paradoxes and contradictions—are laid out for us in the opening paragraph.

Clearly there is an author somewhere who is not the same person as this narrator, and who is directing us moment by moment to accept or reject, to believe or disbelieve, what the narrator tells us.

In order to deal with a viewpoint as complex as this, it will be necessary to deal not only with who speaks to whom in what form, but also with *distance* and *limitation*, subjects treated in chapter 8.

⌒ *The Excursion* ⌒

JOY WILLIAMS

Jenny lies a little. She is just a little girl, a child with fears. She fears that birds will fly out of the toilet bowl. Starlings with slick black wings. She fears trees and fishes and the bones in meat. She lies a little but it is not considered serious. Sometimes it seems she forgets where she is. She is lost in a place that is not her childhood. Sometimes she will say to someone, Mrs. Coogan at the Capt'n Davy Nursery School, for example, that her mother is dead, her father is dead, even her dog Tonto is dead. She will say that she has no toys, that she lives with machinery she cannot run, that she lives in a house with no windows, no view of the street, that she lives with strangers. She has to understand everything herself.

Poor Mrs. Coogan! She pats Jenny's shoulder. Jenny wears pretty and expensive dresses with blue sneakers. The effect is charming. She has blond hair falling over a rather low brow and an interesting, mobile face. She does everything too fast. She rushes to bathtimes and mealtimes and even to sleep. She sleeps rapidly with deep, heartbreaking sighs. Such hurry is unnecessary. It is as though she rushes forward to meet even her memories.

Jenny does not know how to play games very well. When the others play, she is still. She stands with her stomach thrust out, watching the others with a cool, inward gaze. Sometimes, something interrupts her, some urgent voice, perhaps, or shout, and she makes a startled, curious skip. Her brown eyes brim with confusion. She turns pale or very red. Yes, sometimes Jenny has bad days. The crayons are dead, the swings are dead, even little Johnny Lewis who sits so patiently on his mat at snacktime will be dead. He is thirsty and when he gets the cup of juice which Mrs. Coogan gives him, Jenny is glad for his sake.

"I am so happy Johnny Lewis got his juice!" Jenny cries.

Poor Mrs. Coogan. The child is such a puzzle.

"I don't care for the swimming," Jenny tells her, even though Mrs. Coogan doesn't take her little group swimming. She takes them for a walk. Down to the corner, where the school bus carrying the older children goes by.

"Perhaps you'll like it when you get a little older, when you get a little better at it," Mrs. Coogan says.

Jenny shakes her head. She thinks of all the nakedness, milling and bobbing and bumping against her in the flat, warm, dark water. She says this aloud.

"Oh my dear," Mrs. Coogan says.

"I don't understand about the swimming," Jenny says.

Jenny's father picks her up at four. In the car, he always has a present for her. Today it is a watch. It is only a toy watch, but it has moving parts and the manufacturer states that if it is not abused it will keep fairly reasonable time.

Mrs. Coogan says to Jenny's father, "All children fib a little. It's their nature. Their lives are incompatible with the limits imposed upon their experience."

Jenny feels no real insecurity while Mrs. Coogan speaks, but she is a little anxious. She is with a man. She doesn't smell very good. Outside other men are striking the locked door with sticks.

"Leña," they call. "Leña."

Jenny's father frowns at Mrs. Coogan. He does not wish to be aware that Jenny lies. To him, it is a terrible risk of oneself to lie. It risks control, peace, self-knowledge, even, perhaps, the proper acceptance of love. He is a thoughtful, reasonable man. He loves his only child. He wills her safe passage through the world. He does not wish to acknowledge that lying gives a beat and structure to Jenny's life that the truth has not yet justified. Jenny's imagination depresses him. He senses an ultimatum in it.

Jenny runs to the car. Her father is not with her. He is behind her. Suddenly the child realizes this and whips around to catch him with her eyes. Once again, she succeeds.

Jenny's mother is in the front seat, checking over her grocery list. Jenny kisses her and shows her the big, colorful watch. A tiny girl sits on a swing within the watch's face. When Jenny winds it, the girl starts swinging, the clock starts to run.

Jenny sits in the back. The car moves out into the street. She hears a mother somewhere crying. Some mother, calling, "Oh come back and let me rock you on your little swing!"

Jenny says nothing. She is propelled by sidereal energies. Loving, for her, will not be a free choosing of her destiny. It will be the discovery of the most fateful part of herself. She is with a man. When he kisses her, he covers her throat with his hand. He rubs his fingers lightly down the tendons of her neck. He holds her neck in his big hand as he kisses her over and over again.

"Raisin Bran or Cheerios?" Jenny's mother asks. "Cheddar or Swiss?"

Jenny is just a little girl. She worries that there will not be enough jam, not enough cookies. When she walks with her mother through the supermarket, she nervously pats her mother's arm.

Now, at home, Jenny reads. She is precocious in this. When she first discovered that she could read, she did not tell anyone about it. The words took on the depths of patient, dangerous animals, and Jenny cautiously lived alone with them for awhile. Now, however, everyone realizes that she can read, and they are very proud of her. Jenny reads in the newspaper that that day in San Luis Obispo, California, a seventeen-year-old girl came out of a clothing store, looked around horrified, screamed, and died. The newspaper said that several years previous to this, the girl's sister had woken early, given a piercing scream, and died. The newspaper said that the parents now fear for the welfare of their other two daughters.

Women suffer from the loss of a secret once known. Jenny will realize this someday. Now, however, she merely thinks, "What is the dread that women have?"

Jenny gets up and goes to her room. A stuffed bear is propped on her bureau. She takes it to the kitchen and gives it some orange juice. Then she takes it to the bathroom and puts it on the toilet seat for a moment. Then she puts it to bed.

Jenny wakes crying in the night and rushes into her parents' room. She is not sure of the time; she is not sure if they will be there. Of course they are there.

Jenny is just a child. On a bedside table are her mother's reading glasses and a little vase of marigolds. Deeply hued, yellow, red and orange. Her parents are very patient. She is a normal little girl with fears, with nightmares. The nightmares do no real harm, that is, they will not alter her life. She is afraid that she is growing, that she will grow too much. She returns to her room after being comforted, holding one of the little flowers.

The man likes flowers, although he dislikes Jenny's childishness. He removes Jenny's skimpy cotton dress. He puts the flowers between her breasts, between her legs. The house is full of flowers. It is Mexico on the Day of the Dead. Millions of marigolds have been woven into carpets and placed on the graves. Jenny's mouth hurts, her stomach hurts. Yes, the man dislikes her childishness. He kneels beside her, his hands on her hips, and forces her to look at his blank, warm face. It is a youthful face, although he is certainly no longer a young man. Jenny had seen him when he was younger, drunk, blue-eyed. It doesn't matter. He doesn't age. He has had other loves and he has behaved similarly with them all. How could it be otherwise? Even so, Jenny knows that she has originated with him, that anything before him was nostalgia for this. Even so, there are letters, variously addressed, interchangeably addressed, it would seem. These letters won't be kept. It isn't the time, but they are here now, in a jumble, littered with the toys. Jenny reads them as though in a dream. This is Jenny! As in a dream too, she is less reasonable but capable of better judgment.

> *I won't stay here. It is a tomb, this town, and the streets are full of whores, women with live mice or snakes or fish in the clear plastic heels of their shoes. Death and the whores are everywhere, walking in these bright, horrible shoes.*

How unhappy Jenny's mother would be if she were to see this letter! She comes into the child's room in the morning and helps her tie her shoes.

"You do it like this," she says, crossing the laces, "and then you do this, you make a bunny ear here, see."

Her mother holds her on her lap while she teaches her to tie her shoes. Jenny is so impatient. She wants to cry as she sees her mother's eager fingers. Jenny's nightie is damp and sweaty. Her mother takes it off and goes to the sink where she washes it with sweet-smelling soap. Then she makes Jenny's breakfast. Jenny is not hungry. She takes the food outside and scatters it on the ground. The grass covers it up. Jenny goes back to her room. Everything is neatly put away. Her mother has made the bed. Jenny takes everything out again, her toy stove and typewriter and phone, her puppets and cars, the costly and minute dollhouse furnishings. Everything is there: a tiny papier-mâché pot roast dinner, lamps, rugs, andirons, fans, everything. The cupboards are full of play bread, the play pool is full of water.

Jenny's face is tense and intimate. She knows everything, but how aimless and arbitrary her knowledge is! For she has only desire; she has always had only the desire for this, her sleek, quiescent lover. He is so cold and so satisfying for there is no discovery in him. She goes to the bed and curls up beside him. He is dark and she is light. There are no shadings in Jenny's world. He is a tall, dark tree rooted in the stubborn night, and she is a flame seeking him—unstable, transparent. They are in Oaxaca. If they opened the shutters they would see the stone town. The town is made of a soft, pale green stone that makes it look as though it has been rained upon for centuries. Shadows in the shape of men fall from the buildings. Everything is cool, almost rotten. In the markets, the fruit beads with water; the fragile feathered skulls of the birds are moist to the touch.

The man sleeks her hair back behind her ears. She is not so pretty now. Her face is uneven, her eyes are closed.

"You're asleep," he says. "You're making love to me in your sleep. *Vete a la chingada.*" He says it slangily and softly, scornfully as any Mexican. She is nothing, nowhere. There is something exquisite in this, in the way, now, that he holds her throat. The pressure is so familiar. She yearns for this.

But he turns from her. He leaves.

Jenny pretends sleep. She plays that she is sleeping. She is fascinated with her sleep where everything takes place as though it were not so. Nothing is concealed. On stationery from the Hotel Principal there is written:

Nobody to blame. Call 228

She sits at a small desk, drinking beer and reading. She is reading about the Aztecs. She notes the goddess TLAZOLTEOTL, the goddess of filth and fecundity, of human moods, sexual love and confession. Jenny sits very straight in the chair. Her neck is long, full, graceful. But she feels out of breath. The high, clear air here makes her pant. The man pants too while he climbs the steep, stone steps of the town. He smokes too much. At night, when they return from drinking, he coughs flecks of blood onto the bathroom mirror. The blood is on the tiles, in the basin. Jenny closes her own mouth tightly as she hears him gag. Breath is outside her, expelled, not doing her any good. She stands beside the man as he coughs. There is not much blood, but it seems to be everywhere, late at night, after they have been drinking, everywhere except on the man's clothes. He is impeccable about his clothes. He always wears a grey lightweight suit and a white shirt. He has two suits and they are both grey, and he has several shirts and they are all white. He is always the same. Even in his nakedness, his force, he is smooth, furled, closed. He is simple to her. There is no other way offered. He offers her the death of his sterility. His sexuality is the source of life, and his curse is death. He offers her nothing except his dying.

She wets her hands and wipes off the mirror. She cannot imagine him dead really. She is just a child embracing the crisis of a woman. The death she sees is that of herself in his emptiness. And he fills her with it. He floods her with emptiness. She grasps his thick, longish hair. She feels as if she is floating through his hair, falling miraculously away from danger into death. Safe at last.

"Jenny, Jenny, Jenny," her mother calls.

"I want a baby," Jenny says. "Can I have a baby?"

"Of course," her mother says, "when you get to be a big girl and fall in love."

Jenny will write on the stationery of the Hotel Principal:

The claims of love and self-preservation are opposed.

The man looks over her shoulder. He is restless, impatient to get going. They are going to the baths outside of town, in the mountains. A waterfall thuds into a long, stone basin which has been artificially heated. It is a private club, crowded with Americans and wealthy Mexicans. When Jenny and the man arrive at the baths, they first go to a tiny stone cubicle where the man strips. He hangs his clothes carefully from the wooden pegs which are fixed in the stone. Jenny looks outside where a red horse grazes from a long, woven tether. There is water trickling over the face of the hillside. There is very little grass. The water sparkles around the horse's hooves. The man turns Jenny from the window and begins to undress her. She is like a little child with artless limbs. He rolls her pants down slowly. He slips her sweater off. He does everything slowly. Her clothes fall to the floor which is wet with something, which smells sweet. With one hand, the man holds her arms firmly behind her back. He doesn't do anything to her. She cannot smell him or even feel his breath. She can see his face which is a little stern but not frightening. It holds no disappointment for her. She tries to move closer to him, but his grip on her arms prevents her. She begins to tremble. Her body feels his stroking, his touch, even though he does nothing. Her body starts to beat, to move in the style of their lovemaking. She becomes confused, the absence of him in her is so strong.

Later, the man goes out to the pool. Jenny hates the baths, but they come here several times a week on the man's insistence. She dresses and goes out to the side of the pool and watches the man swim back and forth. There are many people here, naked or nearly so, tossing miniature footballs back and forth. She sees the man grasp the ankles of a woman and begin to tow her playfully through the water. The woman wears silver earrings. Her hair is silver, her pubic hair is silver. Her mouth is a thickly frosted white. The water foams on her skin in tiny translucent bubbles. The woman laughs and moves her legs up in a scissors grip around the man's waist. Jenny sees him kiss her.

Another man, a Mexican, comes up to Jenny. He is bare-chested and wears white trousers and tall, yellow boots. He absently plucks at his left nipple while he looks at her.

"Ford Galaxie," he says at last. He takes a ring of car keys from his pocket and jerks his head toward the mountains.

"No," Jenny says.

"Galaxie," the Mexican says. "Galaxie. *Rojo.*"

Jenny sees the car, its red shell cold in the black mountains, drawn through the landscape of rock and mutilated maguey. Drawn through, with her inside, quietly transported.

"No," she says. She hates the baths. The tile in the bottom of the pool is arranged in the shape of a bird, a heron with thin legs and a huge, flat head. Her lover stands still in the water now, looking at her, amused.

"Jenny," her mother laughs. "You're such a dreamer. Would you like to go out for supper? You and Daddy and I can go to the restaurant that you like."

For it is just the summer. That is all it is, and Jenny is only five. In the house which they are renting on Martha's Vineyard, there is a dinghy stored in the rafters of the living room. The landlord is supposed to come for it and take it down, but he does not. Jenny positions herself beneath the dinghy and scatters her shell collection over her legs and chest. She pretends that she has been cast out of it and floated to the bottom of the sea.

"Jenny-cake, get up now," her mother says. The child rises heavily from the floor. The same sorrow undergone for nothing is concluded. Again and again, nothing.

"Oh Jenny-cake," her mother says sadly, for Jenny is so quiet, so pale. They have come to the island for the sunshine, for play, to offer Jenny her childhood. Her childhood eludes them all. What is the guide which Jenny follows?

"Let's play hairdresser," her mother says. "I'll be the hairdresser and you be the little girl."

Jenny lets her comb and arrange her hair.

"You're so pretty," her mother says.

But she is so melancholy, so careless with herself. She is bruised everywhere. Her mother parts her hair carefully. She brings out a dish of soapy water and brushes and trims Jenny's nails. She is put in order. She is a tidy little girl in a clean dress going out to supper on a summer night.

"Come on Jenny," her mother urges her. "We want to be back home while it's still light." Jenny moves slowly to the door that her father is holding open for them.

"I have an idea," her mother says, "I'll be a parade and you be the little girl following the parade."

Jenny is so far away. She smiles to keep her mother from prattling so. She is what she will be. She has no energy, no talent, not even for love. She lies face down, her face buried in a filthy sheet. The man lies beside her. She can feel his heart beating on her arm. Pounding like something left out of life. A great machine, a desolate engine, taking over for her, moving her. The machine moves her out the door, into the streets of the town.

There is a dance floor in the restaurant. Sometimes Jenny dances with her father. She dances by standing on top of his shoes while he moves around the floor. The restaurant is quite expensive. The menu is written in chalk on a blackboard which is then rolled from table to table. They go to this restaurant mostly because Jenny likes the blackboard. She can pretend that this is school.

There is a candle on each table, and Jenny blows it out at the beginning of each meal. This plunges their table into deep twilight. Sometimes the waitress relights the candle, and Jenny blows it out again. She can pretend that this is her birthday over and over again. Her parents allow her to do this. They allow her to do anything that does not bring distress to others. This usually works out well.

Halfway through their dinner, they become aware of a quarrel at the next table. A man is shouting at the woman who sits beside him. He does not appear angry, but he is saying outrageous things. The woman sits very straight in her chair and cuts into her food. Once, she puts her hand gently on the side of his head. He does not shrug it off nor does it appear that he allows the caress. The woman's hand falls back in her lap.

"Please don't," the woman says. "We're spoiling the others' dinner."

"I don't care about the others," the man says. "I care about you."

The woman's laugh is high and uneasy. Her face is serene, but her hands tremble. The bones glow beneath her taut skin. There is a sense of blood, decay, the smell of love.

"Nothing matters except you," the man says again. He reaches over and picks up the food from her plate. It is some sort of creamed fish. He squeezes it in his hand and lets it drop on the table between them. It knocks over the flowers, the wine. "What do you care what others think?" he says.

"I don't know why people go out if they're not intending to have a nice time," Jenny's mother whispers. Jenny doesn't speak. The man's curses tease her ears. The reality of the couple, now gone, cheats her eyes. She gazes fixedly at the abandoned table, at the garbage there. Everywhere there is disorder. Even in her parents' eyes.

"Tomorrow we're going sailing," her father says. "It's going to be a beautiful day."

"I would say that woman had a problem there," Jenny's mother says.

Outside, the sunset has dispersed the afternoon's fog. The sun makes long paddle strokes through the clouds. At day's end, the day creaks back to brightness like a swinging boom. Jenny walks down the street between her parents. At the curb, as children do, she takes a little leap into space, supported, for the moment, by their hands.

And now gone for good, this moment. It is night again.

"It's been night for a long time," the man says. He is shaving at the basin. His face, to about an inch below his eyes, is a white mask of lather. His mouth is a dark hole in the mask.

Jenny's dizzy from drinking. The sheets are white, the walls are white. One section of the room has a raised ceiling. It rises handsomely to nothing but a single light bulb, shaded by strips of wood. The frame around the light is very substantial. It is as though the light were caged. The light is like a wild thing up there, pressed against the ceiling, a furious bright creature with slanty wings.

In the room there is a chair, a table, a bureau and a bed. There is a milkshake in a glass on a tin tray. On the surface of the milk, green petals of mold reach out from the sides toward the center.

"Clean yourself up and we'll go out," the man says.

Jenny moves obediently to the basin. She hangs her head over the round black drain. She splashes her hands and face with water. The drain seems very complex.

Grids, mazes, avenues of descent, lacings, and webs of matter. At the very bottom of the drain she sees a pinpoint of light. She's sure of it. Children lie there in that light, sleeping. She sees them so clearly, their small, sweet mouths open in the light.

"We know too much," Jenny says. "We all know too much almost right away."

"Clean yourself up better than that," the man says.

"You go ahead. I'll meet you there," Jenny says. For she has plans for the future. Jenny has lived in nothing if not the future all her life. Time had moved between herself and the man, but only for years. What does time matter to the inevitability of relations? It is inevitability that matters to lives, not love. For had she not always remembered him? And seen him rising from a kiss? Always.

When she is alone, she unties the rope that ties her luggage together. The bag is empty. She has come to this last place with nothing, really. She has been with this man for a long time. There had always been less of her each time she followed him. She wants to do this right, but her fingers fumble with the rope. It is as though her fingers were cold, the rope knotted and soaked with sea water. It is so difficult to arrange. She stops for a moment and then remembers in a panic that she has to go to the bathroom. That was the most important thing to remember. She feels close to tears because she almost forgot.

"I have to go to the bathroom," she cries.

Her mother leads her there.

"This is not a nice bathroom," her mother says. Water runs here only at certain times of the day. It is not running now. There are rags on the floor. The light falling through the window is dirty.

"Help me Mother," Jenny says.

Her stomach is so upset. She is afraid she will soil herself. She wants to get out in the air for a moment and clear her head. Her head is full of lies. Outside the toilet, out there, she remembers, is the deck of the motor sailer. The green sails which have faded to a style of blue are luffing, pounding like boards in the wind. She closes the door to the toilet. Out here is the Atlantic, rough and blue and cold. Of course there is no danger. The engines are on; they are bringing the people back to the dock. The sails have the weight of wood. There is no danger. She is all right. She is just a little girl. She is with her mother and father. They are on vacation. They are cruising around the island with other tourists. Her father has planned an excursion for each day of their vacation. Now they are almost home. No one is behaving recklessly. People sit quietly on the boat or move about measuredly, collecting tackle or coiling lines or helping children into their sweaters.

Jenny sees the man waiting on the dock. The boat's engines whine higher as the boat is backed up, as it bumps softly against the canvas-wrapped pilings. The horrid machine whines higher and higher. She steps off into his arms.

He kisses her as he might another. She finds him rough, hurtful at first, but then his handling of her becomes more gentle, more sure in the knowledge that she is willing.

His tongue moves deeply, achingly in her mouth. His loving becomes autonomous now. It becomes, at last, complete.

Suggestions for Discussion

1. Who speaks? To Whom? In what form?

2. "Excursion" offers an unusual modern use of the *editorial omniscient*. Show how the author sets up a "contract" in the first paragraph that allows her such omniscience. What is the function of phrases like "just a little girl," "is not considered serious," "it seems she forgets," "is not her childhood," and "has to understand everything herself." Whose point(s) of view do these suggest?

3. Are there any limitations at all accepted by this omniscient author? What would it *not* feel appropriate for the narrative to know or do? How does the author limit kinds of authorial knowledge toward the end of the story? What is the effect of this limiting?

4. In spite of the author's omniscience, much of the narrative has an objective, matter-of-fact tone. Why did the author make this choice? How does it characterize, effect the atmosphere?

5. At what point do you first realize that the narrative will leap forward in time? How has the author prepared you to accept this?

6. How does conflict between Jenny's speech, action, and thought, form the core of her story?

 Girl

JAMAICA KINKEAD

Wash the white clothes on Monday and put them on the stone heap; wash the color clothes on Tuesday and put them on the clothesline to dry; don't walk barehead in the hot sun; cook pumpkin fritters in very hot sweet oil; soak your little cloths right after you take them off; when buying cotton to make yourself a nice blouse, be sure that it doesn't have gum on it, because that way it won't hold up well after a wash; soak salt fish overnight before you cook it; is it true that you sing benna in Sunday school?; always eat your food in such a way that it won't turn someone else's stomach; on Sundays try to walk like a lady and not like the slut you are so bent on becoming; don't sing benna in Sunday school; you mustn't speak to wharf-rat boys, not even to give directions; don't eat fruits on the street—flies will follow you; *but I don't sing benna on Sundays at all and never in Sunday school*; this is how to sew on a button; this is how to make a buttonhole for the button you have just sewed on; this is how to hem a dress when you see the hem coming down and so to prevent yourself from looking like the slut I know you are so bent on becoming; this is how you iron your father's khaki shirt so that it doesn't have a crease; this is how you iron your father's khaki pants so that they don't have a crease; this is how you grow okra—far from the house, because okra tree harbors red ants; when you are growing dasheen, make sure it gets plenty of water or else it makes your throat itch when you are eating it; this is how you sweep a corner; this is how you sweep a whole house; this is how you sweep a yard; this is how you smile to someone you don't like too much; this is how you smile to someone you don't like at all; this is how you smile to someone you like completely; this is how you set a table for tea; this is how you set a table for dinner; this is how you set a table for dinner with an important guest; this is how you set a table for lunch; this is how you set a table for breakfast; this is how to behave in the presence of men who don't know you very well, and this way they won't recognize immediately the slut I have warned you against becoming; be sure to wash every day, even if it is with your own spit; don't squat down to play marbles—you are not a boy, you know; don't pick people's flowers—you might catch something; don't throw stones at blackbirds, because it might not be a blackbird at all; this is how to make a bread pudding; this is how to make doukona; this is how to make pepper pot; this is how to make a good medicine for a cold; this is how to make a good medicine to throw away a child before it even becomes a child; this is how to catch a fish; this is how to throw back a fish you don't like, and that way something bad won't fall on you; this is how to bully a man; this is how a man bullies you; this is how to love a man, and if this doesn't work there are other ways, and if they don't work don't feel too bad about giving up; this is how to spit up in the air if you feel like it, and this is how to move quick so that it doesn't fall on you; this is how to make ends meet; always squeeze bread to make sure it's fresh; *but what if the baker won't let me feel the bread?*; you mean to say that after all you are really going to be the kind of woman who the baker won't let near the bread?

Suggestions for Discussion

1. Who speaks in "Girl"? Is it written in the first or second person?

2. To Whom? Even in this short compass, Kincaid manages to create the character of the daughter in such a way that we see her consistent inconsistency. Identify it.

3. In what form? Describe the form as fully as you can.

4. Is the narrator central or peripheral?

5. This very short story is written as a single ongoing sentence. How does it nevertheless have the form of a story? Can you identify conflict, crisis, and resolution?

6. The story contains several details that, if you live in the continental United States, are likely to be obscure to you: *benna, dasheen, doukona.* It's also possible that you can't exactly see *pumpkin fritters, wharf-rat boys, an okra tree, a pepper pot.* How much does it matter? How much do sound, tone, and approximate meaning add to your understanding?

 Hips

SANDRA CISNEROS

I like coffee, I like tea.
I like the boys and the boys like me.
Yes, no, maybe so. Yes, no, maybe so. . .

One day you wake up and they are there. Ready and waiting like a new Buick with the keys in the ignition. Ready to take you where?

They're good for holding a baby when you're cooking, Rachel says, turning the jump rope a little quicker. She has no imagination.

You need them to dance, says Lucy.

If you don't get them you may turn into a man. Nenny says this and she believes it. She is this way because of her age.

That's right, I add before Lucy or Rachel can make fun of her. She is stupid alright, but she *is* my sister.

But most important, hips are scientific, I say repeating what Alicia already told me. It's the bones that let you know which skeleton was a man's when it was a man and which a woman's.

They bloom like roses, I continue because it's obvious I'm the only one who can speak with any authority; I have science on my side. The bones just one day open. Just like that. One day you might decide to have kids, and then where are you going to put them? Got to have room. Bones got to give.

But don't have too many or your behind will spread. That's how it is, says Rachel whose mama is as wide as a boat. And we just laugh.

What I'm saying is who here is ready? You gotta be able to know what to do with hips when you get them, I say making it up as I go. You gotta know how to walk with hips, practice you know—like if half of you wanted to go one way and the other half the other.

That's to lullaby it, Nenny says, that's to rock the baby asleep inside you. And then she begins singing *seashells, copper bells, eevy, ivy, o-ver.*

I'm about to tell her that's the dumbest thing I've ever heard, but the more I think about it. . .

You gotta get the rhythm, and Lucy begins to dance. She has the idea, though she's having trouble keeping her end of the double-dutch steady.

It's gotta be just so, I say. Not too fast and not too slow. Not too fast and not too slow.

We slow the double circles down to a certain speed so Rachel who has just jumped in can practice shaking it.

I want to shake like hoochi-coochie, Lucy says. She is crazy.

I want to move like heebie-jeebie, I say picking up on the cue.

I want to be Tahiti. Or *merengue*. Or electricity.

Or *tembleque*!

Yes, *tembleque*. That's a good one.
And then it's Rachel who starts it:

> *Skip, skip*
> *snake in your hips.*
> *Wiggle around*
> *and break your lip.*

Lucy waits a minute before her turn. She is thinking. Then she begins:

> *The waitress with the big fat hips*
> *who pays the rent with taxi tips. . .*
> *says nobody in town will kiss her on the lips*
> *because. . .*
> *because she looks like Christopher Columbus!*
> *Yes, no, maybe so. Yes, no, maybe so.*

She misses on maybe so. I take a little while before my turn, take a breath, and dive in:

> *Some are skinny like chicken lips.*
> *Some are baggy like soggy Band-Aids*
> *after you get out of the bathtub.*
> *I don't care what kind I get.*
> *Just as long as I get hips.*

Everybody getting into it now except Nenny who is still humming *not a girl, not a boy, just a little baby*. She's like that.

When the two arcs open wide like jaws Nenny jumps in across from me, the rope tick-ticking, the little gold earrings our mama gave her for her First Holy Communion bouncing. She is the color of a bar of naphtha laundry soap, she is like the little brown piece left at the end of the wash, the hard little bone, my sister. Her mouth opens. She begins:

> *My mother and your mother were washing clothes.*
> *My mother punched your mother right in the nose.*
> *What color blood came out?*

Not that old song, I say. You gotta use your own song. Make it up, you know? But she doesn't get it or won't. It's hard to say which. The rope turning, turning, turning.

> *Engine, engine number nine,*
> *running down Chicago line.*
> *If the train runs off the track*
> *do you want your money back?*

Do you want you MONEY back?
Yes, no, maybe so. Yes, no, maybe so. . .

I can tell Lucy and Rachel are disgusted, but they don't say anything because she's *my* sister.

Yes, no, maybe, so. Yes, no, maybe so. . .

Nenny, I say, but she doesn't hear me. She is too many light-years away. She is in a world we don't belong to anymore. Nenny. Going. Going.

Y-E-S spells yes and out you go!

<center>~~~~~~~~~~~~</center>

Suggestions for Discussion

1. "Hips" begins "One day you wake up . . ." Is it written in the second person?

2. How does the narrator's language let us know where she feels strong and authoritative, where vulnerable or defensive?

3. Many people speak to many in this very short space. To whom does the narrator speak the story?

4. In what form is the story? What does the secondary form of skipping-rope rhyme add to that basic story form—how does it help to tell the story?

5. Is skipping rope an action? Is the making up of rhymes an action? How do these characterize?

6. "And then it's Rachel who starts it . . ." (see page 226) Starts what? How does this line operate as a turning point in the story?

Retrospect

1. Analyze the *limited omniscient* voice in "The Things They Carried," "Where Are You Going, Where Have You Been?," "The Point," "Hunters in the Snow," and/or "A Very Old Man With Enormous Wings." How limited is it in each case? How much freedom in time, space and characters' minds has the author allowed her/himself?

2. Examine the second person passage on page 21 of *The Writing Life*. What techniques does Annie Dillard use to get you to accept this picture of "you"?

3. How objective is the author of Mary Robison's "Yours"? How does the author direct your sympathies through this relatively factual account?

4. In John Edgar Wideman's story "The Tambourine Lady" page 113, all three persons—*I, you,* and *she* appear. What is the basic person in which the story is written? What is the affect of the others, how do they alter your perception of the point of view?

Writing Assignments

1. Write a short scene about the birth or death of anything (person, plant, animal, machine, scheme, passion, etc.). Use all five areas of knowledge of the *editorial omniscient author*. Be sure to: Give us the thoughts of more than one character, tell us something about at least one character that he or she doesn't realize, include something from past or future, and deliver a universal truth.

2. Write a love scene, serious or comic, from the *limited omniscient* viewpoint—objective observation and the thoughts of one character. Make this character believe that the other loves her or him, while the external actions make clear to the reader that this is not so.

3. Write about a recent dream, using the viewpoint of the objective author. Without any comment or interpretation whatever, report the events (the more bizarre, the better) as they occur.

4. Write a monologue from the point of view of a mother—your own or imaginary—laying down the rules for her child.

5. Write a letter from a central narrator to another character from whom the narrator wants a great deal of money. Convince us as readers that the money is deserved.

6. Place a character in an uncomfortable social situation and write a passage in the *limited omniscient*, in which his/her dialogue is in sharp contrast to his/her interior monologue.

8

ASSORTED LIARS
Point of View, Part II

- *At What Distance?*

- *With What Limitations?*

As with the chemist at her microscope and the lookout in his tower, fictional point of view always involves the *distance*, close or far, of the perceiver from the thing perceived. Point of view in fiction, however, is immensely complicated by the fact that distance is not only, though it may be partly, spatial. It may also be temporal. Or the distance may be intangible and involve a judgment—moral, intellectual, and/or emotional. More complicated still, the narrator or characters or both may view the action from one distance, the author and reader from another.

At What Distance?

Authorial distance, sometimes called *psychic distance,* is the degree to which we as readers feel on the one hand intimacy and identification with, or on the other hand detachment and alienation from, the characters in a story.

Several of the techniques already described in this book—abstract nouns, summary, typicality, apparent objectivity—can be used to create a feeling of distance and detachment in the reader toward the characters.

It started in the backyards. At first the men concentrated on heat and smoke, and on dangerous thrusts with long forks. Their wives gave them aprons in railroad stripes, with slogans on the front—*Hot Stuff, The Boss*—to spur them on. Then it began to get mixed up who should do the dishes, and you can't fall back on paper plates forever, and around that time the wives got tired of making butterscotch brownies and jello salads with grated carrots in them and wanted to make money instead, and one thing led to another.

Margaret Atwood, "Simmering"

Closeness and sympathy can be achieved by concrete detail, scene, a character's thoughts, and so forth.

She dreams she does not already have three children. A squeeze around the flowers in her hands chokes off three and four and five years of breath. Instantly she is ashamed and frightened in her superstition. She looks for the first time at the preacher, forces humility into her eyes, as if she believes he is, in fact, a man of God. She can imagine God, a small black boy, timidly pulling the preacher's coattail.

Alice Walker, "Roselily"

Or a combination of techniques may make us feel simultaneously sympathetic and detached—a frequent effect of comedy—as in this example:

I'm a dishwasher in a restaurant. I'm not trying to impress anybody. I'm not bragging. It's just what I do. It's not the glamorous job people make it out to be. Sure, you make a lot of dough and everybody looks up to you and respects you, but then again there's a lot of responsibility. It weighs on you. It wears on you. Everybody wants to be a dishwasher these days, I guess, but they'got an idealistic view of it.

Robert McBrearty, "The Dishwasher"

As author you may ask us to identify completely with one character and totally condemn another. One character may judge another harshly while you as author suggest that we should qualify that judgment. If there is also a narrator, that narrator may think himself morally superior while behind his back you make sure that we will think him morally deficient. Further, the four members of the relationship author-reader-character-narrator may operate differently in various areas of value: The character calls the narrator stupid and ugly; the narrator thinks herself ugly but clever; the author and the reader know that she is both intelligent and beautiful.

Any complexity or convolution in the relationship among author, narrator, and characters can make successful fiction. The one relationship in the dialogue in which there must not be any opposition or distance is between author and reader. We may find the characters and/or the narrator bad, stupid, and tasteless and still applaud the book as just, brilliant, and beautiful. But if the hero's agony strikes us as ridiculous, if the comedy leaves us cold—if we say that the *book* is bad, stupid, or tasteless—then we are in opposition to the author's values and reject his or her "point of view" in the sense of "opinion." Ultimately, the reader must accept the essential attitudes and judgments of the author, even if only provisionally, if the fiction is going to work.

I can think of no exception to this rule, and it is not altered by experimental plays and stories in which the writer's purpose is to embarrass, anger, or disgust us. Our acceptance of such experiments rests on our understanding that the writer did want to embarrass, anger, or disgust us, just as we accept being frightened by a horror story because we know that the writer set out to frighten us. If we think the writer is disgusting by accident, ineptitude, or moral depravity, then we are "really" disgusted and the fiction does not work.

It is a frustrating experience for many beginning (and established) authors to find that, whereas they meant the protagonist to appear sensitive, their readers find him self-pitying; whereas the author meant her to be witty, the readers find her vulgar. When this happens there is a failure of authorial or psychic distance: the author did not have sufficient perspective on the character to convince us to share his or her judgment. I recall one class in which a student author had written, with excellent use of image and scene, the story of a young man who fell in love with an exceptionally beautiful young woman, and whose feelings turned to revulsion when he found out she had had a mastectomy. The most vocal feminist in the class loved this story, which she described as "the exposé of a skuzzwort." This was not, from the author's point of view, a successful reading of his story.

SPATIAL AND TEMPORAL DISTANCE

The author's or narrator's attitude may involve distance in time or space or both. When a story begins, "Long ago and far away," we are instantly transported by a tone we recognize as belonging to fairy tale, fantasy, and neverland. Any time you (or your narrator) begin by telling us that the events you are relating took place in the far past, you distance us, making a submerged promise that the events will come to an end, since they "already have."

> That spring, when I had a great deal of potential and no money at all, I took a job as a janitor. That was when I was still very young and spent money very freely, and when, almost every night, I drifted off to sleep lulled by sweet anticipation of that time when my potential would suddenly be realized and there would be capsule biographies of my life on the dust jackets of many books.

> James Alan McPherson, "Gold Coast"

Here a distance in time indicates the attitude of the narrator toward his younger self, and his indulgent, self-mocking tone (*lulled by sweet anticipation of that time when my potential would suddenly be realized*) invites us as readers to identify with the older, narrating self. We know that he is no longer lulled by such fantasies, and, at least for the duration of the story, neither are we. That is, we are close to the narrator, distanced from him as a young man, so that the distance in time also involves distance in attitude.

By contrast, the young protagonist of Frederick Busch's *Sometimes I Live in the Country* is presented in perceptions, vocabulary and syntax that, *even though these are in the third person*, suggest we are inside the child's mind, temporally close to him. At the same time, these techniques distance us psychically, since we are aware of the difference between our own perceptions and way of speaking, and the child's.

> The sky sat on top of their hill. He was between the grass and the black
> air and the stars. Pop's gun was black too and it was colder than the ground.
> It filled his mouth. It was a small barrel but it filled his mouth up. He gagged
> on the gun that stuffed up into his head. He decided to close his eyes. Then
> he opened them. He didn't want to miss anything. He pulled the trigger but
> nothing happened. He didn't want to pull the trigger but he did.

In the next passage, the author makes use of space to establish an impersonal and authoritative tone.

> An unassuming young man was traveling, in midsummer, from his native
> city of Hamburg, to Davos-Platz in the Canton of Grisons, on a three weeks'
> visit.
> From Hamburg to Davos is a long journey—too long, indeed, for so brief a
> stay. It crosses all sorts of country; goes up hill and down dale, descends from
> the plateau of Southern Germany to the shore of Lake Constance, over its
> bounding waves and on across marshes once thought to be bottomless.
>
> Thomas Mann, *The Magic Mountain*

Here Mann distances us from the young man by characterizing him perfunctorily, not even naming him, and describes the place travelogue style, inviting us to take a panoramic view. This choice of tone establishes a remoteness that is emotional as well as geographical, and would do so even if the reader happened to be a native of Grisons. (Eventually we will become intimately involved with Davos and the unassuming young man, who is in for a longer stay than he expects.)

By closing the literal distance between the reader and the subject, the intangible distance can be closed as well.

> Her face was half an inch from my face. The curtain flapped at the open
> window and her pupils pulsed with the coming and going of the light. I know
> Jill's eyes; I've painted them. They're violent and taciturn, a ring of gas-blue
> points like cold explosion to the outside boundary of iris, the whole held
> back with its brilliant lens. A detonation under glass.
>
> Janet Burroway, *Raw Silk*

In the extreme closeness of this focus, we are brought emotionally close, invited to share the narrator's perspective of Jill's explosive eyes.

It will be obvious that using time and space as a means of controlling the reader's emotional closeness or distance involves all the elements of atmosphere discussed in chapter 6. This is true of familiarity, which invites identification with a place, and of strangeness, which alienates. And it is true of summary, which distances, and of scene, which draws us close. If you say, "There were twelve diphtheria outbreaks in Coeville over the next thirty years," you invite us to take a detached historical attitude. But if you say, "He forced his finger into her throat and tilted her toward the light to see, as he'd expected, the grayish membrane reaching toward the roof of her mouth and into her nose," the doctor may remain detached, but we as readers cannot.

There is a grammatical technique, very often misused, involving the switching of tense. Most fiction in English is written in the past tense (*She put her foot on the shovel and leaned all her weight against it*). The author's constant effort is to give this past the immediacy of the present. A story may be written in the present tense (*She puts her foot on the shovel and leans all her weight against it*). The effect of the present tense, somewhat self-consciously, is to reduce distance and increase immediacy: we are there. Generally speaking, the tense once established should not be changed.

> Danforth got home about five o'clock in the morning and fixed himself a peanut butter sandwich. He eats it over the sink, washing it down with half a carton of chocolate milk. He left the carton on the sink and stumbled up to bed.

The change of tense in the second sentence is pointless; it violates the reader's sense of time to have the action skip from past to present and back again and produces no compensating effect.

There are times, however, when a change of tense can be functional and effective. In the story "Gold Coast," we are dealing with two time frames, one having to do with the narrator's earlier experiences as a janitor, and one in which he acknowledges the telling.

> I left the rug on the floor because it was dirty and too large for my new apartment. I also left the two plates given me by James Sullivan, for no reason at all. Sometimes I want to go back to get them, but I do not know how to ask for them or explain why I left them in the first place.

The tense change here is logical and functional: It acknowledges the past of the "story" and the present of the "telling"; it also incidentally reinforces our emotional identification with the older, narrating self.

Sometimes, a shift into the present tense even without a strictly logical justification can achieve the effect of intensity and immediacy, so that the emotional distance between reader and character is diminished.

> When alone he had a dreadful and distressing desire to call someone, but he knew beforehand that with others present it would be still worse. "Another

dose of morphine—to lose consciousness. I will tell him, the doctor, that he must think of something else. It's impossible, impossible, to go on like this."

An hour and another pass like that. But now there's a ring at the doorbell. Perhaps it's the doctor? It is. He comes in fresh, hearty, plump and cheerful.

Leo Tolstoy, *The Death of Ivan Ilyich*

This switch from the past to the present draws us into the character's anguish and makes the doctor's arrival more intensely felt. Notice that Ivan Ilyich's thoughts— "Another dose of morphine"—which occur naturally in the present tense, serve as a transition from past to present so that we are not jolted by the change. In *The Death of Ivan Ilyich*, Tolstoy keeps the whole scene of the doctor's visit in the present tense, while Ivan Ilyich's consciousness is at a pitch of pain, contempt for the doctor, and hatred for his wife; then, as the focus moves to the wife, the tense slips back into the past.

> The thrill of hatred he feels for her makes him suffer from her touch.
> Her attitude towards him and his disease is still the same. Just as the doctor had adopted a certain relation to his patient which he could not abandon, so had she formed one toward him . . . and she could not now change that attitude.

The present tense can be effectively employed to depict moments of special intensity, but it needs both to be saved for those crucial moments and to be controlled so carefully in the transition that the reader is primarily aware of the intensity, rather than the tense.

INTANGIBLE DISTANCE

Spatial and temporal distance, then, can imply distance in the attitude of the teller toward his or her material. But authorial distance may also be implied through *tone* without any tangible counterpart.

The word "tone," applied to fiction, is a metaphor derived from music and also commonly—and metaphorically—used to describe color and speech. When we speak of a "tone of voice" we mean that an attitude is conveyed, and this attitude is determined by the situation and by the relation of the persons involved in the situation. Tone can match, emphasize, alter, or contradict the meaning of the words.

The situation is that Louise stumbles into her friend Judy's apartment, panting, hair disheveled, coat torn, and face blanched. Judy rushes to support her. "You look awful! What happened?" Here the tone conveys alarm, openness, and a readiness to sympathize.

Judy's son wheels in grinning, swinging a baseball bat, shirt torn, mud splattered, and missing a shoe. "You look awful! What happened?" Judy's tone is angry, exasperated.

Louise's ex-boyfriend drops by that night decked out in a plaid polyester sports coat and an electric-blue tie. "You look awful! What happened?" Louise says, her tone light, but cutting, so that he knows she means it.

Judy's husband comes back from a week in Miami and takes off his shirt to model his tan. "You look awful! What happened?" she teases, playful and flirting, so that he knows she means he looks terrific.

In each of these situations the attitude is determined by the situation and the emotional relationships of the persons involved, and in life as in acting the various tones would be conveyed by vocal means—pitch, tempo, plosion, nasality—reinforced by posture, gesture, and facial expression. When we apply the word "tone" to fiction, we tacitly acknowledge that we must do without these helpful signs. The author, of course, may describe pitch, posture, and the like, or may identify a tone as "cutting" or "playful," but these verbal and adverbial aids describe only the tone used among characters, whereas the fictional relationship importantly includes an author who must also convey identification or distance, sympathy or judgment, and who must choose and arrange words so that they match, emphasize, alter, or contradict their inherent meaning.

Tone itself is an intangible, and there are probably as many possible tones as there are possible situations, relationships, and sentences. But in a very general way, we will trust, in literature as in life, a choice of words that seems appropriate in intensity or value to the meaning conveyed. If the intensity or value seems inappropriate, we will start to read between the lines. If a woman putting iodine on a cut says "Ouch," we don't have to search for her meaning. But if the cut is being stitched up without anesthetic, then "Ouch" may convey courage, resignation, and trust. If she says "Ouch" when her lover strokes her cheek, then we read anger and recoil into the word.

In the same way, you as author manipulate intensity and value in your choice of language, sometimes matching meaning, sometimes contradicting, sometimes overstating, sometimes understating, to indicate your attitude to the reader.

> She was a tall woman of imperious mien, handsome, with definite black eyebrows. Her smooth black hair was parted exactly. For a few moments she stood steadily watching the miners as they passed along the railway; then she turned toward the brook course. Her face was calm and set, her mouth was closed with disillusionment.
>
> D. H. Lawrence, "Odor of Chrysanthemums"

There is in this passage no discrepancy between the thing conveyed and the intensity with which it is conveyed, and we take the words at face value, accepting that the woman is as the author says she is. The phrase "imperious mien" has itself an imperious tone about it (I doubt one would speak of a real cool mien). The syntax is as straightforward as the woman herself. (Notice how the rhythm alters with "For a few moments," so that the longest and most flowing clause follows the passing miners.) You might describe the tone of the passage as a whole as "calm and set."

The next example is quite different.

> Mrs. Herriton did not believe in romance, nor in transfiguration, nor in parallels from history, nor in anything that may disturb domestic life. She adroitly changed the subject before Philip got excited.

> E. M. Forster, *Where Angels Fear to Tread*

This is clearly also a woman of "imperious mien," and the author purports, like the first, to be informing us of her actions and attitudes. But unlike the first example, the distance here between the woman's attitude and the author's is apparent. It is possible to "believe in" both romance and transfiguration, which are concepts. If Lawrence should say of the woman in "Odor of Chrysanthemums" that "she did not believe in romance, nor in transfiguration," we would accept it as a straightforward part of her characterization. But how can one believe in parallels? *Belief* is too strong a word for *parallels*, and the discrepancy makes us suspicious. Not to "believe" in "anything that may disturb domestic life" is a discrepancy of a severer order, unrealistic and absurd. The word "adroitly" presents a value judgment, one of praise. But placed as it is between "anything that may disturb domestic life" and "before Philip got excited," it shows us that Mrs. Herriton is manipulating the excitement out of domestic life.

Irony. Discrepancies of intensity and value are ironic. Any time there is a discrepancy between what is said and what we are to accept as the truth, we are in the presence of an irony. There are three basic types of irony.

Verbal Irony is a rhetorical device in which the author (or character) says one thing and means another. The passage from "Dishwasher" at the beginning of this chapter displays verbal irony, where the "glamor" and "responsibility" of the job point up the opposite. Here Mrs. Herriton "adroitly changed the subject" is also a form of verbal irony. When the author goes on to say, "Lilia tried to assert herself, and said that she should go to take care of her mother. It required all Mrs. Herriton's kindness to prevent her," there is further verbal irony in the combination of "required" and "kindness."

Dramatic Irony is a device of plot in which the reader or audience knows more than the character does. The classical example of dramatic irony is *Oedipus Rex*, where the audience knows that Oedipus himself is the murderer he seeks. There is a dramatic irony in "Hunters in the Snow," where the reader understands that with every repetition of "I'm going to the hospital," Kenny slides a little nearer toward death.

Cosmic Irony is an all-encompassing attitude toward life, which takes into account the contradictions inherent in the human condition. The story "Where Are You Going, Where Have You Been?" in which Connie's contemptuous desire to get away from her family is fulfilled, and she is destroyed by it, demonstrates cosmic irony.

Any of these types of irony will inform the author's attitude toward the material and will be reflected in his or her tone. Any of them will involve authorial distance, since the author means, knows, or wishes to take into account—and also intends the reader to understand—something not wholly conveyed by the literal meaning of the words.

Of the two passages quoted above, we may say that the first, from Lawrence, is without irony; the second, from Forster, contains an irony presented by the author, understood by the reader, and directed against the character described. The following passage, again about a woman of imperious mien, is more complex because it introduces the fourth possible member of the narrative relationship, the narrator; and it also involves temporal distance.

> She was a tall woman with high cheekbones, now more emphasized than ever by the loss of her molar teeth. Her lips were finer than most of her tribe's and wore a shut, rather sour expression. Her eyes seemed to be always fixed on the distance, as though she didn't "see" or mind the immediate, but dwelt in the eternal. She was not like other children's grandmothers we knew, who would spoil her grandchildren and had huts "just outside the hedge" of their sons' homesteads. Grandmother lived three hills away, which was inexplicable.
>
> Jonathan Kariara, "Her Warrior"

This paragraph begins, like Lawrence's, without irony, as a strong portrait of a strong woman. Because we trust the consistent tone of the first two sentences, we also accept the teller's simile "as though she didn't see or mind the immediate," which emphasizes without contradicting. Up to this point the voice seems to have the authority of an omniscient author, but in the fourth sentence the identity of the narrator is introduced—one of the woman's grandchildren. Because the past tense is used, and even more, because the language is measured and educated, we instantly understand that the narrator is telling of his childhood perceptions from an adult, temporally distanced perspective. Curiously, the final word of the final sentence presents us with a contradiction of everything we have just found convincing. It cannot be "inexplicable" that this woman lived three hills away, because it has already been explained to us that she lived in deep and essential remoteness.

This irony is not directed primarily against the character of the grandmother but by the narrator against himself as a child. Author, narrator, and reader all concur in an intellectual distance from the child's mind and its faulty perceptions. At the same time, there is perhaps a sympathetic identification with the child's hurt, and therefore a residual judgment of the grandmother.

With What Limitations?

In each of the excerpts in the section "Intangible Distance" we trust the teller of the tale. We may find ourselves in opposition to characters perceived or perceiving, but we identify with the attitudes, straightforward or ironic, of the authors and narrators who present us these characters. We share, at least for the duration of the narrative, their norms.

THE UNRELIABLE NARRATOR

It is also possible to mistrust the teller. Authorial distance may involve not a deliberate attitude taken by the speaker, but distance on the part of the author from the narrator. The answer to the question, *Who speaks?* may itself necessitate a judgment, and again this judgment may imply opposition of the author (and reader) on any scale of value—moral, intellectual, aesthetic, or physical—and to these I would add educational and experiential (probably the list can be expanded further).

If the answer to *Who speaks?* is *a child, a bigot, a jealous lover, an animal, a schizophrenic, a murderer, a liar,* the implications may be that the narrator speaks with limitations we do not necessarily share. To the extent that the narrator displays and betrays such limitations, she or he is an *unreliable narrator*; and the author, without a word to call his own, must let the reader know that the story is not to be trusted.

Here is a fourth woman, imperious and sour, who tells her own story.

> I have always, always, tried to do right and help people. It's a part of my community duty and my duty to God. But I can tell you right now, you don't never gets no thanks for it!. . .
>
> Use to be a big ole fat sloppy woman live cross the street went to my church. She had a different man in her house with her every month! She got mad at me for tellin the minister on her about all them men! Now, I'm doin my duty and she got mad! I told her somebody had to be the pillar of the community and if it had to be me, so be it! She said I was the pill of the community and a lotta other things, but I told the minister that too and pretty soon she was movin away. Good! I like a clean community!

> J. California Cooper, "The Watcher"

We mistrust every judgment this woman makes, but we are also aware of an author we do trust, manipulating the narrator's tone to expose her. The outburst is fraught with ironies, but because the narrator is unaware of them, they are directed against herself. We can hear that interference is being dressed up as *duty*. When she brags in cliche, we agree that she's more of a *pill* than a *pillar*. When she appropriates biblical language—*so be it!*—we suspect that even the minister might agree. Punctuation itself, the self-righteous overuse of the exclamation point, suggests her inappropriate intensity. It occurs to us we'd probably like the look of that "big ole fat sloppy" neighbor; and we know for certain why that neighbor moved away.

In this case the narrator is wholly unreliable, and we're unlikely to accept any judgment she could make. But it is also possible for a narrator to be reliable in some areas of value and unreliable in others. Mark Twain's Huckleberry Finn is a famous case in point. Here Huck has decided to free his friend Jim, and he is astonished that Tom Sawyer is going along with the plan.

> Well, one thing was dead sure; and that was, that Tom Sawyer was in earnest and was actly going to help steal that nigger out of slavery. That was the

thing that was too many for me. Here was a boy that was respectable, and well brung up; and had a character to lose; and folks at home that had characters; and he was bright and not leather-headed; and knowing and not ignorant; and not mean, but kind; and yet here he was, without any more pride, or rightness, or feeling, than to stoop to this business, and make himself a shame, and his family a shame, before everybody. I couldn't understand it, no way at all.

The extended irony in this excerpt is that slavery should be defended by the respectable, the bright, the knowing, the kind, and those of character. We reject Huck's assessment of Tom as well as the implied assessment of himself as worth so little that he has nothing to lose by freeing a slave. Huck's moral instincts are better than he himself can understand. (Notice, incidentally, how Huck's lack of education is communicated by word choice and syntax and how sparse the misspellings are.) So author and reader are in intellectual opposition to Huck the narrator, but morally identify with him.

The unreliable narrator—who has become one of the most popular characters in modern fiction—is far from a newcomer to literature and in fact predates fiction. Every drama contains characters who speak for themselves and present their own cases, and from whom we are partly or wholly distanced in one area of value or another. So we identify with Othello's morality but mistrust his logic, trust Faust's intellect but not his ethics, admire Barney Fife's heart of gold but not his courage. As these examples suggest, the unreliable narrator always presents us with dramatic irony, because we always "know" more than he or she does about the characters, the events, and the significance of both.

AN EXERCISE IN UNRELIABILITY

The following four passages represent narrations by four relatively mad madmen. How mad is each? To whom does each speak? In what form? Which of their statements are reliable? Which are unreliable? Which of them admit to madness? Is the admission reliable? What ironies can you identify, and against whom is each directed? What is the attitude of the author behind the narrator? By what choice and arrangement of words do you know this?

The doctor advised me not to insist too much on looking so far back. Recent events, he says, are equally valuable for him, and above all my fancies and dreams of the night before. But I like to do things in their order, so directly I left the doctor (who was going to be away from Trieste for some time). I bought and read a book on psychoanalysis, so that I might begin from the very beginning, and make the doctor's task easier. It is not difficult to understand, but very boring. I have stretched myself out after lunch in an easy chair, pencil and paper in hand. All the lines have disappeared from my forehead as I sit here with my mind completely relaxed. I seem to be able to see my thoughts as something quite apart from myself. I can watch them rising, falling, their only form of activity. I seize my pencil in order to remind them that it is the duty of thought to manifest itself. At once the wrinkles collect on my brow as I think of the letters that make up every word.

Italo Svevo, *Confessions of Zeno*

Madrid, Februarius the thirtieth

So I'm in Spain. It all happened so quickly that I hardly had time to realize it. This morning the Spanish delegation finally arrived for me and we all got into the carriage. I was somewhat bewildered by the extraordinary speed at which we traveled. We went so fast that in half an hour we reached the Spanish border. But then, nowadays there are railroads all over Europe and the ships go so fast too. Spain is a strange country. When we entered the first room, I saw a multitude of people with shaven heads. I soon realized, though, that these must be Dominican or Capuchin monks because they always shave their heads. I also thought that the manners of the King's Chancellor, who was leading me by the hand, were rather strange. He pushed me into a small room and said: "You sit quiet and don't you call yourself King Ferdinand again or I'll beat the nonsense out of your head." But I knew that I was just being tested and refused to submit.

Nikolai Gogol, *The Diary of a Madman*

Pushed back into sleep as I fight to emerge, pushed back as they drown a kitten, or a child fighting to wake up, pushed back by voices and lullabies and bribes and bullies, punished by tones of voices and by silences, gripped into sleep by medicines and syrups and dummies and dope.

Nevertheless I fight, desperate, like a kitten trying to climb out of the slippysided zinc pail it has been flung in, an unwanted, unneeded cat to drown, better dead than alive, better asleep than awake, but I fight, up and up into the light, greeting dark now as a different land, a different texture, a different state of the Light.

Doris Lessing, *Briefing for a Descent into Hell*

Come into my cell. Make yourself at home. Take the chair; I'll sit on the cot. No? You prefer to stand by the window? I understand. You like my little view. Have you noticed that the narrower the view the more you can see? For the first time I understand how old ladies can sit on their porches for years.

Don't I know you? You look very familiar. I've been feeling rather depressed and I don't remember things very well. I think I am here because of that or because I committed a crime. Perhaps it's both. Is this a prison or a hospital or a prison hospital? A Center for Aberrant Behavior? So that's it. I have behaved aberrantly. In short, I'm in the nuthouse.

Walker Percy, *Lancelot*

UNRELIABILITY IN OTHER VIEWPOINTS

I have said that a narrator cannot be omniscient, although he or she may be reliable. It may seem equally plausible that the phenomenon of unreliability can apply only to a narrator, who is by definition a fallible human being. But the subtleties of authorial distance are such that it is possible to indicate unreliability through virtually any point of view. If, for example, you have chosen a limited omniscient viewpoint including only external observation and the thoughts of one character, then it may be that the character's thoughts are unreliable and that he or she misrepresents external facts. Then you must make us aware through tone that you know more than you have chosen to present. William Golding, in *The Inheritors*, tells his story in the third person, but through the eyes and thoughts of a Neanderthal who has not yet developed the power of deductive reasoning.

> The man turned sideways in the bushes and looked at Lok along his shoulder. A stick rose upright and there was a lump of bone in the middle. Suddenly Lok understood that the man was holding the stick out to him but neither he nor Lok could reach across the river. He would have laughed if it were not for the echo of screaming in his head. The stick began to grow shorter at both ends. Then it shot out to full length again.
> The dead tree by Lok's ear acquired a voice.
> "Clop!"
> His ears twitched and he turned to the tree. By his face there had grown a twig: a twig that smelt of other, and of goose, and of the bitter berries that Lok's stomach told him he must not eat.

The imaginative problem here, imaginatively embraced, is that we must supply the deductive reasoning of which our point of view character is incapable. Lok has no experience of bows or poison arrows, nor of "men" attacking each other, so his conclusions are unreliable. "Suddenly Lok understood" is an irony setting us in opposition to the character's intellect; at the same time, his innocence makes him morally sympathetic. Since the author does not intervene to interpret for us, the effect is very near that of an unreliable narrator.

Other experiments abound. Isaac Loeb Peretz tells the story of "Bontsha the Silent" from the point of view of the editorial omniscient, privy to the deliberations of the angels, but with Yiddish syntax and "universal truths" so questionable that the omniscient voice itself is unreliable. Conversely, Faulkner's *The Sound and the Fury* is told through several unreliable narrators, each with an idiosyncratic and partial perception of the story, so that the cumulative effect is of an omniscient author able not only to penetrate many minds but also to perceive the larger significance.

I'm conscious that this discussion of point of view contains more analysis than advice, and this is because very little can be said to be right or wrong about point of view as long as the reader ultimately identifies with the author; as long, that is, as you make it work. In *Aspects of the Novel* E. M. Forster speaks vaguely, but with undeniable accuracy, of "the power of the writer to bounce the reader into accepting what he says." He then goes on to prove categorically that Dickens's *Bleak House* is a disaster, "Logically all to pieces, but Dickens bounces us, so that we do not mind the shiftings of the view point."

The one imperative is that the reader must bounce with, not against, the author. Virtually any story can be told from virtually any point of view and convey the same attitude of the author.

Suppose, for example, that you are going to write this story: Two American soldiers, one a seasoned corporal and the other a newly arrived private, are sent on a mission in a Far Eastern "police action" to kill a sniper. They track, find, and capture the Oriental, who turns out to be a fifteen-year-old boy. The corporal offers to let the private pull the trigger, but he cannot. The corporal kills the sniper and triumphantly cuts off his ear for a trophy. The young soldier vomits; ashamed of himself, he pulls himself together and vows to do better next time.

Your attitude as author of this story is that war is inhumane and dehumanizing.

You may write the story from the point of view of the editorial omniscient, following the actions of the hunters and the hunted, going into the minds of corporal, private, and sniper, ranging the backgrounds of each and knowing the ultimate pointlessness of the death, telling us, in effect, that war is inhumane and dehumanizing.

Or you may write it from the point of view of the corporal as an unreliable narrator, proud of his toughness and his expertise, condescending to the private, certain the Orientals are animals, glorying in his trophy, betraying his inhumanity.

Between these two extremes of total omniscience and total unreliability, you may take any position of the middle ground. The story might be written in the limited omniscient, presenting the thoughts only of the anxious private and the external actions of the others. It might be written objectively, with a cold and detached accuracy of military detail. It might be written by a peripheral narrator, a war correspondent, from interviews and documents; as a letter home from the private to his girl; as a field report from the corporal; as an interior monologue of the young sniper during the seconds before his death.

Any of these modes could contain your meaning, any of them fulfill your purpose. Your central problem as a writer might prove to be the choosing. But whatever your final choice of point of view in the technical sense, your point of view in the sense of *opinion*—that war is inhumane and dehumanizing—could be suggested.

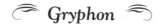

Gryphon

CHARLES BAXTER

ON WEDNESDAY AFTERNOON, between the geography lesson on ancient Egypt's hand-operated irrigation system and an art project that involved drawing a model city next to a mountain, our fourth-grade teacher, Mr. Hibler, developed a cough. This cough began with a series of muffled throat clearings and progressed to propulsive noises contained within Mr. Hibler's closed mouth. "Listen to him," Carol Peterson whispered to me. "He's gonna blow up." Mr. Hibler's laughter—dazed and infrequent—sounded a bit like his cough, but as we worked on our model cities we would look up, thinking he was enjoying a joke, and see Mr. Hibler's face turning red, his cheeks puffed out. This was not laughter. Twice he bent over, and his loose tie, like a plumb line, hung down straight from his neck as he exploded himself into a Kleenex. He would excuse himself, then go on coughing. "I'll bet you a dime," Carol Peterson whispered, "we get a substitute tomorrow."

Carol sat at the desk in front of mine and was a bad person—when she thought no one was looking she would blow her nose on notebook paper, then crumble it up and throw it into the wastebasket—but at times of crisis she spoke the truth. I knew I'd lose the dime.

"No deal," I said.

When Mr. Hibler stood us up in formation at the door just prior to the final bell, he was almost incapable of speech. "I'm sorry, boys and girls," he said. "I seem to be coming down with something."

"I hope you feel better tomorrow, Mr. Hibler," Bobby Kryzanowicz, the faultless brown-noser said, and I heard Carol Peterson's evil giggle. Then Mr. Hibler opened the door and we walked out to the buses, a clique of us starting noisily to hawk and cough as soon as we thought we were a few feet beyond Mr. Hibler's earshot.

Five Oaks being a rural community, and in Michigan, the supply of substitute teachers was limited to the town's unemployed community college graduates, a pool of about four mothers. These ladies fluttered, provided easeful class days, and nervously covered material we had mastered weeks earlier. Therefore it was a surprise when a woman we had never seen came into the class the next day, carrying a purple purse, a checkerboard lunchbox, and a few books. She put the books on one side of Mr. Hibler's desk and the lunchbox on the other, next to the Voice of Music phonograph. Three of us in the back of the room were playing with Heever, the chameleon that lived in the terrarium and on one of the plastic drapes, when she walked in.

She clapped her hands at us. "Little boys," she said, "why are you bent over together like that?" She didn't wait for us to answer. "Are you tormenting an animal? Put it back. Please sit down at your desks. I want no cabals this time of the day." We just stared at her. "Boys," she repeated, "I asked you to sit down."

I put the chameleon in his terrarium and felt my way to my desk, never taking my eyes off the woman. With white and green chalk, she had started to draw a tree on the left side of the blackboard. She didn't look usual. Furthermore, her tree was outsized, disproportionate, for some reason.

"This room needs a tree," she said, with one line drawing the suggestion of a leaf. "A large, leafy, shady, deciduous . . . oak."

Her fine, light hair had been done up in what I would learn years later was called a chignon, and she wore gold-rimmed glasses whose lenses seemed to have the faintest blue tint. Harold Knardahl, who sat across from me, whispered "Mars," and I nodded slowly, savoring the imminent weirdness of the day. The substitute drew another branch with an extravagant arm gesture, then turned around and said, "Good morning. I don't believe I said good morning to all you yet."

Facing us, she was no special age—an adult is an adult—but her face had two prominent lines, descending vertically from the sides of her mouth to her chin. I knew where I had seen those lines before: *Pinocchio*. They were marionette lines. "You may stare at me," she said to us, as a few more kids from the last bus came into the room, their eyes fixed on her, "for a few more seconds, until the bell rings. Then I will permit no more staring. Looking I will permit. Staring, no. It is impolite to stare, and a sign of bad breeding. You cannot make a social effort while staring."

Harold Knardahl did not glance at me, or nudge, but I heard him whisper "Mars" again, trying to get more mileage out of his single joke with the kids who had just come in.

When everyone was seated, the substitute teacher finished her tree, put down her chalk fastidiously on the phonograph, brushed her hands, and faced us. "Good morning," she said. "I am Miss Ferenczi, your teacher for the day. I am fairly new to your community, and I don't believe any of you know me. I will therefore start by telling you a story about myself."

While we settled back, she launched into her tale. She said her grandfather had been a Hungarian prince; her mother had been born in some place called Flanders, had been a pianist, and had played concerts for people Miss Ferenczi referred to as "crowned heads." She gave us a knowing look. "Grieg," she said, "the Norwegian master, wrote a concerto for piano that was," she paused, "my mother's triumph at her debut concert in London." Her eyes searched the ceiling. Our eyes followed. Nothing up there but ceiling tile. "For reasons that I shall not go into, my family's fortunes took us to Detroit, then north to dreadful Saginaw, and now here I am in Five Oaks, as your substitute teacher, for today, Thursday, October the eleventh. I believe it will be a good day: All the forecasts coincide. We shall start with your reading lesson. Take out your reading book. I believe it is called *Broad Horizons*, or something along those lines."

Jeannie Vermeesch raised her hand. Miss Ferenzi nodded at her. "Mr. Hibler always starts the day with the Pledge of Allegiance," Jeannie whined.

"Oh, does he? In that case," Miss Ferenczi said, "you must know it *very* well by now, and we certainly need not spend our time on it. No, no allegiance pledging on the premises today, by my reckoning. Not with so much sunlight coming into the room. A pledge does not suit my mood." She glanced at her watch. "Time *is* flying. Take out *Broad Horizons*."

She disappointed us by giving us an ordinary lesson, complete with vocabulary word drills, comprehension questions, and recitation. She didn't seem to care for the material, however. She sighed every few minutes and rubbed her glasses with a frilly perfumed handkerchief that she withdrew, magician style, from her left sleeve.

After reading we moved on to arithmetic. It was my favorite time of the morning, when the lazy autumn sunlight dazzled its way through ribbons of clouds past the windows on the east side of the classroom, and crept across the linoleum floor. On the playground the first group of children, the kindergartners, were running on the quack grass just beyond the monkey bars. We were doing multiplication tables. Miss Ferenczi had made John Wazny stand up at his desk in the front row. He was supposed to go through the tables of six. From where I was sitting, I could smell the Vitalis soaked into John's plastered hair. He was doing fine until he came to six times eleven and six times twelve. "Six times eleven," he said, "is sixty-eight. Six times twelve is . . ." He put his fingers to his head, quickly and secretly sniffed his fingertips, and said, "seventy-two." Then he sat down.

"Fine," Miss Ferenczi said. "Well now. That was very good."

"Miss Ferenczi!" One of the Eddy twins was waving her hand desperately in the air. "Miss Ferenczi! Miss Ferenczi!"

"Yes?"

"John said that six times eleven is sixty-eight and you said he was right!"

"*Did* I?" She gazed at the class with a jolly look breaking across her marionette's face. "Did I say that? Well, what *is* six times eleven?"

"It's sixty-six!"

She nodded. "Yes. So it is. But, and I know some people will not entirely agree with me, at some times it is sixty-eight."

"When? When is it sixty-eight?"

We were all waiting.

"In higher mathematics, which you children do not yet understand, six times eleven can be considered to be sixty-eight." She laughed through her nose. "In higher mathematics numbers are . . . more fluid. The only thing a number does is contain a certain amount of something. Think of water. A cup is not the only way to measure a certain amount of water, is it?" We were staring, shaking our heads. "You could use saucepans or thimbles. In either case, the water *would be the same*. Perhaps," she started again, "it would be better for you to think that six times eleven is sixty-eight only when I am in the room."

"Why is it sixty-eight," Mark Poole asked, "when you're in the room?"

"Because it's more interesting that way," she said, smiling very rapidly behind her blue-tinted glasses. "Besides, I'm your substitute teacher, am I not?" We all nodded. "Well, then, think of six times eleven equals sixty-eight as a substitute fact."

"A substitute fact?"

"Yes." Then she looked at us carefully. "Do you think," she asked, "that anyone is going to be hurt by a substitute fact?"

We looked back at her.

"Will the plants on the windowsill be hurt?" We glanced at them. There were sensitive plants thriving in a green plastic tray, and several wilted ferns in small clay pots. "Your dogs and cats, or your moms and dads?" She waited. "So," she concluded, "what's the problem?"

"But it's wrong," Janice Weber said, "isn't it?"

"What's your name, young lady?"

"Janice Weber."

"And you think it's wrong, Janice?"

"I was just asking."

"Well, all right. You were just asking. I think we've spent enough time on this matter by now, don't you, class? You are free to think what you like. When your teacher, Mr. Hibler, returns, six times eleven will be sixty-six again, you can rest assured. And it will be that for the rest of your lives in Five Oaks. Too bad, eh?" She raised her eyebrows and glinted herself at us. "But for now, it wasn't. So much for that. Let us go to your assigned problems for today, as painstakingly outlined, I see, in Mr. Hibler's lesson plan. Take out a sheet of paper and write your names in the upper left-hand corner."

For the next half hour we did the rest of our arithmetic problems. We handed them in and went on to spelling, my worst subject. Spelling always came before lunch. We were taking spelling dictation and looking at the clock. "Thorough," Miss Ferenczi said. "Boundary." She walked in the aisles between the desks, holding the spelling book open and looking down at our papers. "Balcony." I clutched my pencil. Somehow, the way she said those words, they seemed foreign, Hungarian, mis-voweled and mis-consonanted. I stared down at what I had spelled. *Balconie.* I turned my pencil upside down and erased my mistake. *Balconey.* That looked better, but still incorrect. I cursed the world of spelling and tried erasing it again and saw the paper beginning to wear away. *Balkony.* Suddenly I felt a hand on my shoulder.

"I don't like that word either," Miss Ferenczi whispered, bent over, her mouth near my ear. "It's ugly. My feeling is, if you don't like a word, you don't have to use it." She straightened up, leaving behind a slight odor of Clorets.

At lunchtime we went out to get our trays of sloppy joes, peaches in heavy syrup, coconut cookies, and milk, and brought them back to the classroom, where Miss Ferenczi was sitting at the desk, eating a brown sticky thing she had unwrapped from tightly rubber-banded wax paper. "Miss Ferenczi," I said, raising my hand. "You don't have to eat with us. You can eat with the other teachers. There's a teachers' lounge," I ended up, "next to the principal's office."

"No, thank you," she said. "I prefer it here."

"We've got a room monitor," I said. "Mrs. Eddy." I pointed to where Mrs. Eddy, Joyce and Judy's mother, sat silently at the back of the room, doing her knitting.

"That's fine," Miss Ferenczi said. "But I shall continue to eat here, with you children. I prefer it," she repeated.

"How come?" Wayne Razmer asked without raising his hand.

"I talked with the other teachers before class this morning," Miss Ferenczi said, biting into her brown food. "There was a great rattling of the words for the fewness of ideas. I didn't care for their brand of hilarity. I don't like ditto machine jokes."

"Oh," Wayne said.

"What's that you're eating?" Maxine Sylvester asked, twitching her nose. "Is it food?"

"It most certainly *is* food. It's a stuffed fig. I had to drive almost down to Detroit to get it. I also bought some smoked sturgeon. And this," she said, lifting some green leaves out of her lunchbox, "is raw spinach, cleaned this morning before I came out here to the Garfield-Murry school."

"Why're you eating raw spinach?" Maxine asked.

"It's good for you," Miss Ferenczi said. "More stimulating than soda pop or smelling salts." I bit into my sloppy joe and stared blankly out the window. An almost invisible moon was faintly silvered in the daytime autumn sky. "As far as food is concerned," Miss Ferenczi was saying, "you have to shuffle the pack. Mix it up. Too many people eat . . . well, never mind."

"Miss Ferenczi," Carol Peterson said, "what are we going to do this afternoon?"

"Well," she said, looking down at Mr. Hibler's lesson plan, "I see that your teacher, Mr. Hibler, has you scheduled for a unit on the Egyptians." Carol groaned. "Yessss," Miss Ferenczi continued, "that is what we will do: the Egyptians. A remarkable people. Almost as remarkable as the Americans. But not quite." She lowered her head, did her quick smile, and went back to eating her spinach.

After noon recess we came back into the classroom and saw that Miss Ferenczi had drawn a pyramid on the blackboard, close to her oak tree. Some of us who had been playing baseball were messing around in the back of the room, dropping the bats and the gloves into the playground box, and I think that Ray Schontzeler had just slugged me when I heard Miss Ferenczi's high-pitched voice quavering with emotion. "Boys," she said, "come to order right this minute and take your seats. I do not wish to waste a minute of class time. Take out your geography books." We trudged to our desks and, still sweating, pulled out *Distant Lands and Their People.* "Turn to page forty-two." She waited for thirty seconds, then looked over at Kelly Munger. "Young man," she said, "why are you still fossicking in your desk?"

Kelly looked as if his foot had been stepped on. "Why am I what?"

"Why are you . . . burrowing in your desk like that?"

"I'm lookin' for the book, Miss Ferenczi."

Bobby Kryzanowicz, the faultless brown-noser who sat in the first row by choice, softly said, "His name is Kelly Munger. He can't ever find his stuff. He always does that."

"I don't care what his name is, especially after lunch," Miss Ferenczi said. "*Where is your book?*"

"I just found it." Kelly was peering into his desk and with both hands pulled at the book, shoveling along in front of it several pencils and crayons, which fell into his lap and then to the floor.

"I hate a mess," Miss Ferenczi said. "I hate a mess in a desk or a mind. It's . . . unsanitary. You wouldn't want your house at home to look like your desk at school, now, would you?" She didn't wait for an answer. "I should think not. A house at home should be as neat as human hands can make it. What were we talking about? Egypt. Page forty-two. I note from Mr. Hibler's lesson plan that you have been discussing the modes of Egyptian irrigation. Interesting, in my view, but not so interesting as what we are about to cover. The pyramids and Egyptian slave labor. A plus on one side, a minus on the other." We had our books open to page forty-two, where there was a picture of a pyramid, but Miss Ferenczi wasn't looking at the book. Instead, she was staring at some object just outside the window.

"Pyramids," Miss Ferenczi said, still looking past the window. "I want you to think about the pyramids. And what was inside. The bodies of the pharaohs, of course, and their attendant treasures. Scrolls. Perhaps," Miss Ferenczi said, with something gleeful but unsmiling in her face, "these scrolls were novels for the pharaohs, helping them to pass the time in their long voyage through the centuries. But then, I am joking." I was looking at the lines on Miss Ferenczi's face. "Pyramids," Miss Ferenczi went on, "were the respositories of special cosmic powers. The nature of a pyramid is to guide cosmic energy forces into a concentrated point. The Egyptians knew that; we have generally forgotten it. Did you know," she asked, walking to the side of the room so that she was standing by the coat closet, "that George Washington had Egyptian blood, from his grandmother? Certain features of the Constitution of the United States are notable for their Egyptian ideas."

Without glancing down at the book, she began to talk about the movement of souls in Egyptian religion. She said that when people die, their souls return to Earth in the form of carpenter ants, or walnut trees, depending on how they behaved—"well or ill"—in life. She said that the Egyptians believed that people act the way they do because of magnetism produced by tidal forces in the solar system, forces produced by the sun and by its "planetary ally," Jupiter. Jupiter, she said, was a planet, as we had been told, but had "certain properties of stars." She was speaking very fast. She said that the Egyptians were great explorers and conquerors. She said that the greatest of all the conquerors, Genghis Khan, had had forty horses and forty young women killed on the site of his grave. We listened. No one tried to stop her. "I myself have been in Egypt," she said, "and have witnessed much dust and many brutalities." She said that an old man in Egypt who worked for a circus had personally shown her an animal in a cage, a monster, half bird and half lion. She said that this monster was called a gryphon and that she had heard about them but never seen them until she traveled to the outskirts of Cairo. She said that Egyptian astronomers had discovered the planet Saturn, but had not seen its rings. She said that the Egyptians were the first to discover that dogs, when they are ill, will not drink from rivers, but wait for rain, and hold their jaws open to catch it.

"She lies."

We were on the school bus home. I was sitting next to Carl Whiteside, who had bad breath and a huge collection of marbles. We were arguing. Carl thought she was lying. I said she wasn't, probably.

"I didn't believe that stuff about the bird," Carl said, "and what she told us about the pyramids? I didn't believe that either. She didn't know what she was talking about."

"Oh, yeah?" I had liked her. She was strange. I thought I could nail him. "If she was lying," I said, "what'd she say that was a lie?"

"Six times eleven isn't sixty-eight. It isn't ever. It's sixty-six, I know for a fact."

"She said so. She admitted it. What else did she lie about?"

"I don't know," he said. "Stuff."

"What stuff?"

"Well." He swung his legs back and forth. "You ever see an animal that was half lion and half bird?" He crossed his arms. "It sounded real fakey to me."

"It could happen," I said. I had to improvise, to outrage him. "I read in this newspaper my mom bought in the IGA about this scientist, this mad scientist in the Swiss Alps, and he's been putting genes and chromosomes and stuff together in test tubes, and he combined a human being and a hamster." I waited, for effect. "It's called a humster."

"You never." Carl was staring at me, his mouth open, his terrible bad breath making its way toward me. "What newspaper was it?"

"The *National Enquirer*," I said, "that they sell next to the cash registers." When I saw his look of recognition, I knew I had bested him. "And this mad scientist," I said, "his name was, um, Dr. Frankenbush." I realized belatedly that this name was a mistake and waited for Carl to notice its resemblance to the name of the other famous mad master of permutations, but he only sat there.

"A man and a hamster?" He was staring at me, squinting, his mouth opening in distaste. "Jeez. What'd it look like?"

When the bus reached my stop, I took off down our dirt road and ran up through the back yard, kicking the tire swing for good luck. I dropped my books on the back steps so I could hug and kiss our dog, Mr. Selby. Then I hurried inside. I could smell Brussels sprouts cooking, my unfavorite vegetable. My mother was washing other vegetables in the kitchen sink, and my baby brother was hollering in his yellow playpen on the kitchen floor.

"Hi, Mom," I said, hopping around the playpen to kiss her, "Guess what?"

"I have no idea."

"We had this substitute today, Miss Ferenczi, and I'd never seen her before, and she had all these stories and ideas and stuff."

"Well. That's good." My mother looked out the window behind the sink, her eyes on the pine woods west of our house. Her face and hairstyle always reminded other people of Betty Crocker, whose picture was framed inside a gigantic spoon on the side of the Bisquick box; to me, though, my mother's face just looked white. "Listen, Tommy," she said, "go upstairs and pick your clothes off the bathroom floor, then go outside to the shed and put the shovel and ax away that your father left outside this morning."

"She said that six times eleven was sometimes sixty-eight!" I said. "And she said she once saw a monster that was half lion and half bird." I waited. "In Egypt, she said."

"Did you hear me?" my mother asked, raising her arm to wipe her forehead with the back of her hand. "You have chores to do."

"I know," I said. "I was just telling you about the substitute."

"It's very interesting," my mother said, quickly glancing down at me, "and we can talk about it later when your father gets home. But right now you have some work to do."

"Okay, Mom." I took a cookie out of the jar on the counter and was about to go outside when I had a thought. I ran into the living room, pulled out a dictionary next to the TV stand, and opened it to the G's. *Gryphon*: "variant of griffin." *Griffin*: "a fabulous beast with the head and wings of an eagle and the body of a lion." Fabulous was right. I shouted with triumph and ran outside to put my father's tools back in their place.

Miss Ferenczi was back the next day, slightly altered. She had pulled her hair down and twisted it into pigtails, with red rubber bands holding them tight one inch from the ends. She was wearing a green blouse and pink scarf, making her difficult to look at for a full class day. This time there was no pretense of doing a reading lesson or moving on to arithmetic. As soon as the bell rang, she simply began to talk.

She talked for forty minutes straight. There seemed to be less connection between her ideas, but the ideas themselves were, as the dictionary would say, fabulous. She said she had heard of a huge jewel, in what she called the Antipodes, that was so brilliant that when the light shone into it at a certain angle it would blind whoever was looking at its center. She said that the biggest diamond in the world was cursed and had killed everyone who owned it, and that by a trick of fate it was called the Hope diamond. Diamonds are magic, she said, and this is why women wear them on their fingers, as a sign of the magic of womanhood. Men have strength, Miss Ferenczi said, but no true magic. That is why men fall in love with women but women do not fall in love with men: they just love being loved. George Washington had died because of a mistake he made about a diamond. Washington was not the first *true* President, but she did say who was. In some places in the world, she said, men and women still live in the trees and eat monkeys for breakfast. Their doctors are magicians. At the bottom of the sea are creatures thin as pancakes which have never been studied by scientists because when you take them up to the air, the fish explode.

There was not a sound in the classroom, except for Miss Ferenczi's voice, and Donna DeShano's coughing. No one even went to the bathroom.

Beethoven, she said, had not been deaf; it was a trick to make himself famous, and it worked. As she talked, Miss Ferenczi's pigtails swung back and forth. There are trees in the world, she said, that eat meat: their leaves are sticky and close up on bugs like hands. She lifted her hands and brought them together, palm to palm. Venus, which most people think is the next closest planet to the sun, is not always closer, and, besides, it is the planet of greatest mystery because of its thick cloud cover. "I know what lies underneath those clouds," Miss Ferenczi said, and waited. After the silence, she said, "Angels. Angels live under those clouds." She said that angels were not invisible to everyone and were in fact smarter than most people. They did not dress in robes as was often claimed but instead wore formal evening clothes, as if they were about to attend a concert. Often angels *do* attend concerts and sit in the aisles where, she said, most people pay no attention to them. She said the most terrible angel had the shape of the Sphinx. "There is no running away from that one," she said. She said that unquenchable fires burn just under the surface of the earth in Ohio, and that the baby Mozart fainted dead away in his cradle when he first heard the sound of a trumpet. She said that someone named Narzim al Harrardim was the greatest writer who ever lived. She said that planets control behavior, and anyone conceived during a solar eclipse would be born with webbed feet.

"I know you children like to hear these things," she said, "these secrets, and that is why I am telling you all this." We nodded. It was better than doing comprehension questions for the readings in *Broad Horizons*.

"I will tell you one more story," she said, "and then we will have to do some arithmetic." She leaned over, and her voice grew soft. "There is no death," she said. "You must never be afraid. Never. That which is, cannot die. It will change into different earthly and unearthly elements, but I know this as sure as I stand here in front of you, and I swear it: you must not be afraid. I have seen this truth with these eyes. I know it because in a dream God kissed me. Here." And she pointed with her right index finger to the side of her head, below the mouth, where the vertical lines were carved into her skin.

Absent-mindedly we all did our arithmetic problems. At recess the class was out on the playground, but no one was playing. We were all standing in small groups, talking about Miss Ferenczi. We didn't know if she was crazy, or what. I looked out beyond the playground, at the rusted cars piled in a small heap behind a clump of sumac, and I wanted to see shapes there, approaching me.

On the way home, Carl sat next to me again. He didn't say much, and I didn't either. At last he turned to me. "You know what she said about the leaves that close up on bugs?"

"Huh?"

"The leaves," Carl insisted. "The meat-eating plants. I know it's true. I saw it on television. The leaves have this icky glue that the plants have got smeared all over them and the insects can't get off 'cause they're stuck. I saw it." He seemed demoralized. "She's tellin' the truth."

"Yeah."

"You think she's seen all those angels?"

I shrugged.

"I don't think she has," Carl informed me. "I think she made that part up."

"There's a tree," I suddenly said. I was looking out the window at the farms along County Road H. I knew every barn, every broken windmill, every fence, every anhydrous ammonia tank, by heart. "There's a tree that's . . . that I've seen . . . "

"Don't you try to do it," Carl said. "You'll just sound like a jerk."

I kissed my mother. She was standing in front of the stove. "How was your day?" she asked.

"Fine."

"Did you have Miss Ferenczi again?"

"Yeah."

"Well?"

"She was fine, Mom," I asked, "can I go to my room?"

"No," she said, "not until you've gone out to the vegetable garden and picked me a few tomatoes." She glanced at the sky. "I think it's going to rain. Skedaddle and do it now. Then you come back inside and watch your brother for a few minutes while I go upstairs. I need to clean up before dinner." She looked down at me. "You're looking a little pale, Tommy." She touched the back of her hand to my forehead and I felt her diamond ring against my skin. "Do you feel all right?"

"I'm fine," I said, and went out to pick the tomatoes.

Coughing mutedly, Mr. Hibler was back the next day, slipping lozenges into his mouth when his back was turned at forty-five minute intervals and asking us how much of the prepared lesson plan Miss Ferenczi had followed. Edith Atwater took the responsibility for the class of explaining to Mr. Hibler that the substitute hadn't always done exactly what he would have done, but we had worked hard even though she talked a lot. About what? he asked. All kinds of things, Edith said. I sort of forgot. To our relief, Mr. Hibler seemed not at all interested in what Miss Ferenczi had said to fill the day. He probably thought it was woman's talk; unserious and not suited for school. It was enough that he had a pile of arithmetic problems from us to correct.

For the next month, the sumac turned a distracting red in the field, and the sun traveled toward the southern sky, so that its rays reached Mr. Hibler's Halloween display on the bulletin board in the back of the room, fading the scarecrow with a pumpkin head from orange to tan. Every three days I measured how much farther the sun had moved toward the southern horizon by making small marks with my black Crayola on the north wall, ant-sized marks only I knew were there, inching west.

And then in early December, four days after the first permanent snowfall, she appeared again in our classroom. The minute she came in the door, I felt my heart begin to pound. Once again, she was different: this time, her hair hung straight down and seemed hardly to have been combed. She hadn't brought her lunchbox with her, but she was carrying what seemed to be a small box. She greeted all of us and talked about the weather. Donna DeShano had to remind her to take her overcoat off.

When the bell to start the day finally rang, Miss Ferenczi looked out at all of us and said, "Children, I have enjoyed your company in the past, and today I am going to reward you." She held up the small box. "Do you know what this is?" She waited. "Of course you don't. It is a tarot pack."

Edith Atwater raised her hand. "What's a tarot pack, Miss Ferenczi?"

"It is used to tell fortunes," she said. "And that is what I shall do this morning. I shall tell your fortunes, as I have been taught to do."

"What's fortune?" Bobby Kryzanowicz asked.

"The future, young man. I shall tell you what your future will be. I can't do your whole future, of course. I shall have to limit myself to the five-card system, the wands, cups, swords, pentacles, and the higher arcanes. Now who wants to be first?"

There was a long silence. Then Carol Peterson raised her hand.

"All right," Miss Ferenczi said. She divided the pack into five smaller packs and walked back to Carol's desk, in front of mine. "Pick one card from each of these packs," she said. I saw that Carol had a four of cups, a six of swords, but I couldn't see the other cards. Miss Ferenczi studied the cards on Carol's desk for a minute. "Not bad," she said. "I do not see much higher education. Probably an early marriage. Many children. There's something bleak and dreary here, but I can't tell you what. Perhaps just the tasks of a housewife life. I think you'll do very well, for the most part." She smiled at Carol, a smile with a certain lack of interest. "Who wants to be next?"

Carl Whiteside raised his hand slowly.

"Yes," Miss Ferenczi said, "let's do a boy." She walked over to where Carl sat. After he picked his five cards, she gazed at them for a long time. "Travel," she said. "Much distant travel. You might go into the Army. Not too much romantic interest here. A late marriage, if at all. Squabbles. But the Sun is in your major arcana, here, yes, that's a very good card." She giggled. "Maybe a good life."

Next I raised my hand, and she told me my future. She did the same with Bobby Kryzanowicz, Kelly Munger, Edith Atwater, and Kim Foor. Then she came to Wayne Razmer. He picked his five cards, and I could see that the Death card was one of them.

"What's your name?" Miss Ferenczi asked.

"Wayne."

"Well, Wayne," she said, you will undergo a *great* metamorphosis, the greatest, before you become an adult. Your earthly element will leap away, into thin air, you sweet boy. This card, this nine of swords here, tells of suffering and desolation. And this ten of wands, well, that's certainly a heavy load."

"What about this one?" Wayne pointed to the Death card.

"That one? That one means you will die soon, my dear." She gathered up the cards. We were all looking at Wayne. "But do not fear," she said. "It's not really death, so much as change." She put the cards on Mr. Hibler's desk. "And now, let's do some arithmetic."

At lunchtime Wayne went to Mr. Faegre, the principal, and told him what Miss Ferenczi had done. During the noon recess, we saw Miss Ferenczi drive out of the parking lot in her green Rambler. I stood under the slide, listening to the other kids coasting down and landing in the little depressive bowl at the bottom. I was kicking stones and tugging at my hair right up to the moment when I saw Wayne come out to the playground. He smiled, the dead fool, and with the fingers of his right hand he was showing everyone how he had told on Miss Ferenczi.

I made my way toward Wayne, pushing myself past two girls from another class. He was watching me with his little pinhead eyes.

"You told," I shouted at him. "She was just kidding."

"She shouldn't have," he shouted back. "We were supposed to be doing arithmetic."

"She just scared you," I said. "You're a chicken. You're a chicken, Wayne. You are. Scared of a little card," I singsonged.

Wayne fell at me, his two fists hammering down on my nose. I gave him a good one in the stomach and then I tried for his head. Aiming my fist, I saw that he was crying. I slugged him.

"She was right," I yelled. "She was always right! She told the truth!" Other kids were whooping. "You were just scared, that's all!"

And then large hands pulled at us, and it was my turn to speak to Mr. Faegre.

In the afternoon Miss Ferenczi was gone, and my nose was stuffed with cotton clotted with blood, and my lip had swelled, and our class had been combined with Mrs. Mantei's sixth-grade class for a crowded afternoon science unit on insect life in ditches and swamps. I knew where Mrs. Mantei lived: she had a new house trailer just down the road from us, at the Clearwater Park. She was no mystery. Somehow she and Mr. Bodine, the other fourth-grade teacher, had managed to fit forty-five desks into the room. Kelly Munger asked if Miss Ferenczi had been arrested, and Mrs. Mantei said, no, of course not. All that afternoon, until the buses came to pick us up, we learned about field crickets and two-striped grasshoppers, water bugs, cicadas, mosquitoes, flies, and moths. We learned about insects' hard outer shell, the exoskeleton, and the usual parts of the mouth, including the labrum, mandible, maxilla, and glossa. We learned about compound eyes and the four-stage metamorphosis from egg to larva to pupa to adult. We learned something, but not much, about mating. Mrs. Mantei drew, very skillfully, the internal anatomy of the grasshopper on the blackboard. We learned about the dance of the honeybee, directing other bees in the hive to pollen. We found out about which insects were pests to man, and which were not. On lined white pieces of paper we made lists of insects we might actually see, then a list of insects too small to be clearly visible, such as fleas; Mrs. Mantei said that our assignment would be to memorize these lists for the next day, when Mr. Hibler would certainly return and test us on our knowledge.

Suggestions for Discussion

1. Who speaks to whom in what form?

2. What temporal distance is established by the language of the first paragraph between the narrator as he tells the story, and his childhood self? How? Find diction that reinforces this distance throughout the story. Where and how is the distance qualified by our seeing through the boy's eyes, in his terms?

3. The phrase with which the story begins, "On Wednesday afternoon," tells us less about time than about the familiarity of the narrator to the scene. What means are used to indicate the period in which the story takes place?

4. The character of Miss Ferenczi is presented directly through her speech, appearance and action; and she is also interpreted and judged by the narrator and other children. Show how our psychic distance from these judgments varies. How do they help create her character?

5. What are the limitations of the boy's understanding? Where does the grown author understand more? Where does he identify with the boy's understanding?

6. Find examples of *dramatic irony*, where we as readers know more than the characters. Does this story also suggest a *cosmic irony*?

7. Compare the psychic distance of the last paragraph of the story with the first. Why does the narrator not remind us that he is an adult looking back on the scene?

Rape Fantasies

MARGARET ATWOOD

The way they're going on about it in the magazines you'd think it was just invented, and not only that but it's something terrific, like a vaccine for cancer. They put it in capital letters on the front cover, and inside they have these questionnaires like the ones they used to have about whether you were a good enough wife or an endomorph or an ectomorph, remember that? with the scoring upside down on page 73, and then these numbered do-it-yourself dealies, you know? RAPE, TEN THINGS TO DO ABOUT IT, like it was ten new hairdos or something. I mean, what's so new about it?

So at work they all have to talk about it because no matter what magazine you open, there it is, staring you right between the eyes, and they're beginning to have it on the television, too. Personally I'd prefer a June Allyson movie anytime but they don't make them any more and they don't even have them that much on the Late Show. For instance, day before yesterday, that would be Wednesday, thank god it's Friday as they say, we were sitting around in the women's lunch room—the lunch room, I mean you'd think you could get some peace and quiet in there—and Chrissy closes up the magazine she's been reading and says, "How about it, girls, do you have rape fantasies?"

The four of us were having our game of bridge the way we always do, and I had a bare twelve points counting the singleton with not that much of a bid in anything. So I said one club, hoping Sondra would remember about the one club convention, because the time before when I used that she thought I really meant clubs and she bid us up to three, and all I had was four little ones with nothing higher than a six, and we went down two and on top of that we were vulnerable. She is not the world's best bridge player. I mean, neither am I but there's a limit.

Darlene passed but the damage was done. Sondra's head went round like it was a ball bearings and she said, "*What* fantasies?"

"Rape fantasies," Chrissy said. She's a receptionist and she looks like one; she's pretty but cool as a cucumber, like she's been painted all over with nail polish, if you know what I mean. Varnished. "It says here all women have rape fantasies."

"For Chrissake, I'm eating an egg sandwich," I said, "and I bid one club and Darlene passed."

"You mean, like some guy jumping you in an alley or something," Sondra said. She was eating her lunch, we all eat our lunches during the game, and she bit into a piece of that celery she always brings and started to chew away on it with this thoughtful expression in her eyes and I knew we might as well pack it in as far as the game was concerned.

"Yeah, sort of like that," Chrissy said. She was blushing a little, you could see it even under her makeup.

"I don't think you should go out alone at night," Darlene said, "you put yourself in a position," and I may have been mistaken but she was looking at me. She's the oldest, she's forty-one though you wouldn't know it and neither does she, but I looked it up in the employees' file. I like to guess a person's age and then look it up to see if I'm right. I let myself have an extra pack of cigarettes if I am, though I'm trying to cut down. I figure it's harmless as long as you don't tell. I mean, not everyone has access to that file, it's more or less confidential. But it's all right if I tell you. I don't expect you'll ever meet her, though you never know, it's a small world. Anyway.

"For *heaven's* sake, it's only *Toronto*," Greta said. She worked in Detroit for three years and she never lets you forget it, it's like she thinks she's a war hero or something, we should all admire her just for the fact that she's still walking this earth, though she was really living in Windsor the whole time, she just worked in Detroit. Which for me doesn't really count. It's where you sleep, right?

"Well, do you?" Chrissy said. She was obviously trying to tell us about hers but she wasn't about to go first, she's cautious, that one.

"I certainly don't," Darlene said, and she wrinkled up her nose, like this, and I had to laugh. "I think it's disgusting." She's divorced, I read that in the file too, she never talks about it. It must've been years ago anyway. She got up and went over to the coffee machine and turned her back on us as though she wasn't going to have anything more to do with it.

"Well," Greta said. I could see it was going to be between her and Chrissy. They're both blondes, I don't mean that in a bitchy way but they do try to outdress each other. Greta would like to get out of Filing, she'd like to be a receptionist too so she could meet more people. You don't meet much of anyone in Filing except other people in Filing. Me, I don't mind it so much, I have outside interests.

"Well," Greta said, "I sometimes think about, you know my apartment? It's got this little balcony, I like to sit out there in the summer and I have a few plants out there. I never bother that much about locking the door to the balcony, it's one of those sliding glass ones, I'm on the eighteenth floor for heaven's sake, I've got a good view of the lake and the CN Tower and all. But I'm sitting around one night in my housecoat, watching TV with my shoes off, you know how you do, and I see this guy's feet, coming down past the window, and the next thing you know he's standing on the balcony, he's let himself down by a rope with a hook on the end of it from the floor above, that's the nineteenth, and before I can even get up off the chesterfield he's inside the apartment. He's all dressed in black with black gloves on"—I knew right away what show she got the black gloves off because I saw the same one—"and then he, well, you know."

"You know what?" Chrissy said, but Greta said, "And afterwards he tells me that he goes all over the outside of the apartment building like that, from one floor to another, with his rope and his hook. . . and then he goes out to the balcony and tosses his rope, and he climbs up it and disappears."

"Just like Tarzan," I said, but nobody laughed.

"Is that all?" Chrissy said. "Don't you ever think about, well, I think about being in the bathtub, with no clothes on. . . "

"So who takes a bath in their clothes?" I said, you have to admit it's stupid when you come to think of it, but she just went on, ". . . with lots of bubbles, what I use is Vitabath, it's more expensive but it's so relaxing, and my hair pinned up, and the door opens and this fellow's standing there. . . "

"How'd he get in?" Greta said.

"Oh, I don't know, through a window or something. Well, I can't very well get out of the bathtub, the bathroom's too small and besides he's blocking the doorway, so I just *lie* there, and he starts to very slowly take his own clothes off, and then he gets into the bathtub with me."

"Don't you scream or anything?" said Darlene. She'd come back with her cup of coffee, she was getting really interested. "I'd scream like bloody murder."

"Who'd hear me?" Chrissy said. "Besides, all the articles say it's better not to resist, that way you don't get hurt."

"Anyway you might get bubbles up your nose," I said, "from the deep breathing," and I swear all four of them looked at me like I was in bad taste, like I'd insulted the Virgin Mary or something. I mean, I don't see what's wrong with a little joke now and then. Life's too short, right?

"Listen," I said, "those aren't *rape* fantasies. I mean, you aren't getting *raped*, it's just some guy you haven't met formally who happens to be more attractive than Derek Cummins"—he's the Assistant Manager, he wears elevator shoes or at any rate they have these thick soles and he has this funny was of talking, we call him Derek Duck—"and you have a good time. Rape is when they've got a knife or something and you don't want to."

"So what about you, Estelle," Chrissy said, she was miffed because I laughed at her fantasy, she thought I was putting her down. Sondra was miffed too, by this time she'd finished her celery and she wanted to tell about hers, but she hadn't got in fast enough.

"All right, let me tell you one," I said. "I'm walking down this dark street at night and this fellow comes up and grabs my arm. Now it so happens that I have a plastic lemon in my purse, you know how it always says you should carry a plastic lemon in your purse? I don't really do it, I tried it once but the darn thing leaked all over my chequebook, but in this fantasy I have one, and I say to him, "You're intending to rape me, right?" and he nods, so I open my purse to get the plastic lemon, and I can't find it! My purse is full of all this junk, Kleenex and cigarettes and my change purse and my lipstick and my driver's licence, you know the kind of stuff; so I ask him to hold out his hands, like this, and I pile all this junk into them and down at the bottom there's the plastic lemon, and I can't get the top off. So I hand it to him and he's very obliging, he twists the top off and hands it back to me, and I squirt him in the eye."

I hope you don't think that's too vicious. Come to think of it, it is a bit mean, especially when he was so polite and all.

"*That's* your rape fantasy?" Chrissy says. "I don't believe it."

"She's a card," Darlene says, she and I are the ones that've been here the longest and she never will forget the time I got drunk at the office party and insisted I was going to dance under the table instead of on top of it, I did a sort of Cossack number but then I hit my head on the bottom of the table—actually it was a desk—when I went to get up, and I knocked myself out cold. She's decided that's the mark of an original mind and she tells everyone new about it and I'm not sure that's fair. Though I did do it.

"I'm being totally honest," I say. I always am and they know it. There's no point in being anything else, is the way I look at it, and sooner or later the truth will out so you might as well not waste the time, right? "You should hear the one about the Easy-Off Oven Cleaner."

But that was the end of the lunch hour, with one bridge game shot to hell, and the next day we spent most of the time arguing over whether to start a new game or play out the hands we had left over from the day before, so Sondra never did get a chance to tell about her rape fanstasy.

It started me thinking though, about my own rape fantasies. Maybe I'm abnormal or something. I mean I have fantasies about handsome strangers coming in through the window too, like Mr. Clean, I wish one would, please god somebody without flat feet and big sweat marks on his shirt, and over five feet five, believe me being tall is a handicap though it's getting better, tall guys are starting to like someone whose nose reaches higher than their belly button. But if you're being totally honest you can't count those as rape fantasies. In a real rape fantasy, what you should feel is this anxiety, like when you think about your apartment building catching on fire and whether you should use the elevator or the stairs or maybe just stick your head under a wet towel, and you try to remember everything you've read about what to do but you can't decide.

For instance, I'm walking along this dark street at night and this short, ugly fellow comes up and grabs my arm, and not only is he ugly, you know, with a sort of puffy nothing face, like those fellows you have to talk to in the bank when your account's overdrawn—of course I don't mean they're all like that—but he's absolutely covered in pimples. So he gets me pinned against the wall, he's short but he's heavy, and he starts to undo himself and the zipper gets stuck. I mean, one of the most significant moments in a girl's life, it's almost like getting married or having a baby or something, and he sticks the zipper.

So I say, kind of disgusted, "Oh for Chrissake," and he starts to cry. He tells me he's never been able to get anything right in his entire life, and this is the last straw, he's going to go jump off a bridge.

"Look," I say, I feel so sorry for him, in my rape fantasies I always end up feeling sorry for the guy, I mean there has to be something *wrong* with them, if it was Clint Eastwood it'd be different but worse luck it never is. I was the kind of little girl who buried dead robins, know what I mean? It used to drive my mother nuts, she didn't like me touching them, because of the germs I guess. So I say, "Listen, I know how you feel. You really should do something about those pimples, if you got rid of them you'd be quite good looking, honest; then you wouldn't have to go around doing stuff like this. I had them myself once," I say, to comfort him, but in fact I did, and it ends up I give him the name of my old dermatologist, the one I had in high school, that was back in Leamington, except I used to go to St. Catharine's for the dermatologist. I'm telling you, I was really lonely when I first came here; I thought it was going to be such a big adventure and all, but it's a lot harder to meet people in a city. But I guess it's different for a guy.

Or I'm lying in bed with this terrible cold, my face is all swollen up, my eyes are red and my nose is dripping like a leaky tap, and this fellow comes in through the window and *he* has a terrible cold too, it's a new kind of flu that's been going around. So he says "I'b goig do rabe you"—I hope you don't mind me holding my nose like this but that's the way I imagine it—and he lets out this terrific sneeze, which slows him down a bit, also I'm no object of beauty myself, you'd have to be some kind of pervert to want to rape someone with a cold like mine, it'd be like raping a bottle of LePages mucilage the way my nose is running. He's looking wildly around the room, and I realize it's because he doesn't have a piece of Kleenex! "Id's ride here," I say, and I pass him the Kleenex, god knows why he even bothered to get out of bed, you'd think if you were going to go around climbing in windows you'd wait till you were healthier, right? I mean, that takes a certain amount of energy. So I ask him why doesn't he let me fix him a NeoCitran and scotch, that's what I always take, you still have the cold but you don't feel it, so I do and we end up watching the Late Show together. I mean, they aren't all sex maniacs, the rest of the time they must lead a normal life. I figure they enjoy watching the Late Show just like anybody else.

I do have a scarier one though. . . where the fellow says he's hearing angel voices that're telling him he's got to kill me, you know, you read about things like that all the time in the papers. In this one I'm not in the apartment where I live now, I'm back in my mother's house in Leamington and the fellow's been hiding in the cellar, he grabs my arm when I go downstairs to get a jar of jam and he's got hold of the axe too, out of the garage, that one is really scary. I mean, what do you say to a nut like that?

So I start to shake but after a minute I get control of myself and I say, is he sure the angel voices have got the right person, because I hear the same angel voices and they've been telling me for some time that I'm going to give birth to the reincarnation of St. Anne who in turn has the Virgin Mary and right after that comes Jesus Christ and the end of the world, and he wouldn't want to interfere with that, would he? So he gets confused and listens some more, and then he asks for a sign and I show him my vaccination mark, you can see it's sort of an odd-shaped one, it got infected because I scratched the top off, and that does it, he apologizes and climbs out the coal chute again, which is how he got in in the first place, and I say to myself there's some advantage in having been brought up a Catholic even though I haven't been to church since they changed the service into English, it just isn't the same, you might as well be a Protestant. I must write to Mother and tell her to nail up that coal chute, it always has bothered me. Funny, I couldn't tell you at all what this man looks like but I know exactly what kind of shoes he's wearing, because that's the last I see of him, his shoes going up the coal chute, and they're the old-fashioned kind that lace up the ankles, even though he's a young fellow. That's strange, isn't it?

Let me tell you though I really sweat until I see him safely out of there and I go upstairs right away and make myself a cup of tea. I don't think about that one much. My mother always said you shouldn't dwell on unpleasant things and I generally agree with that, I mean, dwelling on them doesn't make them go away. Though not dwelling on them doesn't make them go away either, when you come to think of it.

Sometimes I have these short ones where the fellow grabs my arm but I'm really a Kung-Fu expert, can you believe it, in real life I'm sure it would just be a conk on the head and that's that, like getting your tonsils out, you'd wake up and it would be all over except for the sore places, and you'd be lucky if your neck wasn't broken or something, I could never even hit the volleyball in gym and a volleyball is fairly large, you know?—and I just go *zap* with my fingers into his eyes and that's it, he falls over, or I flip him against a wall or something. But I could never really stick my fingers in anyone's eyes, could you? It would feel like hot jello and I don't even like cold jello, just thinking about it gives me the creeps. I feel a bit guilty about that one, I mean how would you like walking aroung knowing someone's been blinded for life because of you?

But maybe it's different for a guy.

The most touching one I have is when the fellow grabs my arm and I say, sad and kind of dignified, "You'd be raping a corpse." That pulls him up short and I explain that I've just found out I have leukaemia and the doctors have only given me a few months to live. That's why I'm out pacing the streets alone at night, I need to think, you know, come to terms with myself. I don't really have leukaemia but in the fantasy I do, I guess I chose that particular disease because a girl in my grade four class died of it, the whole class sent her flowers when she was in the hospital. I didn't understand then that she was going to die and I wanted to have leukaemia too so I could get flowers. Kids are funny, aren't they? Well, it turns out that he has leukaemia himself, and *he* only has a few months to live, that's why he's going around raping people, he's very bitter because he's so young and his life is being taken from him before he's really lived it. So we walk along gently under the street lights, it's spring and sort of misty, and we end up going for coffee, we're happy we've found the only other person in the world who can understand what we're going through, it's almost like fate, and after a while we just sort of look at each other and our hands touch, and he comes back with me and moves into my apartment and we spend our last months together before we die, we just sort of don't wake up in the morning, though I've never decided which one of us gets to die first. If it's him I have to go on and fantasize about the funeral, if it's me I don't have to worry about that, so it just about depends on how tired I am at the time. You may not believe this but sometimes I even start crying. I cry at the ends of movies, even the ones that aren't all that sad, so I guess it's the same thing. My mother's like that too.

The funny thing about these fantasies is that the man is always someone I don't know, and the statistics in the magazines, well, most of them anyway, they say it's often someone you do know, at least a little bit, like your boss or something—I mean, it wouldn't be *my* boss, he's over sixty and I'm sure he couldn't rape his way out of a paper bag, poor old thing, but it might be someone like Derek Duck, in his elevator shoes, perish the thought—or someone you just met, who invites you up for a drink, it's getting so you can hardly be sociable any more, and how are you supposed to meet people if you can't trust them even that basic amount? You can't spend your whole life in the Filing Department or cooped up in your own apart-ment with all the doors and windows locked and the shades down. I'm not what you would call a drinker but I like to go out now and then for a drink or two in a nice place, even if I am by myself, I'm with Women's Lib on that even though I can't agree with a lot of the other things they say. Like here for instance, the wait-ers all know me and if anyone, you know, bothers me. . . I don't know why I'm telling you all this, except I think it helps you get to know a person, especially at first, hearing some of the things they think about. At work they call me the office worry wart, but it isn't so much like worrying, it's more like figuring out what you should do in an emergency, like I said before.

Anyway, another thing about it is that there's a lot of conversation, in fact I spend most of my time, in the fantasy that is, wondering what I'm going to say and what he's going to say, I think it would be better if you could get a conversation going. Like, how could a fellow do that to a person he's just had a long conversa-tion with, once you let them know you're human, you have a life too, I don't see how they could go ahead with it, right? I mean, I know it happens but I just don't understand it, that's the part I really don't understand.

~~~~~~~~~~~

Suggestions for Discussion

1. Who speaks to whom? In what form?

2. How would you describe the *distance* of the narrator to her audience? How does her confessional, chatty tone determine that distance? Does it have the effect she intends?

3. How unreliable is the narrator? In what way?

4. Each of the narrator's tales tends to throw out an incongrous detail—a plastic lemon, Kleenex, dead robins. How do these contribute to the distance, and the comedy?

5. There are no rape fantasies in "Rape Fantasies." What is the story about? What is its conflict?

Retrospect

1. What techniques do the authors use to create authorial or psychic distance in "Where Are You Going, Where Have You Been?," "Yours," "Hunters in the Snow," and "The Excursion"? How is this question related to the question, *Who speaks?*

2. Describe the limitations of the narrator of "Guests of the Nation"? To what extent do these limitations propel the plot? How do they change?

3. Show how the narrator of "My Man Bovanne" is more reliable than her more educated children.

4. Would you describe the speaker in Jamaica Kincaid's "Girl" as an unreliable narrator? Why or why not?

Writing Assignments

1. Choose a crucial incident from a child's life (your own or invented) and write about it from the temporally distanced perspective of an adult narrator.

2. Rewrite the same incident in the child's language from the point of view of the child as narrator.

3. Write a passage from the point of view of a central narrator who is spatially distanced from the events he or she describes. Make the contrast significant—write of a sea voyage from prison, of home from an alien country, of a closet from a mountaintop, or the like.

4. Write a short scene from the point of view of anything nonhuman (a plant, object, animal, Martian, angel). We may sympathize or not with the perceptions of the narrator, but try to imagine or invent the terms, logic, and frame of reference this character would use.

5. Write from the point of view of a narrator who passes scathing judgments on another character, but let us know that the narrator really loves or envies the other.

6. Let your narrator begin with a totally unacceptable premise—illogical, ignorant, bigoted, insane. In the passage, let us gradually come to sympathize with his or her view.

7. Take any assignment you have previously done and recast it from another point of view. This may (but will not simply) involve changing the person in which it is written. Alter the means of perception or point of view character so that we have an entirely different perspective on the events. But let your attitude as author remain the same.

9

IS AND IS NOT

Comparison

- *Types of Metaphor and Simile*

- *Metaphoric Faults to Avoid*

- *Allegory*

- *Symbol*

- *The Objective Correlative*

As the concept of distance implies, every reader reading is a self-deceiver. We simultaneously "believe" a story and know that it is a fiction, a fabrication. Our belief in the reality of the story may be so strong that it produces physical reactions—tears, trembling, sighs, gasps, a headache. At the same time, as long as the fiction is working for us, we know that our submission is voluntary; that we have, as Samuel Taylor Coleridge pointed out, suspended disbelief. "It's just a movie," says the exasperated father as he takes his shrieking six-year-old out to the lobby. For the father the fiction is working; for the child it is not.

The necessity of disbelief was demonstrated for me some years ago with the performance of a play that ended with too "good" a hanging. The harness was too well hidden, the actor too adept at purpling and bloating his face when the trap fell. Consternation rippled through the audience: My God, they've hanged the *actor*. Because the illusion was too like reality, the illusion was destroyed and the audience was jolted from its belief in the story back into the real world of the performance.

Simultaneous belief and awareness of illusion are present in both the content and the craft of literature, and what is properly called artistic pleasure derives from the tension of this *is* and *is not*.

The content of a plot tells us that something happens that does not happen, that people who do not exist behave in such a way, and that the events of life—which we know to be random, unrelated, and unfinished—are necessary, patterned, and come to closure. When someone declares interest or pleasure in a story "because it really happened," he or she is expressing an unartistic and anti-artistic preference, subscribing to the lie that events can be accurately translated into the medium of words. Pleasure in artistry comes precisely when the illusion rings true without, however, destroying the knowledge that it is an illusion.

In the same way, the techniques of every art offer us the tension of things that are and are not alike. This is true of poetry, in which rhyme is interesting because *tend* sounds like *mend* but not exactly like; it is true of music, whose interest lies in variations on a theme; of composition, where shapes and colors are balanced in asymmetry. And it is the fundamental nature of metaphor, from which literature derives.

Just as the content of a work must not be too like life to destroy the knowledge that it is an illusion, so the likenesses in the formal elements of art must not be too much alike. Rich rhyme, in which *tend* rhymes with *contend* and *pretend*, is boring and restrictive, and virtually no poet chooses to write a whole poem in it. Repetitive tunes jingle; symmetrical compositions tend toward decor.

Metaphor is the literary device by which we are told that something is, or is like, something that it clearly is not, or is not exactly like. What a good metaphor does is surprise us with the unlikeness of the two things compared while at the same time convincing us of the aptness or truth of the likeness. In the process it can illuminate the meaning not only of the thing at hand, but of the story and its theme. A bad metaphor fails to surprise or convince or both—and so fails to illuminate.

Types of Metaphor and Simile

The simplest distinction between kinds of comparison, and usually the first one grasped by beginning students of literature, is between *metaphor* and *simile*. A simile makes a comparison with the use of *like* or *as*, a metaphor without. Though this distinction is technical, it is not entirely trivial, for a metaphor demands a more literal acceptance. If you say, "a woman is a rose," you ask for an extreme suspension of disbelief, whereas "a woman is like a rose" is a more sophisticated form, acknowledging the artifice in the statement.

Historically, metaphor preceded simile, originating in a purely sensuous comparison. When we speak of "the eyes of a potato," or "the eye of the needle," we mean simply that the leaf bud and the thread hole *look like* eyes. We don't mean to suggest that the potato or the needle can see. The comparisons do not suggest any essential or abstract quality to do with sight.

Both metaphor and simile have developed, however, so that the resonance of comparison is precisely in the essential or abstract quality that the two objects share. When a writer speaks of "the eyes of the houses" or "the windows of the soul," the comparison of eyes to windows does contain the idea of transmitting vision between the inner and the outer. When we speak of "the king of beasts," we don't mean that a lion wears a crown or sits on a throne (though it is relevant that in children's stories the lion often does precisely that, in order to suggest a primitive physical likeness); we mean that king and lion share abstract qualities of power, position, pride, and bearing.

In both metaphor and simile a physical similarity can yield up a characterizing abstraction. So if "a woman" is either "a rose" or "like a rose," the significance lies not in the physical similarity but in the essential qualities that such similarity implies: slenderness, suppleness, fragrance, beauty, color—and perhaps the hidden threat of thorns.

Every metaphor and simile I have used so far is either a cliché or a dead metaphor (both of which will be discussed later). Each of them may at one time have surprised by their aptness, but by now each has been used so often that the surprise is gone. I wished to use familiar examples in order to clarify that *resonance of comparison depends on the abstractions conveyed in the likeness of the things compared.* A good metaphor reverberates with the essential; this is the writer's principle of choice.

So Flannery O'Connor, in "A Good Man Is Hard to Find," describes the mother as having "a face as round and innocent as a cabbage." A soccer ball is also round and innocent; so is a schoolroom globe; so is a street lamp. But if the mother's face had been as round and innocent as any of these things, she would be a different woman altogether. A cabbage is also rural, heavy, dense, and cheap, and so it conveys a whole complex of abstractions about the woman's class and mentality. There is, on the other hand, no innocence in the face of Shrike, in Nathanael West's *Miss Lonelyhearts,* who "buried his triangular face like a hatchet in her neck."

Sometimes the aptness of a comparison is achieved by taking it from an area of reference relevant to the thing compared. In *Dombey and Son,* Charles Dickens describes the ships' instrument maker, Solomon Gills, as having "eyes as red as if they had been small suns looking at you through a fog." The simile suggests a seascape, whereas in *One Flew Over the Cuckoo's Nest,* Ken Kesey's Ruckly, rendered inert by shock therapy, has eyes "all smoked up and gray and deserted inside like blown fuses." But the metaphor may range further from its original, in which case the abstraction conveyed must strike us as strongly and essentially appropriate. William Faulkner's Emily Grierson in "A Rose for Emily" has "haughty black eyes in a face the flesh of which was strained across the temple and about the eyesockets as you imagine a lighthouse-keeper's face ought to look." Miss Emily has no connection with the sea, but the metaphor reminds us not only of her sternness and self-sufficiency, but also that she has isolated herself in a locked house. The same character as an old woman has eyes that "looked like two pieces of coal pressed into a lump of dough," and the image domesticates her, robs her of her light.

Both metaphors and similes can be *extended,* meaning that the writer continues to present aspects of likeness in the things compared.

There was a white fog. . . standing all around you like something solid. At eight or nine, perhaps, it lifted as a shutter lifts. We had a glimpse of the towering multitude of trees, of the immense matted jungle, with the blazing little ball of sun hanging over it—all perfectly still—and then the shutter came down again, smoothly, as if sliding in greased grooves.

Joseph Conrad, *Heart of Darkness*

Notice that Conrad moves from a generalized image of "something solid" to the specific simile "as a shutter lifts"; reasserts the simile as a metaphor, "then the shutter came down again"; and becomes still more specific in the extension "as if sliding in greased grooves."

Also note that Conrad emphasizes the dumb solidity of the fog by comparing the larger natural image with the smaller manufactured object. This is a technique that contemporary writers have used to effects both comic and profound, as when Frederick Barthleme in *The Brothers* describes a young woman "with a life stretching out in front of her like so many unrented videos" or a man's head "bobbing like an enormous Q-Tip against the little black sky."

In a more usual metaphoric technique, the smaller or more ordinary image is compared with one more significant or intense, as in this example from Louise Erdrich's "Machimanito," where the narrator invokes the names of Anishinabe Indians dead of tuberculosis:

Their names grew within us, swelled to the brink of our lips, forced our eyes open in the middle of the night. We were filled with the water of the drowned, cold and black—airless water that lapped against the seal of our tongues or leaked slowly from the corners of our eyes. Within us, like ice shards, their names bobbed and shifted.

A *conceit*, which can be either metaphor or simile, is a comparison of two things radically and startlingly unlike—in Samuel Johnson's words, "yoked by violence together." A conceit is as far removed as possible from the purely sensuous comparison of "the eyes of the potato." It compares two things that have very little or no immediately apprehensible similarity; and so it is the nature of the conceit to be long. The author must explain to us, sometimes at great length, why these things can be said to be alike. When John Donne compares a flea to the Holy Trinity, the two images have no areas of reference in common, and we don't understand. He must explain to us that the flea, having bitten both the poet and his lover, now has the blood of three souls in its body.

The conceit is more common to poetry than to prose because of the density of its imagery, but it can be used to good effect in fiction. In *The Day of the Locust*, Nathanael West uses a conceit in an insistent devaluation of love. The screenwriter Claude Estee says:

Love is like a vending machine, eh? Not bad. You insert a coin and press home the lever. There's some mechanical activity inside the bowels of the device. You receive a small sweet, frown at yourself in the dirty mirror, adjust your hat, take a firm grip on your umbrella and walk away, trying to look as though nothing had happened.

"Love is like a vending machine" is a conceit; if the writer didn't explain to us in what way love is like a vending machine, we'd founder trying to figure it out. So he goes on to develop the vending machine in images that suggest not "love" but seamy sex. The last image—"trying to look as though nothing had happened"—has nothing to do with the vending machine; we accept it because by this time we've fused the two ideas in our minds.

Tom Robbins employs conceit in *Even Cowgirls Get the Blues*, in a playfully self-conscious, mock-scientific comparison of Sissy Hankshaw's thumbs to a pearl.

> As for the oyster, its rectal temperature has never been estimated, although we must suspect that the tissue heat of the sedentary bivalve is as far below good old 98.6 as that of the busy bee is above. Nonetheless, the oyster, could it fancy, should fancy its excremental equipment a hot item, for what other among Creation's crapping creatures can convert its bodily wastes to treasure?

There is a metaphor here, however strained. The author is attempting to draw a shaky parallel between the manner in which the oyster, when beset by impurities or disease, coats the offending matter with its secretions—and the manner in which Sissy Hankshaw, adorned with thumbs that many might consider morbid, coated the offending digits with glory.

The comparison of pearl and thumbs is a conceit because sensuous similarity is not the point: Sissy's thumbs are not necessarily pale or shiny. The similarity is in the abstract idea of converting "impurities" to "glory."

A *dead metaphor* is one so familiar that it has in effect ceased to be a metaphor; it has lost the force of the original comparison and acquired a new definition. Fowler's *Modern English Usage* uses the word "sift" to demonstrate the dead metaphor, one that has "been used so often that speaker and hearer have ceased to be aware that the words used are not literal."

> Thus, in *The men were sifting the meal* we have a literal use of *sift*; in *Satan hath desired to have you, that he may sift you as wheat*, *sift* is a live metaphor; in *the sifting of evidence*, the metaphor is so familiar that it is about equal chances whether *sifting* or *examination* will be used, and that a sieve is not present to the thought.

English abounds in dead metaphors. *Abounds* is one, where the overflowing of liquid is not present to the thought. When a person *runs* for office, legs are not present to the thought, nor is an arrow when we speak of someone's *aim*, hot stones when we go through an *ordeal*, headgear when someone *caps* a joke. Unlike clichés, dead metaphors enrich the language. There is a residual resonance from the original metaphor but no pointless effort on the part of the mind to resolve the tension of like and unlike. English is fertile with metaphors (including those eyes of the potato and the needle) that have died and been resurrected as idiom, a "manner of speaking."

Metaphoric Faults to Avoid

Comparison is not a frivolity. It is, on the contrary, the primary business of the brain. Some eighteenth-century philosophers spoke of the human mind as a tabula rasa, a blank slate on which sense impressions were recorded, compared, and grouped. Now we're more likely to speak of the mind as a "computer" (notice that both images are metaphors), "storing" and "sorting" "data." What both acknowledge is that comparison is the basis of all learning and all reasoning. When a child burns his hand on the stove and hears his mother say, "It's hot," and then goes toward the radiator and again hears her say, "It's hot," the child learns not to burn his fingers. The implicit real life comparison is meant to convey a fact, and it teaches a mode of behavior. By contrast, the goal of literary comparison is to convey not a fact but a perception, and thereby to enlarge our scope of understanding. When we speak of "the flames of torment," our impulse is comprehension and compassion.

Nevertheless, metaphor is a dirty word in some critical circles, because of the strain of the pursuit. Clichés, mixed metaphors, and similes that are inept, unapt, obscure, or done to death mar good prose and tax the patience of the most willing reader. After eyes have been red suns, burnt-out fuses, lighthouse keepers, and lumps of coal, what else can they be?

The answer is, always something. But because by definition metaphor introduces an alien image into the flow of the story, metaphor is to some degree always self-conscious. Badly handled, it calls attention to the writer rather than the meaning and produces a sort of hiccup in the reader's involvement. A good metaphor fits so neatly that it fuses to and illuminates the meaning; or, like the Robbins passage quoted above, it acknowledges its self-consciousness so as to take the reader into the game. Generally speaking, where metaphors are concerned, less is more and, if in doubt, don't.

(Now I want to analyze the preceding paragraph. It contains at least seven dead metaphors: *alien, flow, handled, calls, fits, fuses,* and *illuminates.* A metaphor is not a foreigner; a story is not water; we do not take comparisons in our fingers; they have no vocal cords; they are not puzzle pieces; they do not congeal; and they give off no light rays. But each of these words has acquired a new definition and so settles into its context without strain. At the same time, the metaphoric echoes of these words make them more interesting than their abstract synonyms: *introduces an image from a different context into the meaning of the story. . . badly written, it makes us aware of the writer. . . a good metaphor is so directly relevant that it makes the meaning more understandable*—these abstract synonyms contain no imagery, and so they make for flatter writing. I have probably used what Fowler speaks of as a "moribund or dormant, but not stone-dead" metaphor when I speak of Robbins "taking the reader into the game." If I were Robbins, I'd probably have said, "inviting the reader to sit down at the literary pinochle table," which is a way of acknowledging that "taking the reader into the game" is a familiar metaphor; that is, it's a way of taking us into the game. I have used one live metaphor—"produces a sort of hiccup in the reader's involvement"—and I think I will leave it there to defend itself.)

There are more don'ts than do's to record for the writing of metaphor and simile, because every good comparison is its own justification by virtue of being apt and original.

To study good metaphor, read. In the meantime, avoid the following:

Cliché metaphors are metaphors on their way to being dead. They are inevitably apt comparisons; if they were not, they wouldn't have been repeated often enough to become clichés. But because they have not acquired new definitions, the reader's mind must make the imaginative leap to an image. The image fails to surprise, and we blame the writer for this expenditure of energy without a payoff. Or, to put it a worse way:

> Clichés are *the last word* in bad writing, and *it's a crying shame* to see all you *bright young things* spoiling your *deathless prose* with phrases as *old as the hills.* You must *keep your nose to the grindstone,* because *the sweet smell of success* only comes to those who *march to the tune of a different drummer.*

It's a sad fact that because you have been born into the twentieth century, you may not say that eyes are like pools or stars, and you should be very wary of saying that they flood with tears. These have been so often repeated that they've become shorthand for emotions (attractions in the first and second instances, grief in the third) without the felt force of those emotions. Anytime you as writer record an emotion without convincing us to feel that emotion, you introduce a fatal distance between author and reader. Therefore, neither may your characters be hawk-eyed nor eagle-eyed; nor may they have ruby lips or pearly teeth or peaches-and-cream complexions or necks like swans or thighs like hams. I once gave a character spatulate fingers—and have been worrying about it ever since. If you sense—and you may—that the moment calls for the special intensity of metaphor, you may have to sift through a whole stock of clichés that come readily to mind. Or it may be time for freewriting, clustering, and giving the mind room to play. Sometimes your internal critic may reject as fantastic the comparison that, on second look, proves fresh and apt.

In any case, *pools* and *stars* have become clichés for *eyes* because they capture and manifest something essential about the nature of eyes. As long as eyes continue to contain liquid and light, there will be a new way of saying so. And a metaphor freshly pursued can even take advantage of the shared writer-reader consciousness of familiar images. Here William Golding, in *The Inheritors*, describes his Neanderthal protagonist's first tears, which mark his evolution into a human being.

> There was a light now in each cavern, lights faint as the starlight reflected in the crystals of a granite cliff. The lights increased, acquired definition, brightened, lay each sparkling at the lower edge of a cavern. Suddenly, noiselessly, the lights became thin crescents, went out, and streaks glistened

on each cheek. The lights appeared again, caught among the silvered curls of the beard. They hung, elongated, dropped from curl to curl and gathered at the lowest tip. The streaks on the cheeks pulsed as the drops swam down them, a great drop swelled at the end of a hair of the beard, shivering and bright. It detached itself and fell in a silver flash.

In this sharply focused and fully extended metaphor of eyes as caverns, Golding asks us to draw on a range of familiar light imagery: starlight, crystal, and crescent moon, silver. The light imagery usually associated with eyes attaches to the water imagery of tears, though neither eyes nor tears are named. There is a submerged acknowledgment of cliché, but there is no cliché; Golding has reinvested the familiar images with their comparative and emotional force.

In both serious and comic writing, the consciousness of the familiar can be a peripheral advantage if you find a new way of exploiting it. It is a cliché to say, "You'll break my heart," but when Linda Ronstadt sings, "Break my mind, break my mind," the heart is still there, and the old image takes on new force. Although you may not say her eyes are like pools, you may probably say *her eyes are like the scummy duck pond out back*, and we'll find it comic partly because we know the cliché is lurking under the scum.

Cliché can also be useful as a device for establishing authorial distance toward a character or narrator. If the author tells us that Rome wasn't built in a day, we're likely to think the author has little to contribute to human insight; but if a character says so, in speech or thought, the judgment attaches to the character rather than to the author.

> The door closed and he turned to find the dumpy figure, surmounted by the atrocious hat, coming toward him. "Well," she said, "*you only live once* and paying a little more for it, I at least won't *meet myself coming and going*."
>
> "Some day I'll start making money . . ."
>
> "I think you're doing fine," she said, drawing on her gloves. "You've only been out of school a year. *Rome wasn't built in a day*."

> Flannery O'Connor, "Everything That Rises Must Converge"

Though you can exploit the familiar by acknowledging it in a new way, it is never sufficient to put a cliché in quotation marks: *They hadn't seen each other for "eons."* Writers are sometimes tempted to do this in order to indicate that they know a cliché when they see one. Unfortunately, quotation marks have no power to renew emotion. All they say is, "I'm being lazy and I know it."

Far-fetched metaphors are the opposite of clichés; they surprise but are not apt. As the dead metaphor *far-fetched* suggests, the mind must travel too far to carry back the likeness, and too much is lost on the way. When such a comparison does work, we speak laudatorily of a "leap of the imagination." But when it does not, what we face is in effect a failed conceit: The explanation of what is alike about these two things does not convince. Very good writers in the search for originality sometimes fetch too far. Ernest Hemingway's talent was not for metaphor, and on the rare occasions that he used a metaphor, he was likely to strain. In this passage from *A Farewell to Arms*, the protagonist has escaped a firing squad and is fleeing the war.

> You had lost your cars and your men as a floorwalker loses the stock of his department in a fire. There was, however, no insurance. You were out of it now. You had no more obligation. If they shot floorwalkers after a fire in the department store because they spoke with an accent they had always had, then certainly the floorwalkers would not be expected to return when the store opened again for business. They might seek other employment; if there was any other employment and the police did not get them.

Well, this doesn't work. We may be willing to see the likeness between stock lost in a department store fire and men and cars lost in a military skirmish; but "they" *don't* shoot floorwalkers as they shoot prisoners of war; and although a foreign accent might be a disadvantage behind enemy lines, it is hard to see how floorwalkers could be killed because of one, although it might make it hard for them to get hired in the first place, if. . . The mind twists trying to find any illuminating or essential logic in the comparison of a soldier to a floorwalker, and fails, so that the protagonist's situation is trivialized in the attempt.

Mixed metaphors are so called because they ask us to compare the original image with things from two or more different areas of reference: *As you walk the path of life, don't founder on the reefs of ignorance.* Life can be a path or a sea, but it cannot be both at the same time. The point of the metaphor is to fuse two images in a single tension. The mind is adamantly unwilling to fuse three.

Separate metaphors or similes too close together, especially if they come from areas of reference very different in value or tone, disturb in the same way the mixed metaphor does. The mind doesn't leap; it staggers.

> They fought like rats in a Brooklyn sewer. Nevertheless her presence was the axiom of his heart's geometry, and when she was away you would see him walking up and down the street dragging his cane along the picket fence like an idle boy's stick.

Any of these metaphors or similes might be acceptable by itself, but rats, axioms, and boys' sticks connote three different areas and tones, and two sentences cannot contain them all.

Mixed metaphors and metaphors too close together may be used for comic or characterizing effect. *The New Yorker* has been amusing its readers for decades with a filler item called "Block That Metaphor." But the laugh is always on the writer/speaker, and put-down humor, like a bad pun, is more likely to produce a snicker than an insight. Just as writers are sometimes tempted to put a cliché in quotation marks, they are sometimes tempted to mix metaphors and then apologize for it, in some such phrase as "to mix the metaphor," or, "if I may be permitted a mixed metaphor." It doesn't work. Don't apologize and don't mix.

Obscure and *overdone metaphors* falter because the author has misjudged the difficulty of the comparison. The result is either confusion or an insult to the reader's intelligence. In the case of obscurity, a similarity in the author's mind isn't getting onto the page. One student described the spines on a prickly pear cactus as being "slender as a fat man's fingers." I was completely confused by this. Was it ironic, that the spines weren't slender at all? Ah no, he said, hadn't I noticed how startling it was when someone with a fleshy body had bony fingers and toes? The trouble here was that the author knew what he meant but had left out the essential abstraction in the comparison, the startling quality of the contrast: "the spines of the fleshy prickly pear, like slender fingers on a fat man."

In this case, the simile was underexplained. It's probably a more common impulse—we're so anxious to make sure the reader gets it—to explain the obvious. In the novel *Raw Silk*, I had the narrator describe quarrels with her husband, "which I used to face with my dukes up in high confidence that we'd soon clear the air. The air can't be cleared now. We live in marital Los Angeles. This is the air—polluted, poisoned." A critic friend pointed out to me that anybody who didn't know about L. A. smog wouldn't get it anyway, and that all the last two words did was ram the comparison down the reader's throat. He was right. "The air can't be cleared now. We live in marital Los Angeles. This is the air." The rewrite is much stronger because it neither explains nor exaggerates; and the reader enjoys supplying the metaphoric link.

Metaphors using *topical references*, including brand names, esoteric objects, or celebrity names, can work as long as a sense of the connection is given; don't rely for effect on knowledge that the reader may not have. To write, "He looked just like Michael Jackson," is to make Jackson do your job; and if the reader happens to be a Beethoven buff, or Hungarian, or reading your story in the twenty-first century, there may be no way of knowing what the reference refers to. "He had the liquid, androgynous movements of Michael Jackson" will convey the sense even for someone who doesn't own a television. Likewise, "She was as beautiful as Theda Bara" may not mean much to you, whereas if I say, "She had the saucer eyes and satin hair of Theda Bara," you'll get it, close enough.

Allegory

Allegory is a narrative form in which comparison is structural rather than stylistic. An allegory is a continuous fictional comparison of events, in which the action of the story represents a different action or a philosophical idea. The simplest illustration of an allegory is a fable, in which, for example, the race between the tortoise and the hare is used to illustrate the philosophical notion that "the race is not always to the swift." Such a story can be seen as an extended simile, with the original figure of the comparison suppressed: The tortoise and the hare represent types of human beings, but people are never mentioned and the comparison takes place in the reader's mind. George Orwell's *Animal Farm* is a less naive animal allegory, exploring ideas about corruption in a democratic society. Muriel Spark's *The Abbey* is a historical allegory, representing, without any direct reference to Richard

Nixon, the events of Nixon's presidential term through allegorical machinations in a nunnery. The plots of such stories are self-contained, but their significance lies in the reference to outside events or ideas.

Allegory is a tricky form. In the hands of Dante, John Bunyan, Edmund Spenser, John Keats, Franz Kafka, Henrik Ibsen, and Samuel Beckett, it has yielded works of the highest philosophical insight. But most allegories seem to smirk. A naive philosophical fable leads to a simpleminded idea that can be stated in a single phrase; a historical allegory relies on our familiarity with, for example, the Watergate scandal or the tribulations of the local football team, and so appeals to a limited and insular readership.

Symbol

A *symbol* differs from metaphor and simile in that it need not contain a comparison. A symbol is an object or event that, by virtue of association, represents something more or something other than itself. Sometimes an object is invested arbitrarily with such meaning, as a flag represents a nation and patriotism. Sometimes a single event stands for a whole complex of events, as the crucifixion of Christ stands as well for resurrection and redemption. Sometimes an object is invested with a complex of qualities through its association with the event, like the cross itself. These symbols are not metaphors; the cross represents redemption but is not similar to redemption, which cannot be said to be wooden or T-shaped. In "Everything That Rises Must Converge" by Flannery O'Connor, the protagonist's mother encounters a black woman wearing the same absurd hat of which she has been so proud. The hat can in no way be said to "resemble" desegregation, but in the course of the story it comes to represent the tenacious nostalgia of gentility and the aspirations of the new black middle class, and therefore the unacknowledged "converging" of equality.

Nevertheless, most literary symbols, including this one, do in the course of the action derive their extra meaning from some sort of likeness on the level of emotional or ideological abstraction. The hat is not "like" desegregation, but the action of the story reveals that both women are able to buy such a hat and choose it; this is a concrete example of equality, and so represents the larger concept of equality.

Margaret Drabble's novel *The Garrick Year* recounts the disillusionment of a young wife and mother who finds no escape from her situation. The book ends with a family picnic in an English meadow and the return home.

> On the way back to the car, Flora dashed at a sheep that was lying in the path, but unlike all the others it did not get up and move: it stared at us instead with a sick and stricken indignation. Flora passed quickly on, pretending for pride's sake that she had not noticed its recalcitrance; but as I passed, walking slowly, supported by David, I looked more closely and I saw curled up and clutching at the sheep's belly a real snake. I did not say anything to David: I did not want to admit that I had seen it, but I did see it,

I can see it still. It is the only wild snake that I have ever seen. In my book on Herefordshire it says that that part of the country is notorious for its snakes. But "Oh, well, so what," is all that one can say, the Garden of Eden was crawling with them too, and David and I managed to lie amongst them for one whole pleasant afternoon. One just has to keep on and to pretend, for the sake of the children, not to notice. Otherwise one might just as well stay at home.

The sheep is a symbol of the young woman's emotional situation. It does resemble her, but only on the level of the abstractions: sickness, indignation, and yet resignation at the fatal dangers of the human condition. There is here a metaphor that could be expressed as such *(she was sick and resigned as the sheep)*, but the strength of the symbol is that such literal expression does not take place: We let the sheep stand in the place of the young woman while we reach out to the larger significance.

A symbol may also begin as and grow from a metaphor, so that it finally contains more qualities than the original comparison. In John Irving's novel *The World According to Garp*, the young Garp mishears the word "undertow" as "under toad" and compares the danger of the sea to the lurking fantasies of his childish imagination. Throughout the novel the "under toad" persists, and it comes symbolically to represent all the submerged dangers of ordinary life, ready to drag Garp under just when he thinks he is swimming under his own power. Likewise, the African continent in *Heart of Darkness* is dark like the barbaric reaches of the soul; but in the course of the novella we come to understand that darkness is shot with light and light with darkness, that barbarity and civilization are inextricably intermixed, and that the heart of darkness is the darkness of the heart.

One important distinction in the use of literary symbols is between those symbols of which the character is aware, and therefore "belong" to him or her, and those symbols of which only writer and reader are aware, and therefore belong to the work. This distinction is often important to characterization, theme, and distance. In the passage quoted from *The Garrick Year*, the narrator is clearly aware of the import of the sheep, and her awareness suggests her intelligence and the final acceptance of her situation, so that we identify with her in recognizing the symbol. The mother in "Everything That Rises Must Converge," on the other hand, does not recognize the hat as a symbol, and this distances us from her perception. She is merely disconcerted and angered that a black woman can dress in the same style she does, whereas for author and reader the coincidence symbolizes a larger convergence.

Sometimes the interplay between these types of symbol—those recognized by the characters and those seen only by writer and reader—can enrich the story in scope or irony. In *The Inheritors*, from which I've quoted several times, the Neanderthal tribe has its own religious symbols—a root, a grave, shapes in the ice cap—that represent its life-cycle worship. But in the course of the action, flood, fire, and a waterfall recall biblical symbols that allow the reader to supply an additional religious interpretation, which the characters would be incapable of doing.

Again, in "Everything That Rises Must Converge," the mother sees her hat as representing, first, her taste and pride, and later the outrageousness of black presumption. For the reader it has the opposite and ironic significance, as a symbol of equality.

Symbols are subject to all the same faults as metaphor: cliché, strain, obscurity, obviousness, and overwriting. For these reasons, and because the word "Symbolism" also describes a particular late-nineteenth-century movement in French poetry, with connotations of obscurity, dream, and magical incantation, *symbolism* as a method has sometimes been treated with scorn in the hard-nosed twentieth century.

Yet is seems to me incontrovertible that the writing process is inherently and by definition symbolic. In the structuring of events, the creation of character and atmosphere, the choice of object, detail, and language, you are selecting and arranging toward the goal that these elements should signify more than their mute material existence. If this were not so, then you would have no principle of choice and might just as well write about any other sets of events, characters, and objects. If you so much as say, "as innocent as a cabbage," the image is minutely symbolic, not a statement of fact but selected to mean something more and something other than itself.

People constantly function symbolically. We must do so because we rarely know exactly what we mean, and if we do we are not willing to express it, and if we are willing we are not able, and if we are able we are not heard, and if we are heard we are not understood. Words are unwieldy and unyielding, and we leap past them with intuition, body language, tone, and symbol. "Is the oven supposed to be on?" he asks. He is only peripherally curious about whether the oven is supposed to be on. He is really complaining: *You're scatterbrained and extravagant with the money I go out and earn.* "If I don't preheat it, the muffins won't crest," she says, meaning: *You didn't catch me this time! You're always complaining about the food, and God knows I wear myself out trying to please you.* "We used to have salade niçoise in the summertime," he recalls, meaning: *Don't be so damn triumphant. You're still extravagant, and you haven't got the class you used to have when we were young.* "We used to keep a garden," she says, meaning: *You're always away on weekends and never have time to do anything with me because you don't love me anymore; I think you have a mistress.* "What do you expect of me!" he explodes, and neither of them is surprised that ovens, muffins, salads, and gardens have erupted. When people say "we quarreled over nothing," this is what they mean—they quarreled over symbols.

The Objective Correlative

But the conflict in a fiction cannot be "over nothing," and as a writer you must search for the concrete external manifestations that are adequate to the inexpressible feeling. T. S. Eliot used the term "objective correlative" to describe this process and this necessity.

> The only way of expressing emotion in the form of art is by finding an
> "objective correlative"; in other words, a set of objects, a situation, a chain of

events which shall be the formula of that particular emotion; such that when the external facts, which must terminate in sensory experience, are given, the emotion is immediately invoked.

The Sacred Wood

Some critics have argued that Eliot's *objective correlative* is really no more than a synonym for *symbol*, but the term and its definition make several important distinctions:

1. An "objective correlative" contains and evokes an *emotion*. Unlike many other sorts of symbols—scientific formulae, notes of music, the letters of the alphabet—the purpose of artistic symbol is to invoke emotion.

2. Some kinds of symbol—religious or political, for example—also arouse emotion, but they do so by virtue of one's acceptance of a general community of belief not specific to the context in which that symbol is used. The wine that represents the blood of Christ will evoke the same general emotion in Venice, Buenos Aires, and New York. But an artistic symbol arouses an emotion specific to the work and does not rely on sympathy or belief outside that work. Mentioning the wine of the Communion ceremony in a story cannot be relied on to produce religious emotion in the reader; indeed, the author may choose to make it arouse some other emotion entirely.

3. The elements of a story are interrelated in such a way that the specific objects, situation, and events produce a specific emotion. The "romance" and "pity" invoked by *Romeo and Juliet* are not the same romance and pity invoked by *Anna Karenina* or *Gone With the Wind*, because the external manifestations in each work (which, being external "terminate in sensory experience") define the nature of the emotion.

4. The objects, situation, and events of a particular work contain its particular effect; conversely, if they do not contain the desired emotional effect, that effect cannot be produced in that work, either by its statement in abstractions or by appeal to outside symbols. The "objective" sensory experience (objects, situation, events) must be "co-relative" to the emotion, each corresponding to the other, for that is the only way of expressing emotion in the form of art.

When literary symbols fail, it is most often in this difficult and essential mutuality. In a typical example, we begin the story in a room of a dying woman alone with her collection of perfume bottles. The story ranges back over her rich and sensuous life, and at the end we focus on an empty perfume bottle. It is meant to move us at her death, but it does not. Yet the fault is not in the perfume bottle. Presumably a perfume bottle may express mortality as well as a hat may express racial equality. The fault is in the use of the symbol, which has not been integrated into the texture of the story. As Bonnie Friedman puts it in *Writing Past Dark*: "Before a thing can be a symbol it must be a thing. It must do its job as a thing in the world before and during and after you have projected all your meaning all over it." In the case of the perfume bottle we would need to be convinced, perhaps, of the importance this woman placed on scent as essence, need to know how the collection has played a part in the conflicts of her life, perhaps need to see her fumbling now toward her favorite, so that we could emotionally equate the spilling or evaporation of the scent with the death of her own spirit.

A symbolic object, situation, or event may err because it is insufficiently integrated into the story, and so seems to exist for its own sake rather than to emanate naturally from the characters' lives. It may err because the objective correlative is inadequate to the emotion it is supposed to evoke. Or it may err because it is too heavy or heavy-handed; that is, the author keeps pushing the symbol at us, nudging us in the ribs to say: Get it? In any of these cases we will say that the symbol is *artificial*—a curious word in the critical vocabulary, analogous to the charge of a *formula* plot, since *art*, like *form*, is a word of praise. All writing is "artificial," and when we charge it with being so, we mean that it isn't artificial enough, that the artifice has not concealed itself so as to give the illusion of the natural, and that the artificer must go back to work.

Signs and Symbols

VLADIMIR NABOKOV

I

For the fourth time in as many years they were confronted with the problem of what birthday present to bring a young man who was incurably deranged in his mind. He had no desires. Man-made objects were to him either hives of evil, vibrant with a malignant activity that he alone could perceive, or gross comforts for which no use could be found in his abstract world. After eliminating a number of articles that might offend him or frighten him (anything in the gadget line for instance was taboo), his parents chose a dainty and innocent trifle: a basket with ten different fruit jellies in ten little jars.

At the time of his birth they had been married already for a long time; a score of years had elapsed, and now they were quite old. Her drab gray hair was done anyhow. She wore cheap black dresses. Unlike other women of her age (such as Mrs. Sol, their next-door neighbor, whose face was all pink and mauve with paint and whose hat was a cluster of brookside flowers), she presented a naked white countenance to the fault-finding light of spring days. Her husband, who in the old country had been a fairly successful businessman, was now wholly dependent on his brother Isaac, a real American of almost forty years' standing. They seldom saw him and had nicknamed him "the Prince."

That Friday everything went wrong. The underground train lost its life current between two stations, and for a quarter of an hour one could hear nothing but the dutiful beating of one's heart and the rustling of newspapers. The bus they had to take next kept them waiting for ages; and when it did come, it was crammed with garrulous high-school children. It was raining hard as they walked up the brown path leading to the sanitarium. There they waited again; and instead of their boy shuffling into the room as he usually did (his poor face blotched with acne, ill-shaven, sullen, and confused), a nurse they knew, and did not care for, appeared at last and brightly explained that he had again attempted to take his life. He was all right, she said, but a visit might disturb him. The place was so miserably under-staffed, and things got mislaid or mixed up so easily, that they decided not to leave their present in the office but to bring it to him next time they came.

She waited for her husband to open his umbrella and then took his arm. He kept clearing his throat in a special resonant way he had when he was upset. They reached the bus-stop shelter on the other side of the street and he closed his umbrella. A few feet away, under a swaying and dripping tree, a tiny half-dead unfledged bird was helplessly twitching in a puddle.

During the long ride to the subway station, she and her husband did not exchange a word; and every time she glanced at his old hands (swollen veins, brown-spotted skin), clasped and twitching upon the handle of his umbrella, she felt the mounting pressure of tears. As she looked around trying to hook her mind onto something, it gave her a kind of soft shock, a mixture of compassion and won-der, to notice that one of the passengers, a girl with dark hair and grubby red toe-nails, was weeping on the shoulder of an older woman. Whom did that woman resemble? She resembled Rebecca Borisovna, whose daughter had married one of the Soloveichiks—in Minsk, years ago.

The last time he had tried to do it, his method had been, in the doctor's words, a masterpiece of inventiveness; he would have succeeded, had not an envious fel-low patient thought he was learning to fly—and stopped him. What he really wanted to do was to tear a hole in his world and escape.

The system of his delusions had been the subject of an elaborate paper in a sci-entific monthly, but long before that she and her husband had puzzled it out for themselves. "Referential mania," Herman Brink had called it. In these very rare cases the patient imagines that everything happening around him is a veiled refer-ence to his personality and existence. He excludes real people from the conspir-acy—because he considers himself to be so much more intelligent than other men. Phenomenal nature shadows him wherever he goes. Clouds in the staring sky transmit to one another, by means of slow signs, incredibly detailed information regarding him. His inmost thoughts are discussed at nightfall, in manual alphabet, by darkly gesticulating trees. Pebbles or stains or sun flecks form patterns represent-ing in some awful way messages which he must intercept. Everything is a cipher and of everything he is the theme. Some of the spies are detached observers, such are glass surfaces and still pools; others, such as coats in store windows, are preju-diced witnesses, lynchers at heart; others again (running water, storms) are hysteri-cal to the point of insanity, have a distorted opinion of him and grotesquely misin-terpret his actions. He must be always on his guard and devote every minute and module of life to the decoding of the undulation of things. The very air he exhales is indexed and filed away. If only the interest he provokes were limited to his immediate surroundings—but alas it is not! With distance the torrents of wild scandal increase in volume and volubility. The silhouettes of his blood corpuscles, magnified a million times, flit over vast plains; and still farther, great mountains of

unbearable solidity and height sum up in terms of granite and groaning firs the ultimate truth of his being.

II

When they emerged from the thunder and foul air of the subway, the last dregs of
the day were mixed with the street lights. She wanted to buy some fish for supper, so
she handed him the basket of jelly jars, telling him to go home. He walked up to the
third landing and then remembered he had given her his keys earlier in the day.

In silence he sat down on the steps and in silence rose when some ten minutes
later she came, heavily trudging upstairs, wanly smiling, shaking her head in depre-
cation of her silliness. They entered their two-room flat and he at once went to the
mirror. Straining the corners of his mouth apart by means of his thumbs, with a
horrible masklike grimace he removed his new hopelessly uncomfortable dental
plate and severed the long tusks of saliva connecting him to it. He read his
Russian-language newspaper while she laid the table. Still reading, he ate the pale
victuals that needed no teeth. She knew his moods and was also silent.

When he had gone to bed, she remained in the living room with her pack of
soiled cards and her old albums. Across the narrow yard where the rain tinkled in
the dark against some battered ash cans, windows were blandly alight and in one
of them a black-trousered man with his bare elbows raised could be seen lying
supine on an untidy bed. She pulled the blind down and examined the photographs. As a baby he looked more surprised than most babies. From a fold in the
album, a German maid they had had in Leipzig and her fat-faced fiance fell out.
Minsk, the Revolution, Leipzig, Berlin, Leipzig, a slanting house front badly out of
focus. Four years old, in a park: moodily, shyly, with puckered forehead, looking
away from an eager squirrel as he would from any other stranger. Aunt Rosa, a
fussy, angular, wild-eyed old lady, who had lived in a tremulous world of bad news,
bankruptcies, train accidents, cancerous growths—until the Germans put her to
death, together with all the people she had worried about. Age six—that was
when he drew wonderful birds with human hands and feet, and suffered from
insomnia like a grown-up man. His cousin, now a famous chess player. He again,
aged about eight, already difficult to understand, afraid of the wallpaper in the
passage, afraid of a certain picture in a book which merely showed an idyllic landscape with rocks on a hillside and an old cart wheel hanging from the branch of a
leafless tree. Aged ten: the year they left Europe. The shame, the pity, the humili-
ating difficulties, the ugly, vicious, backward children he was with in that special
school. And then came a time in his life, coinciding with a long convalescence
after pneumonia, when those little phobias of his which his parents had stub-
bornly regarded as the eccentricities of a prodigiously gifted child hardened as it
were into a dense tangle of logically interacting illusions, making him totally
inaccessible to normal minds.

This, and much more, she accepted—for after all living did mean accepting the
loss of one joy after another, not even joys in her case—mere possibilities of
improvement. She thought of the endless waves of pain that for some reason or
other she and her husband had to endure; of the invisible giants hurting her boy in

some unimaginable fashion; of the incalculable amount of tenderness contained in the world; of the fate of this tenderness, which is either crushed, or wasted, or transformed into madness; of neglected children humming to themselves in unswept corners; of beautiful weeds that cannot hide from the farmer and help-lessly have to watch the shadow of his simian stoop leave mangled flowers in its wake, as the monstrous darkness approaches.

III

It was past midnight when from the living room she heard her husband moan; and presently he staggered in, wearing over his nightgown the old overcoat with astrakhan collar which he much preferred to the nice blue bathrobe he had.

"I can't sleep," he cried.

"Why," she asked, "why can't you sleep? You were so tired."

"I can't sleep because I am dying," he said and lay down on the couch.

"Is it your stomach? Do you want me to call Dr. Solov?"

"No doctors, no doctors," he moaned. "To the devil with doctors! We must get him out of there quick. Otherwise we'll be responsible. Responsible!" he repeated and hurled himself into a sitting position, both feet on the floor, thumping his fore-head with his clenched fist.

"All right," she said quietly, "we shall bring him home tomorrow morning."

"I would like some tea," said her husband and retired to the bathroom.

Bending with difficulty, she retrieved some playing cards and a photograph or two that had slipped from the couch to the floor: knave of hearts, nine of spades, ace of spades, Elsa and her bestial beau.

He returned in high spirits, saying in a loud voice:

"I have it all figured out. We will give him the bedroom. Each of us will spend part of the night near him and the other part on this couch. By turns. We will have the doctor see him at least twice a week. It does not matter what the Prince says. He won't have to say much anyway because it will come out cheaper."

The telephone rang. It was an unusual hour for their telephone to ring. His left slipper had come off and he groped for it with his heel and toe as he stood in the middle of the room, and childishly, toothlessly, gaped at his wife. Having more English than he did, it was she who attended the calls.

"Can I speak to Charlie," said a girl's dull little voice.

"What number you want? No. That is not the right number."

The receiver was gently cradled. Her hand went to her old tired heart.

"It frightened me," she said.

He smiled a quick smile and immediately resumed his excited monologue.

They would fetch him as soon as it was day. Knives would have to be kept in a locked drawer. Even at his worst he presented no danger to other people.

The telephone rang a second time. The same toneless anxious young voice asked for Charlie.

"You have the incorrect number. I will tell you what you are doing: you are turning the letter O instead of the zero."

They sat down to their unexpected festive midnight tea. The birthday present stood on the table. He sipped noisily; his face was flushed; every now and then he imparted a circular motion to his raised glass so as to make the sugar dissolve more thoroughly. The vein on the side of his bald head where there was a large birthmark stood out conspicuously and although he had shaved that morning, a silvery bristle showed on his chin. While she poured him another glass of tea, he put on his spectacles and re-examined with pleasure the luminous yellow, green, red little jars. His clumsy moist lips spelled out their eloquent labels: apricot, grape, peach, plum, quince. He had got to crab apple, when the telephone rang again.

Suggestions for Discussion

1. In the third paragraph of the story we read, "The underground train lost its life current between two stations. . . "; and at the beginning of section II, "they emerged from the thunder and foul air of the subway." How do these metaphors relate to the situation of the story and to its symbolic pattern?

2. Is the "tiny half-dead unfledged bird. . . helplessly twitching in a puddle" at the end of the fourth paragraph of the first section a symbol? Of what?

3. The "referential mania" described on page 278 is the symbolic system of a madman, in which every natural phenomenon means something other and something more than itself. What distance do we take on this system when we first encounter it? How has that distance altered by the end of the story?

4. What place do the following have in the symbolic meaning of the story: The description of Aunt Rosa on page 279? The shadow of the farmer's "simian stoop" at the end of section II on page 280? The old woman's explanation, "you are turning the letter O instead of the zero," on the same page?

5. This is a "Lady or the Tiger" tale, ending with an unanswered and unanswerable question. Why has Nabokov chosen this form for this particular story? Who do *you* think is on the other end of the telephone at the third call? What significance does it have for the symbolic meaning of the story if it should be the wrong-number caller again? The hospital?

6. What techniques does Nabokov use to create psychic distance? Where and how does he draw the reader closer to the characters?

The Ones Who Walk Away from Omelas

URSULA K. LE GUIN

With a clamor of bells that set the swallows soaring, the Festival of Summer came to the city. Omelas, bright-towered by the sea. The rigging of the boats in harbor sparkled with flags. In the streets between houses with red roofs and painted walls, between old moss-grown gardens and under avenues of trees, past great parks and public buildings, processions moved. Some were decorous: old people in long stiff robes of mauve and grey, grave master workmen, quiet, merry women carrying their babies and chatting as they walked. In other streets the music beat faster, a shimmering of gong and tambourine, and the people went dancing, the procession was a dance. Children dodged in and out, their high calls rising like the swallows' crossing flights over the music and singing. All the processions wound towards the north side of the city, where on the great water-meadow called the Green Fields boys and girls, naked in the bright air, with mud-stained feet and ankles and long, lithe arms, exercised their restive horses before the race. The horses wore no gear at all but a halter without bit. Their manes were braided with streamers of silver, gold, and green. They flared their nostrils and pranced and boasted to one another; they were vastly excited, the horse being the only animal who has adopted our ceremonies as his own. Far off to the north and west the mountains stood up half encircling Omelas on her bay. The air of morning was so clear that the snow still crowning the Eighteen Peaks burned with white-gold fire across the miles of sunlit air, under the dark blue of the sky. There was just enough wind to make the banners that marked the racecourse snap and flutter now and then. In the silence of the broad green meadows one could hear the music winding through the city streets, farther and nearer and ever approaching, a cheerful faint sweetness of the air that from time to time trembled and gathered together and broke out into the great joyous clanging of the bells.

Joyous! How is one to tell about joy? How describe the citizens of Omelas?

They were not simple folk, you see, though they were happy. But we do not say the words of cheer much any more. All smiles have become archaic. Given a description such as this one tends to make certain assumptions. Given a description such as this one tends to look next for the King, mounted on a splendid stallion and surrounded by his noble knights, or perhaps in a golden litter borne by great-muscled slaves. But there was no king. They did not use swords, or keep slaves. They were not barbarians. I do not know the rules and laws of their society, but I suspect that they were singularly few. As they did without monarchy and slavery, so they also got on without the stock exchange, the advertisement, the secret police, and the bomb. Yet I repeat that these were not simple folk, not dulcet shepherds, noble savages, bland utopians. They were not less complex than us. The trouble is that we have a bad habit, encouraged by pedants and sophisticates, of considering happiness as something rather stupid. Only pain is intellectual, only evil interesting. This is the treason of the artist: a refusal to admit the banality of evil and the terrible boredom of pain. If you can't lick 'em, join 'em. If it hurts, repeat it. But to praise despair is to condemn delight, to embrace violence is to lose hold of everything else. We have almost lost hold; we can no longer describe a happy man, nor make any celebration of joy. How can I tell you about the people of Omelas? They were not naïve and happy children—though their children were, in fact, happy. They were mature, intelligent, passionate adults whose lives were not wretched. O miracle! but I wish I could describe it better. I wish I could convince you. Omelas sounds in my words like a city in a fairy tale, long ago and far away, once upon a time. Perhaps it would be best if you imagined it as your own fancy bids, assuming it will rise to the occasion, for certainly I cannot suit you all. For instance, how about technology? I think that there would be no cars or helicopters in and above the streets; this follows from the fact that the people of Omelas are happy people. Happiness is based on a just discrimination of what is necessary, what is neither necessary nor destructive, and what is destructive. In the middle category, however—that of the unnecessary but undestructive, that of comfort, luxury, exuberance, etc.—they could perfectly well have central heating, subway trains, washing machines, and all kinds of marvelous devices not yet invented here, floating light-sources, fuelless power, a cure for the common cold. Or they could have none of that: it doesn't matter. As you like it. I incline to think that people from towns up and down the coast have been coming in to Omelas during the last days before the Festival on very fast little trains and double-decked trams and that the train station of Omelas is actually the handsomest building in town, though plainer than the magnificent Farmers' Market. But even granted trains, I fear that Omelas so far strikes some of you as goody-goody. Smiles, bells, parades, horses, bleh. If so, please add an orgy. If an orgy would help, don't hesitate. Let us not, however, have temples from which issue beautiful nude priests and priestesses already half in ecstasy and ready to copulate with any man or woman, lover or stranger, who desires union with the deep godhead of the blood, although that was my first idea. But really it would be better not to have any temples in Omelas—at least, not manned temples. Religion yes, clergy no. Surely the beautiful nudes can just wander about, offering themselves like divine soufflés to the hunger of the needy and the rapture of the flesh. Let them join the processions. Let tambourines be struck above the copulations, and the glory of desire be proclaimed upon the gongs, and (a not unimportant point) let the offspring of these delightful rituals be beloved and looked after by all. One thing I know there is none of in Omelas is guilt. But what else should there be? I thought at first there were no drugs, but that is puritanical. For those who like it, the faint insistent sweetness of *drooz* may perfume the ways of the city, *drooz* which first brings a great lightness and brilliance to the mind and limbs, and then after some hours a dreamy languor, and wonderful visions at last of the very arcana and inmost secrets of the Universe, as well as exciting the pleasure of sex beyond all belief; and it is not habit-forming. For more modest tastes I think there ought to be beer. What else, what else belongs in the joyous city? The sense of victory, surely, the celebration of courage. But as we did without clergy, let us do without soldiers. The joy built upon successful slaughter is not the right kind of joy; it will not do; it is fearful and it is trivial. A boundless and generous contentment, a magnanimous triumph felt not against some outer enemy but in communion with the finest and fairest in the souls of all men everywhere and the splendor of the world's summer: this is what swells the hearts of the people of Omelas, and the victory they celebrate is that of life. I really don't think many of them need to take *drooz*.

Most of the processions have reached the Green Fields by now. A marvelous smell of cooking goes forth from the red and blue tents of the provisioners. The faces of small children are amiably sticky; in the benign grey beard of a man a couple of crumbs of rich pastry are entangled. The youths and girls have mounted their horses and are beginning to group around the starting line of the course. An old woman, small, fat, and laughing, is passing out flowers from a basket, and tall young men wear her flowers in their shining hair. A child of nine or ten sits at the edge of the crowd, alone, playing on a wooden flute. People pause to listen, and they smile, but they do not speak to him, for he never ceases playing and never sees them, his dark eyes wholly rapt in the sweet, thin magic of the tune.

He finishes, and slowly lowers his hands holding the wooden flute.

As if that little private silence were the signal, all at once a trumpet sounds from the pavillion near the starting line: imperious, melancholy, piercing. The horses rear on their slender legs, and some of them neigh in answer. Sober-faced, the young riders stroke the horses' necks and soothe them, whispering, "Quiet, quiet, there my beauty, my hope." They begin to form in rank along the starting line. The crowds along the racecourse are like a field of grass and flowers in the wind. The Festival of Summer has begun.

Do you believe? Do you accept the festival, the city, the joy? No? Then let me describe one more thing.

In the basement under one of the beautiful public buildings of Omelas, or perhaps in the cellar of one of its spacious private homes, there is a room. It has one locked door, and no window. A little light seeps in dustily between cracks in the boards, secondhand from a cobwebbed window somewhere across the cellar. In one corner of the little room a couple of mops, with stiff, clotted, foul-smelling heads, stand near a rusty bucket. The floor is dirt, a little damp to the touch, as cellar dirt usually is. The room is about three paces long and two wide: a mere broom closet or disused tool room. In the room a child is sitting. It could be a boy or a girl. It looks about six, but actually is nearly ten. It is feeble-minded. Perhaps it was born defective, or perhaps it has become imbecile through fear, malnutrition, and neglect. It picks its nose and occasionally fumbles vaguely with its toes or genitals, as it sits hunched in the corner farthest from the bucket and two mops. It is afraid of the mops. It finds them horrible. It shuts its eyes, but it knows the mops are still standing there; and the door is locked; and nobody will come. The door is always locked; and nobody ever comes, except that sometimes—the child has no understanding of time or interval—sometimes the door rattles terribly and opens, and a person, or several people, are there. One of them may come in and kick the child to make it stand up. The others never come close, but peer in at it with frightened, disgusted eyes. The food bowl and the water jug are hastily filled, the door is locked, the eyes disappear. The people at the door never say anything, but the child, who has not always lived in the tool room, and can remember sunlight and its mother's voice, sometimes speaks. "I will be good," it says. "Please let me out. I will be good!" They never answer. The child used to scream for help at night, and cry a good deal, but now it only makes a kind of whining, "eh-haa, eh-haa," and it speaks less and less often. It is so thin there are no calves to its legs; its belly protrudes; it lives on a half-bowl of corn meal and grease a day. It is naked. Its buttocks and thighs are a mass of festered sores, as it sits in its own excrement continually.

They all know it is there, all the people of Omelas. Some of them have come to see it, others are content merely to know it is there. They all know that it has to be there. Some of them understand why, and some do not, but they all understand that their happiness, the beauty of their city, the tenderness of their friendships, the health of their children, the wisdom of their scholars, the skill of their makers, even the abundance of their harvest and the kindly weathers of their skies, depend wholly on this child's abominable misery.

This is usually explained to children when they are between eight and twelve, whenever they seem capable of understanding; and most of those who come to see the child are young people, though often enough an adult comes, or comes back, to see the child. No matter how well the matter has been explained to them, these young spectators are always shocked and sickened at the sight. They feel disgust, which they had thought themselves superior to. They feel anger, outrage, impotence, despite all the explanations. They would like to do something for the child. But there is nothing they can do. If the child were brought up into the sunlight out of that vile place, if it were cleaned and fed and comforted, that would be a good thing, indeed; but if it were done, in that day and hour all the prosperity and beauty and delight of Omelas would wither and be destroyed. Those are the terms. To exchange all the goodness and grace of every life in Omelas for that single, small improvement: to throw away the happiness of thousands for the chance of the happiness of one: that would be to let guilt within the walls indeed.

The terms are strict and absolute; there may not even be a kind word spoken to the child.

Often young people go home in tears, or in a tearless rage, when they have seen the child and faced this terrible paradox. They may brood over it for weeks or years. But as time goes on they begin to realize that even if the child could be released, it would not get much good of its freedom: a little vague pleasure of warmth and food, no doubt, but little more. It is too degraded and imbecile to know any real joy. It has been afraid too long ever to be free of fear. Its habits are too uncouth for it to respond to humane treatment. Indeed, after so long it would probably be wretched without walls about it to protect it, and darkness for its eyes, and its own excrement to sit in. Their tears at the bitter injustice dry when they begin to perceive the terrible justice of reality and to accept it. Yet it is their tears and anger, the trying of their generosity and the acceptance of their helplessness, which are perhaps the true source of the splendor of their lives. Theirs is no vapid, irresponsible happiness. They know that they, like the child, are not free. They know compassion. It is the existence of the child, and their knowledge of its existence, that makes possible the nobility of their architecture, the poignancy of their music, the profundity of their science. It is because of the child that they are so gentle with children. They know that if the wretched one were not snivelling in the dark, the other one, the flute-player, could make no joyful music as the young riders line up in their beauty for the race in the sunlight of the first morning of summer.

Now do you believe in them? Are they more credible? But there is one more thing to tell, and this is quite incredible.

At times one of the adolescent girls or boys who go to see the child does not go home to weep or rage, does not, in fact, go home at all. Sometimes also a man or woman much older falls silent for a day or two, and then leaves home. These people go out into the street, and walk down the street alone. They keep walking, and walk straight out of the city of Omelas, through the beautiful gates. They keep walking across the farmlands of Omelas. Each one goes alone, youth or girl, man or woman. Night falls; the traveler must pass down the village streets, between the houses with yellow-lit windows, and on out into the darkness of the fields. Each alone, they go west or north, towards the mountains. They go on. They leave Omelas, they walk ahead into the darkness, and they do not come back. The place they go towards is a place even less imaginable to most of us than the city of happiness. I cannot describe it at all. It is possible that it does not exist. But they seem to know where they are going, the ones who walk away from Omelas.

Suggestions for Discussion

1. Consider the imagery of the opening paragraph. What abstractions are conveyed by the details? How are verbs used as metaphor?

2. Is "The Ones Who Walk Away from Omelas" an allegory? What situation might it stand for without mentioning?

3. How does the child operate as a symbol? Of what?

4. How do connection and disconnection function in this story? As subject matter? As form? Consider how and whether conflict is central to its structure. Is it a story at all? Who are its characters?

5. Describe the emotion for which "The Ones Who Walk Away from Omelas" is an objective correlative. How do objects, situation, chain of events add up to the "formula of that particular emotion."

6. Who speaks? Who is the "I" in this story? How would you describe the point of view?

7. Describe the indescribable place toward which those who walk away from Omelas go. What does it symbolize?

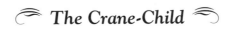

The Crane-Child

DAVID LEAVITT

Jerene found it by accident. She was working in the library one afternoon—wasting time, really—skimming through indexes of psychoanalytic journals and papers in search of something, anything that would give her a clue, a new grounding, that would illuminate the way out of the mammoth, unruly dissertation in which she was lost. Over a period of seven years its subject had changed a dozen times—from child abandonment to the phenomenology of adoption, and onto lost languages, children babbling in their bedrooms. Still her fellowship had been renewed, and would be renewed indefinitely, it seemed, for many of the professors on the philosophy faculty thought her a genius in the raw, a great philosophical mind, while the rest feared she might go off the deep end if they turned her down for money, feared she might come in with a sawed-off shotgun and blow their brains out, like that deranged mathematics graduate student at Stanford. Scanning the index, a little bored, beginning to think about lunch, she read the abstract of a case history that intrigued her. It was in a collection of psychoanalytic papers, shelved in a distant stack. She followed the trail of the call number; took the book from a shelf; read the article quickly the first time, a little anxious, skipping sentences to find the thesis as she had trained herself long ago to do. She read it again, slowly. By the time she was finished she was breathing unevenly, loudly, her foot drumming the dark metal floor of the stacks, her heart pounding.

A baby, a boy, called Michel in the article, was born to a disoriented, possible retarded teenager, the child of a rape. Until he was about two years old, he lived with his mother in a tenement next to a construction site. Every day she stumbled in and around and out of the apartment, lost in her own madness. She was hardly aware of the child, barely knew how to feed or care for him. The neighbors were alarmed at how Michel screamed, but when they went to knock at the door to ask her to quiet him, often she wasn't there. She would go out at all hours, leaving the child alone, unguarded. Then one day, quite suddenly, the crying stopped. The child did not scream, and he did not scream the next night either. For days there was hardly a sound. Police and social workers were called. They found the child lying on his cot by the window. He was alive and remarkably well, considering how severely he appeared to have been neglected. Quietly he played on his squalid cot, stopping every few seconds to look out the window. His play was unlike any they had ever seen. Looking out the window, he would raise his arms, then jerk them to a halt; stand up on his scrawny legs, then fall; bend and rise. He made strange noises, a king of screeching in his throat. What was he doing? the social workers wondered. What kind of play could this be?

Then they looked out the window, where some cranes were in operation, lifting girders and beams, stretching out wrecker balls on their single arms. The child was watching the crane nearest the window. As it lifted, he lifted; as it bent, he bent; as its gears screeched, its motor whirred, the child screeched between his teeth, whirred with his tongue.

They took him away. He screamed hysterically and could not be quieted, so desolate was he to be divided from his beloved crane. Years later, Michel was an adolescent, living in a special institution for the mentally handicapped. He moved like a crane, made the noises of a crane, and although the doctors showed him many pictures and toys, he only responded to the pictures of cranes, only played with the toy cranes. Only cranes made him happy. He came to be known as the "crane-child." And the question Jerene kept coming up against, reading the article, was this: What did it sound like? What did it feel like? The language belonged to Michel alone; it was forever lost to her. How wondrous, how grand those cranes must have seemed to Michel, compared to the small and clumsy creatures who surrounded him. For each, in his own way, she believed, finds what it is he must love, and loves it; the window becomes a mirror; whatever it is that we love, that is who we are.

After Jerene xeroxed the article, she left the library. There was a brisk wind out-doors; she turned her collar up. Some construction was going on nearby—cranes working, lifting beams to the hardhatted men who swarmed the precarious frame of a rising condominium. The cranes looked like a species of gigantic, long-limbed insect. Transfixed, Jerene approached the makeshift wooden fence that surrounded the construction site. There was a crudely cut peephole in the fence, and through it she stared at the vast pit from which the building would rise, watched the cranes lunge and strain. She stood in the deafening roar of the cranes. In the grinding, the churring, the screeching, in the universe of the cranes, the womb of the cranes, she stood there, eyes open, and listened.

～～～～～～～～～～

Suggestions for Discussion

1. Find several clichés. Whose clichés are they? What function do they serve in the story?

2. The child in the article behaves like a crane. What do we know about what this imitation means to him? What does it mean to Jerene?

3. Jerene thinks, "the window becomes a mirror." Does the reader understand this comparison any differently from Jerene? She thinks, "whatever it is we love, that is who we are." Who then is she?

4. Examine the metaphors for the cranes in the closing paragraph. "The Crane-Child" is published in David Leavitt's collection called *The Language of Cranes.* How do you understand the cranes and their "language"? How do the cranes operate as an objective correlative? For what?

Retrospect

1. Find at least a dozen metaphors for writing in the excerpt from Annie Dillard's *The Writing Life* at the end of chapter 1. Make up half a dozen of your own that seem true to the process as you experience it.

2. Consider the watch that Jenny's father gives her in "The Excursion." How does it operate symbolically?

3. Consider the possibility that Gabriel Garcia Marquez' "A Very Old Man With Enormous Wings" is an allegory of "the artist." Does such a possibility enhance or diminish the story for you?

4. The last paragraph of "Gryphon" by Charles Baxter describes in detail an entymology lesson that the children are given after the departure of Miss Ferenczi. What symbolical resonances can you see in this lesson?

5. In Sandra Cisnero's "Hips," how are hips spoken of literally, how are they used in metaphor, and how, ultimately, do they become a symbol? Of what?

Writing Assignments

1. Write a passage using at least three cliché metaphors, finding a way to make each fresh and original.

2. Take any dead metaphor and write a comic or serious scene that reinvests the metaphor with its original comparative force. Here are a few sample suggestions (your own will be better).

    Sifting the evidence. (The lawyer uses a colander, a tea strainer, two coffee filters, and a garlic press to decide the case.)
    Speakeasy. (Chicago, 1916. A young libertine tricks a beautiful but repressed young woman into an illegal basement bar. He thinks drink will loosen her up. What it loosens is not her sensuality but her tongue, and what she says he doesn't want to hear.)
    Peck on the cheek.
    (Alfred Hitchcock has done this one already, perhaps?)

Bus terminal.	Don't spoil your lunch.
Advertising jingle.	Broken home.
Soft shoulders.	Good-bye.

3. Write two one-page scenes, each containing an extended metaphor or simile. In one, compare an ordinary object to something of great size or significance. In the other, compare a major thing or phenomenon to something smaller and more mundane or less intense.

4. Write a short scene involving a conflict between two people over an object. Let the object take on symbolic significance. It may have the same significance to the two people, or a different significance to each.

5. Let an object smaller than a breadbox symbolize hope, redemption, or love to the central character. Let it symbolize something else entirely to the reader.

6. List all the clichés you can think of to describe a pair of blue eyes. Then write a paragraph in which you find a fresh, new metaphor for blue eyes.

7. In an earlier piece you have written, identify a few clichés. Cut them. Replace them with concrete details or more original similes or metaphors.

10

I GOTTA USE WORDS WHEN I TALK TO YOU

Theme

- *Idea and Morality in Theme*

- *How Fictional Elements Contribute to Theme*

- *Developing Theme as You Write*

How does a fiction mean?

Most literature textbooks begin a discussion of theme by warning that theme is not the *message*, not the *moral*, and that the *meaning* of a piece cannot be paraphrased. Theme contains an idea but cannot be stated as an idea. It suggests a morality but offers no moral. Then what is theme, and how as a writer can you pursue that rich resonance?

First of all, theme is what a story is about. But that is not enough, because a story may be "about" a dying Samurai or a quarreling couple or two kids on a trampoline, and those would not be the themes of those stories. A story is also "about" an abstraction, and if the story is significant, that abstraction may be very large; yet thousands of stories are about love, other thousands about death, and still other thousands about both love and death, and to say this is to say little about the theme of any of them.

I think it might be useful to borrow an idea from existentialist philosophy, which asks the question: *What is what is?* That is, what is the nature of that which exists? We might start to understand theme if we ask the question: *What about what it's about?* What does the story have to say about the idea or abstraction that seems to be contained in it? What attitudes or judgments does it imply? Above all, how do the techniques particular to fiction contribute to our experience of those ideas and attitudes in the story?

291

Idea and Morality in Theme

Literature is stuck with ideas in a way other arts are not. Music, paradoxically the most abstract of the arts, creates a logical structure that need make no reference to the world outside itself. It may express a mood, but it need draw no conclusions. Shapes in painting and sculpture may suggest forms in the physical world, but they need not represent the world, and they need not contain a message. But words mean. The grammatical structure of the simplest sentence contains a concept, whatever else it may contain, so that an author who wishes to treat words solely as sound or shape may be said to make strange music or pictures but not literature.

Yet those who choose to deal in the medium of literature consistently denigrate concepts and insist on the value of the particular instance. Here is Vladimir Nabokov's advice to a reader.

> . . . fondle details. There is nothing wrong about the moonshine of generalization *after* the sunny trifles of the book have been lovingly collected. If one begins with a ready-made generalization, one begins at the wrong end and travels away from the book before one has started to understand it.

Joan Didion parallels the idea in an essay on "Why I Write."

> I am not a scholar. I am not in the least an intellectual, which is not to say that when I hear the word "intellectual" I reach for my gun, but only to say that I do not think in abstracts. During the years when I was an undergraduate at Berkeley I tried, with a kind of hopeless late-adolescent energy, to buy some temporary visa into the world of ideas, to forge for myself a mind that could deal with the abstract.
>
> In short I tried to think. I failed. My attention veered inexorably back to the specific, to the tangible, to what was generally considered, by everyone I knew then and for that matter have known since, the peripheral. I would try to contemplate the Hegelian dialect and would find myself concentrating instead on the flowering pear tree outside my window and the particular way the petals fell on the floor.

Didion takes a Socratic stance here, ironically pretending to naïveté and modesty as she equates "thinking" with "thinking in the abstract." Certainly her self-deprecation is ironic in light of the fact that she is not only a novelist but also one of the finest intellects among our contemporary essayists. But she acknowledges an assumption that's both very general and very seriously taken, that *thought* means *dealing with the abstract,* and that abstract thought is more real, central, and valid than specific concrete thought.

What both these passages suggest is that a writer of fiction approaches concepts, abstractions, generalizations, and truths through their particular embodiments—

showing, not telling. "Literature," says John Ciardi, "is never only about ideas, but about the experience of ideas." T. S. Eliot points out that the creation of this experience is of itself an intellectual feat.

> We talk as if thought was precise and emotion was vague. In reality there is precise emotion and there is vague emotion. To express precise emotion requires as great intellectual power as to express precise thought.

The value of the literary experience is that it allows us to judge an idea at two levels of consciousness, the rational and the emotional, simultaneously. The kind of "truth" that can be told through thematic resonance is many-faceted and can acknowledge the competing of many truths, exploring paradox and contradiction.

There is a curious prejudice built into our language that makes us speak of *telling the truth* but *telling a lie*. No one supposes that all conceivable falsehood can be wrapped up in a single statement called "the lie"; lies are manifold, varied, and specific. But truth is supposed to be absolute: the truth, the whole truth, and nothing but the truth. This is, of course, impossible nonsense, and *telling a lie* is a truer phrase than *telling the truth*. Fiction does not have to tell the truth, but a truth.

Anton Chekov wrote that "the writer of fiction should not try to solve such questions as those of God, pessimism and so forth." What is "obligatory for the artist," he said, is not "solving a problem," but "stating a problem correctly." John Keats went even further in pursuing a definition of "the impersonality of genius." "The only means of strengthening one's intellect is to make up one's mind about nothing—to let the mind be a thoroughfare for all thoughts." And he defined genius itself as *negative capability*, "that is when a man is capable of being in uncertainties, mysteries and doubts, without any irritable reaching after fact and reason."

A story, then, speculates on a possible truth. It is not an answer or a law but a supposition, an exploration. Every story reaches in its climax and resolution an interim solution to a specifically realized dilemma. But it offers no ultimate solution.

The contrast with the law here is relevant. Abstract reasoning works toward generalization and results in definitions, laws, and absolute judgments. Imaginative reasoning and concrete thought work toward instances and result in emotional experience, revelation, and the ability to contain life's paradoxes in tension—which may explain the notorious opposition of writers to the laws and institutions of their time. Lawmakers struggle to define a moral position in abstract terms such that it will justly account for every instance to which it is applied. (This is why the language of law is so tedious and convoluted.) Poets and novelists continually goad them by producing instances for which the law does not account and referring by implication to the principle behind and beyond the law. (This is why the language of literature is so dense and compact.)

The idea that is proposed, supposed, or speculated on in a fiction may be simple and idealistic, like the notion in "Cinderella" that the good and beautiful will triumph. Or it may be profound and unprovable, like the theme in *Oedipus Rex* that man cannot escape his destiny but may be ennobled in the attempt. Or it may be deliberately paradoxical and offer no guidelines that can be used in life, as in Jane Austen's *Persuasion*, where the heroine, in order to adhere to her principles, must follow advice given on principles less sound than her own.

In any case, while exploring an idea the writer inevitably conveys an attitude toward that idea. Rust Hills puts it this way.

> . . . coherence in the world [an author] creates is constituted of two concepts he holds, which may be in conflict: one is his world view, his sense of the way the world is; and the other is his sense of morality, the way the world ought to be.

Literature is a persuasive art, and we respond to it with the tautology of literary judgment, that a fiction is "good" if it's "good." No writer who fails to convince us of the validity of his or her vision of the world can convince us of his or her greatness. The Victorians used literature to teach piety, and the Aesthetes asserted that Victorian piety was a deadening lie. Albert Camus believed that no serious writer in the twentieth century could avoid political commitment, whereas for Joyce the true artist could be a God but must not be a preacher. Each of these stances is a moral one. Those who defend escape literature do so on the grounds that people need to escape. Those who defend hardcore pornography argue that we can't prove an uncensored press makes for moral degeneracy, whereas it can be historically demonstrated that a censored press makes for political oppression. Anarchistic, nihilistic, and antisocial literature is always touted as offering a neglected truth. I have yet to hear anyone assert that literature leads to laziness, madness, and brutality and then say that it doesn't matter.

The writer, of course, may be powerfully impelled to impose a limited vision of the world as it ought to be, and even to tie that vision to a social institution, wishing not only to persuade and convince but also to propagandize. But because the emotional force of literary persuasion is in the realization of the particular, the writer is doomed to fail. The greater the work, the more it refers us to some permanent human impulse rather than a given institutional embodiment of that impulse. Fine writing expands our scope by continually presenting a new way of seeing, a further possibility of emotional identification; it flatly refuses to become a law. I am not a Roman Catholic like Gerard Manley Hopkins and cannot be persuaded by his poetry to become one; but in a moment near despair I can drive along an Illinois street in a Chevrolet station wagon and take strength from the lines of a Jesuit in the Welsh wasteland. I am not a communist as Bertolt Brecht was and cannot be convinced by his plays to become one; but I can see the hauteur of wealth displayed on the Gulf of Mexico and recognize, from a parable of the German Marxist, the difference between a possession and a belonging.

In the human experience, emotion, logic, and judgment are inextricably mixed, and we make continual cross-reference between and among them. *You've just got the sulks today.* (I pass judgment on your emotion.) *What do you think of this idea?* (How do you judge this logic?) *Why do I feel this way?* (What is the logic of this emotion?) *It makes no sense to be angry about it.* (I pass judgment on the logic of your emotion.) Literature attempts to fuse three areas of experience organically, denying the force of none of them, positing that no one is more real than the others. This is why I have insisted throughout this book on detail and scene (immediate felt experience), the essential abstractions conveyed therein (ideas), and the attitude implied thereby (judgment).

Not all experience reveals, but all revelation comes through experience. Books aspire to become a part of that revelatory experience, and the books that are made in the form of fiction attempt to do so by re-creating the experience of revelation.

How Fictional Elements Contribute to Theme

Whatever the idea and attitudes that underlie the theme of a story, that story will bring them into the realm of experience through its particular and unique pattern. Theme involves emotion, logic, and judgment, all three—but the pattern that forms the particular experience of that theme is made up of every element of fiction this book has discussed: the arrangement, shape, and flow of the action, as performed by the characters, realized in their details, seen in their atmosphere, from a unique point of view, through the imagery and the rhythm of the language.

This book, for example, contains at least five stories that may be said to have "the generation gap" as a major theme: "Girl," "Where Are You Going, Where Have You Been?" "The Point," "My Man Bovanne," "Gryphon," and (at the end of this chapter) "Ralph the Duck." It could also be argued that "The Use of Force" and "The Excursion" share the theme. Some of these are written from the point of view of a member of the older generation, some from the point of view of the younger. In some conflict is resolved by bridging the gap; in others it is not. The characters are variously poor, middle class, rural, urban, male, female, adolescent, middle-aged, old, black, white. The imagery variously evokes food, drunkenness, schooling, madness, sex, speed, torture, blindness, death, and writing. It is in the different uses of the elements of fiction that each story makes unique what it has to say about, and what attitude it takes toward, the idea of "the generation gap."

What follows is as short a story as you are likely to encounter in print. It is spare in the extreme—almost, as its title suggests, an outline. Yet the author has contrived in this miniscule compass to direct every fictional element we have discussed toward the exploration of several large themes.

A Man Told Me the Story of His Life

GRACE PALEY

Vicente said: I wanted to be a doctor. I wanted to be a doctor with my whole heart.

I learned every bone, every organ in the body. What is it for? Why does it work?

The school said to me: Vicente, be an engineer. That would be good. You understand mathematics.

I said to the school: I want to be a doctor. I already know how the organs connect. When something goes wrong, I'll understand how to make repairs.

The school said: Vicente, you will really be an excellent engineer. You show on all the tests what a good engineer you will be. It doesn't show whether you'll be a good doctor.

I said: Oh, I long to be a doctor. I nearly cried. I was seventeen. I said: But perhaps you're right. You're the teacher. You're the principal. I know I'm young.

The school said: And besides, you're going into the army.

And then I was made a cook. I prepared food for two thousand men.

Now you see me. I have a good job. I have three children. This is my wife, Consuela. Did you know I saved her life?

Look, she suffered pain. The doctor said: What is this? Are you tired? Have you had too much company? How many children? Rest overnight, then tomorrow we'll make tests.

The next morning I called the doctor. I said: She must be operated on immediately. I have looked in the book. I see where her pain is. I understand what the pressure is, where it comes from. I see clearly the organ that is making trouble.

The doctor made a test. He said: She must be operated at once. He said to me: Vicente, how did you know?

I think it would be fair to say that this story is about the waste of Vicente's talent through the bad guidance of authority. I'll start by saying, then, that *waste* and *power* are its central themes. How are the elements of fiction arranged in the story to present them?

The *conflict* is between Vicente and the figures of authority he encounters: teacher, principal, army, doctor. His desire at the beginning of the story is to become a doctor (in itself a figure of authority), and this desire is thwarted by persons of increasing power. In the *crisis action* what is at stake is his wife's life. In this "last battle" he succeeds as a doctor, so that the *resolution* reveals the *irony* of his having been denied in the first place.

The story is told from the *point of view* of a *first-person central narrator,* but with an important qualification. The title, "A Man Told Me the Story of His Life," and the first two words, "Vicente said," posit a *peripheral narrator* reporting what Vicente said. If the story were titled "My Life" and began, "I wanted to be a doctor," Vicente might be making a public appeal, a boast of how wronged he has been. As it is, he told his story privately to the barely sketched author who now wants it known, and this leaves Vicente's modesty intact.

The modesty is underscored by the simplicity of his *speech,* a *rhythm* and word choice that suggest educational *limitations* (perhaps that English is a second language). At the same time, that simplicity helps us *identify* with Vicente morally. Clearly, if he has educational limitations, it is not for want of trying to get an education! His credibility is augmented by *understatement,* both as a youth—"Perhaps you're right. You're the teacher."—and as a man—"I have a good job. I have three children." This apparent acceptance makes us trust him at the same time as it makes us angry on his behalf.

It's consistent with the spareness of the language that we do not have an accumulation of minute or vivid details, but the degree of *specificity* is nevertheless a clue to where to direct our sympathy. In the title Vicente is just "A Man." As soon as he speaks he becomes an individual with a name. "The School," collective and impersonal, speaks to him, but when he speaks it is to single individuals,"the teacher, the principal," and when he speaks of his wife she is personalized as "Consuela."

Moreover, the *sensory details* are so arranged that they relate to each other in ways that give them *metaphoric* and *symbolic significance*. Notice, for example, how Vicente's desire to become a doctor "with my whole heart" is immediately followed by, "I learned every bone, every organ." Here the factual anatomical study refers us back to the heart that is one of those organs, suggesting by implication that Vicente is somebody who knows what a heart is. He knows how things "connect."

An engineer, of course, has to know how things connect and how to make repairs. But so does a doctor, and the authority figures of the school haven't the imagination to see the connection. The army, by putting him to work in a way that involves both connections and anatomical parts, takes advantage of his by-now clear ability to order and organize things—he feeds two thousand men—but it is too late to repair the misdirection of such talents. We don't know what his job is now; it doesn't matter, it's the wrong one.

As a young man Vicente asked, "What is it for? Why does it work?", revealing a natural fascination with the sort of question that would, of course, be asked on an anatomy test. But no such test is given, and the tests that are given are irrelevant. His wife's doctor will "make tests," but like the school authorities he knows less than Vicente does, and so impersonally asks insultingly personal questions. In fact you could say that all the authorities of the story fail the test.

This analysis, which is about two and a half times as long as the story, doesn't begin to exhaust the possibilities for interpretation, and you may disagree with any of my suggestions. But it does indicate how the techniques of characterization, plot, detail, point of view, image, and metaphor all reinforce the themes of waste and power. The story is so densely conceived and developed that it might fairly be titled "Connections," "Tests," "Repairs," "What Is It For?," or "How Did You Know?"—any one could lead us toward the themes of waste and the misguidance of authority.

Not every story is or needs to be as intensely interwoven in its elements as "A Man Told Me the Story of His Life," but the development of theme always involves such interweaving to a degree. It is a standard to work toward.

Developing Theme as You Write

In an essay, your goal is to say as clearly and directly as possible what you mean. In fiction, your goal is to make people and make them do things, and, ideally, never to "say what you mean" at all. Theoretically, an outline can never harm an essay: this is what I have to say, and I'll say it through points A, B, and C. But if a writer sets out to write a story to illustrate an idea, the fiction will almost inevitably be thin. Even if you begin with an outline, as many writers do, it will be an outline of the action and not of your "points." You may not know the meaning of the story until the characters begin to tell you what it is. You'll begin with an image of a person or a situation that seems vaguely to embody something important, and you'll learn as you go what that something is. Likewise, what you mean will emerge in the reading experience and take place in the reader's mind, "not," as the narrator says of Marlow's tales in *Heart of Darkness*, "inside like a kernel but outside, enveloping the tale which brought it out."

But at some point in the writing process, you may find yourself impelled by, under pressure of, or interested primarily in your theme. It will seem that you have set yourself this lonely, austere, and tortuous task because you do have something to say. At this point you will, and you should, begin to let that sorting-comparing-cataloging neocortex of your brain go to work on the stuff of your story. John Gardner describes the process in *The Art of Fiction*.

> Theme, it should be noticed, is not imposed on the story but evoked from within it—initially an intuitive but finally an intellectual act on the part of the writer. The writer muses on the story idea to determine what it is in it that has attracted him, why it seems to him worth telling. Having determined. . . what interests him—and what chiefly concerns the major character. . . he toys with various ways of telling his story, thinks about what has been said before about (his theme), broods on every image that occurs to him, turning it over and over, puzzling it, hunting for connections, trying to figure out—before he writes, while he writes, and in the process of repeated revisions—what it is he really thinks. . . . Only when he thinks out a story in this way does he achieve not just an alternative reality or, loosely, an imitation of nature, but true, firm art—fiction as serious thought.

This process—worrying a fiction until its theme reveals itself, connections occur, images recur, a pattern emerges—is more conscious than readers know, beginning writers want to accept, or established writers are willing to admit. It has become a popular—a cliché—stance for modern writers to claim that they haven't the faintest idea what they meant in their writing. *Don't ask me; read the book. If I knew what it meant, I wouldn't have written it. It means what it says.* When an author makes such a response, it is well to remember that an author is a professional liar. What he or she means is not that there are no themes, ideas, or meanings in the work but that these are not separable from the pattern of fictional experience in which they are embodied. It also means that, having done the difficult writerly job, the writer is now unwilling also to do the critic's work. But beginning critics also resist. Students irritated by the analysis of literature often ask, "How do you know she did that on purpose? How do you know it didn't just happen to come out that way?" The answer is: You don't. But what is on the page is on the page. An author no less than a reader or critic can see an emerging pattern, and the author has both the possibility and the obligation of manipulating it. When you have put something on the page, you have two possibilities, and only two: You may cut it or you are committed to it. Gail Godwin asks:

But what about the other truths you lost by telling it that way?

Ah, my friend, that is my question too. The choice is always a killing one. One option must die so that another may live. I do little murders in my workroom every day.

Often the choice to commit yourself to a phrase, an image, a line of dialogue will reveal, in a minor convulsion of understanding, what you mean. I have written no story or novel in which this did not occur in trivial or dramatic ways. I once sat bolt upright at 4:00 a.m. in a strange town with the realization that my sixty-year-old narrator, in a novel full of images of hands and manipulation, had been lying to me for two hundred pages. Sometimes the realistic objects or actions of a work will begin to take on metaphoric or symbolic associations with your theme, producing a crossing of references, or what Richmond Lattimore calls a "symbol complex." In a novel about a woman who traveled around the world, I employed images of danger- ous water and the danger of losing balance, both physically and mentally. At some point I came up with—or, as it felt, was given—the image of a canal, the lock in which water finds its balance. This unforeseen connection gave me the purest moment of pleasure I had in writing that book. Yet I dare say no reader could iden- tify it as a moment of particular intensity; nor, I hope, would any reader be con- sciously aware that the themes of danger and balance joined there.

Jane Austen once wrote to her sister that the theme of her novel *Mansfield Park* was "ordination." In the two hundred years since that letter, critics have written many times the number of words in the novel trying to explain what she meant. And yet the novel is well understood, forcefully experienced, and intelligently appreciated. The difficulty is not in understanding the book but in applying the "kernel" definition to its multiplicity of ideas and richness of theme.

The fusion of elements into a unified pattern is the nature of creativity, a word devalued in latter years to the extent that it has come to mean a random gush of self-expression. God, perhaps, created out of the void; but in the world as we know it, all creativity, from the sprouting of an onion to the painting of Guernica, is a matter of selection and arrangement. A child learns to draw one circle on top of another, to add two triangles at the top and a line at the bottom, and in this partic- ular pattern of circles, triangles, and lines has made a creature of an altogether dif- ferent nature: a cat! The child draws one square on top of another and connects the corners and has made three dimensions where there are only two. And although these are tricks that can be taught and learned, they partake of the essen- tial nature of creativity, in which several elements are joined to produce not merely a whole that is greater than the sum of its parts, but a whole that is some- thing altogether other. At the conception of a fetus or a short story, there occurs a conjunction of two unlike things, whether cells or ideas, that have never been joined before. Around this conjunction other cells, other ideas accumulate in a deliberate pattern. That pattern is the unique personality of the creature, and if the pattern does not cohere, it miscarries or is stillborn.

The organic unity of a work of literature cannot be taught—or, if it can, I have not discovered a way to teach it. I can suggest from time to time that concrete image is not separate from character, which is revealed in dialogue and point of view, which may be illuminated by simile, which may reveal theme, which is contained in plot as water is contained in an apple. But I cannot tell you how to achieve this; nor, if you achieve it, will you be able to explain very clearly how you have done so. Analysis separates in order to focus; it assumes that an understanding of the parts contributes to an understanding of the whole, but it does not produce the whole. Scientists can determine with minute accuracy the elements, in their proportions, contained in a piece of human skin. They can gather these elements, stir and warm them, but the result will not be skin. A good critic can show you where a metaphor does or does not illuminate character, where the character does or does not ring true in an action. But the critic cannot tell you how to make a character breathe; the breath is talent and can be neither explained nor produced.

No one can tell you what to mean, and no one can tell you how. I am conscious of having avoided the phrase *creative writing* in these pages, largely because all of us who teach creative writing find the words sticking in our throats. I myself would like to see courses taught in creative algebra, creative business administration, creative nursing, and creative history. (I once taught an advanced workshop in Destructive Writing—polemic, invective, libel, gratuitous violence, pornography, propaganda— in which students trying forms of writing they are supposed to avoid proved as creative as any group I ever encountered.) The mystique and the false glamour of the writing profession grow partly out of a mistaken belief that people who can express profound ideas and emotions have ideas and emotions more profound than the rest of us. It isn't so. The ability to express is a special gift with a special craft to support it and is spread fairly equally among the profound, the shallow, and the mediocre.

All the same, I am abashedly conscious that the creative exists—in algebra and nursing as in words—and that it mysteriously surfaces in the trivia of human existence: numbers, bandages, words. In the unified pattern of a fiction there is even something to which the name of magic may be given, where one empty word is placed upon another and tapped with a third, and a flaming scarf or a long-eared hope is pulled out of the tall black heart. The most magical thing about this magic is that once the trick is explained, it is not explained, and the better you understand how it works, the better it will work again.

Birth, death, work, and love continue to occur. Their meanings change from time to time and place to place, and new meanings engender new forms, which capture and create new meanings until they tire, while birth, death, work, and love continue to recur. Something to which we give the name of "honor" seems to persist, though in one place and time it is embodied in choosing to die for your country, in another, choosing not to. A notion of "progress" survives, though it is expressed now in technology, now in ecology, now in the survival of the fittest, now in the protection of the weak. There seems to be something corresponding to the human invention of "love," though it takes its form now in tenacious loyalty, now in letting go.

Ideas are not new, but the form in which they are expressed is constantly renewed, and new forms give life to what used to be called (in the old form) the eternal verities. An innovative writer tries to forge, and those who follow try to perfect, forms that so fuse with meaning that form itself expresses.

∼ Town and Country Lovers ∼

NADINE GORDIMER

I

Dr. Franz-Josef von Leinsdorf is a geologist absorbed in his work; wrapped up in it, as the saying goes—year after year the experience of this work enfolds him, swaddling him away from the landscapes, the cities, and the people, wherever he lives: Peru, New Zealand, the United States. He's always been like that, his mother could confirm from their native Austria. There, even as a handsome small boy he presented only his profile to her: turned away to his bits of rock and stone. His few relaxations have not changed much since then. An occasional skiing trip, listening to music, reading poetry—Rainer Maria Rilke once stayed in his grandmother's hunting lodge in the forests of Styria and the boy was introduced to Rilke's poems while very young.

Layer upon layer, country after country, wherever his work takes him—and now he has been almost seven years in Africa. First the Côte d'Ivoire, and for the past five years, South Africa. The shortage of skilled manpower brought about his recruitment here. He has no interest in the politics of the countries he works in. His private preoccupation-within-the-preoccupation of his work has been research into underground watercourses, but the mining company that employs him in a senior though not executive capacity is interested only in mineral discovery. So he is much out in the field—which is the veld, here—seeking new gold, copper, platinum, and uranium deposits. When he is at home—on this particular job, in this particular country, this city—he lives in a two-roomed flat in a suburban block with a landscaped garden, and does his shopping at a supermarket conveniently across the street. He is not married—yet. That is how his colleagues, and the typists and secretaries at the mining company's head office, would define his situation. Both men and women would describe him as a good-looking man, in a foreign way, with the lower half of his face dark and middle-aged (his mouth is thin and curving, and no matter how close-shaven his beard shows like fine shot embedded in the skin round mouth and chin) and the upper half contradictorily young, with deep-set eyes (some would say grey, some black), thick eyelashes and brows. A tangled gaze: through which concentration and gleaming thoughtfulness perhaps appear as fire and languor. It is this that the women in the office mean when they remark he's not unattractive. Although the gaze seems to promise, he has never invited any one of them to go out with him. There is the general assumption he probably has a girl who's been picked for him, he's bespoken by one of his own kind, back home in Europe where he comes from. Many of these well-educated Europeans have no intention of becoming permanent immigrants; neither the remnant of white colonial life nor idealistic involvement with Black Africa appeals to them.

One advantage, at least, of living in underdeveloped or half-developed countries is that flats are serviced. All Dr. von Leinsdorf has to do for himself is buy his own supplies and cook an evening meal if he doesn't want to go to a restaurant. It is simply a matter of dropping in to the supermarket on his way from his car to his flat after work in the afternoon. He wheels a trolley up and down the shelves, and his simple needs are presented to him in the form of tins, packages, plastic-wrapped meat, cheeses, fruit and vegetables, tubes, bottles. . . . At the cashier's counters where customers must converge and queue there are racks of small items uncategorized, for last-minute purchase. Here, as the coloured girl cashier punches the adding machine, he picks up cigarettes and perhaps a packet of salted nuts or a bar of nougat. Or razor-blades, when he remembers he's running short. One evening in winter he saw that the cardboard display was empty of the brand of blades he preferred, and he drew the cashier's attention to this. These young coloured girls are usually pretty unhelpful, taking money and punching their machines in a manner that asserts with the time-serving obstinacy of the half-literate the limit of any responsibility towards customers, but this one ran an alert glance over the selection of razor-blades, apologized that she was not allowed to leave her post, and said she would see that the stock was replenished "next time." A day or two later she recognized him, gravely, as he took his turn before her counter—"I ahssed them, but it's out of stock. You can't get it. I did ahss about it." He said this didn't matter. "When it comes in, I can keep a few packets for you." He thanked her.

He was away with the prospectors the whole of the next week. He arrived back in town just before nightfall on Friday, and was on his way from car to flat with his arms full of briefcase, suitcase, and canvas bags when someone stopped him by standing timidly in his path. He was about to dodge round unseeingly on the crowded pavement but she spoke. "We got the blades in now. I didn't see you in the shop this week, but I kept some for when you come. So. . . "

He recognized her. He had never seen her standing before, and she was wearing a coat. She was rather small and finely-made, for one of them. The coat was skimpy but no big backside jutted. The cold brought an apricot-graining of warm colour to her cheekbones, beneath which a very small face was quite delicately hollowed, and the skin was smooth, the subdued satiny colour of certain yellow wood. That crêpey hair, but worn drawn back flat and in a little knot pushed into one of the cheap wool chignons that (he recognized also) hung in the miscellany of small goods along with the razor-blades, at the supermarket. He said thanks, he was in a hurry, he'd only just got back from a trip—shifting the burdens he carried, to demonstrate. "Oh shame." She acknowledged his load. "But if you want I can run in and get it for you quickly. If you want."

He saw at once it was perfectly clear that all the girl meant was that she would go back to the supermarket, buy the blades, and bring the packet to him there where he stood, on the pavement. And it seemed that it was this certainty that made him say, in the kindly tone of assumption used for an obliging underling, "I live just across there—*Atlantis*—that flat building. Could you drop them by, for me—number seven-hundred-and-eighteen, seventh floor—"

She had not before been inside one of these big flat buildings near where she worked. She lived a bus- and train-ride away to the West of the city, but this side of the black townships, in a township for people her tint. There was a pool with ferns, not plastic, and even a little waterfall pumped electrically over rocks, in the entrance of the building *Atlantis*; she didn't wait for the lift marked GOODS but took the one meant for whites and a white woman with one of those sausage-dogs on a lead got in with her but did not pay her any attention. The corridors leading to the flats were nicely glassed-in, not draughty.

He wondered if he should give her a twenty-cent piece for her trouble—ten cents would be right for a black; but she said, "Oh no—please, here—" standing outside his open door and awkwardly pushing back at his hand the change from the money he'd given her for the razor-blades. She was smiling, for the first time, in the dignity of refusing a tip. It was difficult to know how to treat these people, in this country; to know what they expected. In spite of her embarrassing refusal of the coin, she stood there, completely unassuming, fists thrust down the pockets of her cheap coat against the cold she'd come in from, rather pretty thin legs neatly aligned, knee to knee, ankle to ankle.

"Would you like a cup of coffee or something?"

He couldn't very well take her into his study-cum-living-room and offer her a drink. She followed him to his kitchen, but at the sight of her pulling out the single chair to drink her cup of coffee at the kitchen table, he said, "No—bring it in here—" and led the way into the big room where, among his books and his papers, his files of scientific correspondence (and the cigar boxes of stamps from the envelopes), his racks of records, his specimens of minerals and rocks, he lived alone.

It was no trouble to her; she saved him the trips to the supermarket and brought him his groceries two or three times a week. All he had to do was to leave a list and the key under the doormat, and she would come up in her lunch-hour to collect them, returning to put his supplies in the flat after work. Sometimes he was home and sometimes not. He bought a box of chocolates and left it, with a note, for her to find; and that was acceptable, apparently, as a gratuity.

Her eyes went over everything in the flat although her body tried to conceal its sense of being out of place by remaining as still as possible, holding its contours in the chair offered her as a stranger's coat is set aside and remains exactly as left until the owner takes it up to go. "You collect?"

"Well, these are specimens—connected with my work."

"My brother used to collect. Miniatures. With brandy and whisky and that, in them. From all over. Different countries."

The second time she watched him grinding coffee for the cup he had offered her she said, "You always do that? Always when you make coffee?"

"But of course. It is no good, for you. Do I make it too strong?"

"Oh it's just I'm not used to it. We buy it ready—you know, it's in a bottle, you just add a bit to the milk or water."

He laughed, instructive: "That's not coffee, that's a synthetic flavouring. In my country we drink only real coffee, fresh, from the beans—you smell how good it is as it's being ground?"

She was stopped by the caretaker and asked what she wanted in the building? Heavy with the *bona fides* of groceries clutched to her body, she said she was working at number 718, on the seventh floor. The caretaker did not tell her not to use the whites' lift; after all, she was not black; her family was very light-skinned.

There was the item "grey button for trousers" on one of his shopping lists. She said as she unpacked the supermarket carrier, "Give me the pants, so long, then," and sat on his sofa that was always gritty with fragments of pipe tobacco, sewing in and out through the four holes of the button with firm, fluent movements of the right hand, gestures supplying the articulacy missing from her talk. She had a little yokel's, peasant's (he thought of it) gap between her two front teeth when she smiled that he didn't much like, but, face ellipsed to three-quarter angle, eyes cast down in concentration with soft lips almost closed, this didn't matter. He said, watching her sew, "You're a good girl"; and touched her.

She remade the bed every late afternoon when they left it and she dressed again before she went home. After a week there was a day when late afternoon became evening, and they were still in the bed.

"Can't you stay the night?"

"My mother," she said.

"Phone her. Make an excuse." He was a foreigner. He had been in the country five years, but he didn't understand that people don't usually have telephones in their houses, where she lived. She got up to dress. He didn't want that tender body to go out in the night cold and kept hindering her with the interruption of his hands; saying nothing. Before she put on her coat, when the body had already disappeared, he spoke, "But you must make some arrangement."

"Oh my mother!" Her face opened to fear and vacancy he could not read.

He was not entirely convinced the woman would think of her daughter as some pure and unsullied virgin. . . "Why?"

The girl said, "S'e'll be scared. S'e'll be scared we get caught."

"Don't tell her anything. Say I'm employing you." In this country he was working in now there were generally rooms on the roofs of flat buildings for tenants' servants.

She said: "That's what I told the caretaker."

She ground fresh coffee beans every time he wanted a cup while he was working at night. She never attempted to cook anything until she had watched in silence while he did it the way he liked, and she learned to reproduce exactly the simple dishes he preferred. She handled his pieces of rock and stone, at first admiring the colours—"It'd make a beautiful ring or necklace, ay." Then he showed her the striations, the formation of each piece, and explained what each was, and how, in the long life of the earth, it had been formed. He named the mineral it yielded, and what that was used for. He worked at his papers, writing, writing, every night, so it did not matter that they could not go out together to public places. On Sundays she got into his car in the basement garage and they drove to the country and picnicked away up in the Magaliesberg, where there was no one. He read or poked about among the rocks; they climbed together, to the mountain pools. He taught her to swim. She had never seen the sea. She squealed and shrieked in the water, showing the gap between her teeth, as—it crossed his mind—she must do when among her own people. Occasionally he had to go out to dinner at the houses of colleagues from the mining company; she sewed and listened to the radio in the flat and he found her in the bed, warm and already asleep, by the time he came in. He made his way into her body without speaking; she made him welcome without a word. Once he put on evening dress for a dinner at his country's consulate; watching him brush one or two fallen hairs from the shoulders of the dark jacket that sat so well on him, she saw a huge room, all chandeliers and people dancing some dance from a costume film—stately, hand-to-hand. She supposed he was going to fetch, in her place in the car, a partner for the evening. They never kissed when either left the flat; he said, suddenly, kindly, pausing as he picked up cigarettes and keys, "Don't be lonely." And added, "Wouldn't you like to visit your family sometimes, when I have to go out?"

He had told her he was going home to his mother in the forests and mountains of his country near the Italian border (he showed her on the map) after Christmas. She had not told him how her mother, not knowing there was any other variety, assumed he was a medical doctor, so she had talked to her about the doctor's children and the doctor's wife who was a very kind lady, glad to have someone who could help out in the surgery as well as the flat.

She remarked wonderingly on his ability to work until midnight or later, after a day at work. She was so tired when she came home from her cash register at the supermarket that once dinner was eaten she could scarcely keep awake. He explained in a way she could understand that while the work she did was repetitive, undemanding of any real response from her intelligence, requiring little mental or physical effort and therefore unrewarding, his work was his greatest interest, it taxed his mental capacities to their limit, exercised all his concentration, and rewarded him constantly as much with the excitement of a problem presented as with the satisfaction of a problem solved. He said later, putting away his papers, speaking out of a silence: "Have you done other kinds of work?" She said, "I was in a clothing factory before. Sportbeau shirts; you know? But the pay's better in the shop."

Of course. Being a conscientious newspaper-reader in every country he lived in, he was aware that it was only recently that the retail consumer trade in this one had been allowed to employ coloureds as shop assistants; even punching a cash register represented advancement. With the continuing shortage of semi-skilled whites a girl like this might be able to edge a little farther into the white-collar category. He began to teach her to type. He was aware that her English was poor, even though, as a foreigner, in his ears her pronunciation did not offend, nor categorize her as it would in those of someone of his education whose mother tongue was English. He corrected her grammatical mistakes but missed the less obvious ones because of his own sometimes exotic English usage—she continued to use the singular pronoun "it" when what was required was the plural "they." Because he was a foreigner (although so clever, as she saw) she was less inhibited than she might have been by the words she knew she misspelled in her typing. While she sat at the typewriter she thought how one day she would type notes for him, as well as making coffee the way he liked it, and taking him inside her body without saying anything, and sitting (even if only through the empty streets of quiet Sundays) beside him in his car, like a wife.

On a summer night near Christmas—he had already bought and hidden a slightly showy but nevertheless good watch he thought she would like—there was a knocking at the door that brought her out of the bathroom and him to his feet, at his work-table. No one ever came to the flat at night; he had no friends intimate enough to drop in without warning. The summons was an imperious banging that did not pause and clearly would not stop until the door was opened.

She stood in the open bathroom doorway gazing at him across the passage into the living-room; her bare feet and shoulders were free of a big bath-towel. She said nothing, did not even whisper. The flat seemed to shake with the strong unhurried blows.

He made as if to go to the door, at last, but now she ran and clutched him by both arms. She shook her head wildly; her lips drew back but her teeth were clenched, she didn't speak. She pulled him into the bedroom, snatched some clothes from the clean laundry laid out on the bed, and got into the wall-cupboard, thrusting the key at his hand. Although his arms and calves felt weakly cold he was horrified, distastefully embarrassed at the sight of her pressed back crouching there under his suits and coat; it was horrible and ridiculous. *Come out!* he whispered. *No! Come out!* She hissed: *Where? Where can I go?*

Never mind! Get out of there!

He put out his hand to grasp her. At bay, she said with all the force of her terrible whisper, baring the gap in her teeth: *I'll throw myself out the window.*

She forced the key into his hand like the handle of a knife. He closed the door on her face and drove the key home in the lock, then dropped it among coins in his trouser pocket.

He unslotted the chain that was looped across the flat door. He turned the serrated knob of the Yale lock. The three policemen, two in plain clothes, stood there without impatience although they had been banging on the door for several minutes. The big dark one with an elaborate moustache held out in a hand wearing a plaited gilt ring some sort of identity card.

Dr. von Leinsdorf said quietly, the blood coming strangely back to legs and arms, "What is it?"

The sergeant told him they knew there was a coloured girl in the flat. They had had information; "I been watching this flat three months, I know."

"I am alone here." Dr. von Leinsdorf did not raise his voice.

"I know, I know who is here. Come—" And the sergeant and his two assistants went into the living-room, the kitchen, the bathroom (the sergeant picked up a bottle of after-shave cologne, seemed to study the French label), and the bedroom. The assistants removed the clean laundry that was laid upon the bed and then turned back the bedding, carrying the sheets over to be examined by the sergeant under the lamp. They talked to one another in Afrikaans, which the Doctor did not understand. The sergeant himself looked under the bed, and lifted the long curtains at the window. The wall-cupboard was of the kind that has no knobs; he saw that it was locked and began to ask in Afrikaans, then politely changed to English, "Give us the key."

Dr. von Leinsdorf said, "I'm sorry, I left it at my office—I always lock and take my keys with me in the mornings."

"It's no good, man, you better give me the key."

He smiled a little, reasonably. "It's on my office desk."

The assistants produced a screwdriver and he watched while they inserted it where the cupboard doors met, gave it quick, firm but not forceful leverage. He heard the lock give.

She had been naked, it was true, when they knocked. But now she was wearing a long-sleeved T-shirt with an appliquéd butterfly motif on one breast, and a pair of jeans. Her feet were still bare; she had managed, by feel, in the dark, to get into some of the clothing she had snatched from the bed, but she had no shoes. She had perhaps been weeping behind the cupboard door (her cheeks looked stained) but now her face was sullen and she was breathing heavily, her diaphragm contracting and expanding exaggeratedly and her breasts pushing against the cloth. It made her appear angry; it might simply have been that she was half-suffocated in the cupboard and needed oxygen. She did not look at Dr. von Leinsdorf. She would not reply to the sergeant's questions.

They were taken to the police station where they were at once separated and in turn led for examination by the district surgeon. The man's underwear was taken away and examined, as the sheets had been, for signs of his seed. When the girl was undressed, it was discovered that beneath her jeans she was wearing a pair of men's briefs with his name on the neatly-sewn laundry tag; in her haste, she had taken the wrong garment to her hiding-place.

Now she cried, standing there before the district surgeon in a man's underwear.

He courteously pretended not to notice. He handed briefs, jeans, and T-shirt round the door, and motioned her to lie on a white-sheeted high table where he placed her legs apart, resting in stirrups, and put into her where the other had made his way so warmly a cold hard instrument that expanded wider and wider. Her thighs and knees trembled uncontrollably while the doctor looked into her and touched her deep inside with more hard instruments, carrying wafers of gauze.

When she came out of the examining room back to the charge office, Dr. von Leinsdorf was not there; they must have taken him somewhere else. She spent what was left of the night in a cell, as he must be doing; but early in the morning she was released and taken home to her mother's house in the coloured township by a white man who explained he was the clerk of the lawyer who had been engaged for her by Dr. von Leinsdorf. Dr. von Leinsdorf, the clerk said, had also been bailed out that morning. He did not say when, or if she would see him again.

A statement made by the girl to the police was handed in to Court when she and the man appeared to meet charges of contravening the Immorality Act in a Johannesburg flat on the night of—December, 19—. *I lived with the white man in his flat. He had intercourse with me sometimes. He gave me tablets to take to prevent me becoming pregnant.*

Interviewed by the Sunday papers, the girl said, "I'm sorry for the sadness brought to my mother." She said she was one of nine children of a female laundry worker. She had left school in Standard Three because there was no money at home for gym clothes or a school blazer. She had worked as a machinist in a factory and a cashier in a supermarket. Dr. von Leinsdorf taught her to type his notes.

Dr. Franz-Josef von Leinsdorf, described as the grandson of a baroness, a cultured man engaged in international mineralogical research, said he accepted social distinctions between people but didn't think they should be legally imposed. "Even in my own country it's difficult for a person from a higher class to marry one from a lower class."

The two accused gave no evidence. They did not greet or speak to each other in Court. The Defence argued that the sergeant's evidence that they had been living together as man and wife was hearsay. (The woman with the dachshund, the caretaker?) The magistrate acquitted them because the State failed to prove carnal intercourse had taken place on the night of — December, 19—.

The girl's mother was quoted, with photograph, in the Sunday papers: "I won't let my daughter work as a servant for a white man again."

II

The farm children play together when they are small; but once the white children go away to school they soon don't play together any more, even in the holidays. Although most of the black children get some sort of schooling, they drop every year farther behind the grades passed by the white children; the childish vocabulary, the child's exploration of the adventurous possibilities of dam, koppies, mealie lands, and veld—there comes a time when the white children have surpassed these with the vocabulary of boarding-school and the possibilities of inter-school sports matches and the kind of adventures seen at the cinema. This usefully coincides with the age of twelve or thirteen; so that by the time early adolescence is reached, the black children are making, along with the bodily changes common to all, an easy transition to adult forms of address, beginning to call their old playmates *missus* and *baasie*—little master.

The trouble was Paulus Eysendyck did not seem to realize that Thebedi was now simply one of the crowd of farm children down at the kraal, recognizable in his sister's old clothes. The first Christmas holidays after he had gone to boarding-school he brought home for Thebedi a painted box he had made in his wood-work class. He had to give it to her secretly because he had nothing for the other children at the kraal. And she gave him, before he went back to school, a bracelet she had made of thin brass wire and the grey-and-white beans of the castor-oil crop his father cultivated. (When they used to play together, she was the one who had taught Paulus how to make clay oxen for their toy spans.) There was a craze, even in the *platteland* towns like the one where he was at school, for boys to wear elephant-hair and other bracelets beside their watch-straps; his was admired, friends asked him to get similar ones for them. He said the natives made them on his father's farm and he would try.

When he was fifteen, six feet tall, and tramping round at school dances with the girls from the "sister" school in the same town; when he had learnt how to tease and flirt and fondle quite intimately these girls who were the daughters of prosperous farmers like his father; when he had even met one who, at a wedding he had attended with his parents on a nearby farm, had let him do with her in a locked storeroom what people did when they made love—when he was as far from his childhood as all this, he still brought home from a shop in town a red plastic belt and gilt hoop ear-rings for the black girl, Thebedi. She told her father the missus had given these to her as a reward for some work she had done—it was true she sometimes was called to help out in the farmhouse. She told the girls in the kraal that she had a sweetheart nobody knew about, far away, away on another farm, and they giggled, and teased, and admired her. There was a boy in the kraal called Njabulo who said he wished he could have brought her a belt and ear-rings.

When the farmer's son was home for the holidays she wandered far from the kraal and her companions. He went for walks alone. They had not arranged this; it was an urge each followed independently. He knew it was she, from a long way off. She knew that his dog would not bark at her. Down at the dried-up river-bed where five or six years ago the children had caught a leguaan one great day—a creature that combined ideally the size and ferocious aspect of the crocodile with the harmlessness of the lizard—they squatted side by side on the earth bank. He told her traveller's tales: about school, about the punishments at school, particularly, exaggerating both their nature and his indifference to them. He told her about the town of Middleburg, which she had never seen. She had nothing to tell but she prompted with many questions, like any good listener. While he talked he twisted and tugged at the roots of white stinkwood and Cape willow trees that looped out of the eroded earth around them. It had always been a good spot for children's games, down there hidden by the mesh of old, ant-eaten trees held in place by vigorous ones, wild asparagus bushing up between the trunks, and here and there prickly-pear cactus sunken-skinned and bristly, like an old man's face, keeping alive sapless until the next rainy season. She punctured the dry hide of a prickly-pear again and again with a sharp stick while she listened. She laughed a lot at what he told her, sometimes dropping her face on her knees, sharing amusement with the cool shady earth beneath her bare feet. She put on her pair of shoes—white sandals, thickly Blanco-ed against the farm dust—when he was on the farm, but these were taken off and laid aside, at the river-bed.

One summer afternoon when there was water flowing there and it was very hot she waded in as they used to do when they were children, her dress bunched modestly and tucked into the legs of her pants. The schoolgirls he went swimming with at dams or pools on neighbouring farms wore bikinis but the sight of their dazzling bellies and thighs in the sunlight had never made him feel what he felt now, when the girl came up the bank and sat beside him, the drops of water beading off her dark legs the only points of light in the earth-smelling, deep shade. They were not afraid of one another, they had known one another always; he did with her what he had done that time in the storeroom at the wedding, and this time it was so lovely, so lovely, he was surprised. . . and she was surprised by it, too—he could see in her dark face that was part of the shade, with her big dark eyes, shiny as soft water, watching him attentively: as she had when they used to huddle over their teams of mud oxen, as she had when he told her about detention weekends at school.

They went to the river-bed often through those summer holidays. They met just before the light went, as it does quite quickly, and each returned home with the dark—she to her mother's hut, he to the farmhouse—in time for the evening meal. He did not tell her about school or town any more. She did not ask questions any longer. He told her, each time, when they would meet again. Once or twice it was very early in the morning; the lowing of the cows being driven to graze came to them where they lay, dividing them with unspoken recognition of the sound read in their two pairs of eyes, opening so close to each other.

He was a popular boy at school. He was in the second, then the first soccer team. The head girl of the "sister" school was said to have a crush on him; he didn't particularly like her, but there was a pretty blonde who put up her long hair into a kind of doughnut with a black ribbon round it, whom he took to see films when the schoolboys and girls had a free Saturday afternoon. He had been driving tractors and other farm vehicles since he was ten years old, and as soon as he was eighteen he got a driver's licence and in the holidays, this last year of his school life, he took neighbours' daughters to dances and to the drive-in cinema that had just opened twenty kilometers from the farm. His sisters were married, by then; his parents often left him in charge of the farm over the weekend while they visited the young wives and grandchildren.

When Thebedi saw the farmer and his wife drive away on a Saturday afternoon, the boot of their Mercedes filled with fresh-killed poultry and vegetables from the garden that it was part of her father's work to tend, she knew that she must come not to the river-bed but up to the house. The house was an old one, thick-walled, dark against the heat. The kitchen was its lively thoroughfare, with servants, food supplies, begging cats and dogs, pots boiling over, washing being damped for ironing, and the big deep-freezer the missus had ordered from town, bearing a crocheted mat and a vase of plastic irises. But the dining-room with the bulging-legged heavy table was shut up in its rich, old smell of soup and tomato sauce. The sitting-room curtains were drawn and the T.V. set silent. The door of the parents' bedroom was locked and the empty rooms where the girls had slept had sheets of plastic spread over the beds. It was in one of these that she and the farmer's son stayed together whole nights—almost: she had to get away before the house servants, who knew her, came in at dawn. There was a risk someone would discover her or traces of her presence if he took her to his own bedroom, although she had looked into it many times when she was helping out in the house and knew well, there, the row of silver cups he had won at school.

When she was eighteen and the farmer's son nineteen and working with his father on the farm before entering a veterinary college, the young man Njabulo asked her father for her. Njabulo's parents met with hers and the money he was to pay in place of the cows it is customary to give a prospective bride's parents was settled upon. He had no cows to offer; he was a labourer on the Eysendyck farm, like her father. A bright youngster; old Eysendyck had taught him brick-laying and was using him for odd jobs in construction, around the place. She did not tell the farmer's son that her parents had arranged for her to marry. She did not tell him, either, before he left for his first term at the veterinary college, that she thought she was going to have a baby. Two months after her marriage to Njabulo, she gave birth to a daughter. There was no disgrace in that; among her people it is customary for a young man to make sure, before marriage, that the chosen girl is not barren, and Njabulo made love to her then. But the infant was very light and did not quickly grow darker as most African babies do. Already at birth there was on its head a quantity of straight, fine floss, like that which carries the seeds of certain weeds in the veld. The unfocused eyes it opened were grey flecked with yellow. Njabulo was the matt, opaque coffee-grounds colour that has always been called black; the colour of Thebedi's legs on which beaded water looked oyster-shell blue, the same colour as Thebedi's face, where the black eyes, with their interested gaze and clear whites, were so dominant.

Njabulo made no complaint. Out of his farm labourer's earnings he bought from the Indian store a cellophane-windowed pack containing a pink plastic bath, six napkins, a card of safety pins, a knitted jacket, cap and booties, a dress, and a tin of Johnson's Baby Powder, for Thebedi's baby.

When it was two weeks old Paulus Eysendyck arrived home from the veterinary college for the holidays. He drank a glass of fresh, still-warm milk in the childhood familiarity of his mother's kitchen and heard her discussing with the old house-servant where they could get a reliable substitute to help out now that the girl Thebedi had had a baby. For the first time since he was a small boy he came right into the kraal. It was eleven o'clock in the morning. The men were at work in the lands. He looked about him, urgently; the women turned away, each not wanting to be the one approached to point out where Thebedi lived. Thebedi appeared, coming slowly from the hut Njabulo had built in white man's style, with a tin chimney, and a proper window with glass panes set in straight as walls made of unfired bricks would allow. She greeted him with hands brought together and a token movement representing the respectful bob with which she was accustomed to acknowledge she was in the presence of his father or mother. He lowered his head under the doorway of her home and went in. He said, "I want to see. Show me."

She had taken the bundle off her back before she came out into the light to face him. She moved between the iron bedstead made up with Njabulo's checked blankets and the small wooden table where the pink plastic bath stood among food and kitchen pots, and picked up the bundle from the snugly-blanketed grocer's box where it lay. The infant was asleep; she revealed the closed, pale, plump tiny face, with a bubble of spit at the corner of the mouth, the spidery pink hands stirring. She took off the woollen cap and the straight fine hair flew up after it in static electricity, showing gilded strands here and there. He said nothing. She was watching him as she had done when they were little, and the gang of children had trodden down a crop in their games or transgressed in some other way for which he, as the farmer's son, the white one among them, must intercede with the farmer. She disturbed the sleeping face by scratching or tickling gently at a cheek with one finger, and slowly the eyes opened, saw nothing, were still asleep, and then, awake, no longer narrowed, looked out at them, grey with yellowish flecks, his own hazel eyes.

He struggled for a moment with a grimace of tears, anger, and self-pity. She could not put out her hand to him. He said, "You haven't been near the house with it?"

She shook her head.

"Never?"

Again she shook her head.

"Don't take it out. Stay inside. Can't you take it away somewhere. You must give it to someone—"

She moved to the door with him.

He said, "I'll see what I will do. I don't know." And then he said: "I feel like killing myself."

Her eyes began to glow, to thicken with tears. For a moment there was the feeling between them that used to come when they were alone down at the river-bed.

He walked out.

Two days later, when his mother and father had left the farm for the day, he appeared again. The women were away on the lands, weeding, as they were employed to do as casual labour in the summer; only the very old remained, propped up on the ground outside the huts in the flies and the sun. Thebedi did not ask him in. The child had not been well; it had diarrhoea. He asked where its food was. She said, "The milk comes from me." He went into Njabulo's house, where the child lay; she did not follow but stayed outside the door and watched without seeing an old crone who had lost her mind, talking to herself, talking to the fowls who ignored her.

She thought she heard small grunts from the hut, the kind of infant grunt that indicates a full stomach, a deep sleep. After a time, long or short she did not know, he came out and walked away with plodding stride (his father's gait) out of sight, towards his father's house.

The baby was not fed during the night and although she kept telling Njabulo it was sleeping, he saw for himself in the morning that it was dead. He comforted her with words and caresses. She did not cry but simply sat, staring at the door. Her hands were cold as dead chickens' feet to his touch.

Njabulo buried the little baby where farm workers were buried, in the place in the veld the farmer had given them. Some of the mounds had been left to weather away unmarked, others were covered with stones and a few had fallen wooden crosses. He was going to make a cross but before it was finished the police came and dug up the grave and took away the dead baby: someone—one of the other labourers? their women?—had reported that the baby was almost white, that, strong and healthy, it had died suddenly after a visit by the farmer's son. Pathological tests on the infant corpse showed intestinal damage not always consistent with death by natural causes.

Thebedi went for the first time to the country town where Paulus had been to school, to give evidence at the preparatory examination into the charge of murder brought against him. She cried hysterically in the witness box, saying yes, yes (the gilt hoop ear-rings swung in her ears), she saw the accused pouring liquid into the baby's mouth. She said he had threatened to shoot her if she told anyone.

More than a year went by before, in that same town, the case was brought to trial. She came to Court with a new-born baby on her back. She wore gilt hoop ear-rings; she was calm; she said she had not seen what the white man did in the house.

Paulus Eysendyck said he had visited the hut but had not poisoned the child.

The Defence did not contest that there had been a love relationship between the accused and the girl, or that intercourse had taken place, but submitted there was no proof that the child was the accused's.

The judge told the accused there was strong suspicion against him but not enough proof that he had committed the crime. The Court could not accept the girl's evidence because it was clear she had committed perjury either at this trial or at the preparatory examination. There was the suggestion in the mind of the Court that she might be an accomplice in the crime; but, again, insufficient proof.

The judge commended the honourable behaviour of the husband (sitting in court in a brown-and-yellow-quartered golf cap bought for Sundays) who had not rejected his wife and had "even provided clothes for the unfortunate infant out of his slender means."

The verdict on the accused was "not guilty."

The young white man refused to accept the congratulations of press and public and left the Court with his mother's raincoat shielding his face from photographers. His father said to the press, "I will try and carry on as best I can to hold up my head in the district."

Interviewed by the Sunday papers, who spelled her name in a variety of ways, the black girl, speaking in her own language, was quoted beneath her photograph: "It was a thing of our childhood, we don't see each other anymore."

***

Suggestions for Discussion

1. What is "Town and Country Lovers" about? Decide on three things it says about what it's about.

2. How much authorial distance is created in the opening pages of the story, how, and why? Consider the use of summary, tone, concrete details, and the protagonist's thoughts as revealed through the limited omniscient point of view. How and why is the distance handled differently in the "country lovers" story?

3. Part I stays mainly in Leinsdorf's mind, but occasionally also reveals the thoughts of the unnamed girl. Identify several examples of this. Does Gordimer succeed in "bouncing" the reader from one point of view to another? What does it add to the exploration of the theme? Why doesn't Gordimer give the girl a name?

4. Show how the irony of the sentence "He has no interest in the politics of the country he works in," operates in the theme of both parts of the story. Find other examples of irony in the narrative voice.

5. How often in this two-part story is the behavior of one character surprising to another—or to you? How often does your sympathy or identification change? What is the function of these swings of judgment?

6. What concrete details operate as symbols of the assumed and impassable barrier between the races under apartheid?

7. How does the dialogue (direct and indirect) of the girl, Leinsdorf, and the girl's mother at the end of part I relate to the comments of the judge, Paulus' father, and Thebedi at the end of Part II? What do these speeches have to do with the theme?

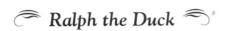

Ralph the Duck

FREDERICK BUSCH

I woke up at 5:25 because the dog was vomiting. I carried seventy-five pounds of heaving golden retriever to the door and poured him onto the silver, moonlit snow. "Good boy," I said because he'd done his only trick. Outside he retched, and I went back up, passing the sofa on which Fanny lay. I tiptoed with enough weight on my toes to let her know how considerate I was while she was deserting me. She blinked her eyes. I swear I heard her blink her eyes. Whenever I tell her that I hear her blink her eyes, she tells me I'm lying; but I can hear the damp slap of lash after I have made her weep.

In bed and warm again, noting the red digital numbers (5:29) and certain that I wouldn't sleep, I didn't. I read a book about men who kill each other for pay or for their honor. I forget which, and so did they. It was 5:45, the alarm would buzz at 6:00, and I would make a pot of coffee and start the wood stove; I would call Fanny and pour her coffee into her mug; I would apologize because I always did, and then she would forgive me if I hadn't been too awful—I didn't think I'd been that bad— and we would stagger through the day, exhausted but pretty sure we were all right, and we'd sleep that night, probably after sex, and then we'd awaken in the same bed to the alarm at 6:00, or the dog, if he'd returned to the frozen deer carcass he'd been eating in the forest on our land. He loved what made him sick. The alarm went off, I got into jeans and woolen socks and a sweatshirt, and I went downstairs to let the dog in. He'd be hungry, of course.

I was the oldest college student in America, I thought. But of course I wasn't. There were always ancient women with their parchment for skin who graduated at seventy-nine from places like Barnard and the University of Georgia. I was only forty-two, and I hardly qualified as a student. I patrolled the college at night in a Bronco with a leaky exhaust system, and I went from room to room in the classroom buildings, kicking out students who were studying or humping in chairs— they'd do it anywhere—and answering emergency calls with my little blue light winking on top of the truck. I didn't carry a gun or a billy, but I had a flashlight that took six batteries and I'd used it twice on some of my overprivileged northeastern-playboy part-time classmates. On Tuesdays and Thursdays I would awaken at 6:00 with my wife, and I'd do my homework, and work around the house, and go to school at 11:30 to sit there for an hour and a half while thirty-five stomachs growled with hunger and boredom, and this guy gave instruction about books.

Because I was on the staff, the college let me take a course for nothing every term. I was getting educated, in a kind of slow-motion way—it would have taken me something like fifteen or sixteen years to graduate, and I would no doubt get an F in gym and have to repeat—and there were times when I respected myself for it. Fanny often did, and that was fair incentive.

I am not unintelligent. *You are not an unintelligent writer,* my professor wrote on my paper about Nathaniel Hawthorne. We had to read short stories, I and the other students, and then we had to write little essays about them. I told how I saw Kafka and Hawthorne in similar light, and I was not unintelligent, he said. He ran into me at dusk one time, when I answered a call about a dead battery and found out it was him. I jumped his Buick from the Bronco's battery, and he was looking me over, I could tell, while I clamped onto the terminals and cranked it up. He was a tall, handsome guy who never wore a suit. He wore khakis and sweaters, loafers or sneaks, and he was always talking to the female students with the brightest hair and best builds. But he couldn't get a Buick going on an ice-cold night, and he didn't know enough to look for cells going bad. I told him he was going to need a new battery and he looked me over the way men sometimes do with other men who fix their cars for them.

"Vietnam?"

I said, "Too old."

"Not at the beginning. Not if you were an adviser. So-called. Or one of the Phoenix Project fellas?"

I was wearing a watch cap made of navy wool and an old Marine fatigue jacket. Slick characters like my professor like it if you're a killer or at least a onetime middleweight fighter. I smiled like I knew something. "Take it easy," I said, and I went back to the truck to swing around the cemetery at the top of the campus. They'd been known to screw in down-filled sleeping bags on horizontal stones up there, and the dean of students didn't want anybody dying of frostbite while joined at the hip to a matriculating fellow resident of our northeastern camp for the overindulged.

He blinked his high beams at me as I went. "You are not an unintelligent driver," I said.

Fanny had left me a bowl of something made with sausages and sauerkraut and potatoes, and the dog hadn't eaten too much more than his fair share. He watched me eat his leftovers and then make myself a king-sized drink composed of sourmash whiskey and ice. In our back room, which is on the northern end of the house, and cold for sitting in that close to dawn, I sat and watched the texture of the sky change. It was going to snow, and I wanted to see the storm come up the valley. I woke up that way, sitting in the rocker with its loose right arm, holding a watery drink, and thinking right away of the girl I'd convinced to go back inside. She'd been standing outside her dormitory, looking up at a window that was dark in the midst of all those lighted panes—they never turned a light off, and often left the faucets run half the night—crying onto her bathrobe. She was barefoot in shoe-pacs, the brown ones so many of them wore unlaced, and for all I know she was naked under the robe. She was beautiful, I thought, and she was somebody's red-headed daughter, standing in a quadrangle how many miles from home weeping.

"He doesn't love anyone," the kid told me. "He doesn't love his wife—I mean his ex-wife. And he doesn't love the ex-wife before that, or the one before that. And you know what? He doesn't love me. I don't know anyone who *does*!"

"It isn't your fault if he isn't smart enough to love you," I said, steering her toward the truck.

She stopped. She turned. "You know him?"

I couldn't help it. I hugged her hard, and she let me, and then she stepped back, and of course I let her go. "Don't you *touch* me! Is this sexual harassment? Do you know the rules? Isn't this sexual harassment?"

"I'm sorry," I said at the door to the truck. "But I think I have to be able to give you a grade before it counts as harassment."

She got in. I told her we were driving to the dean of students' house. She smelled like marijuana and something very sweet, maybe one of those coffee-with-cream liqueurs you don't buy unless you hate to drink.

As the heat of the truck struck her, she started going kind of clay-gray-green, and I reached across her to open the window.

"You touched my breast!" she said.

"It's the smallest one I've touched all night, I'm afraid."

She leaned out the window and gave her rendition of my dog.

But in my rocker, waking up, at whatever time in the morning in my silent house, I thought of her as someone's child. Which made me think of ours, of course. I went for more ice, and I started on a wet breakfast. At the door of the dean of students' house, she'd turned her chalky face to me and asked, "What grade would you give me, then?"

It was a week composed of two teachers locked out of their offices late at night, a Toyota with a flat and no spare, an attempted rape on a senior girl walking home from the library, a major fight outside a fraternity house (broken wrist and significant concussion), and variations on breaking-and-entering. I was scolded by the director of nonacademic services for embracing a student who was drunk; I told him to keep his job, but he called me back because I was right to hug her, he said, and also wrong, but what the hell, and would I please stay. I thought of the fringe benefits—graduation in only sixteen years—so I went back to work.

My professor assigned a story called "A Rose for Emily," and I wrote him a paper about the mechanics of corpse fucking, and how, since she clearly couldn't screw her dead boyfriend, she was keeping his rotten body in bed because she truly loved him. I called the paper "True Love." He gave me a B and wrote *See me, pls*. In his office after class, his feet up on his desk, he trimmed a cigar with a giant folding knife he kept in his drawer.

"You got to clean the hole out," he said, "or they don't draw."

"I don't smoke," I said.

"Bad habit. Real *habit*, though. I started in smoking 'em in Georgia, in the service. My C.O. smoked 'em. We collaborated on a brothel inspection one time, and we ended up smoking these with a couple of women." He waggled his eyebrows at me, now that his malehood was established.

"Were the women smoking them too?"

He snorted laughter through his nose while the greasy smoke came curling off his thin, dry lips. "They were pretty smoky, I'll tell ya!" Then he propped his feet—he was wearing cowboy boots that day—and he sat forward. "It's a little hard to explain. But—hell. You just don't say *fuck* when you write an essay for a college prof. Okay?" Like a scoutmaster with a kid he'd caught in the outhouse jerking off: "All right? You don't wanna do that."

"Did it shock you?"

"Fuck, no, it didn't shock me. I just told you. It violates certain proprieties."

"But if I'm writing it to you, like a letter—"

"You're writing it for posterity. For some mythical reader someplace, not just me. You're making a *statement*."

"Right. My statement said how hard it must be for a woman to fuck with a corpse."

"And a point worth making. I said so. Here."

"But you said I shouldn't say it."

"No. Listen. Just because you're talking about fucking, you don't have to say *fuck*. Does that make it any clearer?"

"No."

"I wish you'd lied to me just now," he said.

I nodded. I did too.

"Where'd you do your service?" he asked.

"Baltimore. Baltimore, Maryland."

"What's in Baltimore?"

"Railroads. I liaised on freight runs of army material. I killed a couple of bums on the rod with my bare hands, though."

He snorted again, but I could see how disappointed he was. He'd been banking on my having been a murderer. Interesting guy in one of my classes, he must have told some terrific woman at an overpriced meal: I just *know* the guy was a rubout specialist in the Nam, he had to have said. I figured I should come to work wearing my fatigue jacket and a red bandanna tied around my head. Say "Man" to him a couple of times, hang a fist in the air for grief and solidarity, and look terribly worn, exhausted by experiences he was fairly certain that he envied me. His dungarees were ironed, I noticed.

On Saturday we went back to the campus because Fanny wanted to see a movie called *The Seven Samurai*. I fell asleep, and I'm afraid I snored. She let me sleep until the auditorium was almost empty. Then she kissed me awake. "Who was screaming in my dream?" I asked her.

"Kurosawa," she said.

"Who?"

"Ask your professor friend."

I looked around, but he wasn't there. "Not an un-weird man," I said.

We went home and cleaned up after the dog and put him out. We drank a little Spanish brandy and went upstairs and made love. I was fairly premature, you might say, but one way and another by the time we fell asleep we were glad to be there with each other, and glad that it was Sunday coming up the valley toward us, and nobody with it. The dog was howling at another dog someplace, or at the moon, or maybe just his moon-thrown shadow on the snow. I did not strangle him when I opened the back door and he limped happily past me and stumbled up the stairs. I followed him into our bedroom and groaned for just being satisfied as I got into bed. You'll notice I didn't say fuck.

He stopped me in the hall after class on a Thursday, and asked me How's it goin, just one of the kickers drinking sour beer and eating pickled eggs and watching the tube in a country bar. How's it goin. I nodded. I wanted a grade from the man, and I did want to learn about expressing myself. I nodded and made what I thought was a smile. He'd let his mustache grow out and his hair grow longer. He was starting to wear dark shirts with lighter ties. I thought he looked like someone in *The Godfather*. He still wore those light little loafers or his high-heeled cowboy boots. His corduroy pants looked baggy. I guess he wanted them to look that way. He motioned me to the wall of the hallway, and he looked and said, "How about the Baltimore stuff?"

I said "Yeah?"

"Was that really true?" He was almost blinking, he wanted so much for me to be a damaged Vietnam vet just looking for a bell tower to climb into and start firing from. The college didn't have a bell tower you could get up into, though I'd once spent an ugly hour chasing a drunken ATO down from the roof of the observatory. "You were just clocking through boxcars in Baltimore?"

I said, "Nah."

"I thought so!" He gave a kind of sigh.

"I killed people," I said.

"You know, I could have sworn you did," he said.

I nodded, and he nodded back. I'd made him so happy.

The assignment was to write something to influence somebody. He called it Rhetoric and Persuasion. We read an essay by George Orwell and "A Modest Proposal" by Jonathan Swift. I liked the Orwell better, but I wasn't comfortable with it. He talked about "niggers," and I felt him saying it two ways.

I wrote "Ralph the Duck."

Once upon a time, there was a duck named Ralph who didn't have any feathers on either wing. So when the cold wind blew, Ralph said, Brr, and shivered and shook.

What's the matter? Ralph's mommy asked.

I'm cold, Ralph said.

Oh, the mommy said. Here. I'll keep you warm.

So she spread her big, feathery wings, and hugged Ralph tight, and when the cold wind blew, Ralph was warm and snuggly, and fell fast asleep.

The next Thursday, he was wearing canvas pants and hiking boots. He mentioned kind of casually to some of the girls in the class how whenever there was a storm he wore his Lake District walking outfit. He had a big, hairy sweater on. I kept waiting for him to make a noise like a mountain goat. But the girls seemed to like it. His boots made a creaky squeak on the linoleum of the hall when he caught up with me after class.

"As I told you," he said, "it isn't unappealing. It's just—not a college theme."

"Right," I said. "Okay. You want me to do it over?"

"No," he said. "Not at all. The D will remain your grade. But I'll read something else if you want to write it."

"This'll be fine," I said.

"Did you understand the assignment?"

"Write something to influence someone—Rhetoric and Persuasion."

We were at his office door and the redheaded kid who had gotten sick in my truck was waiting for him. She looked at me like one of us was in the wrong place, which struck me as accurate enough. He was interested in getting into his office with the redhead, but he remembered to turn around and flash me a grin he seemed to think he was known for.

Instead of going on shift a few hours after class, the way I'm supposed to, I told my supervisor I was sick, and I went home. Fanny was frightened when I came in, because I don't get sick and I don't miss work. She looked at my face and she grew sad. I kissed her hello and went upstairs to change. I always used to change my clothes when I was a kid, as soon as I came home from school. I put on jeans and a flannel shirt and thick wool socks, and I made myself a dark drink of sourmash. Fanny poured herself some wine and came into the cold northern room a few minutes later. I was sitting in the rocker, looking over the valley. The wind was lining up a lot of rows of cloud so that the sky looked like a baked trout when you lift the skin off. "It'll snow," I said to her.

She sat on the old sofa and waited. After a while, she said, "I wonder why they always call it a mackerel sky?"

"Good eating, mackerel," I said.

Fanny said, "Shit! You're never that laconic unless you feel crazy. What's wrong? Who'd you punch out at the playground?"

"We had to write a composition," I said.

"Did he like it?"

"He gave me a D."

"Well, you're familiar enough with D's. I never saw you get this low over a grade."

"I wrote about Ralph the Duck."

She said, "You did?" She said, "Honey." She came over and stood beside the rocker and leaned into me and hugged my head and neck. "Honey," she said. "Honey."

It was the worst of the winter's storms, and one of the worst in years. That afternoon they closed the college, which they almost never do. But the roads were jammed with snow over ice, and now it was freezing rain on top of that, and the only people working at the school that night were the operator who took emergency calls and me. Everyone else had gone home except the students, and most of them were inside. The ones who weren't were drunk, and I kept on sending them in and telling them to act like grown-ups. A number of them said they were, and I really couldn't argue. I had the bright beams on, the defroster set high, the little blue light winking, and a thermos of sourmash and hot coffee that I sipped from every time I had to get out of the truck or every time I realized how cold all that wetness was out there.

About eight o'clock, as the rain was turning back to snow and the cold was worse, the roads impossible, just as I was done helping a county sander on the edge of the campus pull a panel truck out of a snowbank, I got the emergency call from the college operator. We had a student missing. The roommates thought the kid was headed for the quarry. This meant I had to get the Bronco up on a narrow road above the campus, above the old cemetery, into all kinds of woods and rough track that I figured would be choked with ice and snow. Any kid up there would really have to want to be there, and I couldn't go in on foot, because you'd only want to be there on account of drugs, booze, or craziness, and either way I'd be needing blankets and heat, and then a fast ride down to the hospital in town. So I dropped into four-wheel drive to get me up the hill above the campus, bucking snow and sliding on ice, putting all the heater's warmth up onto the windshield because I couldn't see much more than swarming snow. My feet were still cold from the tow job, and it didn't seem to matter that I had on heavy socks and insulated boots I'd coated with waterproofing. I shivered, and I thought of Ralph the Duck.

I had to grind the rest of the way, from the cemetery, in four-wheel low, and in spite of the cold I was smoking my gearbox by the time I was close enough to the quarry—they really did take a lot of rocks for the campus buildings from there—to see I'd have to make my way on foot to where she was. It was a kind of scooped-out shape, maybe four or five stories high, where she stood—well, wobbled is more like it. She was as chalky as she'd been the last time, and her red hair didn't catch the light anymore. It just lay on her like something that had died on top of her head. She was in a white nightgown that was plastered to her body. She had her arms crossed as if she wanted to be warm. She swayed, kind of, in front of the big, dark, scooped-out rock face, where the trees and brush had been cleared for trucks and earthmovers. She looked tiny against all the darkness. From where I stood, I could see the snow driving down in front of the lights I'd left on, but I couldn't see it near her. All it looked like around her was dark. She was shaking with the cold, and she was crying.

I had a blanket with me, and I shoved it down the front of my coat to keep it dry for her, and because I was so cold. I waved. I stood in the lights and I waved. I don't know what she saw—a big shadow, maybe. I surely didn't reassure her, because when she saw me she backed up, until she was near the face of the quarry. She couldn't go any farther.

I called, "Hello! I brought a blanket. Are you cold? I thought you might want a blanket."

Her roommates had told the operator about pills, so I didn't bring her the coffee laced with mash. I figured I didn't have all that much time, anyway, to get her down and pumped out. The booze with whatever pills she'd taken would make her die that much faster.

I hated that word. Die. It made me furious with her. I heard myself seething when I breathed. I pulled my scarf and collar up above my mouth. I didn't want her to see how close I might come to wanting to kill her because she wanted to die.

I called, "Remember me?"

I was closer now. I could see the purple mottling of her skin. I didn't know if it was cold or dying. It probably didn't matter much to distinguish between them right now, I thought. That made me smile. I felt the smile, and I pulled the scarf down so she could look at it. She didn't seem awfully reassured.

"You're the sexual harassment guy," she said. She said it very slowly. Her lips were clumsy. It was like looking at a ventriloquist's dummy.

"I gave you an A," I said.

"When?"

"It's a joke," I said. "You don't want me making jokes. You want me to give you a nice warm blanket, though. And then you want me to take you home."

She leaned against the rock face when I approached. I pulled the blanket out, then zipped my jacket back up. The snow had stopped, I realized, and that wasn't really a very good sign. It felt like an arctic cold descending in its place. I held the blanket out to her, but she only looked at it.

"You'll just have to turn me in," I said. "I'm gonna hug you again."

She screamed, "No more! I don't want any more hugs!"

But she kept her arms on her chest, and I wrapped the blanket around her and stuffed a piece into each of her tight, small fists. I didn't know what to do for her feet. Finally, I got down on my haunches in front of her. She crouched down too, protecting herself.

"No," I said. "No, You're fine."

I took off the woolen mittens I'd been wearing. Mittens keep you warmer than gloves because they trap your hand's heat around the fingers and palms at once. Fanny had knitted them for me. I put a mitten as far onto each of her feet as I could. She let me. She was going to collapse, I thought.

"Now, let's go home," I said. "Let's get you better."

With her funny, stiff lips, she said,"I've been very self-indulgent and weird and I'm sorry. But I'd really like to die." She sounded so reasonable that I found myself nodding in agreement as she spoke.

"You can't just die," I said.

"Aren't I dying already? I took all of them, and then she giggled like a child, which of course is what she was. I borrowed different ones from other people's rooms. See, this isn't some teenage cry for like help. Understand? I'm seriously interested in death and I have to like stay out here a little longer and fall asleep. All right?"

"You can't do that," I said. "You ever hear of Vietnam?"

"I saw that movie," she said. "With the opera in it? *Apocalypse?* Whatever."

"I was there!" I said. "I killed people! I helped to kill them! And when they die, you see their bones later on. You dream about their bones and blood on the ends of the splintered ones, and this kind of mucous stuff coming out of their eyes. You probably heard of guys having dreams like that, didn't you? Whacked-out Vietnam vets? That's me, see? So I'm telling you, I know about dead people and their eye-balls and everything falling out. And people keep dreaming about the dead people they knew, see? You can't make people dream about you like that! It isn't fair!"

"You dream about me?" She was ready to go. She was ready to fall down, and I was going to lift her up and get her to the truck.

"I will," I said. "If you die."

"I want you to," she said. Her lips were hardly moving now. Her eyes were closed. "I want you all to."

I dropped my shoulder and put it into her waist and picked her up and carried her down to the Bronco. She was talking, but not a lot, and her voice leaked down my back. I jammed her into the truck and wrapped the blanket around her better and then put another one down around her feet. I strapped her in with the seat belt. She was shaking, and her eyes were closed and her mouth open. She was breathing. I checked that twice, once when I strapped her in, and then again when I strapped myself in and backed up hard into a sapling and took it down. I got us into first gear, held the clutch in, leaned over to listen for breathing, heard it—shallow panting, like a kid asleep on your lap for a nap—and then I put the gear in and howled down the hillside on what I thought might be the road.

We passed the cemetery. I told her that was a good sign. She didn't respond. I found myself panting too, as if we were breathing for each other. It made me dizzy, but I couldn't stop. We passed the highest dorm, and I dropped the truck into four-wheel high. The cab smelled like burnt oil and hot metal. We were past the chapel now, and the observatory, the president's house, then the bookstore. I had the blue light winking and the V-6 roaring, and I drove on the edge of out-of-control, sens-ing the skids just before I slid into them, and getting back out of them as I needed to. I took a little fender off once, and a bit of the corner of a classroom building, but I worked us back on course, and all I needed to do now was negotiate the sharp left turn around the Administration Building past the library, then floor it for the straight run to the town's main street and then the hospital.

I was panting into the mike, and the operator kept saying, "Say again?"

I made myself slow down some, and I said we'd need stomach pumping, and to get the names of the pills from her friends in the dorm, and I'd be there in less than five or we were crumpled up someplace and dead.

"Roger," the radio said. "Roger all that." My throat tightened and tears came into my eyes. They were helping us, they'd told me: Roger.

I said to the girl, whose head was slumped and whose face looked too blue all through its whiteness, "You know, I had a girl once. My wife, Fanny. She and I had a small girl one time."

I reached over and touched her cheek. It was cold. The truck swerved, and I got my hands on the wheel. I'd made the turn past the Ad Building using just my left. "I can do it in the dark," I sang to no tune I'd ever learned. "I can do it with one hand." I said to her, "We had a girl child, very small. Now, I do *not* want you dying."

I came to the campus gates doing fifty on the ice and snow, smoking the engine, grinding the clutch, and I bounced off a wrought iron fence to give me the curve going left that I needed. On a pool table, it would have been a bank shot worth applause. The town cop picked me up and got out ahead of me and let the street have all the lights and noise it could want. We banged up to the emergency room entrance and I was out and at the other door before the cop on duty, Elmo St. John, could loosen his seat belt. I loosened hers, and I carried her into the lobby of the ER. They had a gurney, and doctors, and they took her away from me. I tried to talk to them, but they made me sit down and do my shaking on a dirty sofa decorated with drawings of little spinning wheels. Somebody brought me hot coffee, I think it was Elmo, but I couldn't hold it.

"They won't," he kept saying to me. "They won't."

"What?"

"You just been sitting there for a minute and a half like St. Vitus dancing, telling me, Don't let her die. Don't let her die."

"Oh."

"You all *right?*"

"How about the kid?"

"They'll tell us soon."

"She better be all right."

"That's right."

"She—somebody's gonna have to tell me plenty if she isn't."

"That's right."

"She better not die this time," I guess I said.

Fanny came downstairs to look for me. I was at the northern windows, looking through the mullions down the valley to the faint red line along the mounds and little peaks of the ridge beyond the valley. The sun was going to come up, and I was looking for it.

Fanny stood behind me. I could hear her. I could smell her hair and the sleep on her. The crimson line widened, and I squinted at it. I heard the dog limp in behind her, catching up. He panted and I knew why his panting sounded familiar. She put her hands on my shoulders and arms. I made muscles to impress her with, and then I let them go, and let my head drop down until my chin was on my chest.

"I didn't think you'd be able to sleep after that," Fanny said.

"I brought enough adrenaline home to run a football team."

"But you hate being a hero, huh? You're hiding in here because somebody's going to call, or come over, and want to talk to you—her parents for shooting sure, sooner or later. Or is that supposed to be part of the service up at the playground? Saving their suicidal daughters. Almost dying to find them in the woods and driving too fast for *any* weather, much less what we had last night. Getting their babies home. The bastards." She was crying. I knew she would be, sooner or later. I could hear the soft sound of her lashes. She sniffed and I could feel her arm move as she felt for the tissues on the coffee table.

"I have them over here," I said. "On the windowsill."

"Yes." She blew her nose, and the dog thumped his tail. He seemed to think it one of Fanny's finer tricks, and he had wagged for her for thirteen years whenever she'd done it. "Well, you're going to have to talk to them."

"I will," I said. "I will." The sun was in our sky now, climbing. We had built the room so we could watch it climb. "I think that jackass with the smile, my prof? She showed up a lot at his office, the last few weeks. He called her my advisee, you know? The way those guys sound about what they're achieving by getting up and shaving and going to work and saying the same thing every day? Every year? Well, she was his advisee, I bet. He was shoving home the old advice."

"She'll be okay," Fanny said. "Her parents will take her home and love her up and get her some help." She began to cry again, then she stopped. She blew her nose, and the dog's tail thumped. She kept a hand between my shoulder and my neck. "So tell me what you'll tell a waiting world. How'd you talk her out?"

"Well, I didn't, really. I got up close and picked her up and carried her is all."

"You didn't say *anything*?"

"Sure I did. Kid's standing in the snow outside of a lot of pills, you're gonna say something."

"So what'd you *say*?"

"I told her stories," I said. "I did Rhetoric and Persuasion."

Fanny said, "Then you go in early on Thursday, you go in half an hour early, and you get that guy to jack up your grade."

⌒⌒⌒⌒⌒⌒⌒⌒⌒⌒

Suggestions for Discussion

1. What is "Ralph the Duck" about? What does it say about what it's about?

2. Consider the following in their relation to the theme of "Ralph the Duck":
    • "He loved what made him sick." (See page 314.)
    • not unintelligent
    • grades
    • "and I did want to learn about expressing myself." (See page 318.)
    • sexual harassment
    • Rhetoric and Persuasion

3. What does Ralph the Duck symbolize to the narrator and his wife? Does it operate differently as a symbol in the story?

4. Describe the plot of "Ralph the Duck." What is the relation of the theme to the plot?

5. Take any passage of dialogue from the story and show how it does more than one thing at a time.

6. Apart from "the generation gap," show how "Ralph the Duck" shares a theme with some other story in this book, and show how the treatment of this theme differs in the various elements of fiction.

Retrospect

1. Consider the question "Where are you going?" in the title of Joyce Carol Oates' story. How does the question relate plot to theme?

2. What does Denis Johnson's "Car Crash While Hitchhiking" say about what's real? How do characterization, atmosphere, incident, and imagery contribute to this theme?

3. Joy Williams "Excursion" begins with the statement, "Jenny lies a little." What does the story have to say about lies and how does it say it? What do you consider the central theme of the story?

4. In Charles Baxter's "Gryphon," how are the words *crazy, fabulous, and knowledge* explored, and how is our usual understanding of those words altered?

5. What is "The Ones Who Walk Away from Omelas" about, and what does it say about what it's about?

6. Consider the themes of insanity, secret communication, helplessness, and chance in "Signs and Symbols."

7. Which of the stories in this volume offer an inversion of a "truth" that you ordinarily accept about, for instance, the nature of reality, sanity, time, goodness? How successfully does each offer its alternative truth?

8. Consider images of children and childhood in "Hips," "Girl," "The Tambourine Lady," and "The Crane-Child." How do these different images inform the themes of the stories?

Writing Assignments

These five exercises are arranged in order of ascending difficulty. The first is the easiest, and it is likely to produce a bad story. If it produces a bad story, it will be invaluably instructive to you, and you will be relieved of the onus of ever doing it again. If it produces a good story, then you have done something else, something more, and something more original than the assignment asks for. If you prefer to do exercise 4 or 5, then you may already have doomed yourself to the writing craft and should prepare to be very poor for a few years while you discover what place writing will have in your life.

1. Take a simple but specific political, religious, scientific, or moral idea. It may be one already available to us in a formula of words, or it may be one of your own, but it should be possible to state it in less than ten words. Write a short story that illustrates the idea. Do not state the idea at all. Your goals are two: that the idea should be perfectly clear to us so that it could be extracted as a moral or message, and that we should feel we have experienced it.

2. Take as your title a common proverb or maxim, such as *power corrupts, honesty is the best policy, walk softly and carry a big stick, haste makes waste.* Let the story make the title ironic, that is, explore a situation in which the advice or statement does not apply.

3. Taking as a starting point some incident or situation from your own life, write a story with one of the following themes: nakedness, blindness, thirst, noise, borders, chains, clean wounds, washing, the color green, dawn. The events themselves may be minor (a story about a slipping bicycle chain may ultimately be more effective than one about a chain gang). Once you have decided on the structure of the story, explore everything you think, know, or believe about your chosen theme and try to incorporate that theme in imagery, dialogue, event, character, and so forth.

4. Identify the belief you hold most passionately and profoundly. Write a short story that explores an instance in which this belief is untrue.

5. Write a short story that you have wanted to write all term and have not written because you knew it was too big for you and you would fail. You may fail. Write it anyway.

11

PLAY IT AGAIN, SAM

Revision

- *Worry It and Walk Away*

- *Criticism*

- *Revision Questions*

- *An Example of the Revision Process*

The creative process is not all inventive; it is partly corrective, critical, nutritive, and fostering—a matter of getting this creature to be the best that it can be. William C. Knott, in *The Craft of Fiction*, cogently observes that "anyone can write—and almost everyone you meet these days is writing. However, only the writers know how to rewrite. It is this ability alone that turns the amateur into a pro."

Revising is a process more dreaded than dreadful. The resistance to rewriting is, if anything, greater than the resistance to beginning in the first place. Yet the chances are that once you have committed yourself to a first draft, you'll be unable to leave it in an unfinished and unsatisfying state. You'll be unhappy until it's right. Making it right will involve a second commitment, to seeing the story fresh and creating it again with the advantage of this re-vision.

You may have to "see-again" more than once. The process of revision involves external and internal insight; you'll need your conscious critic, your creative instinct, and readers you trust. You may need each of them several times, not necessarily in that order.

Worry It and Walk Away

To write your first draft, you banished the internal critic. Now make the critic welcome. Revision is work, but the strange thing is that you may find you can concentrate on the work for much longer than you could play at freedrafting. It has occurred to me that writing a first draft is very like tennis or softball—I have to be psyched for it, energy level up, alert, on my toes. A few hours is all I can manage, and at the end of it I'm wiped out. Revision is like careful carpentry, and if I'm under a deadline or just determined to get this thing crafted and polished, I can be good for twelve hours of it.

The first round of rewrites is probably a matter of letting your misgivings surface. Focus for a while on what seems awkward, overlong, undeveloped, flat, or flowery. Tinker. Tighten. Sharpen. More important at this stage than finishing any given page or phrase is that you're getting to know your story in order to open it to new possibilities. You will also get tired of it; you may feel stuck.

Then put it away. *Put it away.* Don't look at it for a matter of days or weeks— until you feel fresh on the project. In addition to getting some distance on your story, you're mailing it to your unconscious. Carolyn Bly says, "Here is the crux of it: between the conscious and unconscious mind we are more complex and given to concept than we are in the conscious mind."

"Complex" means that you can begin to see your story organically; "concept" means that you may discover what it is really about.

Rollo May, in *The Courage to Create*, makes a similar point.

> Everyone uses from time to time such expressions as, "a thought pops up," an idea comes "from the blue" or "dawns" or "comes as though out of a dream," or "it suddenly hit me." These are various ways of describing a common experience: the breakthrough of ideas from some depth below the level of awareness.

May describes getting stuck doing research on a psychological study; the evidence contradicted his theory that children rejected by their mothers would universally display symptoms of anxiety. He sat for long hours moiling and baffled, "caught by an insoluble problem."

> Late one day, putting aside my books and papers in the little office I used in that shelter house, I walked down the street toward the subway. I was tired. I tried to put the whole troublesome business out of my mind. About fifty feet away from the entrance to the Eighth Street station, it suddenly struck me "out of the blue," as the not-unfitting expression goes, that those young women who didn't fit my hypothesis were all from the proletarian class. . . I saw at that instant that it is not rejection by the mother that is the original trauma which is the source of anxiety; it is rather rejection that is lied about.

Here, May solves a logical problem not by consciously working it out, but by letting it go. In the process he sees a new connection and realizes what his project is about—not rejection after all, but dishonesty.

It is my experience that such connections and such realizations occur over and over again in the course of writing a short story or novel. Often I will believe that because I know who my characters are and what happens to them, I know what my story is about—and often I find I'm wrong, or that my understanding is shallow or incomplete.

In the first draft of my most recent novel, for instance, I opened with the sentence, "It took a hundred and twelve bottles of champagne to see the young Poindexters off to Arizona." A page later one character whispered to another that the young Mr. Poindexter in question had "consumption." I worked on this book for a year (taking my characters off to Arizona where they dealt with the desert heat, lack of water, alcoholism, loss of religion, and the development of mining interests and the building trade) before I saw the connection between "consumption" and "champagne." When I understood that simple link, I understood the overarching theme— surely latent in the idea from the moment it had taken hold of me—between tuberculosis, spiritual thirst, consumerism, and addiction, all issues of "consumption."

It might seem dismaying that you should see what your story is about only after you have written it. Try it; you'll like it. Nothing is more exhilarating than the discovery that a complex pattern has lain in your mind ready to unfold.

Note that in the early stages of revision, both the worrying and the walking away are necessary. Perhaps it is bafflement itself that plunges us to the unconscious space where the answer lies.

Criticism

Once you have thought your story through, drafted it, and worked on it to the best of your ability, someone else's eyes can help to refresh the vision of your own. Wise professionals rely on the help of an agent or editor at this juncture (although even the wisest still smart at censure); anyone can rely on the help of friends, family, or classmates. The trick to making good use of criticism is to be utterly selfish about it. Be greedy for it. Take it all in. Ultimately you are the laborer, the arbiter, *and* the boss in any dispute about your story, so you can afford to consider any problem and any solution. Most of us feel not only committed to what we have put on the page, but also defensive on its behalf—wanting, really, only to be told that it is a work of genius or, failing that, to find out that we have gotten away with it. Therefore, the first exigency of revision is that you learn to hear, absorb, and accept criticism.

It used to be popular to speak of "constructive criticism" and "destructive criticism," but these are misleading terms, suggesting that positive suggestions are useful and negative criticism useless. In practice the opposite is usually the case. You're likely to find that the most constructive thing a reader can do is say *I don't believe this, I don't like this, I don't understand this,* pointing to precisely the passages that made you uneasy. This kind of laying-the-finger-on-the-trouble-spot produces an inward groan, but it's also satisfying; you know just where to go to work. Often the most destructive thing a reader can do is offer you a positive suggestion—*Why don't you have him crash the car?*— that is irrelevant to your vision of the story. Be suspicious of praise that is too extravagant, of blame that is too general. If your impulse is to defend the story or yourself, still

the impulse. Behave as if bad advice were good advice, and give it serious consideration. You can reject it after you have explored it for anything of use it may offer.

Once again, walk away—Kenneth Atchity, in *A Writer's Time*, advises compul-
sory "vacations" at crucial points in the revising process—and let the criticism
cook until you feel ready, impatient, to get back to writing.

When you feel that you have acquired enough distance from the story to see it
anew, go back to work. Make notes of your plans, large and small. Talk to yourself
in your journal about what you want to accomplish and where you think you have
failed. Let your imagination play with new images or passages of dialogue. Keep a
copy of the story as it is so that you can always go back to the original, and then be
ruthless with another copy. Eudora Welty advises cutting sections apart and then
pinning them back together so that they can be easily re- and re-arranged.

Revision Questions

As you plan the revision and as you rewrite, you will know (and your critics will
tell you) what problems are unique to your story. There are also general, almost
universal, pitfalls that you can avoid if you ask yourself the following questions:

What is my story about?   Another way of saying this is: *What is the pattern of
change?* Once this pattern is clear, you can check your draft to make sure you've
included all the crucial moments of discovery and decision. Is there a crisis action?

Are there irrelevant scenes?   Remember that it is a common impulse to try to
cover too much ground. Tell your story in the fewest possible scenes; cut down on
summary and unnecessary flashback. These dissipate energy and lead you to tell
rather than show.

Why should the reader turn from the first page to the second?   Is the language fresh?
Are the characters alive? Does the first sentence, paragraph, page introduce real
tension? If it doesn't, you have probably begun at the wrong place. If you are
unable to find a way to introduce tension on the first page, you may have to doubt
whether you have a story after all.

Is it original?   Almost every writer thinks first, in some way or other, of the
familiar, the usual, the given. This character is a stereotype, that emotion is too
easy, that phrase is a cliché. First-draft laziness is inevitable, but it is also a way of
being dishonest. A good writer will comb the work for clichés and labor to find the
exact, the honest, and the fresh.

Is it clear?   Although ambiguity and mystery provide some of our most profound pleasures in literature, beginning writers are often unable to distinguish
between mystery and muddle, ambiguity and sloppiness. You may want your character to be rich with contradiction, but we still want to know whether that character is male or female, black or white, old or young. We need to be oriented on the
simplest level of reality before we can share your imaginative world. Where are we?
When are we? Who are they? How do things look? What time of day or night is it?
What's the weather? What's happening?

Is it self-conscious?   Probably the most famous piece of advice to the rewriter is William Faulkner's "kill all your darlings." When you are carried away with the purple of your prose, the music of your alliteration, the hilarity of your wit, the profundity of your insights, then the chances are that you are having a better time writing than the reader will have reading. No reader will forgive you, and no reader should. Just tell the story. The style will follow of itself if you just tell the story.

Where is it too long?   Most of us, and even the best of us, write too long. We are so anxious to explain every nuance, cover every possible aspect of character, action, and setting that we forget the necessity of stringent selection. In fiction, and especially in the short story, we want sharpness, economy, and vivid, telling detail. More than necessary is too much. I have been helped in my own tendency to tell all by a friend who went through a copy of one of my novels, drawing a line through the last sentence of about every third paragraph. Then in the margin he wrote, again and again, "Hit it, baby, and get out." That's good advice for anyone.

Where is it undeveloped in character, imagery, theme?   In any first, second, or third draft of a manuscript there are likely to be necessary passages sketched, skipped, or skeletal. What information is missing, what actions are incomplete, what motives obscure, what images inexact? Where does the action occur too abruptly so that it loses its emotional force?

Where is it too general?   Originality, economy, and clarity can all be achieved through the judicious use of significant detail. Learn to spot general, vague, and fuzzy terms. Be suspicious of yourself anytime you see nouns like *someone* and *everything*, adjectives like *huge* and *handsome*, adverbs like *very* and *really*. Seek instead a particular thing, a particular size, an exact degree.

Although the dread of "starting over" is a real and understandable one, the chances are that the rewards of revising will startlingly outweigh the pains. Sometimes a character who is dead on the page will come to life through the addition of a few sentences or significant details. Sometimes a turgid or tedious paragraph can become sharp with a few judicious cuts. Sometimes dropping page one and putting page seven where page three used to be can provide the skeleton of an otherwise limp story. And sometimes, often, perhaps always, the difference between an amateur rough-cut and a publishable story is in the struggle at the rewriting stage.

An Example of the Revision Process

Short story writer Stephen Dunning won the 1990 "World's Best Short Story Contest" with a tight, complex, and evocative story that illustrates most of the principles discussed in this book. "Wanting to Fly" has, in two hundred and forty-five words, eight characters, a power struggle that builds and comes to a crisis, dialogue that reveals character and moves the action, a strong voice, irony, metaphor, and a pattern of change that reveals a theme.

Assuming that a story of such density was not "tossed off," I asked Dunning if he would share his revision process with other writers. What follows are four (of perhaps nine or ten) versions of the story, with Dunning's generous notes. He says:

Mornings I often fast-write, try to hang onto my dreams. Not "free-write," but go so fast I leave censors behind, stumble and goof, hoping to trick myself into a little chunk I like. A word or an image. (Much less often, an "idea.")

Very inefficient! I collect fast-writes (I do them on processor now, for speed) and when I have a stack, I search for chunks of language that interest me. I do this search with high-lighters in hand—pink, for hot items, yellow, for "maybe," green that means "Huh?" Things that puzzle me, but might be important. Obsessions, for example. I highlight words, phrases, images, "talk," mistakes. (Unproved theory of mine: write fast enough, make enough mistakes, you can track your obsessions. They leak out on you.)

How much do I glean?

As little as possible. I've learned, a few words per page. An occasional sentence.

I type these little chunks fresh, set them up in their new environment. Then I doodle, connecting items with lines, starring something special. Now I'm ready to "practice writing," which is what practicing writers do.

How? By answering my own questions: Why does this interest me? What else can I say about it? What does it remind me of? What would _____ (Mother, my childhood sweetheart, Jesus, my mean sister, Winston Churchill—plug in someone who fits) say about this?

In a journal entry dated "somewhere around Halloween 1989," Dunning produced the "fast-write" (what I've referred to in this book as freedrafting) that provided the seeds of the story "Wanting to Fly." The fast-write passage is reproduced here exactly as it came from his word processor, "stumble and goofs" intact.

Version 1

fqast write from dreamsone is a computer dream. it's twenty two fifty eighjt st clair with the mansion full of statues, hedges. thje magraw boiys danny, oliver, the disapproving one with glasses in the mansion games i did ook, better than the midget biully k but often last withj danny ollie. a bunch of othjer boys, the skinny lop-jawed one who spit at me in fooitball. the golden moment, facing him down. leary, he weas. hius name. stsate fair time, aboiut ten guys playing ball leary was spitting and and tried to tackle me on the rocks, us others, us good guys, would try not to, ill fighjt you fair and square. god, i was good. the other boys waiting. leary backing down. some superboy hero! the evenings when the magraws had to go, id fly over into the mansion. crosbys'. sail from our back porch, go low over the hedges between crosbys and us, soar arouind statues, swoop along hedges. then poull up into resting places, a sectret birdself, something i swear i did, i was a bird, i flew. i restded on statues and tree limbs. i can see the hedges and statues. did the dream go bad? at some pooint i wasn't in it, but watching. dozens of little figures, Boschian. a camera scan a huge painting made up of hundreds of little vignettes of weird, gnome like, devilish flyuers. pictogfraphs, almost, but lots of soaring and dipping. i know it was not the way it shoild be. i was watching, helpless to make everone everhything stop. the other flyers shoildn't be there. my place to fly. the night wqas purple and i love the lightness and speed of my flying. then the dream ended, I tried to identify the wonder of it. it seemed to end on Where did these wondrous things come from? They weren't the neightborhood boys. not worried///tjhere at the ened.

This first-draft-of-something-or-other clearly draws on both dreams and memory. In the second version (which Dunning says is four or five drafts editings into a possible story) the author has achieved a gently ironic distance on the character of the boy, but it is interesting to note that he has provided a "frame" with a writer in it—something that many writers do, sometimes in an early version, sometimes in a final publication. Perhaps the introduction of an autobiographical element in the frame helps of itself to find authorial distance. By now the bird-boy of the dream has transmogrified into a human cannonball.

Version 2

Leroy slid open the bottom drawer where they kept his costumes. The white and red looked shabby; the silver looked ok. Nylon, and shiny. He thought of something he wanted to write.

"Part four," he wrote. "I always wanted to fly."

I was eight years old, in third, in Mrs. McKissup's third grade, when my father took me to State Fair. In the grandstand, after the horse races, sitting close to the track and the infield stage, we saw a man in silver tights and big handlebar moustache shot from a cannon. The name I remember is "The Great Zambini," but that doesn't look exactly right. Later my father gave me names like "The Flying Weenie" and "Zamboosi, the Goosey."

That same night of the State Fair I tried to paint my BVD longies with the gold paint in the tiny spray can Mother used to gild the birdcage. Right over my belly button I made a spot the size of a golden apple before the paint ran out. When my father saw it he paddled my ass with his hairbrush. That May, for my ninth birthday, Mother gave me a silver-grey t-shirt with a picture of Halley's comet flashing in red across the front.

Leroy got up from the table to get a beer. In the Lucky Lager six-pack, Carmen had set two cans of Diet Pepsi. Hint, hint, lay off the sauce. Leroy rolled his eyes and twisted out one of the beers. Well, that was like her, fairly comical.

I could fly in that shirt. Summer evenings in the eerie dusk after supper I wheeled around the neighborhood, content to fly alone. Daytimes at Duncan Frenzel's house I pumped the backyard tire swing higher than anyone and learned how to fly out from it just right before the swing reached the top of its arc. I flew out three or four feet beyond Duncan. At school in the sixth grade me and two buddies took over the primary grades' slide and slid down on our stocking feet, launching off from the lip to see who could jump farthest. Mrs. McKissup came over to tell us to let the little children use the slide. When Mrs. McKissup's back was turned, we went back to the slide, and before that day is out, of course, the three of us are in Mr. Beaver's office.

He calls us "childish" and "selfish." This happens again, he'll have to call our parents. Duncan giggles then, and gets a dirty look. When Mr. Beaver asks what would we do if we were trying to run a decent school, we both giggle. Maybe we had the same idea. Mine was to get rid of Mrs. McKissup and let our student teacher teach. She was beautiful, like a model.

My father heard about it anyway and beat me with the hairbrush until finally I cried and spit "I hate you!" in his face.

The summer between seventh and eight, Philip Callum and me made a slide from a refrigerator carton and nailed it onto the Callum's back porch roof. It hung out two feet past the edge of the roof. Mrs. Callum worked at the Police Department, and I called her there when Philip landed wrong and broke his ankle. I didn't know the ankle was broke, just that Philip was screaming like crazy and couldn't walk. Before she got home, I tore the slide off the roof, and it wasn't until the first rain that Mr. Callum found out that his porch roof sprinkled like a watering can. After the phone call on that, Daddy beat me hard with the hairbrush. This is like ten days after.

That was my last beating. As long as I was still there, he never beat me. I think that in some serious way Mother told him not to, and he listened. I felt he could do what he wanted to her, but not to me. Later, once I'd run away and started coming home to visit, my father and I got along.

I was visiting after New Year's, home from Ice Capades, when he drowned. January fifth. Out ice-fishing with Arn Bower, he went out further than he should. He knew it was thin. He broke through and came up under the ice. I saw his face before they got him out.

I cancelled the gig I had starting mid-January. I was tired anyway.

Then I remember maybe once a day Arn would call on my mother. They'd drink a few. Arn would put his arms around her, holding her what seemed more than she wanted, but it was hard to tell. Sometimes I watched from outside, saw Mother push Arn's hands from her legs and breasts. But she didn't push hard or seem not to like it when he started again. I always made plenty of noise so Mother could get herself arranged before I come in.

Before, when I was fifteen, I saw the ad for Wallace's World Carnival coming to Anoka. I left a note for Mother, saying I was going to hitch-hike to my Aunt's, at White Bear Lake. I took the Selby-Lake streetcar the opposite direction to the end of the line, and thumbed to Anoka.

I slept that night in the back end of a truck that hauled the ferris wheel; I left the following night in the cab of that same truck. Willie Farley drove, another runaway named Annette sat in the middle, and me against the side door. I'd got hired as roustabout. I'd help put up the rides and tents, clean up after the animals. A dollar a day, food, sleep wherever I could.

He got the next-to-last beer. How long since he'd thought about Annette! Writing was terrific that way, making you remember things.

Willie was my best friend for two years. Long before Annette left to go home to Anoka, Willie got her drunk on dago red and held her head in his lap, in case she tried to get away. It was Willie's plan to help me lose my cherry. "It's time, Little Buddy, don't use it, you lose it."

"How's Annette going to like it?"

How about you think about your own end, you let me take handle Annette here?"

Then after Willie got her so drunk she didn't know which end was up, he held her head while I pumped myself into her. I'd like myself better if I said I didn't enjoy it, but I did. Annette hardly seemed to notice.

Then Willie left us, going off to get some food. I lay alongside Annette, my right hand under her sweatshirt on her chest. Later she threw up. I got her drinks of water and told what had happened. She already sort of knew. She cried and then we slept there restlessly. At dawn we woke up together, she said she loved me and made me do it to her again. This time was nice. I was full of the wonder of sex, thinking it would be even better if you loved the girl you were making love to, and I didn't love Annette. She never had enough in her mind.

Willie was glad to have Annette shift over on to me. I was up to three dollars a day when Salazar, The Silver Bullet, joined our show, expanded for a two-week stay outside Memphis. In his first flight Salazar broke through his net—It was terrible rotted—and smashed his face bad. Lost half his nose, some teeth, broke his cheekbone and jaw. Willie and Old Man Wallace himself had four hours to talk me into doing the night show. "You're the right size," Old Man Wallace said. Salazar had a small barrel to his cannon. "You bail me out on this one, you're on your way to the big time." With help from Alex the Alligator Man we hauled the gun to a nearby high school football field and rigged a good net. The two of them told me what they thought was true about cannon-balling. Before that night was over, I'd found out they didn't know beans. I can say these three things. You have to push off of the plunger and you have to stretch out in flight. You have to land some way you don't break your bones. Otherwise, it's easy if you have the nerve and don't mind the jolts to your joints.

Carmen came in from her hymns. Leroy hoped she'd say something, like "What you writing there, Leroy?" Anything. But her face was shiny with the humidity and her joy. She was still in Beulah Land. "Oh, the singin was so fine, Leroy, you should of heard us sing."

"I've been writing, here," he said.

"They're raising money for a new organ," Carmen said.

"Praise the Lord, we need it."

Leroy turned back to his notebook. "Annette found some silver tights," he said aloud, thinking that might catch her. He wrote that down and went on.

. . . a silver bowling jacket that she took the name off, and a silver spray for my hair. By showtime, I could have flown without the cannon. It was partly knowing that Annette was there, but it was also inevitable: me being a human cannonball was what had to happen because I was me. My father's Flying Weenie. Because of all those nights and dream-times of flying, and the flight from Philip Callum's porch roof. I spelled inevitable in the fifth grade bee but sat down next-to-last on paranoid, putting in a y even though I knew better.

Polly Pineo won. I wanted her to win. I don't know exactly what I thought would happen if she won, but I know I was glad when she did.

I never saw that Salazar again. Old Man Wallace bought the cannon. Or said
he did. They used me wherever the space laid out right. Willie and I fixed up
Salazar's old cannon until I could fly one hundred fifty feet.
Annette went home, but there were other girls and women everywhere.

Dunning confesses that the second version puzzles him, and that it's possible "the market" was beginning to play a role. "My hunch is: I was trying to get a piece both for the PEN Syndicated Fiction Award" (which Dunning has won twice) "and for the World's Best Short Short Story Contest. Both contests have word limits—PEN's 2,500 and WBSSSC's severe 250."

Dunning also felt that both contests had "taboos, stated or inferred." Perhaps for that reason he drew back in a subsequent long version from the narrator's loss of virginity to a—stronger, in my opinion—bittersweet kissing scene. Gone also are the characters of the writer and his girlfriend Carmen, and the whole frame with its writer writing. The boy's story is sharpened and tightened, but otherwise remains substantially the same.

It's interesting that at this point Dunning began to title his versions, a clue that he had a sense of shape and theme. The progression of titles indicates a subtle shift of emphasis, from "Flying," to "I Always Wanted to Fly," to "Wanting to Fly."

By the time he came to write the penultimate version, Dunning knew he was aiming for the 250-word maximum demanded by the World's Best Short Short Story Contest. He had drastically pruned and condensed. "Note a shift to the present," he says, "a fine way to cut words." One consequence of the shortening is that characters are squashed to sketches ("Bye-bye, Annette: In longer versions she was prominent; here she's a walk-on.") Yet this distilling represents a natural process of characterization, and the richness of the earlier portraits no doubt contributes to the vividness of the later one.

This version of Dunning's story is reproduced as a facsimile of his working manuscript. He says, "Here the inked numbers in the upper right corner indicate that with my pen editings, I've cut 338 to 307. (Lord, Lord! Another 57 to go.)"

Version 3

WORLD'S BEST SHORT STORY CONTEST
991/620/551/496/418/400/369/362/338

I always wanted to fly.

338
31
———
307

At State Fair we see a man [with] in silver tights and [a] handlebar moustache shot from a cannon, [a name like] ''The Great Zambini''?
[Driving home] Father calls me [names like] ''Zamboosi, the Goosey'' and
''Flying Weenie.'' [But] That night, when I paint my BVD's
with Ma's birdcage spray, he paddles me good.

My ninth birthday Ma gives me a silver-grey t-shirt
with Halley's comet [flashing] across the front. I can fly
in that shirt. (Arms out stiff, I tilt around the neigh-
borhood.) [~~Duncan Frenzel and I use~~ ~catches Duncan and me on~] the kindergarten
slide.] Mrs McKissup comes over: ''Now you big boys, let
the children use it.''

[We don't listen.] Before long we're in Mr. Beaver's
office.

''Childish,'' he says. ''Selfish.'' Duncan giggles,
(~~and gets a look~~.) Mr. Beaver asks what *we'd* do if we was
trying to run a decent school. We both giggle, and Father
gets the (~~old~~) call. He beats me with his hairbrush.
(~~We nail it good to Frenzel's porch roof, but~~) ~nailed good to F's roof~ Our refrigerator-carton slide ∧ isn't steady. Duncan lands
wrong, screaming and hollering, and I call the police,
(~~where his ma works.~~) (~~Turns out~~) the ankle was broke. When
it rains, Mr. Frenzel's (~~porch~~) roof sprinkles like a
watering can.
~That was my last beating.~
~~The last time Father beats me is for that~~.

Wallace's Carnival hires me to assemble rides (~~tents
and clean after animals.~~) A dollar a day, food, sleep
where I can. ~Next day~ We leave for Toledo ~~the next day~~, Willie Farley driving the ferris-wheel truck, [another runaway
named Annette in the middle, me against the door.]

It's Willie teaches me to fly.
[Annette knows other things.]

And I've been flying ever since. Once I'm famous, Father and me get along fine. I'm home from Cole Brothers
when he drowns. [January fifth,] ice-fishing with Arn
Bower. [Father knows the ice is thin, but breaks through

and comes up under it](Before they get him out,)I see his face, mouth open and lopsided, a giant perch.

Arn Bower starts keeping Ma company,(and that's good.) Wherever I fly there's women for me.

The final award-winning and publishied version of Dunning's story is so dense that it verges on that hybrid form, the prose poem.

"At some point," he says, "there's tension between the stuff (language, content) and the form. One effect, unfortunate, is sentences that sound more like telegrams than art. But another effect comes from the demands of the form, inviting the writer to imaginative uses of language. Not *altogether* different from writing a haiku or a sonnet, is it? In the third version I wrote:
We don 't listen. Before long we're in Mr. Beaver's office.
Trying to hang onto the stuff ánd still honing the piece, the final version reads:
In two minutes Duncan and me're in Beaver's office.
A slender nine words instead of ten! The final version has a little more stuff and shows (images) more than it tells. It's more specific—*In two minutes* instead of *Before long*—adding a word!; names (*Duncan and me*), and has that lovely contraction (*me + are into me're*)
Makes me smile even now."

Final Version

☞ Wanting to Fly ☜

At State Fair a man in silver tights and handlebar moustache—some name like The Great Zambini—blasts from a cannon. Driving home, Father calls me "Goosey Zamboosi" and "Flying Weenie." But later, when I spray my BVD's with Ma's birdcage paint, he paddles me good.

Again.

For my ninth birthday, Ma gives me a silver-grey t-shirt with Halley's comet flashing across. I can fly in that shirt—arms stiff, tilting. Then Mrs. McKissup catches us on the kindergarten slide. "You boys! Let the children use it."

In two minutes Duncan and me're in Beaver's office.

"Childish," Mr. Beaver says. "Selfish." Duncan giggles. "What would you do, you're trying to run a decent school?" We both giggle.

Father uses the hairbrush.

Duncan and me nail a refrigerator-carton to Frenzels' porch roof. Duncan falls awful hard, grabbing his ankle. "It's broke," he hollers. I run for his ma. Next rain the Frenzels' roof sprinkles like a watering can.

My last beating ever.

Wallace's Carnival hires me to assemble rides—dollar a day, food, sleep anywhere I can. We head for Toledo, Willie Farley driving the ferris-wheel truck. It's Willie teaches me cannon-flying. I get pretty famous.

Then of course Father and me get along. I'm home from Cole Brothers when Father drowns, ice-fishing with Arn Bower. Before they hook him, I see his face—mouth open and lopsided, a giant perch.

Arn Bower starts keeping Ma company, and that's good. There's women wherever I fly.

What you have just read is the story of a story, with Dunning as hero trying to catch a little bit of a literal dream, wrestling it, messing up, sidetracked, persistent, pulled by contradictory forces (the dream, the market), learning as he goes, changing as the thing he is making changes. If you think that is a lot of trouble to go to for two hundred and fifty words, think again. That's what writing is.

I remember that in my freshman English class at the University of Arizona, Patrick McCarthy was trying to impress us with how hard we ought to work. He described his own struggle the night before, till two a.m., for a single paragraph. He was a powerful storyteller, and he made it grindingly awful. I was appalled. I put up my hand. "But doesn't it," I asked cheerfully, "get easier?"

McCarthy thought a moment. "No," he said. "It doesn't get easier. It gets better."

And that's the truth of it. There are fine professional writers who never, as a contemporary said of Shakespeare, "blot a word." (Twentieth-century translation: blip a word.) But they are precious few, and you and I are not among them. The minute we get comfortable doing something, we'll do something else; the minute we reach our standards, we'll raise them. The reward will probably not be fame or money or even an intense life replete with talk of illusion and reality, art and death. More likely the reward will be, now and then, some such thing as a "lovely contraction." It'll be enough.

Unlike Stephen Dunning's "Wanting to Fly," the short story "The Bath" by Raymond Carver underwent major expansion in the revision process, and the new version was published as "A Small, Good Thing." In an interview with Larry McCaffrey and Sinda Gregory, Carver said, "In my own mind I consider them to be really two entirely different stories, not just different versions of the same story; it's hard to even look on them as coming from the same source." Both versions, or both stories, are reprinted here.

The Bath

RAYMOND CARVER

Saturday afternoon the mother drove to the bakery in the shopping center. After looking through a loose-leaf binder with photographs of cakes taped onto the pages, she ordered chocolate, the child's favorite. The cake she chose was decorated with a spaceship and a launching pad under a sprinkling of white stars. The name Scotty would be iced on in green as if it were the name of the spaceship.

The baker listened thoughtfully when the mother told him Scotty would be eight years old. He was an older man, this baker, and he wore a curious apron, a heavy thing with loops that went under his arms and around his back and then crossed in front again where they were tied in a very thick knot. He kept wiping his hands on the front of the apron as he listened to the woman, his wet eyes examining her lips as she studied the samples and talked.

He let her take her time. He was in no hurry.

The mother decided on the spaceship cake, and then she gave the baker her name and her telephone number. The cake would be ready Monday morning, in plenty of time for the party Monday afternoon. This was all the baker was willing to say. No pleasantries, just this small exchange, the barest information, nothing that was not necessary.

Monday morning, the boy was walking to school. He was in the company of another boy, the two boys passing a bag of potato chips back and forth between them. The birthday boy was trying to trick the other boy into telling what he was going to give in the way of a present.

At an intersection, without looking, the birthday boy stepped off the curb, and was promptly knocked down by a car. He fell on his side, his head in the gutter, his legs in the road moving as if he were climbing a wall.

The other boy stood holding the potato chips. He was wondering if he should finish the rest or continue on to school.

The birthday boy did not cry. But neither did he wish to talk anymore. He would not answer when the other boy asked what it felt like to be hit by a car. The birthday boy got up and turned back for home, at which time the other boy waved good-bye and headed off for school.

The birthday boy told his mother what had happened. They sat together on the sofa. She held his hands in her lap. This is what she was doing when the boy pulled his hands away and lay down on his back.

Of course, the birthday party never happened. The birthday boy was in the hospital instead. The mother sat by the bed. She was waiting for the boy to wake up. The father hurried over from his office. He sat next to the mother. So now the both of them waited for the boy to wake up. They waited for hours, and then the father went home to take a bath.

The man drove home from the hospital. He drove the streets faster than he should. It had been a good life till now. There had been work, fatherhood, family. The man had been lucky and happy. But fear made him want a bath.

He pulled into the driveway. He sat in the car trying to make his legs work. The child had been hit by a car and he was in the hospital, but he was going to be all right. The man got out of the car and went up to the door. The dog was barking and the telephone was ringing. It kept ringing while the man unlocked the door and felt the wall for the light switch.

He picked up the receiver. He said, "I just got in the door!"

"There's a cake that wasn't picked up."

This is what the voice on the other end said.

"What are you saying?" the father said.

"The cake," the voice said. "Sixteen dollars."

The husband held the receiver against his ear, trying to understand. He said, "I don't know anything about it."

"Don't hand me that," the voice said.

The husband hung up the telephone. He went into the kitchen and poured himself some whiskey. He called the hospital.

The child's condition remained the same.

While the water ran into the tub, the man lathered his face and shaved. He was in the tub when he heard the telephone again. He got himself out and hurried through the house, saying, "Stupid, stupid," because he wouldn't be doing this if he'd stayed where he was in the hospital. He picked up the receiver and shouted, "Hello!"

The voice said, "It's ready."

The father got back to the hospital after midnight. The wife was sitting in the chair by the bed. She looked up at the husband and then she looked back at the child. From an apparatus over the bed hung a bottle with a tube running from the bottle to the child.

"What's this?" the father said.

"Glucose," the mother said.

The husband put his hand to the back of the woman's head.

"He's going to wake up," the man said.

"I know," the woman said.

In a little while the man said, "Go home and let me take over."

She shook her head. "No," she said.

"Really," he said. "Go home for a while. You don't have to worry. He's sleeping, is all."

A nurse pushed open the door. She nodded to them as she went to the bed. She took the left arm out from under the covers and put her fingers on the wrist. She put the arm back under the covers and wrote on the clipboard attached to the bed.

"How is he?" the mother said.

"Stable," the nurse said. Then she said, "Doctor will be in again shortly."

"I was saying maybe she'd want to go home and get a little rest," the man said. "After the doctor comes."

"She could do that," the nurse said.

The woman said, "We'll see what the doctor says." She brought her hand up to her eyes and leaned her head forward.

The nurse said, "Of course."

The father gazed at his son, the small chest inflating and deflating under the covers. He felt more fear now. He began shaking his head. He talked to himself like this. The child is fine. Instead of sleeping at home, he's doing it here. Sleep is the same wherever you do it.

The doctor came in. He shook hands with the man. The woman got up from the chair.

"Ann," the doctor said and nodded. The doctor said, "Let's just see how he's doing." He moved to the bed and touched the boy's wrist. He peeled back an eyelid and then the other. He turned back the covers and listened to the heart. He pressed his fingers here and there on the body. He went to the end of the bed and studied the chart. He noted the time, scribbled on the chart, and then he considered the mother and the father.

This doctor was a handsome man. His skin was moist and tan. He wore a three-piece suit, a vivid tie, and on his shirt were cufflinks.

The mother was talking to herself like this. He has just come from somewhere with an audience. They gave him a special medal.

The doctor said, "Nothing to shout about, but nothing to worry about. He should wake up pretty soon." The doctor looked at the boy again. "We'll know more after the tests are in."

"Oh, no," the mother said.

The doctor said, "Sometimes you see this."

The father said, "You wouldn't call this a coma, then?"

The father waited and looked at the doctor.

"No, I don't want to call it that," the doctor said. "He's sleeping. It's restorative. The body is doing what it has to do."

"It's a coma," the mother said. "A kind of coma."

The doctor said, "I wouldn't call it that."

He took the woman's hands and patted them. He shook hands with the husband.

The woman put her fingers on the child's forehead and kept them there for a while. "At least he doesn't have a fever," she said. Then she said, "I don't know. Feel his head."

The man put his fingers on the boy's forehead. The man said, "I think he's supposed to feel this way."

The woman stood there awhile longer, working her lip with her teeth. Then she moved to her chair and sat down.

The husband sat in the chair beside her. He wanted to say something else. But there was no saying what it should be. He took her hand and put it in his lap. This made him feel better. It made him feel he was saying something. They sat like that for a while, watching the boy, not talking. From time to time he squeezed her hand until she took it away.

"I've been praying," she said.

"Me too," the father said. "I've been praying too."

A nurse came back in and checked the flow from the bottle.

A doctor came in and said what his name was. This doctor was wearing loafers.

"We're going to take him downstairs for more pictures," he said. "And we want to do a scan."

"A scan?" the mother said. She stood between this new doctor and the bed.

"It's nothing," he said.

"My God," she said.

Two orderlies came in. They wheeled a thing like a bed. They unhooked the boy from the tube and slid him over onto the thing with wheels.

It was after sunup when they brought the birthday boy back out. The mother and father followed the orderlies into the elevator and up to the room. Once more the parents took up their places next to the bed.

They waited all day. The boy did not wake up. The doctor came again and examined the boy again and left after saying the same things again. Nurses came in. Doctors came in. A technician came in and took blood.

"I don't understand this," the mother said to the technician.

"Doctor's orders," the technician said.

The mother went to the window and looked out at the parking lot. Cars with their lights on were driving in and out. She stood at the window with her hands on the sill. She was talking to herself like this. We're into something now, something hard.

She was afraid.

She saw a car stop and a woman in a long coat get into it. She made believe she was that woman. She made believe she was driving away from here to someplace else.

The doctor came in. He looked tanned and healthier than ever. He went to the bed and examined the boy. He said, "His signs are fine. Everything's good."

The mother said, "But he's sleeping."

"Yes," the doctor said.

The husband said, "She's tired. She's starved."

The doctor said, "She should rest. She should eat. Ann," the doctor said.

"Thank you," the husband said.

He shook hands with the doctor and the doctor patted their shoulders and left.

"I suppose one of us should go home and check on things," the man said. "The dog needs to be fed."

"Call the neighbors," the wife said. "Someone will feed him if you ask them to."

She tried to think who. She closed her eyes and tried to think anything at all. After a time she said, "Maybe I'll do it. Maybe if I'm not here watching, he'll wake up. Maybe it's because I'm watching that he won't."

"That could be it," the husband said.

"I'll go home and take a bath and put on something clean," the woman said.

"I think you should do that," the man said.

She picked up her purse. He helped her into her coat. She moved to the door, and looked back. She looked at the child, and then she looked at the father. The husband nodded and smiled.

She went past the nurses' station and down to the end of the corridor, where she turned and saw a little waiting room, a family in there, all sitting in wicker chairs, a man in a khaki shirt, a baseball cap pushed back on his head, a large woman wearing a housedress, slippers, a girl in jeans, hair in dozens of kinky braids, the table littered with flimsy wrappers and styrofoam and coffee sticks and packets of salt and pepper.

"Nelson," the woman said. "Is it about Nelson?"

The woman's eyes widened.

"Tell me now, lady," the woman said. "Is it about Nelson?"

The woman was trying to get up from her chair. But the man had his hand closed over her arm.

"Here, here," the man said.

"I'm sorry," the mother said. "I'm looking for the elevator. My son is in the hospital. I can't find the elevator."

"Elevator is down that way," the man said, and he aimed a finger in the right direction.

"My son was hit by a car," the mother said. "But he's going to be all right. He's in shock now, but it might be some kind of coma too. That's what worries us, the coma part. I'm going out for a little while. Maybe I'll take a bath. But my husband is with him. He's watching. There's a chance everything will change when I'm gone. My name is Ann Weiss."

The man shifted in his chair. He shook his head.

He said, "Our Nelson."

She pulled into the driveway. The dog ran out from behind the house. He ran in circles on the grass. She closed her eyes and leaned her head against the wheel. She listened to the ticking of the engine.

She got out of the car and went to the door. She turned on lights and put on water for tea. She opened a can and fed the dog. She sat down on the sofa with her tea.

The telephone rang.

"Yes!" she said. "Hello!" she said.

"Mrs. Weiss," a man's voice said.

"Yes," she said. "This is Mrs. Weiss. Is it about Scotty?" she said.

"Scotty," the voice said. "It is about Scotty," the voice said. "It has to do with Scotty, yes."

A Small, Good Thing

RAYMOND CARVER

Saturday afternoon she drove to the bakery in the shopping center. After looking through a loose-leaf binder with photographs of cakes taped onto the pages, she ordered chocolate, the child's favorite. The cake she chose was decorated with a space ship and launching pad under a sprinkling of white stars at one end of the cake, and a planet made of red frosting at the other end. His name, SCOTTY, would be in raised green letters beneath the planet. The baker, who was an older man with a thick neck, listened without saying anything when she told him the child would be eight years old next Monday. The baker wore a white apron that looked like a smock. Straps cut under his arms, went around in back and then to the front again where they were secured under his heavy waist. He wiped his hands on his apron as he listened to her. He kept his eyes down on the photographs and let her talk. He let her take her time. He'd just come to work and he'd be there all night, baking, and he was in no real hurry.

She gave the baker her name, Ann Weiss, and her telephone number. The cake would be ready on Monday morning, just out of the oven, in plenty of time for the child's party that afternoon. The baker was not jolly. There were no pleasantries between them, just the minimum exchange of words, the necessary information. He made her feel uncomfortable, and she didn't like that. While he was bent over the counter with the pencil in his hand, she studied his coarse features and wondered if he'd ever done anything else with his life besides be a baker. She was a mother and thirty-three years old, and it seemed to her that everyone, especially someone the baker's age—a man old enough to be her father—must have children who'd gone through this special time of cakes and birthday parties. There must be that between them, she thought. But he was abrupt with her, not rude, just abrupt. She gave up trying to make friends with him. She looked into the back of the bakery and could see a long, heavy wooden table with aluminum pie pans stacked at one end, and beside the table a metal container filled with empty racks. There was an enormous oven. A radio was playing country-western music.

The baker finished printing the information on the special order card and closed up the binder. He looked at her and said, "Monday morning." She thanked him and drove home.

On Monday morning, the birthday boy was walking to school with another boy. They were passing a bag of potato chips back and forth and the birthday boy was trying to find out what his friend intended to give him for his birthday that afternoon. Without looking, he stepped off the curb at an intersection and was immediately knocked down by a car. He fell on his side with his head in the gutter and his legs out in the road. His eyes were closed, but his legs began to move back and forth as if he were trying to climb over something. His friend dropped the potato chips and started to cry. The car had gone a hundred feet or so and stopped in the middle of the road. A man in the driver's seat looked back over his shoulder. He waited until the boy got unsteadily to his feet. The boy wobbled a little. He looked dazed, but okay. The driver put the car into gear and drove away.

The birthday boy didn't cry, but he didn't have anything to say about anything either. He wouldn't answer when his friend asked him what it felt like to be hit by a car. He walked home, and his friend went on to school. But after the birthday boy was inside his house and was telling his mother about it, she sitting beside him on the sofa, holding his hands in her lap, saying, "Scotty, honey, are you sure you feel all right, baby?" thinking she would call the doctor anyway, he suddenly lay back on the sofa, closed his eyes, and went limp. When she couldn't wake him up, she hurried to the telephone and called her husband at work. Howard told her to remain calm, remain calm, and then he called an ambulance for the child and left for the hospital himself.

Of course, the birthday party was cancelled. The child was in the hospital with a mild concussion and suffering from shock. There'd been vomiting, and his lungs had taken in fluid which needed pumping out that afternoon. Now he simply seemed to be in a very deep sleep—but no coma, Doctor Francis had emphasized; no coma, when he saw the alarm in the parents' eyes. At eleven o'clock that Monday night when the boy seemed to be resting comfortably enough after the many X-rays and the lab work, and it was just a matter of his waking up and coming around, Howard left the hospital. He and Ann had been at the hospital with the child since that morning, and he was going home for a short while to bathe and to change clothes. "I'll be back in an hour," he said. She nodded. "It's fine," she said. "I'll be right here." He kissed her on the forehead, and they touched hands. She sat in a chair beside the bed and looked at the child. She was waiting for him to wake up and be all right. Then she could begin to relax.

Howard drove home from the hospital. He took the wet, dark streets very fast, then caught himself and slowed down. Until now, his life had gone smoothly and to his satisfaction—college, marriage, another year of college for the advanced degree in business, a junior partnership in an investment firm. Fatherhood. He was happy and, so far, lucky—he knew that. His parents were still living, his brothers and his sister were established, his friends from college had gone out to take their places in the world. So far he had kept away from any real harm, from those forces he knew existed and that could cripple or bring down a man, if the luck went bad, if things suddenly turned. He pulled into the driveway and parked. His left leg began to tremble. He sat in the car for a minute and tried to deal with the present situation in a rational manner. Scotty had been hit by a car and was in the hospital, but he was going to be all right. He closed his eyes and ran his hand over his face. In a minute, he got out of the car and went up to the front door. The dog was barking inside the house. The telephone rang and rang while he unlocked the door and fumbled for the light switch. He shouldn't have left the hospital, he shouldn't have. "God dammit!" he said. He picked up the receiver and said, "I just walked in the door!"

"There's a cake here that wasn't picked up," the voice on the other end of the line said.

"What are you saying?" Howard asked.

"A cake," the voice said. "A sixteen dollar cake."

Howard held the receiver against his ear, trying to understand. "I don't know anything about a cake," he said. "Jesus, what are you talking about?"

"Don't hand me that," the voice said.

Howard hung up the telephone. He went into the kitchen and poured himself some whiskey. He called the hospital. But the child's condition remained the same; he was still sleeping and nothing had changed there. While water poured into the tub, Howard lathered his face and shaved. He'd just stretched out in the tub and closed his eyes when the telephone began to ring. He hauled himself out, grabbed a towel, and hurried through the house, saying "Stupid, stupid," for having left the hospital. But when he picked up the receiver and shouted, "Hello!" there was no sound at the other end of the line. Then the caller hung up.

He arrived back at the hospital a little after midnight. Ann still sat in the chair beside the bed. She looked at Howard, and then she looked back at the child. The child's eyes stayed closed, the head was still wrapped in bandages. His breathing was quiet and regular. From an apparatus over the bed hung a bottle of glucose with a tube running from the bottle to the boy's arm.

"How is he?" Howard said. "What's all this?" waving at the glucose and the tube.

"Doctor Francis's orders," she said. "He needs nourishment. He needs to keep up his strength. Why doesn't he wake up, Howard? I don't understand, if he's all right."

Howard put his hand against the back of her head. He ran his fingers through her hair. "He's going to be all right. He'll wake up in a little while. Doctor Francis knows what's what."

After a time he said, "Maybe you should go home and get some rest. I'll stay here. Just don't put up with this creep who keeps calling. Hang up right away."

"Who's calling?" she asked.

"I don't know who, just somebody with nothing better to do than call up people. You go on now."

She shook her head. "No," she said, "I'm fine."

"Really," he said. "Go home for a while, and then come back and spell me in the morning. It'll be all right. What did Doctor Francis say? He said Scotty's going to be all right. We don't have to worry. He's just sleeping now, that's all."

A nurse pushed the door open. She nodded at them as she went to the bedside. She took the left arm out from under the covers and put her fingers on the wrist, found the pulse, and then consulted her watch. In a little while she put the arm back under the covers and moved to the foot of the bed where she wrote something on a clipboard attached to the bed.

"How is he?" Ann said. Howard's hand was a weight on her shoulder. She was aware of the pressure from his fingers.

"He's stable," the nurse said. Then she said, "Doctor will be in again shortly. Doctor's back in the hospital. He's making rounds right now."

"I was saying maybe she'd want to go home and get a little rest," Howard said. "After the doctor comes," he said.

"She could do that," the nurse said. "I think you should both feel free to do that, if you wish." The nurse was a big Scandinavian woman with blond hair. There was the trace of an accent in her speech.

"We'll see what the doctor says," Ann said. "I want to talk to the doctor. I don't think he should keep sleeping like this. I don't think that's a good sign." She brought her hand up to her eyes and let her head come forward a little. Howard's grip tightened on her shoulder, and then his hand moved to her neck where his fingers began to knead the muscles there.

"Doctor Francis will be here in a few minutes," the nurse said. Then she left the room.

Howard gazed at his son for a time, the small chest quietly rising and falling under the covers. For the first time since the terrible minutes after Ann's telephone call to him at his office, he felt a genuine fear starting in his limbs. He began shaking his head, trying to keep it away. Scotty was fine, but instead of sleeping at home in his own bed he was in a hospital bed with bandages around his head and a tube in his arm. But this help was what he needed right now.

Doctor Francis came in and shook hands with Howard, though they'd just seen each other a few hours before. Ann got up from the chair. "Doctor?"

"Ann," he said and nodded. "Let's just first see how he's doing," the doctor said. He moved to the side of the bed and took the boy's pulse. He peeled back one eyelid and then the other. Howard and Ann stood beside the doctor and watched. Then the doctor turned back the covers and listened to the boy's heart and lungs with his stethoscope. He pressed his fingers here and there on the abdomen. When he was finished he went to the end of the bed and studied the chart. He noted the time, scribbled something on the chart, and then looked at Howard and Ann.

"Doctor, how is he?" Howard said. "What's the matter with him exactly?"

"Why doesn't he wake up?" Ann said.

The doctor was a handsome, big-shouldered man with a tanned face. He wore a three-piece suit, a striped tie, and ivory cuff-links. His grey hair was combed along the sides of his head, and he looked as if he had just come from a concert. "He's all right," the doctor said. "Nothing to shout about, he could be better, I think. But he's all right. Still, I wish he'd wake up. He should wake up pretty soon." The doctor looked at the boy again. "We'll know some more in a couple of hours, after the results of a few more tests are in. But he's all right, believe me, except for that hairline fracture of the skull. He does have that."

"Oh, no," Ann said.

"And a bit of a concussion, as I said before. Of course, you know he's in shock," the doctor said. "Sometimes you see this in shock cases."

"But he's out of any real danger?" Howard said. "You said before he's not in a coma. You wouldn't call this a coma then, would you, doctor?" Howard waited. He looked at the doctor.

"No, I don't want to call it a coma," the doctor said and glanced over at the boy once more. "He's just in a very deep sleep. It's a restorative, a measure the body is taking on its own. He's out of any real danger, I'd say that for certain, yes. But we'll know more when he wakes up and the other tests are in. Don't worry," the doctor said.

"It's a coma," Ann said. "Of sorts."

"It's not a coma yet, not exactly," the doctor said. "I wouldn't want to call it a coma. Not yet anyway. He's suffered shock. In shock cases this kind of reaction is common enough; it's a temporary reaction to bodily trauma. Coma. Well, coma is a deep, prolonged unconsciousness that could go on for days, or weeks even. Scotty's not in that area, not as far as we can tell anyway. I'm certain his condition will show improvement by morning. I'm betting that it will anyway. We'll know more when he wakes up, which shouldn't be long now. Of course, you may do as you like, stay here or go home for a time. But by all means feel free to leave the hospital for a while if you want. This is not easy, I know." The doctor gazed at the boy again, watching him, and then he turned to Ann and said, "You try not to worry, little mother.

Believe me, we're doing all that can be done. It's just a question of a little more time now." He nodded at her, shook hands with Howard again, and then he left the room.

Ann put her hand over her child's forehead. "At least he doesn't have a fever," she said. Then she said, "My God, he feels so cold though. Howard? Is he supposed to feel like this. Feel his head."

Howard touched the child's temples. His own breathing had slowed. "I think he's supposed to feel this way right now," he said. "He's in shock, remember? That's what the doctor said. The doctor was just in here. He would have said something if Scotty wasn't okay."

Ann stood there a while longer, working her lip with her teeth. Then she moved over to her chair and sat down.

Howard sat in the chair next to her chair. They looked at each other. He wanted to say something else and reassure her, but he was afraid too. He took her hand and put it in his lap, and this made him feel better, her hand being there. He picked up her hand and squeezed it. Then he just held her hand. They sat like that for a while, watching the boy and not talking. From time to time he squeezed her hand. Finally, she took her hand away.

"I've been praying," she said.

He nodded.

She said, "I almost thought I'd forgotten how, but it came back to me. All I had to do was close my eyes and say, 'Please, God, help us,—help Scotty'; and then the rest was easy. The words were right there. Maybe if you prayed too," she said to him.

"I've already prayed," he said. "I prayed this afternoon, yesterday afternoon, I mean, after you called, while I was driving to the hospital. I've been praying," he said.

"That's good," she said. For the first time now, she felt they were together in it, this trouble. She realized with a start it had only been happening to her and to Scotty. She hadn't let Howard into it, though he was there and needed all along. She felt glad to be his wife.

The same nurse came in and took the boy's pulse again and checked the flow from the bottle hanging above the bed.

In an hour another doctor came in. He said his name was Parsons, from Radiology. He had a bushy moustache. He was wearing loafers, a western shirt, and a pair of jeans.

"We're going to take him downstairs for more pictures," he told them. "We need to do some more pictures, and we want to do a scan."

"What's that?" Ann said. "A scan?" She stood between this new doctor and the bed. "I thought you'd already taken all your X-rays."

"I'm afraid we need some more," he said. "Nothing to be alarmed about. We just need some more pictures, and we want to do a brain scan on him."

"My God," Ann said.

"It's perfectly normal procedure in cases like this," this new doctor said. "We just need to find out for sure why he isn't back awake yet. It's normal medical procedure, and nothing to be alarmed about. We'll be taking him down in a few minutes," this doctor said.

In a little while two orderlies came into the room with a gurney. They were black-haired, dark-complexioned men in white uniforms, and they said a few words to each other in a foreign tongue as they unhooked the boy from the tube and moved him from his bed to the gurny. Then they wheeled him from the room. Howard and Ann got on the same elevator. Ann stood beside the gurny and gazed at the child. She closed her eyes as the elevator began its descent. The orderlies stood at either end of the gurny without saying anything, though once one of the men made a comment to the other in their own language, and the other man nodded slowly in response.

Later that morning, just as the sun was beginning to lighten the windows in the waiting room outside the X-ray department, they brought the boy out and moved him back up to his room. Howard and Ann rode up on the elevator with him once more, and once more they took up their places beside the bed.

They waited all day, but still the boy did not wake up. Occasionally one of them would leave the room to go downstairs to the cafeteria to drink coffee and then, as if suddenly remembering and feeling guilty, get up from the table and hurry back to the room. Doctor Francis came again that afternoon and examined the boy once more and then left after telling them he was coming along and could wake up any minute now. Nurses, different nurses than the night before, came in from time to time. Then a young woman from the lab knocked and entered the room. She wore white slacks and a white blouse and carried a little tray of things which she put on the stand beside the bed. Without a word to them, she took blood from the boy's arm. Howard closed his eyes as the woman found the right place on the boy's arm and pushed the needle in.

"I don't understand this," Ann said to the woman.

"Doctor's orders," the young woman said. "I do what I'm told to do. They say draw that one, I draw. What's wrong with him, anyway?" she said. "He's a sweetie."

"He was hit by a car," Howard said. "A hit and run."

The young woman shook her head and looked again at the boy. Then she took her tray and left the room.

"Why won't he wake up?" Ann said. "Howard? I want some answers from these people."

Howard didn't say anything. He sat down again in the chair and crossed one leg over the other. He rubbed his face. He looked at his son and then he settled back in the chair, closed his eyes, and went to sleep.

Ann walked to the window and looked out at the parking lot. It was night and cars were driving into and out of the parking lot with their lights on. She stood at the window with her hands gripping the sill and knew in her heart that they were into something now, something hard. She was afraid, and her teeth began to chatter until she tightened her jaws. She saw a big car stop in front of the hospital and someone, a woman in a long coat, got into the car. For a minute she wished she were that woman and somebody, anybody, was driving her away from here to somewhere else, a place where she would find Scotty waiting for her when she stepped out of the car, ready to say *Mom* and let her gather him in her arms.

In a little while Howard woke up. He looked at the boy again, and then he got up from the chair, stretched, and went over to stand beside her at the window.

They both stared out at the parking lot. They didn't say anything. But they seemed to feel each other's insides now, as though the worry had made them transparent in a perfectly natural way.

The door opened and Doctor Francis came in. He was wearing a different suit and tie this time. His gray hair was combed along the sides of his head, and he looked as if he had just shaved. He went straight to the bed and examined the boy. "He ought to have come around by now. There's just no good reason for this," he said. "But I can tell you we're all convinced he's out of any danger. We'll just feel better when he wakes up. There's no reason, absolutely none, why he shouldn't come around. Very soon. Oh, he'll have himself a dilly of a headache when he does, you can count on that. But all of his signs are fine. They're as normal as can be."

"Is it a coma then?" Ann asked.

The doctor rubbed his smooth cheek. "We'll call it that for the time being, until he wakes up. But you must be worn out. This is hard. Feel free to go out for a bite," he said. "It would do you good. I'll put a nurse in here while you're gone, if you'll feel better about going. Go and have yourselves something to eat."

"I couldn't eat," Ann said. "I'm not hungry."

"Do what you need to do, of course," the doctor said. "Anyway, I wanted to tell you that all the signs are good, the tests are positive, nothing at all negative, and just as soon as he wakes up he'll be over the hill."

"Thank you, doctor," Howard said. He shook hands with the doctor again. The doctor patted Howard's shoulder and went out.

"I suppose one of us should go home and check things," Howard said. "Slug needs to be fed, for one thing."

"Call one of the neighbors," Ann said. "Call the Morgans. Anyone will feed a dog if you ask them to."

"All right," Howard said. After a while he said, "Honey why don't you do it? Why don't you go home and check on things, and then come back? It'll do you good. I'll be right here with him. Seriously," he said. "We need to keep up our strength on this. We'll want to be here for a while even after he wakes up."

"Why don't you go?" she said. "Feed Slug. Feed yourself."

"I already went," he said. "I was gone for exactly an hour and fifteen minutes. You go home for an hour and freshen up. Then come back. I'll stay here."

She tried to think about it, but she was too tired. She closed her eyes and tried to think about it again. After a time she said, "Maybe I will go home for a few minutes. Maybe if I'm not just sitting right here watching him every second he'll wake up and be all right. You know? Maybe he'll wake up if I'm not here. I'll go home and take a bath and put on clean clothes. I'll feed Slug. Then I'll come back."

"I'll be right here," he said. "You go on home, honey, and then come back. I'll be right here keeping an eye on things." His eyes were bloodshot and small, as if he'd been drinking for a long time. His clothes were rumpled. His beard had come out again. She touched his face, and then she took her hand back. She understood he wanted to be by himself for a while, to not have to talk or share his worry for a time. She picked up her purse from the nightstand, and he helped her into her coat.

"I won't be gone long," she said.

"Just sit and rest for a little while when you get home," he said. "Eat something. Take a bath. After you get out of the bath, just sit for a while and rest. It'll do you a world of good, you'll see. Then come back down here," he said. "Let's try not to worry. You heard what Doctor Francis said."

She stood in her coat for a minute trying to recall the doctor's exact words, looking for any nuances, any hint of something behind his words other than what he had said. She tried to remember if his expression had changed any when he bent over to examine the child. She remembered the way his features had composed themselves as he rolled back the child's eyelids and then listened to his breathing.

She went to the door where she turned and looked back. She looked at the child, and then she looked at the father. Howard nodded. She stepped out of the room and pulled the door closed behind her.

She went past the nurses' station and down to the end of the corridor, looking for the elevator. At the end of the corridor she turned to her right where she found a little waiting room where a Negro family sat in wicker chairs. There was a middle-aged man in a khaki shirt and pants, a baseball cap pushed back on his head. A large woman wearing a house dress and slippers was slumped in one of the chairs. A teenaged girl in jeans, hair done in dozens of little braids, lay stretched out in one of the chairs smoking a cigarette, her legs crossed at the ankles. The family swung their eyes to her as she entered the room. The little table was littered with hamburger wrappers and styrofoam cups.

"Franklin," the large woman said as she roused herself. "Is about Franklin?" Her eyes widened. "Tell me now, lady," the woman said. "Is about Franklin?" She was trying to rise from her chair, but the man had closed his hand over her arm.

"Here, here," he said. "Evelyn."

"I'm sorry," Ann said. "I'm looking for the elevator. My son is in the hospital, and now I can't find the elevator."

"Elevator is down that way, turn left," the man said as he aimed a finger.

The girl drew on her cigarette and stared at Ann. Her eyes were narrowed to slits, and her broad lips parted slowly as she let the smoke escape. The Negro woman let her head fall on her shoulder and looked away from Ann, no longer interested.

"My son was hit by a car," Ann said to the man. She seemed to need to explain herself. "He has a concussion and a little skull fracture, but he's going to be all right. He's in shock now, but it might be some kind of coma too. That's what really worries us, the coma part. I'm going out for a little while, but my husband is with him. Maybe he'll wake up while I'm gone."

"That's too bad," the man said and shifted in the chair. He shook his head. He looked down at the table, and then he looked back at Ann. She was still standing there. He said, "Our Franklin, he's on the operating table. Somebody cut him. Tried to kill him. There was a fight where he was at. At this party. They say he was just standing and watching. Not bothering nobody. But that don't mean nothing these days. Now he's on the operating table. We're just hoping and praying, that's all we can do now." He gazed at her steadily.

Ann looked at the girl again, who was still watching her, and at the older woman who kept her head down, but whose eyes were now closed. Ann saw the lips moving silently, making words. She had an urge to ask what those words were. She wanted to talk more with these people who were in the same kind of waiting she was in. She was afraid, and they were afraid. They had that in common. She would have liked to have said something else about the accident, told them more about Scotty, that it had happened on the day of his birthday, Monday, and that he was still unconscious. Yet she didn't know how to begin. She stood there looking at them without saying anything more.

She went down the corridor the man had indicated and found the elevator. She stood for a minute in front of the closed doors, still wondering if she was doing the right thing. Then she put out her finger and touched the button.

She pulled into the driveway and cut the engine. She closed her eyes and leaned her head against the wheel for a minute. She listened to the ticking sounds the engine made as it began to cool. Then she got out of the car. She could hear the dog barking inside the house. She went to the front door, which was unlocked. She went inside and turned on lights and put on a kettle of water for tea. She opened some dog food and fed Slug on the back porch. The dog ate in hungry little smacks. It kept running into the kitchen to see that she was going to stay. As she sat down on the sofa with her tea, the telephone rang.

"Yes!" she said as she answered. "Hello!"

"Mrs. Weiss," a man's voice said. It was five o'clock in the morning, and she thought she could hear machinery or equipment of some kind in the background.

"Yes, yes! What is it?" she said. "This is Mrs. Weiss. This is she. What is it, please?" She listened to whatever it was in the background. "Is it Scotty, for Christ's sake?"

"Scotty," the man's voice said. "It's about Scotty, yes. It has to do with Scotty, that problem. Have you forgotten about Scotty?" the man said. Then he hung up.

She dialed the hospital's number and asked for the third floor. She demanded information about her son from the nurse who answered the telephone. Then she asked to speak to her husband. It was, she said, an emergency.

She waited, turning the telephone cord in her fingers. She closed her eyes and felt sick to her stomach. She would have to make herself eat. Slug came in from the back porch and lay down near her feet. He wagged his tail. She pulled at his ear while he licked her fingers. Howard was on the line.

"Somebody just called here," she said. She twisted the telephone cord. "He said, he said it was about Scotty." She cried.

"Scotty's fine," Howard told her. "I mean he's still sleeping. There's been no change. The nurse has been in twice since you've been gone. They're in here every thirty minutes or so. A nurse or else a doctor. He's all right."

"Somebody called, he said it was about Scotty," she said.

"Honey, you rest for a little while, you need the rest. Then come back here. It must be that same caller I had. Just forget it. Come back down here after you've rested. Then we'll have breakfast or something."

"Breakfast," she said. "I don't want any breakfast."

"You know what I mean," he said. "Juice, something, I don't know. I don't know anything, Ann. Jesus, I'm not hungry either. Ann, it's hard to talk now. I'm standing here at the desk. Doctor Francis is coming again at eight o'clock this morning. He's going to have something to tell us then, something more definite. That's what one of the nurses said. She didn't know any more than that. Ann? Honey, maybe we'll know something more then. At eight o'clock. Come back here before eight. Meanwhile, I'm right here and Scotty's all right. He's still the same," he added.

"I was drinking a cup of tea," she said, "when the telephone rang. They said it was about Scotty. There was a noise in the background. Was there a noise in the background on that call you had, Howard?"

"I don't remember," he said. "Maybe the driver of the car, maybe he's a psychopath and found out about Scotty somehow. But I'm here with him. Just rest like you were going to do. Take a bath and come back by seven or so, and we'll talk to the doctor together when he gets here. It's going to be all right, honey. I'm here, and there are doctors and nurses around. They say his condition is stable."

"I'm scared to death," she said.

She ran water, undressed, and got into the tub. She washed and dried quickly, not taking the time to wash her hair. She put on clean underwear, wool slacks, and a sweater. She went into the living room where the dog looked up at her and let its tail thump once against the floor. It was just starting to get light outside when she went out to the car.

She drove into the parking lot of the hospital and found a space close to the front door. She felt she was in some obscure way responsible for what had happened to the child. She let her thoughts move to the Negro family. She remembered the name "Franklin" and the table that was covered with hamburger papers, and the teenaged girl staring at her as she drew on her cigarette. "Don't have children," she told the girl's image as she entered the front door of the hospital. "For God's sake, don't."

She took the elevator up to thĺe third floor with two nurses who were just going on duty. It was Wednesday morning, a few minutes before seven. There was a page for a Doctor Madison as the elevator doors slid open on the third floor. She got off behind the nurses, who turned in the other direction and continued the conversation she had interrupted when she'd gotten into the elevator. She walked down the corridor to the little alcove where the Negro family had been waiting. They were gone now, but the chairs were scattered in such a way that it looked as if people had just jumped from them the minute before. The table top cluttered with the same cups and papers, the ashtray was filled with cigarette butts.

She stopped at the nurses' station just down the corridor from the waiting room. A nurse was standing behind the counter, brushing her hair and yawning.

"There was a Negro man in surgery last night," Ann said. "Franklin was his name. His family was in the waiting room. I'd like to inquire about his condition."

A nurse who was sitting at the desk behind the counter looked up from a chart in front of her. The telephone buzzed and she picked up the receiver, but she kept her eyes on Ann.

"He passed away," said the nurse at the counter. The nurse held the hairbrush and kept looking at her. "Are you a friend of the family or what?"

"I met the family last night," Ann said. "My own son is in the hospital. I guess he's in shock. We don't know for sure what's wrong. I just wondered about Mr. Franklin, that's all. Thank you." She moved down the corridor. Elevator doors the same color as the walls slid open and a gaunt, bald man in white pants and white canvas shoes pulled a heavy cart off the elevator. She hadn't noticed these doors last night. The man wheeled the cart out into the corridor and stopped in front of the room nearest the elevator and consulted a clipboard. Then he reached down and slid a tray out of the cart. He rapped lightly on the door and entered the room. She could smell the unpleasant odors of warm food as she passed the cart. She hurried past the other station without looking at any of the nurses and pushed open the door to the child's room.

Howard was standing at the window with his hands behind his back. He turned around as she came in.

"How is he?" she said. She went over to the bed. She dropped her purse on the floor beside the nightstand. She seemed to have been gone a long time. She touched the child's face. "Howard?"

"Doctor Francis was here a little while ago," Howard said. She looked at him closely and thought his shoulders were bunched a little.

"I thought he wasn't coming until eight o'clock this morning," she said quickly.

"There was another doctor with him. A neurologist."

"A neurologist," she said.

Howard nodded. His shoulders were bunching, she could see that. "What'd they say, Howard? For Christ's sake, what'd they say? What is it?"

"They said they're going to take him down and run more tests on him, Ann. They think they're going to operate, honey. Honey, they are going to operate. They can't figure out why he won't wake up. It's more than just shock or concussion, they know that much now. It's in his skull, the fracture, it has something, something to do with that, they think. So they're going to operate. I tried to call you, but I guess you'd already left the house."

"Oh, God," she said. "Oh, please, Howard, please," she said, taking his arms.

"Look!" Howard said then. "Scotty! Look, Ann!" He turned her toward the bed.

The boy had opened his eyes, then closed them. He opened them again now. The eyes stared straight ahead for a minute, then moved slowly in his head until they rested on Howard and Ann, then traveled away again.

"Scotty," his mother said, moving to the bed.

"Hey, Scott," his father said. "Hey, son."

They leaned over the bed. Howard took the child's hand in his hands and began to pat and squeeze the hand. Ann bent over the boy and kissed his forehead again and again. She put her hands on either side of his face. "Scotty, honey, it's mommy and daddy," she said. "Scotty?"

The boy looked at them, but without any sign of recognition. Then his eyes scrunched closed, his mouth opened, and he howled until he had no more air in his lungs. His face seemed to relax and soften then. His lips parted as his last breath was puffed through his throat and exhaled gently through the clenched teeth.

The doctors called it a hidden occlusion and said it was a one-in-a-million circumstance. Maybe if it could have been detected somehow and surgery undertaken immediately, it could have saved him. But more than likely not. In any case, what would they have been looking for? Nothing had shown up in the tests or in the X-rays. Doctor Francis was shaken. "I can't tell you how badly I feel. I'm so very sorry, I can't tell you," he said as he led them into the doctors' lounge. There was a doctor sitting in a chair with his legs hooked over the back of another chair, watching an early morning TV show. He was wearing a green delivery room outfit, loose green pants and green blouse, and a green cap that covered his hair. He looked at Howard and Ann and then looked at Doctor Francis. He got to his feet and turned off the set and went out of the room. Doctor Francis guided Ann to the sofa, sat down beside her and began to talk in a low, consoling voice. At one point he leaned over and embraced her. She could feel his chest rising and falling evenly against her shoulder. She kept her eyes open and let him hold her. Howard went into the bathroom, but he left the door open. After a violent fit of weeping, he ran water and washed his face. Then he came out and sat down at the little table that held a telephone. He looked at the telephone as though deciding what to do first. He made some calls. After a time, Doctor Francis used the telephone.

"Is there anything else I can do for the moment?" he asked them.

Howard shook his head. Ann stared at Doctor Francis as if unable to comprehend his words.

The doctor walked them to the hospital's front door. People were entering and leaving the hospital. It was eleven o'clock in the morning. Ann was aware of how slowly, almost reluctantly she moved her feet. It seemed to her that Doctor Francis was making them leave, when she felt they should stay, when it would be more the right thing to do, to stay. She gazed out into the parking lot and then turned around and looked back at the front of the hospital. She began shaking her head. "No, no," she said. "I can't leave him here, no." She heard herself say that and thought how unfair it was that the only words that came out were the sort of words used on TV shows where people were stunned by violent or sudden deaths. She wanted her words to be her own. "No," she said, and for some reason the memory of the Negro woman's head lolling on the woman's shoulder came to her. "No," she said again.

"I'll be talking to you later in the day," the doctor was saying to Howard. "There are still some things that have to be done, things that have to be cleared up to our satisfaction. Some things that need explaining."

"An autopsy," Howard said.

Doctor Francis nodded.

"I understand," Howard said. Then he said, "Oh, Jesus. No, I don't understand, Doctor. I can't, I can't. I just can't."

Doctor Francis put his arm around Howard's shoulders. "I'm sorry. God, how I'm sorry." He let go of Howard's shoulders and held out his hand. Howard looked at the hand, and then he took it. Doctor Francis put his arms around Ann once more. He seemed full of some goodness she didn't understand. She let her head rest on his shoulder, but her eyes stayed open. She kept looking at the hospital. As they drove out of the parking lot, she looked back at the hospital once more.

At home, she sat on the sofa with her hands in her coat pockets. Howard closed the door to the child's room. He got the coffee maker going and then he found an empty box. He had thought to pick up some of the child's things. But instead he sat down beside her on the sofa, pushed the box to one side, and leaned forward, arms between his knees. He began to weep. She pulled his head over into her lap and patted his shoulder. "He's gone," she said. She kept patting his shoulder. Over his sobs she could hear the coffee maker hissing in the kitchen. "There, there," she said tenderly. "Howard, he's gone. He's gone and now we'll have to get used to that. To being alone."

In a little while Howard got up and began moving aimlessly around the room with the box, not putting anything into it, but collecting some things together on the floor at one end of the sofa. She continued to sit with her hands in her coat pockets. Howard put the box down and brought coffee into the living room. Later, Ann made calls to relatives. After each call had been placed and the party had answered, Ann would blurt out a few words and cry for a minute. Then she would quietly explain, in a measured voice, what had happened and tell them about arrangements. Howard took the box out to the garage where he saw the child's bicycle. He dropped the box and sat down on the pavement beside the bicycle. He took hold of the bicycle awkwardly so that it leaned against his chest. He held it, the rubber pedal sticking into his chest. He gave the wheel a turn.

Ann hung up the telephone after talking to her sister. She was looking up another number, when the telephone rang. She picked it up on the first ring.

"Hello," she said, and she heard something in the background, a humming noise. "Hello!" she said. "For God's sake," she said. "Who is this? What is it you want?"

"Your Scotty, I got him ready for you," the man's voice said. "Did you forget him?"

"You evil bastard!" she shouted into the receiver. "How can you do this, you evil son of a bitch?"

"Scotty," the man said. "Have you forgotten about Scotty?" Then the man hung up on her.

Howard heard the shouting and came in to find her with her head on her arms over the table, weeping. He picked up the receiver and listened to the dial tone.

Much later, just before midnight, after they had dealt with many things, the telephone rang again.

"You answer it," she said. "Howard, it's him, I know." They were sitting at the kitchen table with coffee in front of them. Howard had a small glass of whisky beside his cup. He answered on the third ring.

"Hello," he said. "Who is this? Hello! Hello!" The line went dead. "He hung up," Howard said. "Whoever it was."

"It was him," she said. "That bastard. I'd like to kill him," she said. "I'd like to shoot him and watch him kick," she said.

"Ann, my God," he said.

"Could you hear anything?" she said. "In the background? A noise, machinery, something humming?"

"Nothing, really. Nothing like that," he said. "There wasn't much time. I think there was some radio music. Yes, there was a radio going, that's all I could tell. I don't know what in God's name is going on," he said.

She shook her head. "If I could, could get, my hands, on him." It came to her then. She knew who it was. Scotty, the cake, the telephone number. She pushed the chair away from the table and got up. "Drive me down to the shopping center," she said. "Howard."

"What are you saying?"

"The shopping center. I know who it is who's calling. I know who it is. It's the baker, the son-of-a-bitching baker, Howard. I had him bake a cake for Scotty's birthday. That's who's calling. That's who has the number and keeps calling us. To harass us about the cake. The baker, that bastard."

They drove out to the shopping center. The sky was clear and stars were out. It was cold, and they ran the heater in the car. They parked in front of the bakery. All of the shops and stores were closed, but there were cars at the far end of the lot in front of the cinema. The bakery windows were dark, but when they looked through the glass they could see a light in the back room and, now and then, a big man in an apron moving in and out of the white, even light. Through the glass she could see the display cases and some little tables with chairs. She tried the door. She rapped on the glass. But if the baker heard them he gave no sign. He didn't look in their direction.

They drove around behind the bakery and parked. They got out of the car. There was a lighted window too high up for them to see inside. A sign near the back door said, "The Pantry Bakery, Special Orders." She could hear faintly a radio playing inside and something—an oven door?—creak as it was pulled down. She knocked on the door and waited. Then she knocked again, louder. The radio was turned down and there was a scraping sound now, the distinct sound of something, a drawer, being pulled open and then closed.

Someone unlocked the door and opened it. The baker stood in the light and peered out at them. "I'm closed for business," he said. "What do you want at this hour? It's midnight. Are you drunk or something?"

She stepped into the light that fell through the open door. He blinked his heavy eyelids as he recognized her.

"It's you," he said.

"It's me," she said. "Scotty's mother. This is Scotty's father. We'd like to come in."

The baker said, "I'm busy now. I have work to do."

She had stepped inside the doorway anyway. Howard came in behind her. The baker moved back. "It smells like a bakery in here. Doesn't it smell like a bakery in here, Howard?"

"What do you want?" the baker said. "Maybe you want your cake? That's it, you decided you want your cake. You ordered a cake, didn't you?"

"You're pretty smart for a baker," she said. "Howard, this is the man who's been calling us. This is the baker man." She clenched her fists. She stared at him fiercely. There was a deep burning inside her, an anger that made her feel larger than herself, larger than either of these men.

"Just a minute here," the baker said. "You want to pick up your three day old cake? That it? I don't want to argue with you, lady. There it sits over there, getting stale. I'll give it to you for half of what I quoted you. No. You want it? You can have it. It's no good to me, no good to anyone now. It cost me time and money to make that cake. If you want it, okay, if you don't, that's okay too. I have to get back to work." He looked at them and rolled his tongue behind his teeth.

"More cakes," she said. She knew she was in control of it, of what was increasing her. She was calm.

"Lady, I work sixteen hours a day in this place to earn a living," the baker said. He wiped his hands on his apron. "I work night and day in here, trying to make ends meet." A look crossed Ann's face that made the baker move back and say, "No trouble now." He reached to the counter and picked up a rolling pin with his right hand and began to tap it against the palm of his other hand. "You want the cake or not? I have to get back to work. Bakers work at night," he said again. His eyes were small, mean-looking, she thought, nearly lost in the bristly flesh around his cheeks. His neck was thick with fat.

"We know bakers work at night," Ann said. "They make phone calls at night too. You bastard," she said.

The baker continued to tap the rolling pin against his hand. He glanced at Howard. "Careful, careful," he said to Howard.

"My son's dead," she said with a cold, even finality. "He was hit by a car Monday morning. We've been waiting with him until he died. But of course, you couldn't be expected to know that, could you? Bakers can't known everything. Can they, Mr. Baker? But he's dead. He's dead, you bastard!" Just as suddenly as it had welled in her the anger dwindled, gave way to something else, a dizzy feeling of nausea. She leaned against the wooden table that was sprinkled with flour, put her hands over her face and began to cry, her shoulders rocking back and forth. "It isn't fair," she said. "It isn't, isn't fair."

Howard put his hand at the small of her back and looked at the baker. "Shame on you," Howard said to him. "Shame."

The baker put the rolling pin back on the counter. He undid his apron and threw it on the counter. He looked at them, and then he shook his head slowly. He pulled a chair out from under a card table that held papers, and receipts, an adding machine and a telephone directory. "Please sit down," he said. "Let me get you a chair," he said to Howard. "Sit down now, please." The baker went into the front of the shop and returned with two little wrought-iron chairs. "Please sit down you people."

Ann wiped her eyes and looked at the baker. "I wanted to kill you," she said. "I wanted you dead."

The baker had cleared a space for them at the table. He shoved the adding machine to one side, along with the stacks of note paper and receipts. He pushed the telephone directory onto the floor, where it landed with a thud. Howard and Ann sat down and pulled their chairs up to the table. The baker sat down too.

"I don't blame you," the baker said, putting his elbows on the table. "First. Let me say how sorry I am. God alone knows how sorry. Listen to me. I'm just a baker. I don't claim to be anything else. Maybe once, maybe years ago I was a different kind of human being. I've forgotten, I don't know for sure. But I'm not any longer, if I ever was. Now I'm just a baker. That don't excuse my offense, I know. But I'm deeply sorry. I'm sorry for your son, and I'm sorry for my part in this. Sweet, sweet Jesus," the baker said. He spread his hands out on the table and turned them over to reveal his palms. "I don't have any children myself, so I can only imagine what you must be feeling. All I can say to you now is that I'm sorry. Forgive me, if you can," the baker said. "I'm not an evil man, I don't think. Not evil, like you said on the phone. You got to understand that what it comes down to is I don't know how to act anymore, it would seem. Please," the man said, "let me ask you if you can find it in your hearts to forgive me?"

It was warm inside the bakery. In a minute, Howard stood up from the table and took off his coat. He helped Ann from her coat. The baker looked at them for a minute and then nodded and got up from the table. He went to the oven and turned off some switches. He found cups and poured coffee from an electric coffee maker. He put a carton of cream on the table, and a bowl of sugar.

"You probably need to eat something," the baker said. "I hope you'll eat some of my hot rolls. You have to eat and keep going. Eating is a small, good thing in a time like this," he said.

He served them warm cinnamon rolls just out of the oven, the icing still runny. He put butter on the table and knives to spread the butter. Then the baker sat down at the table with them. He waited. He waited until they each took a roll from the platter and began to eat. "It's good to eat something," he said, watching them. "There's more. Eat up. Eat all you want. There's all the rolls in the world in here."

They ate rolls and drank coffee. Ann was suddenly hungry, and the rolls were warm and sweet. She ate three of them, which pleased the baker. Then he began to talk. They listened carefully. Although they were tired and in anguish, they listened to what the baker had to say. They nodded when the baker began to speak of loneliness, and the sense of doubt and limitation that had come to him in his middle years. He told them what it was like to be childless all these years. To repeat the days with the ovens endlessly full and endlessly empty. The party food, the celebrations he'd worked over. Icing knuckle-deep. The tiny wedding couples stuck into cakes. Hundreds of them, no, thousands by now. Birthdays. Just imagine all those candles burning. He had a necessary trade. He was a baker. He was glad he wasn't a florist. It was better to be feeding people. This was a better smell anytime than flowers.

"Smell this," the baker said, breaking open a dark loaf. "It's a heavy bread, but rich." They smelled it, then he had them taste it. It had the taste of molasses and coarse grains. They listened to him. They ate what they could. They swallowed the dark bread. It was like daylight under the fluorescent trays of light. They talked on into the early morning, the high pale cast of light in the windows, and they did not think of leaving.

∽∽∽∽∽∽∽∽∽∽

Suggestions for Discussion

1. Larry McCaffrey and Sinda Gregory speak of the period in which Raymond Carver rewrote "The Bath" as a time of "opening up" for the author, in which he explores "more interior territory using less constricted language." "A Small, Good Thing" begins this process of opening up immediately. Compare the first scenes of the two versions. How does the fuller language alter your perception of the characters, the atmosphere?

2. In interview, Carver said that the story of "The Bath" "hadn't been told originally, it had been messed around with, condensed and compressed. . . to highlight the qualities of menace that I wanted to emphasize." He also said, "there's a lot more optimism" in "A Small, Good Thing" How is the later story more optimistic, less menacing?

3. What is the effect of the addition of the driver's hesitation? Of names for the father, the Doctor? Howard's thoughts on the way home? Details of the boy's condition? The discussion of prayer?

4. Compare the paragraphs beginning "The mother went to the window" on page 343 and "Ann walked to the window" on page 350. How do the details in the later version bring us closer to the character?

5. The mother's confrontation with the family in the waiting room (pages 344 and 352) is dramatically different in the later version. How? How does the kind of connection these characters make function in each version?

6. How does the addition of the scene in the bakery at the end of the story alter its theme?

7. An adaptation of "A Small, Good Thing" was included in the Robert Altman film "Short Cuts," based on several of Carver's stories. See the film and consider how the story is further altered by revisions made for the film. For example, the driver of the car that hits the boy is changed from a man to a woman, and one we know in another context. How does this alter the ultimate atmosphere, theme, and our sympathies and judgments?

Retrospect

Pick any story in this book that dissatisfied you. Imagine that you are the editor of a magazine that is going to publish it. What suggestions for revision would you make to the author?

Writing Assignments

1. If you did assignment 4 in chapter 2 (the postcard short story), rewrite your story, making it at least three times as long, so that the development enriches the action and the characters.

2. Choose any other story you wrote this term; rewrite it, improving it any way you can, but also cutting its original length by at least one quarter.

3. Pick a passage from your journal and use Stephen Dunning's method (page 332) of highlighting "words, phrases, images, talk, mistakes." Cluster and/or freedraft a passage from some of these highlightings. Rewrite the passage. Put it away for a few days. Is it a story? Rewrite it. Put it away. Rewrite it.

4. A class project: Spend about a half-hour in class writing a scene that involves a conflict between two characters. Make a copy of what you write. Take one copy home and rewrite it. Send the other copy home with another class member for him or her to make critical comments and suggestions. Compare your impulses with those of your reader. On the following day, forgive your reader. On the day after that, rewrite the passage once more, incorporating any of the reader's suggestions that prove useful.

APPENDIX A

NARRATIVE TECHNIQUES
Workshop Symbol Code

Format

Manuscripts should be double-spaced, with generous margins, on one side of 8½-by 11-inch white paper. If you use a typewriter, it should have a new black ribbon and well-cleaned keys; if a computer, make sure your printout is easily legible. Title and author's name and address (or class identification) should appear on a cover page. Most editors and teachers now accept copies from a copy machine; make sure they're clear. Always keep a copy of your work.

The symbols listed here are a suggested shorthand for identifying common errors in usage and style. A few of the marks are standard copyediting and proofreading symbols.

Usage

sp.	Misspelling.
gram.	Grammar at fault. Consult Strunk's Elements of Style, Fowler's Modern English Usage, or any good grammar text.
¶	Paragraph. Begin a new one here.
⟶	No new paragraph needed.
⍊	Comma needed. Insert one here.
⌿	No comma needed.
p/c	You have used a possessive for a contraction or vice versa. *Its, their,* and *your* are possessives. *It's, they're,* and *you're* are contractions of *it is, they are,* and *you are.* They're going to take their toll if you're not sure of your usage.

p/p   Participial phrase at the beginning of a sentence must refer to the grammatical subject. "Failing to understand this, your prose will read awkwardly," means that your prose fails to understand.

s/i   Split infinitives tend to always read awkwardly. Try to immediately correct it and to never do it again.

T   A pointless change of tense. It leaves the reader not knowing *when* s/he is.

n/s   Not a sentence. Technique okay if effective, otherwise not. Here, not.

tr.   Transpose. This can refer to letters, words, phrases, sentences, whole paragraphs.

Insert a space here (between words, paragraphs, etc.).

Style

V   This is definitely vague. Or, you have used a generalization or an abstraction where you need a concrete detail. Specify. See pages 58-64.

A   Use the active voice. If "she was happy" or "she felt happy," she was not nearly as happy as if she laughed, grinned, jumped, or threw her arms around a tree. See pages 64-67.

un.   Unnecessary. Delete.

↕   Compress this passage to half the words for twice the strength. You're writing *long*.

?   Either you are confusing or the reader is confused or both. What do you really mean?

awk.   Awkward. This sentence is related to the auk, a thickbodied, short-necked bird without grace. Restyle.

R   Repetition to unintended or undesirable effect.

∝   Cliché.

m/m   Mixed metaphor. See page 271.

o/w
o/s
o/i }   Overwritten, overstated, overinsistent. You're straining. Lower the key to raise the effect.

conv.   In the exceedingly likely and, one might say, almost inevitable event, in view of your enrollment in this class, that you are not Henry James, the use of convoluted language is considerably less than certain to contribute to the augmenting of your intended effect. Simplify.

coy
pomp.
prec.
pret. }   Coy, pompous, precious, pretentious—all meaning that you are enjoying yourself more than the reader is. No reader will forgive you.

chron.   Chronology unnecessarily violated. "She sat down after having crossed to the couch." Except for very special effects, let the reader's mind follow events in their order.

d/t   Unnecessary dialogue tag. "'Shut your stupid mouth,' he said angrily." We do not need to be told that he said this angrily. If he said it sweetly, then we would probably need to be told. See pages 145.

dial.   Dialect is overwritten. You are probably misspelling too much, so that your character sounds stupid rather than regional. Let the syntax do the work; keep misspellings and grammatical mistakes to a minimum. See pages 143–144.

int.   Author intrusion. You are explaining, judging, or interpreting too much. Show us, and let us understand and judge.

p.v.   You have violated point of view, bouncing from one mind to another in a way the reader is not prepared for. See page 204.

APPENDIX B

SUGGESTIONS FOR FURTHER READING

Most of the following books were written by writers for writers; all can be useful to the practicing storyteller.

Aristotle, *The Poetics*. The first extant work of literary criticism, and the essay from which all later criticism derives. There are numerous good translations.

Atchity, Kenneth. *A Writer's Time: A Guide to the Writer's Process from Vision Through Revision*, Norton, 1988. Atchity focuses on the problem every writer complains about most, and offers startling perceptions and helpful directions for finding and apportioning time.

Barzun, Jacques. *On Writing, Editing, and Publishing*. University of Chicago Press, 1986. Is it possible to be elegant, irascible, practical and witty, at the same time, at the full stretch of each? Read it and see.

Bernays, Anne, and Pamela Painter. *What If? Writing Exercises for Fiction Writers*. HarperCollins, 1995. Bernays and Painter identify more than seventy-five situations that a writer may face and provide exercises for each; included are student examples and clear descriptions of objectives. Useful and provocative.

Block, Lawrence, *Telling Lies for Fun & Profit*, Quill, William Morrow, 1981. Lively, often wry counsel on subjects from marketing to modifiers, pen names to plagiarism, writing fast, and faking it.

Bly, Carol. *The Passionate, Accurate Story*. Milkweed Editions, 1990. A genuine original, this book makes a thoughtful plea for value in writing and writing from your values. It combines the insights of literary technique, therapy, and ethics. Since it is written in the form of interlocking stories, it reads quickly and entertainingly.

Booth, Wayne C. *The Rhetoric of Fiction*. University of Chicago Press, 2nd ed. 1983. This is a thorough, brilliant, and difficult discussion of point of view, which well repays the effort of its reading.

Brande, Dorothea. *Becoming a Writer*. J. P. Tarcher, 1981. For those who are over-meticulous, or who have a hard time getting to the typewriter, Brande's mind-freeing exercises may be enormously helpful.

Brown, Rita Mae. *Starting From Scratch: A Different Kind of Writer's Manual*. Bantam, 1988. It is different, in its upbeat energy and reassurance.

Burke, Carol and Molly Best Tinsley, *The Creative Process*, St Martin's Press, 1993. Nicely balanced between explanation and exercises, this book seeks to jog the writer's imagination in fiction, poetry and the essay forms.

Cassill, R.V. *Writing Fiction, 2nd Ed*. Prentice, Hall 1975. This wise book and its even better first edition are out of print and likely to be long since purloined from your library shelf. Complain to the publisher.

Dillard, Annie. *The Writing Life*. Harper and Row, 1989. This stunningly written account of "your day's triviality" touches drudgery itself with luminous significance. Every writer should read it. Also recommended is Dillard's *Living by Fiction*. Harper, 1982.

Edwards, Betty. *Drawing on the Right Side of the Brain*. J. P. Tarcher, rev. ed. 1989. Although it is aimed at the artist rather than the writer, this book offers invaluable help for writers as well, in the ability to think spatially and vividly.

Elbow, Peter. *Writing Without Teachers*. Oxford, 1973. Elbow is excellent on how to keep going, growing, and cooking when you haven't the goads of teacher and deadline. *Writing with Power*, 1981, is not aimed specifically at the imaginative writer, but still has useful advice, and a good section on revising.

Forster, E. M. *Aspects of the Novel*. Harcourt, Brace, Jovanovich, 1956. Forster delivered these Clark Lectures at Trinity College, Cambridge, England, in 1927. They are talkative, informal, and informative; still the best analysis of literature from a writer's point of view. A must.

Friedman, Bonnie. *Writing Past Dark*. HarperCollins, 1993. If you think writing is a lonely task, and you can only afford one book, buy this one.

Gardner, John. *The Art of Fiction: Notes on Craft for Young Writers*. Alfred A. Knopf, 1984. A new classic among books on writing. Gardner's advice is based on his experience as a teacher of creative writing and is addressed to "the serious beginning writer." The book is clear, practical, and a delight to read. Also recommended is Gardner's *On Becoming a Novelist*. HarperCollins, 1985.

Gass, William. *Fiction and the Figures of Life*. David R. Godine, 1979. Gass writes of character, language, philosophy and form, from acute angles in stunning prose. A joy to read.

Goldberg, Natalie. *Writing Down the Bones*. Shambala, 1986; and *Wild Mind*. Bantam, 1990. Goldberg is the guru of can-do, encouraging the writer with short, pithy, personal, and cheerful cheerings-on.

Hills, Rust. *Writing in General and the Short Story in Particular*. Houghton Mifflin 1987. A former literary editor of Esquire Magazine, Hills has written a breezy, enjoyable guide to fictional technique with good advice on every page.

Huddle, David. *The Writing Habit: Essays*. Peregrine Smith Books, 1991. Huddle has a level voice and a sound sense of what it is to live with the habit. He is kind without sentimentality; strongly recommended.

Hughes, Elaine Farris. *Writing from the Inner Self*. HarperCollins, 1991. This book imaginatively makes connections between writing and meditation, leading you through exercises that involve awareness of the body, feelings, observations, and memories in order to enrich the imagination.

James, Henry. *The House of Fiction*. Greenwood, 1973. The master of indirection goes directly to the heart of the house of fiction.

Jason, Philip K., and Allan B. Lefcowitz. *Creative Writer's Handbook*, 2nd ed. Prentice-Hall, 1994. A comprehensive, thoughtful and readable guide to craft.

Lamott, Ann. *Bird by Bird: Instructions on Writing and Life*. Pantheon, 1994. Ms. Lamott believes that writing "can help you make sense of the world and give you direction," and this book is designed to help writers get "a little work done every day for the rest of their lives."

Macdonald, Ross. *Self-Portrait: Ceaselessly Into the Past*. Capra Press, 1981. An anecdotal, lively and provocative memoir of a writing life.

Madden, David. *Revising Fiction: A Handbook for Fiction Writers*. New American Library, 1988. Although it is too weighty to operate as a handbook, this volume, uniquely devoted to the art of revising, shows the process convincingly and in full. Also useful as a reference tool is Madden's *A Primer of the Novel for Readers and Writers*. Scarecrow Press, 1980.

May, Rollo. *The Courage to Create*. Bantam 1984. A philosophic classic on the subject.

Minot, Stephen. *Three Genres*, 4th ed. Prentice-Hall, 1988. This text covers the writing of poetry, fiction, and drama, so that each is necessarily treated briefly. Nevertheless, Minot is direct and insightful, well worth reading.

Nelson, Victoria. *On Writer's Block: A New Approach to Creativity*, Houghton Mifflin, 1993. Among the new breed of writers' books that use the insights of psychology and therapy, this is exceptionally helpful. Nelson is sensible as well as sensitive. Her suggestions work.

Olsen, Tillie. *Silences*. Delacorte Press, 1978. Eloquent essays, of which the title piece is a must.

Pack, Robert and Jay Parini, eds. *Writers on Writing*. Middlebury College Press, 1991. Described by the editors as a "celebration," this volume collects 25 eloquent essays by established writers who offer advice and experience practical, witty, confessional, flip, moving and/or profound.

Plimpton, George. *The Writer's Chapbook: A Compendium of Fact, Opinion, Wit, and Advice from the 20th Century's Preeminent Writers*. Penguin, 1989. Edited from the famous *Paris Review* interviews.

Rico, Gabriele Lusser. *Writing the Natural Way*, J. P. Tarcher, 1983. Describes in full the technique of clustering and offers useful techniques for freeing the imagination.

Schneider, Pat, *The Writer as an Artist: A New Approach to Writing Alone and With Others* Lowell House/Chicago Books, 1993. Both optimistic and rigorous, Schneider bases advice and exercises on the belief that "If you can think, you can write."

Shelnutt, Eve. *The Writing Room*. Longstreet Press, 1989. A wide-ranging, outspoken, often persuasive discussion of the crafts of fiction and poetry, with examples, analyses and exercises.

Sloane, William. *The Craft of Writing*, edited by Julia Sloane. W. W. Norton, 1983. This book was culled posthumously from the notes of one of the great teachers of fiction writing. The advice he gives is solid and memorable, and the reader's only regret is that there isn't more.

Stafford, William. *Writing the Australian Crawl*, ed. Donald Hall, Univ. of Michigan Press, 1978. The poet has affable and practical advice for fiction writers too; and *You Must Revise Your Life*. University of Michigan, 1986; an inspiriting potpourri of poems, essays, and interviews on writing.

Stern, Jerome. *Making Shapely Fiction*. Norton, 1991. A witty, useful guide. Stern illustrates various possible shapes for stories; he includes a cogent list of *don'ts* and discusses the elements of good writing in dictionary form so you can use the book as a handy reference.

Strunk, William C., and E. B. White. *The Elements of Style*, 3rd ed. Macmillan, 1979. Strunk provides the rules for correct usage and vigorous writing in this briefest and most useful of handbooks.

Ueland, Barbara. *If You Want to Write*. Greywolf Press, 1987. "Everybody is talented. Everybody is original," Ueland says, and she says it convincingly, in this book that holds up very well since its first edition in 1938.

Welty, Eudora. *One Writer's Beginnings*. Harvard press, 1984. One of the best autobiographies ever offered by a writer; moving, funny and full of insight.

Williams, Joseph M. *Style*, HarperCollins, 1994. This is a well-written, readable book that deals with such subjects as mechanics, clarity, coherence and elegance. Comforting to have at hand.

Willis, Meredith Sue, Personal Fiction Writing, Teachers & Writers Collaborative, 1984. *Blazing Pencils*, 1990, and *Deep Revision*, 1993. The last especially is a splendid extended view of revision as a creative process in itself, with lots of "Do This" suggestions and acknowledgment of the computer's usefulness to the reviser.

Woodruff, Jay, ed., *A Piece of Work: Five Writers Discuss Their Revisions*, Univ. of Iowa Press, 1993. Poets and fiction writers (including Tobias Wolff and Joyce Carol Oates whose short stories are included in this volume) discuss their drafts, their writing processes, and much more of interest.

Ziegler, Alan. *The Writing Workshop* (in two volumes). Teachers and Writers Collaborative, 1981 and 1984. The author calls these useful books a "survey course" in writing. They are mainly intended for teachers of writing but can be adapted to use as a self-teaching tool; they're full of interesting practical advice.

Zinsser, William, ed., *Inventing the Truth: The Art and Craft of Memoir*, Houghton Mifflin 1988. Although this series of talks, originally given at the New York Public Library, is not aimed at the fiction writer, they shine with hints on how to use the subject matter of your life, from five fine writers: Annie Dillard, Toni Morrison, Russell Baker, Alfred Kazin, and Lewis Thomas.

Marketing

Of the guides and services offered to writers, three of the most helpful follow.

Associated Writing Programs (Tallwood House, Mail Stop 1E3, George Mason University, Fairfax, VA 22030). Those enrolled in the creative writing program of a college or university that is a member of AWP are automatically members.

Others can join for a reasonable fee. AWP's services include a magazine, *The AWP Chronicle*, a catalog of writing programs, a placement service, an annual meeting, and a number of awards and publications. The organization is probably the nearest thing to a "network" of writers in the nation, and can provide contact with other writers, as well as valuable information on prizes, programs, presses, and the ideas current in the teaching of writing.

Poets & Writers, Inc. (72 Spring St., New York, NY 10012). Poets & Writers issues a bimonthly magazine that has articles of high quality and interest to writers, and provides information on contests and on magazines and publishers soliciting manuscripts. The organization also has a number of useful publications that are periodically revised: the *Directory of American Poets and Fiction Writers*, *Literary Agents: A Writer's Guide*, and *Author and Audience: A Readings and Workshops Guide*; and an annual listing called *Writers' Conferences*.

Writer's Market, Writer's Digest Books (Cincinnati). A new edition comes out each year with practical advice on how to sell manuscripts as well as lists of book and magazine publishers, agents, foreign markets, and other services for writers.

ACKNOWLEDGMENTS

Margaret Atwood, "Rape Fantasies" first appeared in Chatelaine Magazine, copyright © 1977. Reprinted by permission of Margaret Atwood and the Canadian Publishers, McClelland & Stewart, Toronto.

Toni Cade Bambara, "My Man Bovanne" from *Gorilla, My Love* by Toni Cade Bambara. Reprinted by permission of Random House, Inc.

Charles Baxter, "Gryphon" from *Through The Safety Net* by Charles Baxter. Copyright © 1985 by Charles Baxter. Reprinted by permission of Viking Penguin, a division of Penguin Books USA Inc.

Frederick Busch, "Ralph the Duck" from *Absent Friends* by Frederick Busch. Copyright © 1986 by Frederick Busch. Reprinted by permission of Random House, Inc.

Raymond Carver, "The Bath" from *What We Talk About When We Talk About Love* by Raymond Carver. Copyright © 1981 by Raymond Carver. Reprinted by permission of Random House, Inc.

Raymond Carver, "A Small Good Thing" from *Cathedral* by Raymond Carver. © 1985 by Raymond Carver. Reprinted by permission of Random House, Inc.

Sandra Cisneros, "Hips" from *The House on Mango Street* by Sandra Cisneros. Copyright © 1984 by Sandra Cisneros. Published by Vintage Books, a division of Random House, Inc., New York; published in hardcover by Alfred A. Knopf in 1994. Reprinted by permission of Susan Bergholz Literary Services, New York.

Charles D'Ambrosio, "The Point." Copyright © 1990 by Charles D'Ambrosio. Originally published in *The New Yorker*. Reprinted by permission of Mary Evans Inc.

Stephen Dunning, "Wanting to Fly" and Drafts by Stephen Dunning. Copyright © 1990 by Stephen Dunning. Reprinted by permission of the author.

Annie Dillard, excerpts from "The Writing Life" by Annie Dillard. Copyright © 1989 by Annie Dillard. Reprinted by permission of HarperCollins Publishers, Inc.

Bonnie Friedman, "Message from a Cloud of Flies: On Distraction" from *Writing Past Dark* by Bonnie Friedman. Copyright © 1993 by Bonnie Friedman. Reprinted by permission of HarperCollins Publishers, Inc.

Gabriel Garcia Marquez, "A Very Old Man With Enormous Wings" from *Leaf Storm and Other Stories* by Gabriel Garcia Marquez. Copyright © 1971 by Gabriel Garcia Marquez. Reprinted by permission of HarperCollins Publishers, Inc.

Nadine Gordimer, "Town and Country Lovers" from *A Soldier's Embrace* by Nadine Gordimer. Copyright © 1980 by Nadine Gordimer. Reprinted by permission of Viking Penguin, a division of Penguin Books USA Inc.

Denis Johnson, "Car Crash While Hitchhiking" from *Jesus' Son* by Denis Johnson. © 1992 by Denis Johnson. Reprinted by permission of Farrar, Straus and Giroux, Inc.

Jamaica Kincaid, "Girl" from *At the Bottom of the River* by Jamaica Kincaid. Copyright © 1978, 1979, 1982, 1983 by Jamaica Kincaid. Reprinted by permission of Farrar, Straus and Giroux, Inc.

David Leavitt, "The Crane Child" from *The Lost Language of Cranes* by David Leavitt. Copyright © 1986 by David Leavitt. Reprinted by permission of Alfred A. Knopf.

Ursula K. Le Guin, "The Ones Who Walk Away from Omelas." First appeared in *New Dimensions 3*. Copyright © 1973 by Ursula K. Le Guin. Reprinted by permission of the author and Virginia Kidd Literary Agency.

Gabriel Garcia Marquez, "A Very Old Man with Enormous Wings" from *Leaf Storm and Stories* by Gabriel Garcia Marquez, translated by Gregory Rabassa. Reprinted by permission of HarperCollins Publishers, Inc.

Vladimir Nabokov, "Signs and Symbols" from *Nabokov's Dozen* by Vladimir Nabokov. Reprinted by permission of Doubleday & Company, Inc.

Joyce Carol Oates, "Where Are You Going, Where Have You Been?" from *The Wheel of Love and Other Stories* by Joyce Carol Oates. Copyright © 1970 by Joyce Carol Oates. Reprinted by permission of John Hawkins & Associates, Inc.

Tim O'Brien, "The Things They Carried" from *The Things They Carried* by Tim O'Brien. Reprinted by permission of Houghton Mifflin Co./Seymour Lawrence.

Frank O'Connor, "Guests of the Nation" from *The Collected Stories of Frank O'Connor* by Frank O'Connor. Copyright © 1951 by Frank O'Connor. Reprinted by permission of Random House, Inc. (U.S. rights) and Writers House Inc. (Canadian).

Grace Paley, "A Man Told Me the Story of His Life" from *Later the Same Day* by Grace Paley. Copyright © 1985 by Grace Paley. Reprinted by permission of Farrar, Straus and Giroux, Inc.

Mary Robison, "Yours" from *An Amateur's Guide to the Night* by Mary Robison. Copyright © 1983 by Mary Robison. Reprinted by permission of Random House, Inc.

John Edgar Wideman, "The Tambourine Lady" from *Fever: 12 Stories* by John Edgar Wideman. © 1989 by John Edgar Wideman. Reprinted by permission of Henry Holt and Company.

Joy Williams, "The Excursion" from *Taking Care* by Joy Williams. Copyright © 1982 by Joy Williams. Reprinted by permission of Random House, Inc.

William Carlos Williams, "The Use of Force" from *The Farmer's Daughters* by William Carlos Williams. Reprinted by permission of New Directions Publishing Corporation.

Tobias Wolff, "Hunters in the Snow" from *In the Garden of the North American Martyrs* by Tobias Wolff. Copyright © 1981 by Tobias Wolff. Reprinted by permission of The Ecco Press.

INDEX